THE ANNOTATED
GLIMPSES
OF
UNFAMILIAR JAPAN

BY

LAFCADIO HEARN

VOLUME II

Edited By

Hayato Tokugawa

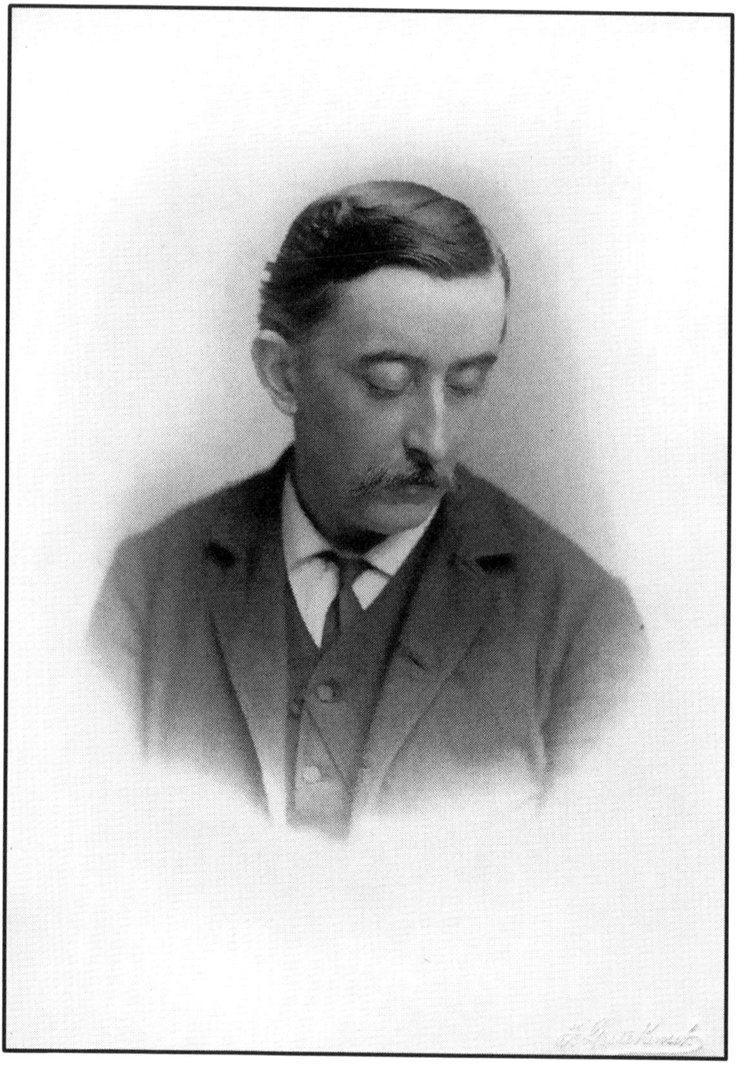

THE ANNOTATED
GLIMPSES
OF UNFAMILIAR JAPAN

BY

LAFCADIO HEARN

IN TWO VOLUMES
(ILLUSTRATED)

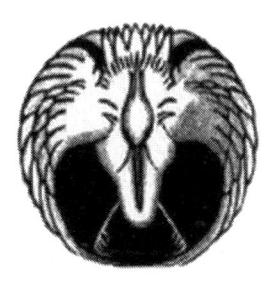

VOLUME. II

The Second Volume of
The Lafcadio Hearn's Japan Series
(Annotated)

EDITED BY

HAYATO TOKUGAWA

Japanese Translations by Soseki S. and Saito H.

SHISEI-DŌ PUBLICATIONS
Tajimi, Japan and San Francisco, California

THE ANNOTATED *GLIMPSES OF UNFAMILIAR JAPAN, BY LAFCADIO HEARN, VOLUME II*, Edited by Hayato Tokugawa.

© Copyright 2014 by Hayato Tokugawa.

All rights reserved under International and Pan-American Copyright Conventions. Published in the United States and Japan by Shisei-Dō Publications. No part of this publication may be reproduced or utilized in any form or by any means, electronic or mechanical, including photocopying, recording, or by any information storage and retrieval system without prior written permission of the author or publisher, except in the case of brief quotations embodied in critical articles or reviews.

The original version of this work, *Glimpses of Unfamiliar Japan, Volume II*, by Lafcadio Hearn, Copyright 1894, is in the public domain.

The illustration on page 170 is © Hayato Tokugawa. All other illustrations are in the public domain.

Cover Design © by Hayato Tokugawa.

Cover art is by Hayato Tokugawa based on Thirty-six Views of Mt. Fuji - The Great Wave by Hokusai Katsushika (1760-1849).

ShiseiDoPublications@yahoo.com

FIRST EDITION

FOR MY WIFE AOI:

MY MUSE, MY INSPIRATION
AND MY TRANSLATOR.
A CONSTANT SOURCE OF NEW THINGS
FROM OLD JAPAN.

AUTHOR'S DEDICATION

TO THE FRIENDS
WHOSE KINDNESS ALONE RENDERED POSSIBLE
MY SOJOURN IN THE ORIENT, —

PAYMASTER MITCHELL McDONALD, U.S.N.[1]

AND

BASIL HALL CHAMBERLAIN, ESQ.[2]
Emeritus Professor of Philology and Japanese in the
Imperial University of Tokyō

I DEDICATE THESE VOLUMES

IN TOKEN OF

AFFECTION AND GRATITUDE

TABLE OF CONTENTS

Editor's Preface xi
Author's Preface xiii
Introduction xvii
XVI In a Japanese Garden 3
XVII The Household Shrine 49
XVIII Of Women's Hair 83
XIX From the Diary of an English Teacher 99
XX Two Strange Festivals 153
XXI By the Sea of Japan 167
XXII Of A Dancing Girl 187
XXIII From Hōki to Oki 213
XXIV Of Souls 277
XXV Of Ghosts and Goblins 287
XXVI The Japanese Smile 303
XXVII Sayōnara 329
APPENDIX A 339
Notes 349

x

EDITOR'S PREFACE

GLIMPSES OF UNFAMILIAR JAPAN, originally copyrighted in 1894, published by Houghton Mifflin Company, and printed by The Riverside Press, Cambridge, Massachusetts, is the first book offered by Shisei-Dō Publications in our annotated series of works by Lafcadio Hearn relative to Japan. Unfortunately, outside of Japan where Hearn still maintains a high degree of popularity, his sizeable volume of work has gradually grown more obscure with the passage of time, known principally in the West to only a minor, select group of students of Japanese culture and history, and sadly lacking in accessibility to a new, modern reading audience. It is our intention to introduce Lafcadio Hearn, and particularly his works on Japan, to a wider range of contemporary readers who are curious to know about Japanese history, religion, and culture, particularly that of the Edo and Meiji eras.

With that in mind, we were faced with a definite challenge; that being, how to present Lafcadio Hearn's books to contemporary readers when they were written in a style of English prose that used a vocabulary and grammar now often regarded as archaic, or at best, old fashioned; and which make reference to many things, both Western and Japanese, which are unfamiliar to twenty-first century readers? At the same time, we sought to preserve the author's own unique style, which both fascinated and endeared his late nineteenth and early twentieth century readers. We have endeavored then to update the vocabulary and grammar in order to better reflect modern usage, and so facilitate the reader's understanding of the book's content and purpose. We did this however only when we felt it necessary, in order that we not impinge on Hearn's unique style, which was written for the ear, rather than the eye. As we read the original book, we did so aloud and listened carefully, so that in our editing, we would not detract from the personal experience he offers his audience; as though he were speaking to each person directly, telling his stories.

We have offered explanations of the various references that Hearn made; especially those references that are now no longer common knowledge, or that we felt required further explanation because they simply are not known to the West; thus, enhancing the reader's understanding of Japan, its people, its culture, and the author himself; and we hope, encouraging the reader to research and read further about those references they find of interest.

With reference to the use of Japanese words in the text, whenever possible we have allowed Hearn's hyphenated construction of words to stand, as they provide the reader with a good indication of their pronunciation. When practical, we have also utilized the Wade-Giles System for the Romanization[3] of Japanese, particularly since this work was first produced in the nineteenth century when the system was most widely in use. We have therefore, not utilized the more modern Romanization system used in *Kenkyusha's New English-Japanese Dictionary*, with its use of apostrophes after n at the end of a syllable that is followed by a vowel or y.

Further, we have provided graphic illustrations, when possible, of the things and places the author is describing, as well as actual scenes from Hearn's Japan, the Japan of the Meiji period. We did this, not because the author's words are lacking, but because in many cases, what he describes simply no longer exists or can only be found in museums; and because it is our desire that the reader have the opportunity to see the very things that Hearn saw and so feel more a part of his experiences.

We hope you enjoy this new, augmented presentation of *Glimpses of Unfamiliar Japan*, and find it, as we did, some of the best of Lafcadio Hearn.

HAYATO TOKUGAWA
Tajimi, Japan

AUTHOR'S PREFACE

IN THE INTRODUCTION to his charming *Tales of Old Japan*, Mr. Mitford[4] wrote in 1871: "The books which have been written of late years about Japan have either been compiled from official records, or have contained the sketchy impressions of passing travelers. Of the inner life of the Japanese, the world at large knows little: their religion, their superstitions, their ways of thought, the hidden springs by which they move — all these are as yet mysteries."

This invisible life referred to by Mr. Mitford is the Unfamiliar Japan of which I have been able to obtain a few glimpses. The reader may, perhaps, be disappointed by their rarity; for a residence of little more than four years among the people — even by one who tries to adopt their habits and customs — scarcely suffices to enable the foreigner to begin to feel at home in this world of strangeness. No one can feel more than the author himself, how little has been accomplished in these volumes, and how much remains to do.

The popular religious ideas, especially the ideas derived from Buddhism, and the curious superstitions touched upon in these sketches are little shared by the educated classes of "New Japan." Except with regard to his characteristic indifference toward abstract ideas in general, and metaphysical speculation in particular, the

Occidentalized[i] Japanese of today stands almost on the intellectual plane of the cultivated Parisian or Bostonian. But he is inclined to treat with undue contempt all concepts of the supernatural; and toward the great religious questions of the hour, his attitude is one of perfect apathy. Rarely does his university training in modern philosophy compel him to attempt any independent study of relationships, either sociological or psychological. For him, superstitions are simply superstitions; their relation to the emotional nature of the people does not interest him at all.[ii] And this is not only because he thoroughly understands that people, but because the class to which he belongs is still unreasoningly, though quite naturally, ashamed of its older beliefs. Most of us who now call ourselves agnostics can recollect the feelings with which, in the period of our fresh emancipation from a faith far more irrational than Buddhism, we looked back upon the gloomy theology of our fathers. Intellectual Japan has become agnostic within only a few decades; and the suddenness of this mental revolution adequately explains the principal, though perhaps not all the causes, of the present attitude of the upper class toward Buddhism. For the time being, it certainly borders on intolerance; and while such is the feeling even toward religion, as distinguished from superstition, the feeling toward superstition as distinguished from religion must be something stronger still.

But the rare charm of Japanese life, so different from that of all other lands, is not to be found in its Europeanized circles. It is to be found among the great common people, who represent in Japan, as in all countries, the national virtues, and who still cling to their delightful old customs, their picturesque clothes, their Buddhist images, their household shrines, their beautiful and touching worship of ancestors. This is the life of which a foreign observer can never weary, if fortunate and sympathetic enough to enter into it — the life that forces him sometimes to doubt whether the course of our boasted Western progress is really in the direction of moral development. Each day, while the years pass, there will be revealed to him some strange and unsuspected beauty in it. Like other life, it has its darker side; yet, even this is brightness compared with the darker side of Western existence. It has its foibles, its follies, its vices, its cruelties; yet the more one sees of it, the more one marvels at its extraordinary goodness, its miraculous patience, its never-failing courtesy, its simplicity of heart, its intuitive charity. And to our own larger Western

---

[i] Editor's Footnote: Meaning "Westernized." The term "Occident" refers to the West; that is, the countries of Europe and America. While the author used the term extensively in the original volumes, it has most often been replaced in this text with more contemporary terms.

[ii] Author's Footnote: In striking contrast to this indifference is the strong, national, farseeing conservatism of Viscount Tōrio — a noble exception. [See "The Japanese Smile," in *Glimpses of Unfamiliar Japan*, vol. II.]

comprehension, its commonest superstitions, however scorned at Tōkyō, have the rarest value as fragments of the unwritten literature of its hopes, its fears, its experience with right and wrong — its primitive efforts to find solutions for the riddle of the Unseen. How much the lighter and kindlier superstitions of the people add to the charm of Japanese life can, indeed, be understood only by one who has long resided in the interior. A few of their beliefs are sinister — such as that in demon-foxes, which public education is rapidly dispelling; but a large number are comparable for beauty of fancy even to those Greek myths in which our noblest poets of today still find inspiration; while many others, which encourage kindness to the unfortunate, and kindness to animals, can never have produced anything but the happiest moral results. The amusing presumption of domestic animals, and the comparative fearlessness of many wild creatures in the presence of man; the white clouds of gulls that hover around each incoming steamer in expectation of a handout of crumbs; the whirring of doves from temple eaves to pick up the rice scattered for them by pilgrims, the familiar storks of ancient public gardens; the deer of holy shrines, awaiting cakes and caresses; the fish which raise their heads from sacred lotus ponds when the stranger's shadow falls upon the water — these and a hundred other pretty sights are due to fancies which, though called superstitions, teach in simplest form the sublime truth of the Unity of Life. And even when considering beliefs less attractive than these — superstitions of which the grotesqueness may provoke a smile — the impartial observer would do well to bear in mind the words of Lecky:[5]

> *Many superstitions do undoubtedly answer to the Greek conception of slavish "fear of the Gods," and have been productive of unspeakable misery to mankind; but there are very many others of a different tendency. Superstitions appeal to our hopes as well as our fears. They often meet and gratify the inmost longings of the heart. They offer certainties where reason can only afford possibilities or probabilities. They supply conceptions on which the imagination loves to dwell. They sometimes impart even a new sanction to moral truths. Creating wants which they alone can satisfy, and fears which they alone can quell, they often become essential elements of happiness; and their consoling efficacy is most felt in the languid or troubled hours when it is most needed. We owe more to our illusions than to our knowledge. The imagination, which is altogether constructive, probably contributes more to our happiness than the reason, which in the sphere of speculation is mainly critical and destructive. The rude charm which, in the hour of danger or distress, the savage clasps so confidently to his breast, the sacred picture which is believed to shed a hallowing and protecting influence over the poor man's cottage, can bestow a more real consolation in the darkest hour of human suffering than can be afforded by the grandest theories of philosophy... No error can be more grave than to*

imagine that when a critical spirit is abroad the pleasant beliefs will all remain, and the painful ones alone will perish.

That the critical spirit of modernized Japan is now indirectly aiding rather than opposing the efforts of foreign bigotry to destroy the simple, happy beliefs of the people, and substitute those cruel superstitions which the West has long intellectually outgrown — the fancies of an unforgiving God and an everlasting hell — is surely to be regretted. More than a hundred and sixty years ago, Kaempfer[6] wrote of the Japanese: "In the practice of virtue, in purity of life and outward devotion, they far outdo the Christians." And except where native morals have suffered by foreign contamination, as in the open ports, these words are true of the Japanese today. My own conviction, and that of many impartial and more experienced observers of Japanese life, is that Japan has nothing whatever to gain by conversion to Christianity, either morally or otherwise, but very much to lose.

Of the twenty-seven sketches composing these volumes, four were originally purchased by various newspaper syndicates, and reappear in a considerably altered form, and six were published in the *Atlantic Monthly* (1891 - 1893). The remainder, forming the bulk of the work, are new.

L.H.
KUMAMOTO, KYŪSHŪ, JAPAN, May, 1894.

INTRODUCTION

Glimpses of Unfamiliar Japan is regarded by many admirers, authorities, and critics as Lafcadio Hearn's seminal work with regard to Old Japan and things Japanese; after all, it truly was the first popularly published book that told the West, in beautiful language, of the wonders that he saw there. These two volumes and the essays therein, many of which were published separately world-wide, truly gave the West its first glimpses of a part of the world and a country of which little was known but that fascinated everyone.

In Volume Two of *The Annotated Glimpses of Unfamiliar Japan*, as in Volume One, we have the opportunity to explore Japan right along with Hearn; however this time, the locations are not those destined to become popular tourist attractions, but rather islands, towns, and villages, on the west coast of Japan, the Japanese sea, which still remain relatively unknown to outsiders and even to many Japanese. Along the way, he tells some "ghostly" stories and describes many of the old-fashioned customs and beliefs of the people he finds there.

But even before these travels and tales begin, he invites us into the garden at his home on Kitabori-cho in Matsué, just a few streets northwest of a hill where stands Matsué Castle, and which has been lovingly preserved by the people of the city and opened to the public. There we are treated to a tour and an explanation of some of the basics of Japanese ornamental gardening, an introduction to some of the creatures that inhabit his yard, along with some wonderful old stories.

Hearn then moves on to a very informative essay on Shintō, a primer of sorts, and then provides us with a comparative look at both Japanese Buddhism and Shintō, and how both religions approach their respective esteems for the dead.

If you have ever been intrigued by the hairstyles of Japanese women, particularly those seen in the old ukiyo-e prints and antique photographs, Lafcadio Hearn next takes us on a *tour de force* of the myriad of Meiji styles and their complexities, and tells a "ghostly" story involving his wife's own hairstylist and a head which, detached from its body, travels about on its own.

During the Meiji era, education was paramount to Japan's future positon in the world and Lafcadio Hearn was part of the process of bringing the youth of the nation first into the late 19th century and then the twentieth. With the fondest of memories, Hearn tells us of his early days as a teacher in Matsué and introduces us to some of his favorite pupils in a way that is both endearing and humorous; yet, ultimately tragic.

He then changes direction, introducing the reader to two special Japanese festivals, that of the New Year and another which follows a month later, Setsubun; at the same time he introduces us to some fascinating, if not so benevolent, spirits associated with them. He then moves on to tell us a bit about Japanese dancing girls, geisha, and concludes that chapter with a touching story of a renowned dancer from the past.

Later we are treated to a discussion of the fascinating concept of multiple souls in one person, and a winter visit to some ghosts, goblins, and Japanese Hell — Jogoku.

Our visit with Hearn concludes with a serious essay on the meaning of the (then) seemingly omnipresent smile of the Japanese people and then makes some ominous predictions for Japan's future, followed by his farewell to Matsue; which was marked by love and respect from his students and the town; yet, again was marred by tragedy, and described as only he could express it.

We hope you enjoy this new enhanced presentation of Volume II of *Glimpses of Unfamiliar Japan*, and find it, as we did, some of the best of Lafcadio Hearn.

THE ANNOTATED
GLIMPSES OF UNFAMILIAR JAPAN
VOLUME II

2

XVI

IN A JAPANESE GARDEN

I

MY LITTLE TWO-STORY HOUSE by the Ōhashigawa River, although as dainty as a bird cage, proved much too small for comfort at the approach of the hot season; the rooms being scarcely higher than steamship cabins, and so narrow that an ordinary mosquito net could not be suspended in them. I was sorry to lose the beautiful lake view, but I found it necessary to move to the northern part of the city, onto a very quiet street behind the decaying castle.[7] My new home is a *katchiū-yashiki*, the ancient residence of some samurai of high rank. It is shut off from the street, or rather roadway which skirts the castle moat, by a long, high wall topped with tiles. One climbs to the gate, which is almost as large as that of a temple courtyard, by a low, broad flight of stone steps. Projecting from the wall, to the right of the gate, is a lookout window, heavily barred, like a big wooden cage. There, in feudal days, armed retainers kept keen watch on all who passed by; invisible watch, for the bars are set so closely that a face behind them cannot be seen from the road. Inside the gate, the approach to the house is also walled in on both sides, so that the visitor, unless privileged, could see in front of him, only the house entrance, always closed with white *shoji.*[8] Like all samurai homes, the residence itself is only one story high, but there are fourteen rooms within, and these are high, spacious, and beautiful. Sadly, there is no lake view nor any charming panorama.

Part of the O-Shiroyama,[i] with the castle on its summit, half concealed by a grove of pines, may be seen above the top of the front wall, but only part. Scarcely a hundred yards behind the house rise densely wooded hills which cut off not only the horizon but a large slice of the sky as well. There is however, fair compensation for this confinement in the form of a pretty garden, or rather, a series of garden spaces, which surround the house on three sides and are overlooked by broad verandas; and from one certain veranda I can enjoy the view of two gardens at once. Hedges of bamboo and woven rushes, with wide, gateless openings in their middle, mark the boundaries of the three divisions of the pleasure grounds; but these structures are not intended to serve as fences; they are ornamental and only indicate where one style of landscape gardening ends and another begins.[9]

---

[i] The castle mountain; more specifically, the Honorable Castle Mountain.

II

Now a few words about Japanese gardens in general.

After having learned, merely by seeing something about the Japanese manner of arranging flowers (for the practical knowledge of the art requires years of study and experience, besides a natural, instinctive sense of beauty), one can then only consider European ideas of floral decoration as vulgar. This observation is not the result of any hasty enthusiasm, but a conviction settled by long residence in the interior of the country. I have come to understand the unspeakable loveliness of a solitary spray of blossoms arranged as only a Japanese expert knows how to arrange it; not by simply poking the spray into a vase, but by perhaps one whole hour's labor of trimming, posing, and the most delicate manipulation. Therefore, I cannot think now of what we Western people call a "bouquet" as anything but a vulgar, murdering of flowers; an outrage on the sense of color, a brutality and an abomination. Somewhat in the same way, and for similar reasons, after having learned what an old Japanese garden is, I can remember our most expensive gardens at home only as ignorant displays of what wealth can accomplish in the creation of incongruities that violate nature.

A Japanese garden is not a flower garden and neither is it made for the purpose of cultivating plants. In nine cases out of ten, there is nothing in it resembling a flowerbed. Some gardens may contain scarcely a twig of green; some have nothing green at all and consist entirely of rocks, pebbles and sand; although, these are exceptional.[i] As a rule, a Japanese garden is a landscape garden; yet, its existence does not depend on any fixed allowance of space. It may cover one acre or many acres. It may also be only ten feet square. It may, in extreme cases, be much less; for, a certain kind of Japanese garden can be made small enough to put in a *tokonoma*.[10] Such a garden, in a container no larger than a fruit dish, is called *koniwa* or *tokoniwa*, and may occasionally be seen in the *tokonoma* of humble, little houses so closely squeezed between other structures that they have no ground in which to cultivate an outdoor garden. (I say "an outdoor garden," because there are indoor gardens, both upstairs and downstairs, in some large Japanese houses.) The *tokoniwa* is usually made in some curious bowl or shallow carved box, or quaintly shaped container that is impossible to describe by any English word. Created within are minuscule hills with minuscule houses on them, and microscopic ponds and streams spanned by tiny humped bridges; and strange, wee plants do the duty of trees and curiously formed pebbles stand for rocks. There are tiny *tōrō*,[ii] perhaps a tiny *torii*[11] as well. In short, a charming and living model of a Japanese landscape.

---

[i] Author's Footnote: Such as the garden attached to the abbot's palace at Tokuwamonji, cited by Mr. Conder, which was made to commemorate the legend of stones which bowed themselves in agreement to the doctrine of Buddha. At Togo-ike, in Tottori-ken [Tottori Province], I saw a very large garden consisting almost entirely of stones and sand. The impression which the designer had intended to convey was that of approaching the sea over the edge of a dune, and the illusion was beautiful.

[ii] *Tōrō* are traditional Japanese stone lanterns, introduced to Japan at the same time as was Buddhism, in the 6th century. The *ishi-doro*, or stone lantern, is the most common type one is likely to see, gracing gardens, temples and shrines throughout Japan. *Ishi-doro* come in many different sizes and shapes, but common to them all is a hollowed upper part, made to hold candles, oil lamps, and now electric lights, which are lighted on special occasions. The 2000 *ishi-doro*, which line the approaches to the Kasuga Shrine in Nara, are perhaps the most famous in Japan.

Another fact of prime importance to remember is that, in order to comprehend the beauty of a Japanese garden, it is necessary to understand, or at least to learn to understand, the beauty of stones. Not of stones quarried by the hand of man, but of stones shaped only by nature. Until you can feel, keenly feel, that stones have character, that stones have tones and values, the whole artistic meaning of a Japanese garden cannot be revealed to you. In the foreigner, however aesthetic as he may be, this feeling needs to be cultivated by study. It is inborn in the Japanese; the soul of the nation comprehends nature infinitely better than we do: at least in her visible forms. Being a Westerner, however, the true sense of the beauty of stones can only be appreciated by you through long familiarity with the Japanese use and choice of them. If you live in the heartland, the character of the lessons to be acquired exist everywhere around you.

You cannot walk through a street without observing tasks and problems in the aesthetics of stones for you to master. At the approaches to temples, by the side of roads, before holy groves, and in all parks and pleasure grounds, as well as in all cemeteries, you will notice large, irregular, flat slabs of natural rock, mostly from the river beds and thus water-worn, sculptured with *kanji*, but otherwise uncut. These have been set up as votive tablets, as commemorative monuments, as tombstones, and are much more costly than the ordinary cut-stone columns and *haka*[1] chiseled with the figures of deities in relief. Again, you will see in front of most of the shrines, no, even on the grounds of nearly all large homes, great irregular blocks of granite or other hard rock, worn by the action of torrents, and converted into water basins (*chodzu-bachi*) by cutting a circular hollow in the top. These are common examples of the utilization of stones, even in the poorest villages; and if you have any natural artistic sentiment, you cannot fail to discover, sooner or later, how much more beautiful these natural forms are than any shapes from the hand of the stonecutter.

It is also probable that you will become so familiar, at last, to the sight of inscriptions cut on rock surfaces, especially if you travel much through the country, that you will often find yourself involuntarily looking for texts or other carvings where there are none, and could not possibly be; as if *kanji* belonged by natural law to rock formation.

Stones will perhaps begin to assume for you a certain individual or characteristic aspect, to suggest moods and sensations, as they do to the Japanese. Indeed, Japan is particularly a land of suggestive shapes in stone, as high volcanic lands are apt

---

[1] *Haka* (墓), a Japanese family grave; also used to refer to the tombstone of the grave.

to be; and such shapes without doubt addressed themselves to the imagination of the people at a time long before the date of that archaic text which tells of demons in Izumo "who made rocks, and the roots of trees, and leaves, and the foam of the green waters to speak."

As might be expected in a country where the suggestiveness of natural forms is thus recognized, there are in Japan, many curious beliefs and superstitions concerning stones. In almost every province, there are famous stones that are supposed to be sacred or haunted, or to possess miraculous powers, such as the Women's Stone at the temple of Hachiman at Kamakura,[12] and the Sesshō-seki, or Death Stone of Nasu,[13] and the Wealth-giving Stone at Enoshima, to which pilgrims pay reverence. There are even legends of stones having shown sensibility, like the tradition of the Nodding Stones, which bowed down before the monk Daita when he preached to them the word of Buddha; or, the ancient story from the *Kojiki*, that the Emperor O-Jin, being augustly intoxicated, "struck with his august staff a great stone in the middle of the Ohosaka Road, upon which the stone ran away!"[i]

---

[i] Author's Footnote: The *Kojiki*, translated by Professor B. H. Chamberlain, p. 254.

Stones are valued for their beauty; and large stones, selected for their shape, may have an aesthetic value of hundreds of dollars. Large stones form the skeleton, or framework, in the design of old Japanese gardens. Not only is every stone chosen with an eye for its particular expressiveness of form, but every stone in the garden or about the premises has its separate and individual name, indicating its purpose or its decorative duty. But I can only tell you a little, a very little, about the folklore of a Japanese garden. If you want to know more about stones and their names; and about the philosophy of gardens, read the unique essay of Mr. Conder on the *Art of Landscape Gardening in Japan*,[i] and his beautiful book on the *Japanese Art of Floral Decoration*; and also the brief but charming chapter on gardens in Morse's *Japanese Homes*.[ii]

III

No effort is made to create an impossible or purely ideal landscape in the Japanese garden. Its artistic purpose is to faithfully copy the attractions of a real landscape, and to convey the real impression that a real landscape communicates. Therefore, it is a picture and a poem at the same time; perhaps even more a poem than a picture; for, as nature's scenery, in its varying aspects, affects us with sensations of joy, solemnity, grimness, or of sweetness, of force or of peace, so must the true expression of it in the labor of the landscape gardener, create not merely an impression of beauty, but a mood in the soul.

The grand old landscape gardeners, those Buddhist monks who first introduced the art to Japan, and subsequently devel-

---

[i] Author's Footnote: Since this paper was written, Mr. Conder has published a beautiful, illustrated volume, *Landscape Gardening in Japan*, by Josiah Conder, F.R.I.B.A., (Tōkyō, 1893). A photographic supplement to the work gives views of the most famous gardens in the capital and elsewhere.

[ii] Author's Footnote: The observations of Dr. Rein [Johannes Justus Rein, January 27, 1835 – January 23, 1918, a German geographer and Japanologist] on Japanese gardens are not to be recommended, in respect either to accuracy or to comprehension of the subject. Rein spent only two years in Japan, the larger part of which time he devoted to the study of the lacquer industry, the manufacture of silk and paper, and other practical matters. On these subjects his work is justly valued; but, his chapters on Japanese manners and customs, art, religion, and literature show extremely little acquaintance with those topics.

oped it into an almost occult science, carried their theory yet further than this. They believed that it was possible to express moral lessons in the design of a garden; and abstract ideas such as chastity, faith, piety, contentment, calm, and married bliss. Gardens were therefore designed according to the character of the owner, whether poet, warrior, philosopher, or priest. In those ancient gardens (sadly, the art is passing away under the destructive influence of the utterly commonplace Western taste), both a mood of nature and some rare Asian concept of a mood of man were expressed.

I do not know what human sentiment the main part of my garden was intended to reflect and there is no one to tell me. Those who made it passed away many generations ago, in the eternal rebirth of souls; however, as a poem of nature, it does not require an interpreter. It occupies the front portion of the grounds, facing south, and extends west to the edge of the northern section of the garden, from which it is partially separated by a curious screen-fence structure. There are large rocks in it, heavily covered in moss; many fantastic basins of stone for holding water, stone lamps green with the years; and a *shachihoko*, like one sees at the peaked corners of castle roofs: a great stone fish, an idealized porpoise, with its nose in the ground and its tail in the air.[1] There are miniature hills, with old trees on them; there are long slopes of green, shadowed by flowering shrubs, like riverbanks; and there are green knolls like small islands. All these green hills rise from spaces of pale yellow sand, as smooth as the surface of silk and imitating the curves and meanderings of the course of a river. These spaces of sand are not to be walked on; they are much too beautiful for that. The least speck of dirt would mar their effect; and it requires the trained skill of an experienced gardener (he is a delightful old man) to keep them in perfect form. However, they are crossed in various directions by lines of flat, uncut rock slabs, placed at slightly irregular distances from one another, exactly like steppingstones across a brook. The whole effect is that of the shores of a still stream in some lovely, lonesome, drowsy place.

The garden is so secluded that there is nothing to break the illusion. High walls and fences shut out streets and adjacent things; the shrubs and the trees rising and thickening toward the

---

[1] Author's Footnote: This attitude of the *shachihoko* is somewhat common, thus, the common expression *shachihoko dai*, signifying "to stand on one's head."

boundaries, conceal even the roofs of the neighboring *katchiu-yashiki*. The quivering shadows of leaves on the sunned sand are softly beautiful and the faintly sweet scent of flowers comes with every breath of warm air; and there is a humming of bees.

IV

According to Buddhism, all existence is divided into *hijō*, things without desire, such as stones and trees; and *ujō*, things having desire, such as men and animals. This division does not, so far as I know, find expression in the written philosophy of gardens, but it is a convenient one. The folklore of my little domain relates both to the inanimate and the animate. In natural order, the *hijō* may be considered first, beginning with a solitary shrub near the entrance of the *yashiki*, and close to the gate of the first garden.

Within the front gateway of almost every old samurai house, and usually near the entrance of the dwelling itself, there is a small tree with large, peculiar leaves. The name of this tree in Izumo is *tegashiwa*, and there is one beside my door. What the scientific name of it is I do not know, nor am I quite sure of the etymology of the Japanese name; however, there is a word, *tegashi*, meaning a bond for the hands; and the shapes of the leaves of the *tegashiwa* somewhat resembles the shape of a hand.

In old days, when a samurai retainer was obliged to leave his home in order to accompany his *daimyō*[14] to Edo,[i] it was customary, just before his departure, to set a baked *tai*[ii], served on a *tegashiwa* leaf, in front of him. After this farewell meal, the leaf on which the *tai* had been served, was hung up above the door as a charm to bring the departed samurai safely back again. This pretty superstition about the leaves of the *tegashiwa* had its origin not only in their shape but also in their movement. Stirred by a wind, they seemed to beckon, not in our Western manner, but in

---

[i] Edo (江戸), meaning "bay-entrance" or "estuary", and sometimes also spelled as Yedo or Yeddo, is the former name of Tōkyō, and was the seat of power for the Tokugawa Shōgunate which ruled Japan from 1603 to 1868.

[ii] Author's Footnote: The magnificent perch called *tai* (*Serranus marginalis*), which is very common along the Izumo coast, is not only justly prized as the most delicate of Japanese fish, but is also held to be an emblem of good fortune. It is a ceremonial gift at weddings and on congratulatory occasions. The Japanese also call it "the king of fishes."

the way that a Japanese signs to his friend to come, by gently waving his hand up and down with the palm towards the ground.

Another shrub to be found in most Japanese gardens is the *nanten*,[1] about which there exists a very curious belief. If you have an evil dream, a dream which predicts bad luck, you should whisper it to the *nanten* early in the morning, and then it will never come true.[ii] There are two varieties of this graceful plant: one which bears red berries and one which bears white. The

---

[1] Author's Footnote: *Nandina domestica*.

[ii] Author's Footnote: In Izumo, they say that the most lucky of dreams is a dream of *Fuji*, the Sacred Mountain. Next in order of good omens is dreaming of a falcon (*taka*). The third best subject of a dream is the eggplant (*nasubi*). To dream of the sun or of the moon is very lucky; but it is still more so to dream of stars. For a young wife, it is most fortunate to dream of swallowing a star: this signifies that she will become the mother of a beautiful child. To dream of a cow is a good omen; to dream of a horse is lucky, but it signifies traveling. To dream of rain or fire is good. Some dreams are held in Japan, as in the West, "to go by contraries." Therefore, to dream of having one's house burned up, or of funerals, or of being dead, or of talking to the ghost of a dead person, is good. Some dreams which are good for women mean the reverse when dreamed by men; for example, it is good for a woman to dream that her nose bleeds, but for a man this is very bad. To dream of much money is a sign of loss to come. To dream of the *koi*, or any freshwater fish, is the most unlucky of all. This is curious, for in other parts of Japan, the *koi* is a symbol of good fortune.

latter is rare. Both kinds grow in my garden. The common variety is placed closed to the veranda (perhaps for the convenience of dreamers); the other occupies a little flowerbed in the middle of the garden, together with a small citron tree.

This very dainty citron tree is called "Buddha's Fingers,"[i] because of the wonderful shape of its fragrant fruit. Near it stands a kind of laurel, with long, thin leaves as glossy as bronze. It is called *yuzuri-ha*[ii] by the Japanese, and is almost as common in the gardens of old samurai homes as the *tegashiwa* itself. It is believed to be a tree of good fortune because none of its leaves ever falls off before a new one, growing behind it has developed; thus, the *yuzuri-ha* symbolizes hope that the father will not pass away before his son has become a vigorous man, well able to succeed him as the head of the family. On every New Year's

---

[i] Author's Footnote: *Tebushukan: Citrus sarkodactilis.*
[ii] Author's Footnote: *Yuzuru* means to resign in favor of another; *ha* signifies a leaf. The botanical name, as given in Hepburn's dictionary is *Daphniphillum macropodum.*

Day, therefore, the leaves of the *yuzuri-ha*, mingled with fern fronds, are attached to the *shimenawa*[15] which is then suspended in front of every Izumo home.

V

The trees, like the shrubs, have their curious poetry and legends. Like the stones, each tree has its special landscape name according to its position and purpose in the composition. Just as rocks and stones form the skeleton of the ground plan of a garden, so pines form the framework of its foliage design. They give body to the whole. In this garden, there are five pines; not pines tormented into fantastic forms, but pines made wondrously picturesque by long and tireless care and judicious trimming. The object of the gardener has been to develop to the utmost possible degree, their natural tendency toward rugged line and massing of foliage; that spiny, somber-green foliage which Japanese art is never weary of imitating in metal inlay or golden lacquer. The pine is a symbolic tree in this land of symbolism. Ever green, it is at once the emblem of unflinching purpose and of vigorous old age; and its needle-shaped leaves are credited with the power of driving away demons.

There are two *sakuranoki*,[i] Japanese cherry trees; those trees whose blossoms, as Professor Chamberlain so justly observes, are "Beyond comparison more lovely than anything Europe has to show." Many varieties are cultivated and loved; those in my garden bear blossoms of the most delicate pink: a flushed white. When, in spring, the trees flower, it is as though fleecy masses of clouds, faintly tinged by sunset, have floated down from the highest sky to fold themselves around the branches. This comparison is no poetic exaggeration; neither is it original: it is an ancient Japanese description of the most marvelous floral exhibition which nature is capable of making. The reader who has never seen a cherry tree blossoming in Japan cannot possibly imagine the delight of the spectacle. There are no green leaves: these come later. There is only one glorious burst of blossoms, veiling every twig and bough in their delicate mist; and the soil beneath each tree is deeply covered out of sight by fallen petals, as though by a drift of pink snow.

These are cultivated cherry trees. There are others which put forth their leaves before their blossoms, such as the *yamazakura*, or mountain cherry.[ii] This too, however, has its poetry of beauty and of symbolism. As the great Shintō writer and poet Motowori sang:[16]

Shikishima no
Yamato-gokoro wo
Hito-towaba,
Asa-hi niou
Yamasakura hana.[iii]

---

[i] Author's Footnote: *Cerasus pseudo-cerasus* (Lindley).

[ii] Author's Footnote: About this mountain cherry there is a humorous saying which illustrates the Japanese love of puns. In order to fully appreciate it, the reader should know that Japanese nouns have no distinction of singular or plural. The word *ha*, as pronounced, may signify either "leaves" or "teeth;" and the word *hana*, either "flowers" or "nose." The *yamasakura* put forth its *ha* (leaves) before its *hana* (flowers). Therefore, a man whose *ha* (teeth) project in advance of his *hana* (nose) is called a *yamasakura*. Prognathism [having the jaws projecting beyond the upper face] is not uncommon in Japan, especially among the lower classes.

[iii] Author's Footnote: "If one should ask you concerning the heart of a true Japanese, point to the wild cherry flower glowing in the sun."

Whether cultivated or uncultivated, the Japanese cherry trees are emblems. Those that are planted in old samurai gardens were not cherished for their loveliness alone. Their spotless blossoms were regarded as symbolizing that delicacy of sentiment and blamelessness of life, belonging to high courtesy and true knightliness. "As the cherry flower is first among flowers," says an old proverb, "so should the warrior be the first among men."

Shading the western end of this garden, and projecting its smooth, dark limbs above the awning of the veranda, is a superb *umenoki* (Japanese plum tree); very old, and originally planted, no doubt as in other gardens, for the sake of the sight of its blossoming. The flowering of the *umenoki*,[1] in the earliest spring, is scarcely less astonishing than that of the cherry tree, which does not blossom for a full month later; and the blossoming of both is celebrated by popular holidays. Nor are these, although the most famed, the only flowers that are loved. The wisteria, the *convolvulus* (morning glory, moonflower), the peony, each in its season, form displays of blooming lovely enough to draw whole populations out of the cities into the countryside to see them. In Izumo, the blossoming of the peony is especially marvelous. The

---

[1] Author's Footnote: There are three noteworthy varieties: one bearing red, one pink and white, and one producing pure white flowers.

Plum Gateway," by Hiroshi Yoshida (1935).

most famous place for this spectacle is the little island of Daikonshima, in the grand Naka-umi lagoon, about an hour's sailing from Matsué. In May, the entire island burns crimson with peonies and even the boys and girls of the public schools are given a holiday so that they may enjoy the sight.

Although the plum flower is certainly a rival in beauty to the *sakura-no-hana*, the Japanese compare a woman's beauty, physical beauty, to the cherry flower, never to the plum flower. Womanly virtue and sweetness, on the other hand, are compared to the *ume-no-hana*, never to the cherry blossom. It is a great mistake to state, as some writers have done, that the Japanese never think of comparing a woman to trees and flowers. For grace, a maiden is likened to a slender willow;[i] for youthful charm, to the cherry tree in bloom; for sweetness of heart, to the blossoming plum tree. No, the old Japanese poets have compared woman to all beautiful things. They have even sought metaphors from flowers for her various poses and movements, as in the verse:

Tateba shakuyaku;[ii]
Suwareba botan;
Aruku sugatawa
Himeyuri[iii] *no hana.*[iv]

Why, even the names of the most humble country girls are often those of beautiful trees or flowers prefixed by the honorific "O":[v] O-Matsu (Pine), O-Také (Bamboo), O-Umé (Plum), O-Hana (Blossom), O-Iné (Ear of Young Rice), not to speak of the professional flower names of dancing girls and of

---

[i] Author's Footnote: The expression *yanagi-goshi*, "a willow-waist," is one of several in common use comparing slender beauty to the willow tree.

[ii] Author's Footnote: *Peonia albiflora*. The name signifies the delicacy of beauty. The simile of the *botan* (the tree peony) can be fully appreciated only by one who is acquainted with the Japanese flower.

[iii] Author's Footnote: Some say *keshiyuri* (poppy) instead of *himeyuri*. The latter is a graceful species of lily, *Lilium callosum*.

[iv] Author's Footnote: "Standing, she is a *shakuyaku*; seated she is a *botan*; and the charm of her figure in walking is the charm of a *himeyuri*."

[v] Author's Footnote: In the higher classes of Japanese society today, the honorific "O" is not, as a rule, used before the names of girls, and showy appellations are not given to daughters. Even among the poor, respectable classes, names resembling those of geisha, etc., are in disfavor; but, those cited above are good, honest, everyday names.

joro.[17] It has been argued with considerable force that the origin of certain tree names borne by girls, must be sought in the folk conception of the tree as an emblem of longevity, happiness, or good fortune, rather than in any popular idea of the beauty of the tree itself. But however this may be, proverb, poem, song, and popular speech today yield ample proof that the Japanese comparisons of women to trees and flowers are in no way inferior to our own in aesthetic sentimentality.

VI

That trees, at least Japanese trees, have souls, cannot seem an unnatural idea to one who has seen the blossoming of the *umenoki* and the *sakuranoki*. This is a popular belief in Izumo and elsewhere. It is not in accord with Buddhist philosophy, and yet, in a certain sense it strikes one as being much closer to cosmic truth than the old Western orthodox notion of trees as "things created for the use of man." Furthermore, there exist several odd superstitions about particular trees, not unlike certain West Indian beliefs which have had a good influence in stopping the destruction of valuable timber. Japan, like the tropical world, has its goblin trees. Of these, the *enoki* (*Celtis willdenowiana*) and the *yanagi* (drooping willow) are deemed especially ghostly, and are now rarely to be found in old Japanese gardens. Both are believed to have the power of haunting. "*Enoki ga bakeru*," is the Izumo saying. You will find in a Japanese dictionary the word "*bakeru*" translated by such terms as "to be transformed," "to be metamorphosed," "to be changed," etc.; but the belief about these trees is very unique and cannot be explained by any such rendering of the verb "*bakeru*." The tree itself does not change form or place, but a specter called *Ki-no-o-baké* disengages itself from the tree and walks about in various forms.[1] Most often, the

---

[1] Author's Footnote: Mr. Satow [Sir Ernest Mason Satow (June 30, 1843 – August 26, 1929), known in Japan as "アーネスト・サトウ" (Ānesuto Satō), a British scholar, diplomat and Japanologist.] has found in Hirata, a belief to which this seems to some extent similar, the curious Shintō doctrine "according to which a divine being throws off portions of itself by a process of fissure, thus producing what are called *waki-mi-tama*, parted sprits with separate functions." The great god of Izumo, Oho-kuni-nushi-no-kami, is said by Hirata to have three such "parted spirits:" his rough spirit (*ara-mi-tama*) that punishes, his gentle spirit (*nigi-mi-tama*) that pardons, and his benedictory

shape assumed by the phantom is that of a beautiful woman. The tree specter seldom speaks and seldom ventures very far away from its tree. If approached, it immediately shrinks back into the trunk or the foliage. It is said that if either an old *yanagi* or a young *enoki* is cut, blood will flow from the gash. When such trees are very young, it is not believed that they have supernatural habits; but rather, they become more dangerous the older they grow.

There is another pretty legend, recalling the old Greek drama of *dryads*,[i] about a willow tree which grew in the garden of a samurai of Kyōto. Because of its weird reputation, the tenant of the house wanted to cut it down; but another samurai dissuaded him, saying, "Instead, sell it to me so that I can plant it in my garden. That tree has a soul; it is cruel to destroy its life." Consequently, purchased and transplanted, the *yanagi* flourished well in its new home and its spirit, out of gratitude, took the form of a beautiful woman, and became the wife of the samurai who had befriended it and a charming boy was the result of this union. A few years later, the *daimyō* to whom the ground

---

or benevolent spirit (*saki-mi-tama*) that blesses. There is a Shintō story that the rough spirit of this god once met the gentle spirit without recognizing it.

[i] Tree nymphs in Greek mythology.

belonged, gave orders that the tree should be cut down. Then the wife wept bitterly, and for the first time, revealed to her husband the whole story. "And now," she added, "I know that I must die; but our child will live, and you will always love him. This thought is my only consolation." The astonished and terrified husband sought in vain to keep her. Bidding him farewell forever, she vanished into the tree. Needless to say, the samurai did everything in his power to persuade the *daimyō* to give up his intention. The *daimyō* wanted the tree for the reparation of a great Buddhist temple, the San-jiu-san-gen-dō.[i] The tree was cut down; but, having fallen, it suddenly became so heavy that three hundred men could not move it. Then the child, taking a branch in his little hand, said, "Come," and the tree followed him, gliding along the ground to the courtyard of the temple.

Although said to be a *bakemono-ki*, the *enoki* sometimes receives highest religious honors; for the spirit of the god Kōjin,[18] to whom old dolls are dedicated, is supposed to live within certain very ancient *enoki* trees; and in front of these are placed shrines where people pray.

VII

The second garden, on the north side, is my favorite. It contains no large growths. It is paved with blue pebbles and its center is occupied by a small pond; a miniature lake fringed with rare plants, and containing a small island with tiny mountains and dwarf peach trees, pines, and azaleas, some of which are perhaps more than a century old, although scarcely more than a foot high. Nevertheless, this work, seen as it was intended to be seen, does not look like a miniature at all. From a certain corner of the guestroom, looking out on it, the appearance is that of a real lakeshore with a real island beyond it, a stone's throw away. So clever the art of the ancient gardener who designed all this, and who has been sleeping for a hundred years under the cedars of Gessho-ji, that the illusion can be detected only from the *zashiki*[ii] by the presence of an *ishidōrō*, or stone lamp, on the

---

[i] Author's Footnote: Perhaps the most impressive of all the Buddhist temples in Kyōto. It is dedicated to Kwannon of the Thousand Hands, and is said to contain 33,333 of her images.

[ii] A *zakishi* is the guestroom of a samurai house.

island. The size of the *ishidōrō* betrays the false perspective; and I do not think it was placed there when the garden was made.

Here and there at the edge of the pond, and almost level with the water, are large flat stones, on which one may either stand or squat, to watch the residents of the pond or to tend the water plants. There are beautiful water lilies (*Nuphar Japonica*), whose bright green leaf-disks float smoothly on the surface, and many lotus plants of two kinds: those which bear pink and those which bear pure white flowers. There are iris plants growing along the bank, whose blossoms are a prismatic violet; and there are various ornamental grasses, ferns, and mosses. But the pond is essentially a lotus pond; the lotus plants make up its greatest charm. It is a delight to watch every phase of their marvelous growth; from the first unrolling of the leaf to the fall of the last flower. On rainy days, especially, the lotus plants are worth observing. Their great, cup-shaped leaves, swaying high above the pond, catch the rain and hold it a while; but always after the water in the leaf reaches a certain level, the stem bends and empties the leaf with a loud splash; and then straightens again. Rainwater on a lotus leaf is a favorite subject with Japanese metalworkers, and only metalwork can reproduce the effect; for the motion and color of water moving on the green, sleek surfaces are exactly those of quicksilver.

VIII

The third garden, which is very large, extends beyond the enclosure containing the lotus pond to the foot of the wooded hills that form the northern and northeastern boundary of this old samurai residence. Formerly, all this broad level space was occupied by a bamboo grove; but it is now little more than an abundance of grasses and wild flowers. In the northeast corner, there is a magnificent well, from which ice-cold water is brought into the house through a most ingenious little aqueduct of bamboo pipes; and in the northwestern end, veiled by tall weeds, there stands a very small stone shrine of Inari, with two proportionately small stone foxes sitting in front of it. Shrine and images are chipped, broken, and thickly patched with dark green moss. But on the east side of the house, one little square of soil belonging to this large part of the garden is still cultivated. It is devoted entirely to chrysanthemum plants, which are shielded from heavy rain and strong sun by slanting frames of light wood, fashioned like *shōji*, with panes of white paper, and supported like awnings on thin posts of bamboo. I can venture to add nothing to what has already been written about these marvelous products of Japanese horticulture; but there is a little story relating to chrysanthemums, which I will attempt to tell.

There is one place in Japan where it is thought unlucky to cultivate chrysanthemums, for reasons which will presently appear; and that place is in the pretty, little city of Himeji,[19] in the province of Harima. Himeji contains the ruins of a great castle with thirty turrets; and a *daimyō* used to live there, whose income was one hundred and fifty-six thousand *koku*[20] of rice. Now, in the house of one of that *daimyō's* chief retainers, there was a maidservant, from a good family, whose name was O-Kiku. The name "Kiku" signifies a chrysanthemum flower. Many precious things were entrusted to her care, and among others, ten valuable dishes of gold. One of these was suddenly lost and could not be found. The girl, being responsible for the care of the dishes, and not knowing how to prove her innocence, drowned herself in a well. From then on, her ghost, returning nightly, could be heard counting the dishes with slow sobs:

"*Ichi-mai…Ni-mai…San-mai…Yo-mai…Go-mai…Raku-mai…Shichi-mai…Hachi-mai…Ku-mai…*"

Then a cry of despair would be heard and a loud burst of weeping; and again the girl's voice pitifully counting the dishes, "One, two, three, four, five, six, seven, eight, nine."

Her spirit passed into the body of a strange little insect, whose head faintly resembles that of a ghost with long, disheveled hair. It is called *O-Kiku-mushi*, or "the fly of O-Kiku"; and it is found, they say, nowhere except in Himeji. A famous play was written about O-Kiku, which is still acted in all the popular theaters, entitled *Banshu O-Kiku-no-Sara-ya-shiki*; or, *The Manor of the Dish of O-Kiku of Banshu.*

Some say that Banshu is only the corruption of the name of an ancient district of Tokyō (Edo), where the story should have been set. The people of Himeji say that part of their city, now called Go-Ken-Yashiki, is identical to the site of the ancient manor. What is certainly true is that to cultivate chrysanthemum flowers in that part of Himeji called Go-Ken-Yashiki, is considered unlucky because the name of O-Kiku means "Chrysanthemum." Therefore, nobody, I am told, ever cultivates chrysanthemums there.

IX

Now, about the *ujō*, or things having desire, which inhabit these gardens. There are four species of frogs: three that dwell in

"Shinkei 36 Kaisen," (Kiku) by Tsukioka Yoshitoshi (1889).

the lotus pond, and one that lives in the trees. The tree frog is a very pretty little creature, exquisitely green. It has a shrill cry, almost like the note of a *semi*[1] and it is called *amagaeru*, or "the rain frog," because, like its relatives in other countries, its croaking is an omen of rain. The pond frogs are called *babagaeru*, *shinagaeru*, and *Tono-san-gaeru*. Of these, the first variety is the largest and the ugliest: its color is very disagreeable and its full name ("*babagaeru*" being a good abbreviation) is quite as offensive as its color. The *shinagaeru*, or "striped frog," is not handsome, except by comparison with the previously mentioned creature. But the *Tono-san-gaeru*, named after a famed *daimyō* who left behind a memory of great splendor, is beautiful: its color is a fine bronze-red.

Besides these varieties of frogs, an uncouth, google-eyed thing lives in the garden which although called *hikigaeru*, I believe is a toad. "*Hikigaeru*" is the term ordinarily used for a bullfrog. This creature enters the house almost daily to be fed and seems to have no fear even of strangers. My people consider it a luck-bringing visitor; and it is credited with the power of drawing all the mosquitoes out of the room into its mouth by simply sucking its breath in. As much as it is cherished by gardeners and others, there is a legend about a goblin toad of old times, which, by sucking in its breath, drew men, not insects into its mouth.

The pond is inhabited by many small fish; *imori* or newts, with bright, red bellies; and multitudes of little water beetles, called *maimaimushi*, which pass their entire time by gyrating on the surface of the water so rapidly that it is almost impossible to clearly distinguish their shape. A man who runs about aimlessly to and fro, under the influence of excitement, is compared to a *maimaimushi*. And, there are some beautiful snails, with yellow stripes on their shells. Japanese children have a charm-song which is supposed to have power to make the snail put out its horns:

---

[1] *Semi* is Japanese for cicada, an insect in the order *Hemiptera* in the superfamily *Cicdoidea*, with large, wide eyes and transparent, veined wings. There are about 2,500 species of cicada around the world. In the early Japanese novel, *Genji Monogatari (Tales of Genji)*, the main character poetically compares one of his many love interests to a cicada because of the way she delicately sheds her scarf, the way a cicada sheds it shell when molting. *Semi* are also a frequent subject for *haiku*.

Daidaimushi,[i] *daidaimushi,*
tsuno chitto dashare!
Ame kaze fuku kara
tsuno chitto dashare![ii]

The playground of the children of the better classes has always been the family garden, just as that of the poor children is the temple courtyard. It is in the garden that the little ones first learn something of the wonderful life of plants and the marvels of the insect world; and also they are first taught those pretty legends and songs about birds and flowers, which form such a charming part of Japanese folklore. Since the home training of the child is left mostly to the mother, lessons of kindness to animals are taught early, and the results are strongly marked in later life. It is true, however, that Japanese children are not entirely free from that unconscious tendency to cruelty characteristic of children in all countries, as a remnant of primitive instincts. But, in this regard, the great moral difference between the sexes is strongly marked from the earliest years. The tenderness of the woman-soul appears even in the child. Little Japanese girls who play with insects or small animals rarely hurt them; and generally set them free after they have provided a reasonable amount of amusement. Little boys are not nearly so good when out of the sight of parents or guardians. If seen doing anything cruel, a child is made to feel ashamed of the act and hears the Buddhist warning, "Thy future birth will be unhappy, if thou dost cruel things."[21]

Somewhere among the rocks in the pond, lives a small tortoise; left in the garden, probably, by the previous tenants of the house. It is very pretty, but manages to remain invisible for weeks at a time. In popular mythology, the tortoise is the servant of the deity Kompira;[iii] and if a pious fisherman finds a tortoise, he writes on its back characters signifying "Servant of the Deity Kompira," and then gives it a drink of *saké* and sets it free. It is supposed to be very fond of *saké*.

---

[i] Author's Footnote: *Daidaimushi* in Izumo. The dictionary word is *dedemushi*. The snail is supposed to be very fond of wet weather; and one who goes out much in the rain is compared to a snail: *dedemushi no yona*.

[ii] Author's Footnote: "Snail, snail, put out your horns a little: it rains and the wind is blowing, so put out your horns, just for a little while."

[iii] Author's Footnote: A Buddhist deity, but within recent times identified by Shintō with the god Kotohira.

"Urashima and Dragon Palace," by Gekko Ogata (1893).

Some say that only the land tortoise, or "stone tortoise," is the servant of Kompira, and the sea tortoise, or turtle, is the servant of the Dragon Empire beneath the sea. The turtle is said to have the power to create, with its breath, a cloud, fog, or a magnificent palace. It figures in the beautiful old folktale of *Urashima*.[1] All tortoises are supposed to live for a thousand years; therefore, one of the most frequent symbols of longevity in Japanese art is a tortoise. The tortoise most commonly represented by native painters and metalworkers has a peculiar tail, or rather, a multitude of small tails, extending behind it like the fringe of a straw raincoat (*mino*) thus it is called *minogamé*. Now, some of the tortoises kept in the sacred ponds of Buddhist temples attain an extraordinary age, and certain water plants attach themselves to the creatures' shells and stream behind them when they walk. The myth of the *minogamé* is supposed to

---

[1] Author's Footnote: See Professor Chamberlain's version of it in *The Japanese Fairytale Series*, with charming illustrations by a native artist. [Also refer to *Out of the East*, also by Lafcadio Hearn.]

have had its origin in old artistic efforts to represent the appearance of such tortoises with plants fastened on their shells.

X

Early in summer, the frogs are surprisingly numerous; and after dark, are noisy beyond description; but, week by week their nightly clamor grows more feeble, as their numbers diminish under the attacks of many enemies. A large family of snakes, some fully three feet long, make occasional inroads into the colony. The victims often utter piteous cries, which are promptly responded to, whenever possible, by some inmate of the house, and many a frog has been saved by my servant-girl, who, by a gentle tap with a bamboo stick, compels the snake to let its prey go. These snakes are beautiful swimmers. They make themselves quite free about the garden; but they come out only on hot days. None of my people would think of injuring or killing one of them; indeed, in Izumo it is said that to kill a snake is unlucky. "If you kill a snake without provocation," a peasant assured me, "you will afterwards find its head in the *komebitsu* (the box in which cooked rice is kept) when you take off the lid."

But the snakes devour comparatively few frogs. Impudent kites[22] and crows are their most implacable destroyers; and there is a very pretty weasel which lives under the *kura* (storeroom), which does not hesitate to take either fish or frogs out of the pond, even when the lord of the manor is watching. There is also a cat who poaches in my preserve; a gaunt outlaw, a master thief, who I have made many vain attempts to reclaim from vagabondage. Partly because of the immorality of this cat, and partly because it happens to have a long tail, it has the evil reputation of being a *nekomata*, or goblin cat.

It is true that in Izumo some kittens are born with long tales; but it is very seldom that they are allowed to grow up with long tails. For the natural tendency of cats is to become goblins and this tendency to metamorphosis can only be prevented by cutting off their tails in kittenhood. Cats are magicians, tails or no tails, and have the power of making corpses dance. Cats are ungrateful. "Feed a dog for three days," says a Japanese proverb, "and he will remember your kindness for three years; feed a cat for three years, and she will forget your kindness in three days." Cats are mischievous: they tear the *tatami* mats,[23] make holes in the *shōji*, and sharpen their claws on the pillars of *tokonoma*. Cats are under a curse: only the cat and the venomous serpent did not weep at the death of Buddha; and they will never enter the bliss of the *Gokuraku* (paradise). For all these reasons, and others too numerous to tell, cats are not much loved in Izumo and are compelled to pass the greater part of their lives out of doors.

XI

Not less than eleven varieties of butterflies have visited the neighborhood of the lotus pond within the past few days. The most common variety is snowy white. It is supposed to be especially attracted by the *na*, or rapeseed plant; and when little girls see it they sing:

> *Chō-chō, chō-chō, na no ha ni tomare;*
> *Na no ha ga iyenara, te ni tomare.*[1]

But the most interesting insects are certainly the *semi* (cicadae). These Japanese tree crickets are much more extraordinary singers than even the wonderful cicadae of the tropics and much less boring; for, there is a different species of *semi*, with a totally different song, for almost every month during the whole warm season. There are, I believe, seven kinds; but I have become familiar with only four. The first to be heard in my trees

---

[1] Author's Footnote: "Butterfly, little butterfly, light upon the *na* leaf. But if you do not like the *na* leaf, light, I pray you, upon my head."

is the *natsuzemi* or summer *semi*: it makes a sound like the Japanese syllable *ji*, beginning wheezily, slowly swelling into a shrill crescendo, like the blowing of steam, and then dying away in another wheeze. This *j-i-i-iiiiiiiii* is so deafening that when two or three *natsuzemi* come close to the window, I am forced to make them go away. Happily, the *natsuzemi* is soon succeeded by the *minminzemi*, a much finer musician, whose name is derived from its wonderful note. It is said "to chant like a Buddhist priest reciting the *kyō*;"[24] and certainly, on hearing it the first time, one can hardly believe that one is listening to a mere cicada. The *minminzemi* is followed, early in autumn, by a beautiful green *semi*, the *higurashi*, which makes a uniquely clear sound, like the rapid ringing of a small bell, "*kana-kana-kana-kana-kana*;" however, the most astonishing visitor of all comes still later: the *tsuku-tsuku-bōshi*.[1] I believe that this creature can have no rival in the whole world of cicadae: its music is exactly like the song of a bird. Its name, like that of the *minminzemi*, is an imitation of its sound; but in Izumo, the sounds of its chant are given like so:

"Cicada and Lotus," by Gekko Ogata.

---

[1] Author's Footnote: *Bōshi* means "a hat"; *tsukeru*, "to put on." But this etymology is more than doubtful.

> "*Tsuku-tsuku uisu,*[i]
> *Tsuku-tsuku uisu,*
> *Tsuku-tsuku uisu;*
> *Ui-ōsu,*
> *Ui-ōsu,*
> *Ui-ōsu,*
> *Ui-ōs-s-s-s-s-s-s-su.*"

However, the *semi* are not the only musicians of the garden. Two remarkable creatures aid their orchestra. The first is a beautiful, bright green grasshopper, known to the Japanese by the curious name of *hotoke-no-uma*, or "the horse of the dead." This insect's head really bears some resemblance in shape to the head of a horse, hence the name. It is a strangely friendly creature, allowing itself to be taken in hand without struggling, and generally making itself quite at home in the house, which it often enters. It makes a very thin sound, which the Japanese write as a repetition of the syllables *jun-ta*; and the name *junta* is sometimes given to the grasshopper itself.

The other insect is also a green grasshopper, somewhat larger, and much more shy; it is called *gisu*,[ii] because of its chant:

> *Chon,*
> *Gisu;*
> *Chon,*
> *Gisu;*
> *Chon,*
> *Gisu;*
> *Chon…(ad libitum).*

Several lovely species of dragonflies (*tombō*) hover about the pond on hot, bright days. One variety, the most beautiful creature of its kind that I ever saw, gleaming with indescribable metallic colors, and ghostly thin, is called *Tenshi-tombō*, "the Emperor's dragonfly." There is another, the largest of Japanese dragonflies, but somewhat rare, which is much sought after by children as a plaything. It is said of this species that there are

---

[i] Author's Footnote: Some say "*Chokko-chokko-uisu.*" "*Uisu*" would be pronounced in English very much like "weece," the final u being silent. "*Uiōsu*" would be something like "we-oce."

[ii] Author's Footnote: Pronounced almost like "geese."

33

many more males than females. What I can vouch for as true is that, if you catch a female, the male can be almost immediately attracted by exposing the captive. Boys, accordingly, try to secure a female, and when one is captured, they tie it with a thread to some branch, and sing a curious little song, of which these are the original words:

> *Konna[i] dansho Korai o*
> *Adsuma no metō ni makete*
> *Nigeru wa haji dewa naikai?*

Which means, "You, the male, King of Korea, do you not feel shame to flee away from the Queen of the east?" (This taunt is an allusion to the story of the conquest of Korea by the Empress Jin-gō.)[25] The male invariably comes, and is also caught. In Izumo, the first seven words of the original song have been corrupted into "*konna unjo Korai abura no mito;*" and the name of the male dragonfly, *unjo*, and that of the female, *mito*, are derived from two words of the corrupted version.

"Dragonfly," by Bairei Kono (1844 – 1895).

---

[i] Author's Footnote: Contraction of *kore naru*.

XII

On warm nights, all sorts of uninvited guests invade the house in multitudes. Two varieties of mosquitoes do their utmost to make life unpleasant, and these have learned the wisdom of not approaching a lamp too closely; however, hosts of curious and harmless things cannot be prevented from seeking their death in the flame. The most numerous victims of all, which come as thick as a shower of rain, are called *sanemori*. At least, they are called that in Izumo, where they do much damage to growing rice.

Now, the name *sanemori* is an illustrious one; that of a famous warrior of old times, belonging to the Genji clan. There is a legend that, while he was fighting with an enemy on horseback, his own steed slipped and fell in a rice field, and he was consequently overpowered and slain by his enemy. He became a rice-devouring insect, which is still respectfully called, by the peasants of Izumo, *sanemori-san*. On certain summer nights, they light fires in the rice fields, to attract the insect; and beat gongs and sound bamboo flutes, chanting all the while, "O Sanemori, augustly agree to come here!" A *kannushi*[26] performs a religious rite, and a straw figure, representing a horse and rider, is then either burned or thrown into a neighboring river or canal. By this ceremony, it is believed that the fields are cleared of the insect.

"Bijin and Mosquito Net," by Eisen Ikeda (1790 - 1848).

This tiny creature is almost exactly the size and color of a rice husk. The legend concerning it may have arisen from the fact that its body, together with the wings, bears some resemblance to the helmet of a Japanese warrior.[i]

Next in number among the victims of fire are the moths, some of which are very strange and beautiful. The most remarkable is an enormous creature popularly called *okori-chōchō*, or the "*ague*[ii] moth," because there is a superstitious belief that it brings intermittent fever into any house it enters. It has a body quite as heavy, and almost as powerful, as that of the largest hummingbird, and its struggles, when caught in the hand, are surprising in their force. It makes a very loud whirring sound while flying. The wings of one, which I examined, measured, outspread, five inches from tip to tip; yet, seemed small in proportion to the heavy body. They were richly mottled with dusky browns and silver grays of various tones.

Many flying night-comers, however, avoid the lamp. Most fantastic of all visitors is the *tōrō* or *kamakiri*, called *kamakaké* in Izumo; a bright green praying mantis, extremely feared by children for its capacity to bite — it is very large. I have seen specimens over six inches long. The eyes of the *kamakaké* are a brilliant black at night, but by day they appear grass-colored, like the rest of the body. The mantis is very intelligent and surprisingly aggressive. I saw one attacked by a strong frog easily put its enemy to flight. Subsequently it fell prey to other

---

[i] Author's Footnote: A related legend attaches to the *shiwan*, a little yellow insect which preys on cucumbers. The *shiwan* is said to have once been a physician, who, being detected in an amorous intrigue, had to fly for his life; but as he went, his foot caught in a cucumber vine, so that he fell and was overtaken and killed. His ghost became an insect, the destroyer of cucumber vines.

In the zoological mythology and plant mythology of Japan, there exist many legends offering a curious resemblance to the old Greek tales of metamorphoses. Some of the most remarkable bits of such folklore have originated, however, in comparatively modern time. The legend of the crab called *heikegani*, found at Nagato, is an example. The souls of the Taira warriors who perished in the great naval battle of Dan-no-ura (now Seto-Nakai), in 1185, are supposed to have been transformed into *heikegani*. The shell of the *heikegani* is certainly surprising. It is wrinkled into the likeness of a grim face, or rather into exact semblance of one of those black, iron visors or masks, which feudal warriors wore in battle, and which are shaped like frowning faces.

[ii] A noun meaning malarial fever, chills, or a fit of shivering.

inhabitants of the pond, but it required the combined efforts of several frogs to defeat the monstrous insect; and even then, the battle was decided only when the *kamakaké* had been dragged into the water.

Other visitors are beetles of many colors and a type of small roach called *goki-kaburi*, meaning "one whose head is covered with a bowl." It is alleged that the *goki-kaburi* likes to eat human eyes, and is therefore the abhorred enemy of Ichibata-sama, Yakushi-Nyorai of Ichibata, by whom diseases of the eye are healed. To kill the *goki-kaburi* is consequently thought to be a meritorious act in the sight of this Buddha. Always welcome are the beautiful fireflies (*hotaru*), which enter quite noiselessly, and immediately seek the darkest place in the house: slow glimmering, like sparks moved by a gentle wind. They are supposed to be very fond of water; therefore, children sing this little song to them:

> *Hataru kõe midzu nomashõ;*
> *Achi no midzu wa nigaizo;*
> *Kochi no midzu wa amaizo.*[1]

A pretty, gray lizard, quite different from some which usually haunt the garden, also makes its appearance at night and pursues

---

[1] Author's Footnote: "Come, firefly, I will give you water to drink. The water of that place is bitter; the water here is sweet."

its prey along the ceiling. Sometimes, an extraordinarily large centipede attempts the same thing, but with less success, and has to be seized with a pair of fire tongs and thrown into the darkness outside. Very rarely, an enormous spider appears. This creature seems harmless. If captured, it will pretend to be dead, until certain that it is not watched, then it will run away with surprising swiftness if it gets a chance. It is hairless and very different from the tarantula or *fukurogumo*. It is called *miyamagumo*, or "mountain spider."

There are four other kinds of spiders common to the neighborhood: *tenagakumo*, or "long-armed spider;" *hiratakumo*, or "flat spider;" *jikumo*, or "earth spider;" and *totatekumo*, or "door-shutting spider." Most spiders are considered evil beings. The people say that a spider seen anywhere at night should be killed; for, all spiders that show themselves after dark are goblins. While people are awake and watchful, such creatures make themselves small; but, when everybody is fast asleep, then they assume their true goblin shape and become monstrous.

"Ghost and Spider," by Kinsen Suzuki (1867-1945).

XIII

The high wood of the hill behind the garden is full of bird life. There live wild *uguisu*, owls, wild doves, too many crows, and a queer bird that makes weird noises at night: long, deep sounds of *hoo, hoo*. It is called *awamakidori* or the "millet-sowing bird," because when the farmers hear its cry, they know that it is time to plant the millet. It is quite small and brown, extremely shy; and so far as I can learn, altogether nocturnal in its habits.

But rarely, very rarely, a far stranger cry is heard in those trees at night: a voice like one crying in pain the syllables "*ho-to-to-gi-su.*" The cry and the name of the bird are one and the same: *hototogisu*.

It is a bird of which weird things are told; for, they say it is not really a creature of this living world, but a night wanderer from the Land of Darkness. In the Meido[27] its home is among those sunless mountains of Shide,[28] over which all souls must pass to reach the place of judgment. Once a year it comes; the end of the fifth month by the antique counting of moons. The peasants, hearing its voice, say to one another, "Now we must sow the rice; for, the Shide-no-taosa is with us." The word *taosa* signifies the head man of a *mura* or village, as villages were governed in the old days; but why the *hototogisu* is called the "Taosa of Shide" I do not know. Perhaps it is thought to be a soul from some shadowy hamlet of the Shide hills, where ghosts like to rest on their weary way to the realm of Emma, the King of Death.

Its cry has been interpreted in various ways. Some state that the *hototogisu* does not really repeat its own name, but asks, "*Honzon kaketaka?*" (Has the *honzon*[1] been suspended?). Others, resting their interpretation on the wisdom of the Chinese, claim that the bird's speech signifies, "Surely it is better to return home." This, at least, is true: that all who journey far from their native place, and hear the voice of the *hototogisu* in other distant provinces, are seized with the sickness of longing for home.

---

[1] Author's Footnote: By *honzon* is here meant the sacred *kakemono*, or picture, exposed to public view in the temples only on the birthday of the Buddha, which is the eighth day of the old fourth month. *Honzon* also means the principle image in a Buddhist temple.

Only at night, the people say, is its voice heard, and most often on the nights of great moons; and it chants while hovering high out of sight, of which a poet has written of it this way:

*Hito koe wa.
Tsuki ga naitaka
Hototogisu!*[i]

And another has written:

*Hototogisu
Nakitsuru kata wo.
Nagamureba,
Tada ariake no
Tsuki zo nokoreru.*[ii]

"Bush Warbler and Bamboo," by Seitei (Shotei) Watanabe (1851 - 1918).

The city dweller may pass a lifetime without hearing the *hototogisu*. Caged, the little creature will remain silent and die. Poets often wait vainly in the dew, from sunset until dawn, to hear the strange cry which has inspired so many exquisite verses;

---

[i] Author's Footnote: "A solitary voice! Did the Moon cry? T'was but the *hototogisu*."

[ii] Author's Footnote: "When I gaze towards the place where I heard the *hototogisu* cry, lo! There is naught save the wan morning moon."

but those who have heard, have found it so mournful that they have compared it to the cry of one wounded suddenly to death.

Hototogisu
Chi ni naku koe wa
Ariake no
Tsuki yori hokani
Kiku hito mo nashi.[i]

Concerning Izumo owls, I will content myself with citing a composition by one of my Japanese students:

The owl is a hateful bird that sees in the dark. Little children who cry are frightened by the threat that the owl will come to take them away; for the owl cries, "Ho! Ho! Sorotto kōka! Sorotto kōka!" which means, "Thou! Must I enter slowly?" It also cries, "Noritsuke hose! Ho! Ho!" which means, "Do thou make the starch to use in washing tomorrow?" And when the women hear that cry, they know that tomorrow will be a fine day. It also cries, "Tototo," "The man dies," and "Kōto-kokko," "The boy dies." So people hate it. And crows hate it so much that it is used to catch crows. The farmer puts an owl in the rice field; and all the crows come to kill it, and they get caught fast in the snares. This should teach us not to give way to our dislikes for other people.

The kites which hover over the city all day do not live in the neighborhood. Their nests are far away on the blue peaks; but they pass much of their time by catching fish and in stealing from backyards. They pay the woods and the garden swift and sudden piratical visits; and their sinister cry, *pi-yoroyoro, pi-yoroyoro,* sounds periodically over the town from dawn until sundown. They certainly are the most insolent of all feathered creatures; more insolent than even their fellow robbers, the crows. A kite will drop five miles to snatch a *tai* fish out of a fish-seller's bucket, or a fried cake out of child's hand, and then shoot back to the clouds before the victim of the theft has time to bend down for a stone to throw. Hence the saying, "to look as

---

[i] Author's Footnote: "Save only the morning moon, none heard the heart's-blood cry of the *hototogisu.*"

surprised as if one's *aburagé*[i] had been snatched from one's hand by a kite."

Moreover, there is no telling what a kite may think is good to steal. For example, my neighbor's servant girl went to the river the other day, wearing in her hair, a string of small scarlet beads made of rice grains, prepared and dyed in a certain ingenious way. A kite landed on her head, tore away, and then swallowed the string of beads! But it is great fun to feed these birds with dead rats or mice, which have been caught in traps overnight and subsequently drowned. The instant a dead rat is exposed to view, a kite pounces from the sky to carry it away. Sometimes a crow may beat the kite, but the crow must be able to get to the woods very swiftly indeed, in order to keep his prize.

The children sing this song:

Tobi, tobi, maute mise!
Ashita no ba ni
Karasu ni kakushite
Nezumi yaru.[ii]

The mention of dancing refers to the beautiful balancing motion of the kite's wings in flight. By suggestion, this motion is artistically compared to the graceful swaying of a *maiko*,[29] or dancing girl, extending her arms and waving the long wide sleeves of her silken robe.

Although there is a sizable colony of crows in the woods behind my house, the headquarters of the crow army is in the pine grove of the ancient castle grounds, visible from my front rooms. To see the crows all flying home at the same hour every evening is an interesting spectacle, and popular imagination has found an amusing comparison for it in the hurry-scurry of people running to a fire. This explains the meaning of a song which children sing to the crows returning to their nests:

Ato no karasu saki ine,
Ware ga iye ga yakeru ken,
Hayō inde midzu kake,

---

[i] Author's Footnote: A sort of doughnut made of bean flour or tofu.
[ii] Author's Footnote: "Kite, kite, let me see you dance, and tomorrow evening, when the crows do not know, I will give you a rat."

Midzu ga nakya yarozo,
Amattara ko ni yare,
Ko ga nakya modose.[1]

"Winter Crow," by Kyosai Kawanabe 1831-1889.

Confucianism seems to have discovered virtue in the crow. There is a Japanese proverb, "*Karasu ni hampo no ko ari,*" meaning that the crow performs the filial duty or *hampo*; or, more literally, "the filial duty of *hampo* exists in the crow." "*Hampo*" means literally, "to return a feeding." The young crow is said to repay its parents' care by feeding them when it becomes strong.

Another example of filial piety[30] is provided by the dove. "*Hato ni sanshi no rei ari,*" "the dove sits three branches below its parent;" or, more literally, "has the three-branch etiquette to perform."

The cry of the wild dove (*yamabato*), which I hear almost daily from the woods, is the most sweetly plaintive sound that ever reached my ears. The Izumo peasants say that the bird

---

[1] Author's Footnote: "O tardy crow, hasten forward! Your house is on fire. Hurry to throw water upon it. If there be no water, I will give you. If you have too much, give it to your child. If you have no child, then give it back to me."

utters these words, which it certainly seems to do, if one listens to it after having learned the alleged syllables:

> *Tété*
>   *poppō*
> *Kaka*
>   *Poppō*
> *Tété*
>   *poppō*
> *Kaka*
>   *Poppō*
> *Tété*…(sudden pause).

"*Tété*" is the baby word for "father," and *kaka* for "mother;" and "*poppō*" signifies, in infantile speech, "the bosom."[1]

Wild *uguisu*[31] also frequently sweeten my summer with their song, and sometimes come very near the house, apparently attracted by the chant of my caged pet. The *uguisu* is very common in this province. It haunts all the woods and the sacred groves in the neighborhoods of the city. I never made a journey in Izumo during the warm season without hearing its note from some shadowy place. But, there are *uguisu*, and *uguisu*. There are *uguisu* to be had for one or two yen, but the finely trained, cage-bred singer may command not less than a hundred yen.

It was at a little village temple that I first heard one curious belief about this delicate creature. In Japan, the coffin in which a corpse is borne to burial, is totally unlike a Western coffin. It is a surprisingly small, square box, wherein the dead is placed in a sitting posture. How any adult corpse can be put into so small a space may well be an enigma to foreigners. In cases of pronounced *rigor mortis*[32] the work of getting the body into the coffin is difficult even for the professional *dōshin-bozu* a person who prepares a body for burial|. But the devout followers of Nichiren[33] claim that after death, their bodies will remain perfectly flexible; and the dead body of an *uguisu*, they insist, likewise never stiffens, for this little bird is of their faith, and

---

[1] Author's Footnote: The words "papa" and "mamma" exist in Japanese baby language, but their meaning is not at all what might be supposed. "*Mamma*," or, with the usual honorific, "*O-Mamma*," means "boiled rice." "*Papa*" means "tobacco."

passes its life in singing praises to the *Sutra of the Lotus of the Good Law*.

XIV

I have already become a little too fond of my dwelling place. Each day, after returning from my college duties, and exchanging my teacher's uniform for the infinitely more comfortable Japanese robe, I find more than compensation for the weariness of five class hours in the simple pleasure of squatting on the shaded veranda overlooking the gardens. Those antique garden walls, heavily covered in moss below their ruined tiled tops, seem to shut out even the murmur of the city's life. There are no sounds but the voices of birds, the shrilling of *semi*, or at long, lazy intervals, the solitary splash of a diving frog. No, those walls seclude me from much more than city streets. Outside them hums the changed Japan of telegraphs, newspapers, and steamships; inside dwell the all-relaxing peace of nature and the dreams of the sixteenth century. There is a charm of quaintness in the very air, a faint sense of something unseen and sweet all around one; perhaps the gentle haunting of dead ladies who looked like the ladies of the old picture books, and who lived here when all this was new. Even in the summer light, touching

45

the gray, strange shapes of stone, moving through the foliage of the long-loved trees, there is the tenderness of a phantom caress. These are the gardens of the past. The future will know them only as dreams, creations of a forgotten art, whose charm no genius may reproduce.

Of the human tenants here, no creature seems to be afraid. The little frogs resting on the lotus leaves scarcely flinch from my touch; the lizards sun themselves with easy reach of my hand; the water snakes glide across my shadow without fear; bands of *semi* establish their deafening orchestra on a plum branch just above my head, and a praying mantis insolently poses on my knee. Swallows and sparrows not only build their nests on my roof, but even enter my rooms without concern (one swallow has actually built its nest in the ceiling of the bathroom) and the weasel steals fish under my very eyes without any scruples of conscience. A wild *uguisu* perches on a cedar by the window, and in a burst of savage sweetness, challenges my caged pet to a contest in song; and always, through the golden air, from the green twilight of the mountain pines, there sings to me the plaintive, caressing, delicious call of the *yamabato:*

Tété
poppō
Kaka

> *Poppō*
> *Tété*
> *poppō*
> *Kaka*
> *Poppō*
> *Tété...*

No European dove has such a cry. He who can hear, for the first time, the voice of the *yamabato* without feeling a new sensation in his heart, little deserves to live in this happy world.

Yet all this — the old *katchiū-yashiki* and its gardens — will without doubt have vanished forever before many years.[1] Already, a multitude of gardens, more spacious and more beautiful than mine, have been converted into rice fields or bamboo groves; and the quaint Izumo city, touched at last by some long-projected railway line, perhaps even within the present decade, will swell and change, grow commonplace, and demand these grounds for the building of factories and mills. Not from here alone, but from all the land, the ancient peace and the ancient charm seem doomed to pass away; for, impermanency is the nature of things, more particularly in Japan; and the changes and the changers will also be changed until there is no place found for them — regret is vanity. The dead art that made the beauty of this place was the art also, of that faith to which belongs the all-consoling text, "Verily, even plants and trees, rocks and stones, all shall enter into Nirvana."

---

[1] Of this, Lafcadio Hearn was very wrong. His house has been lovingly preserved to this day in Matsué, with a museum next to it. The house is open year round and the entry fee is a modest 300 *yen*.

"Bird on a Persimmon Tree," by Seitei (Shotei) Watanabe, c. 1900.

XVII

THE HOUSEHOLD SHRINE

I

IN JAPAN there are two forms of the Religion of the Dead: that which belongs to Shintō and that which belongs to Buddhism. The first is the ancient cult commonly called ancestor worship; but, the term ancestor worship seems to me much too confined for the religion which pays reverence not only to those ancient gods believed to be the fathers of the Japanese nation, but also to a host of deified sovereigns, heroes, princes, and illustrious men. Within comparatively recent times the great *daimyō* of Izumo, for example, were deified; and the peasants of Shimane still pray before the shrines of the Matsudaira. Moreover, Shintō, like the faiths of Greece and of Rome, has its deities of the elements and special deities who preside over all the various affairs of life. Therefore, ancestor worship, though still a striking feature of Shintō, does not by itself constitute the state religion;[34] neither does the term fully describe the Shintō cult of the dead; a cult which in Izumo retains its ancient character more than in other parts of Japan.

Here I may presume, though not an Asian scholar, to say something about the state religion of Japan, that ancient faith of Izumo, which, although even more deeply rooted in national life

49

than Buddhism, is far less known to the Western world. Little has been written in English about Shintō which gives the least idea of what Shintō is, except in special works by such men of scholarship as Chamberlain and Satow: works which the Western reader, unless himself a specialist, is not likely to become familiar with outside of Japan. Much about its ancient traditions and rites may be learned from the works of the scholars just mentioned; however, as Mr. Satow himself acknowledges, a definite answer to the question, "What is the nature of Shintō?" is still difficult to give. How to define the common element in the six kinds of Shintō which are known to exist, and some of which no foreign scholar has yet been able to examine for lack of time, authorities, or of opportunity?

Even in its modern, external forms, Shintō is amply complex enough to challenge the united powers of the historian, linguist, and anthropologist; merely to trace the numerous lines of its evolution, and to determine the sources of its various elements; prehistoric polytheisms and fetishisms, traditions of dubious origin, philosophical concepts from China, Korea, and elsewhere, all mingled with Buddhism, Taoism, and Confucianism. The so-called "Revival of Pure Shintō," an effort aided by the government to restore the religion to its ancient simplicity by divesting it of foreign characteristics, and especially of every sign or token of Buddhist origin, resulted in (so far as the stated purpose was concerned) in the destruction of priceless art, and in leaving the enigma of origins as complicated as before. Thus, Shintō had been too profoundly modified in the course of fifteen centuries of change, to be modified by an edict. For the same reason scholarly efforts to define its relation to national ethics by mere historical and philosophical analysis, as well seek to define the ultimate secret of life by the elements of the body that it animates, must fail. Yet, when the result of such efforts are closely combined with a deep knowledge of Japanese thought and feeling, the thought and sentiment, not of a special class, but of the people at large, then indeed, all that Shintō was and is may be fully comprehended. This may be accomplished, I think, through the united labor of European and Japanese scholars.

Nevertheless, something of what Shintō signifies, in the simple poetry of its beliefs, in the home training of the child; in the reverence of filial piety before the tablets of ancestors, may be learned during a residence of some years among the people by one who lives their life and adopts their manners and customs. With such experience, he can at least claim the right to express his own concept of Shintō.

II

Those far-seeing rulers of the Meiji era, who disestablished Buddhism to strengthen Shintō, without doubt knew they were giving new strength, not only to a faith in perfect harmony with their own state policy, but also to one possessing in itself, a far more profound vitality than the foreign religion, which although omnipotent as an art influence, had never found deep root in the intellectual soil of Japan. Buddhism was already in decay, although transplanted from China scarcely more than thirteen centuries before; while Shintō, though doubtlessly older by many thousands of years, seems instead to have gained rather than to have lost strength through all the periods of change. Eclectic, like the genius of the nation, it had appropriated and assimilated all forms of foreign thought, which could aid its material expression or fortify its ethics. Buddhism had attempted to absorb its gods, even as it had adopted previously the ancient deities of Brahmanism; but Shintō, while seeming to yield, was really only borrowing strength from its rival. This marvelous vitality of Shintō is due to the fact that in the course of its long development, out of unrecorded beginnings, it became, and below the surface still remains, a religion of the heart. Whatever the origin of its rites and traditions is, its ethical spirit has become identified with all the deepest and best emotions of the nation. Hence, in Izumo especially, the attempt to create a Buddhist-Shintōism resulted only in the formation of a Shintō-Buddhism.

The secret, living force of Shintō today, that force which repels missionary efforts at proselytizing, means something much more profound than tradition, worship, or ceremonialism. Shintō may yet, without loss of real power, survive all these. Certainly, the expansion of the popular mind through education, the influences of modern science, must compel modification or abandonment of many ancient Shintō concepts; but, the ethics of Shintō will surely endure. For Shintō signifies character in the higher sense: courage, courtesy, honor, and above all things, loyalty. The spirit of Shintō is the spirit of filial piety, the zest for duty, and the readiness to surrender life for a principle without a thought of why. It is the obedience of the child and the sweetness of the Japanese woman. Likewise, it is also conservatism; the healthy constraint on the national tendency to cast away the value of the entire past in rash eagerness to assimilate too much of the foreign present. It is religion; but religion transformed into hereditary moral impulse: religion transformed into ethical instinct. It is the whole emotional life of the nation, – the Soul of Japan.

The child is born Shintō. Home teaching and school training only give expression to what is innate. They do not plant new seeds, they do not advance the ethical sense transmitted as an ancestral trait. Even as a Japanese infant inherits such ability to handle a writing brush as can never be acquired by Western fingers, so does it inherit ethical sensitivity totally different from our own. Ask a class of Japanese students, young students of fourteen to sixteen, to tell their dearest wishes; and if they trust you, perhaps nine out of ten will answer, "To die for His Majesty, Our Emperor." The wish soars from the heart, as pure as any wish for martyrdom that was ever born. How much this sense of loyalty may or may not have been weakened in such great centers as Tokyō by the new agnosticism, and by the rapid growth of other nineteenth century ideas among the student class, I do not know; but in the country, it remains as natural to boyhood as joy. It is also unreasoning, unlike those loyal sentiments with us, the results of more mature knowledge and settled conviction. Never does the Japanese youth ask himself why; the beauty of self-sacrifice alone is the all-sufficing motive. Such ecstatic loyalty is a part of the national life. It is in the blood, inherent as the instinct of the ant to perish for its little republic, as unconscious as the loyalty of bees to their queen. It is Shintō.

The readiness to sacrifice one's own life for loyalty's sake, for the sake of a superior, for the sake of honor, which has distinguished the nation in modern times, would seem also to have been a national characteristic from the earliest period of its independent existence. Long before the era of established feudalism, when honorable suicide became a matter of rigid etiquette, not only for warriors, but even for women and little children, the giving of one's life for one's prince, even when the sacrifice could benefit nothing, was held as a sacred duty. Among various incidents which might be cited from the ancient *Kojiki*, the following is not the least impressive:

> *Prince Mayowa, at the age of only seven years, having killed his father's slayer, fled into the house of a nobleman, Omi Tsubura. Then Prince Oho-hatsuse raised an army, and besieged that house. And the arrows that were shot were numerous*

like the ears of the reeds. And Omi Tsubura came forth himself, and having taken off the weapons with which he was girded, did bow eight times, and said, "The maiden-princess Kara, my daughter whom you have decided to court, is at your service. Again I will present to you five granaries. Though a vile slave of a nobleman exerting his utmost strength in the fight can scarcely hope to conquer, yet must he die rather than desert a prince who, trusting him, has entered into his house."

Having so spoken, he again took his weapons and went to fight again. Then, their strength being exhausted, and their arrows gone, he said to the prince, "My hands are wounded and our arrows are gone. We can no longer fight. What shall be done?"

The Prince replied, "There is nothing more to do. Kill me." So Omi Tsubura stabbed the Prince to death with his sword, and then immediately killed himself by cutting off his own head.

Thousands of equally strong examples could easily be quoted from later Japanese history, including many which occurred even within the memory of the living. Nor was it only that to die for people might become a sacred duty; in certain circumstances, conscience dictated that it was no less a duty to die for a purely personal conviction. He who held any opinion which he believed of vital importance would, when other means failed, write his views in a farewell letter and then take his own life; in order to call attention to his beliefs and to prove their sincerity. Such an incident occurred only last year in Tōkyō,[1] when a young lieutenant of militia, Ōhara Takayoshi, killed himself by *hara-kiri* in the cemetery of Saitokuji, leaving a letter stating as the reason for his act, his hope to force public recognition of the danger to Japanese independence from the growth of Russian power in the North Pacific. But a much more touching sacrifice, in May of the same year, a sacrifice conceived in the purest and most innocent spirit of loyalty, was that of the young girl Yoko Hatakeyama, who after the attempt to assassinate the Czarevitch [Nicholas],[35] traveled from Tōkyō to Kyōto and there killed herself before the gate of the Kenchō [Kenchōji],[ii] merely as a vicarious atonement

---

[i] Author's Footnote: This was written early in 1892.
[ii] Kencho (Enshō-ji, 延勝寺) was a former Buddhist monastery in northeastern Kyōto, Japan, endowed by Emperor Konoe in fulfillment of a sacred vow. It is known as one of the "Six Victorious Temples," *Rokusho* (六勝寺).

for the incident which had cause shame to Japan and grief to the Father of the people: His Sacred Majesty the Emperor.[i]

III

As to its external forms, modern Shintō is indeed difficult to analyze; but through all the intricate textures of irrelevant beliefs so thickly interwoven around it, indications of its earliest character are still easily distinguished. In certain ancient rites, in its archaic prayers, texts, and symbols, in the history of its shrines, and even in many of the innocent ideas of its poorest worshippers, it is plainly revealed as the most ancient of all forms of worship: that which Herbert Spencer[36] terms "the root of all religions," devotion to the dead. Indeed, it has been frequently so explained by its own greatest scholars and theologians.

Its deities are ghosts: all the dead become deities. In his *Tama no mihashira*,[ii] the great commentator Hirata[37] says, "The spirits of the dead continue to exist in the unseen world which is everywhere around us, and they all become gods of varying character and degree of influence. Some reside in temples built

---

[i] More accurately, when Nicholas cut his trip to Japan short in spite of Emperor Meiji's apology, Yuko Hatakeyama, a young seamstress, slit her throat with a razor in front of the Kyōto Prefectural Office as an act of public contrition, and soon died in a hospital. Japanese media at the time labeled her as *"retsujo,"* literally "valiant woman," and praised her patriotism. For a touching personal account of this incident and Yuko Hatakeyama, refer to Hearn's book, *Out of the East*, Chapter XI, "Yuko: A Reminiscence."
[ii] *The True Pillar of Spirit*

in their honor; others hover near their tombs; and they continue to render services to their prince, parents, wife, and children, just as when living."[i] And they do more than this, for they control the lives and the actions of men. "Every human action," says Hirata, "is the work of a god."[ii] And Motowori[38], scarcely less famous an exponent of pure Shintō doctrine writes, "All the moral ideas which a man requires, are implanted in his bosom by the gods, and are of the same nature with those instincts which compel him to eat when he is hungry or to drink when he is thirsty."[iii]

With this doctrine of intuition, no Ten Commandments are required, no fixed code of ethics; and the human conscience is declared to be the only necessary guide. Even though every action is "the work of a *kami*," still each man has within him the power to distinguish the righteous impulse from the unrighteous, the influence of the good deity from that of the evil. No moral teacher is so infallible as one's own heart. "To have learned that there is no way (*michi*),[iv] says Motowori, "to be learned and practiced, is really to have learned the Way of the Gods."[v] Hirata

---

[i] Author's Footnote: Quoted from Mr. Satow's masterly essay, "The Revival of Pure Shintō," published in the *Transactions of the Asiatic Society of Japan*. By "gods" are not necessarily meant benevolent *kami*. Shintō has no devils; but it has its "bad gods" as well as good deities.

[ii] Author's Footnote: Satow, "The Revival of Pure Shinto."

[iii] Author's Footnote: *Ibid*.

[iv] Author's Footnote: In the sense of a moral path; i.e., an ethical system.

[v] Author's Footnote: Satow, "The Revival of Pure Shintō." The whole force of Motowori's words will not be fully understood unless the reader knows that the term Shintō is of comparatively modern origin in Japan, having been

writes, "If you desire to practice true virtue, learn to stand in awe of the Unseen; and that will prevent you from doing wrong. Make a vow to the Gods who rule over the Unseen, and cultivate the conscience (*ma-gokoro*) implanted in you; and then you will never wander from the way."

How this spiritual self-culture may be best acquired, the same great teacher has stated with almost equal brevity, "Devotion to the memory of ancestors is the mainspring of all virtues. No one who discharges his duty to them will ever be disrespectful to the gods or to his living parents. Such a man will be faithful to his prince, loyal to his friends, and kind and gentle to his wife and children."[1]

How far are these antique beliefs removed from the ideas of the nineteenth century? Certainly not so far that we can afford to smile at them. The faith of the primitive man and the knowledge of the most profound psychologist may meet in strange harmony on the threshold of the same ultimate truth, and the thought of a child may repeat the conclusions of a Spencer or a Schopenhauer.[39] Are not our ancestors in truth our *kami*? Is not every action indeed the work of the dead who dwell within us? Have not our impulses and tendencies, our capacities and weaknesses, our heroisms and timidities, been created by those vanished myriads from whom we received the all-mysterious bequest of life? Do we still think of that infinitely complex something, which is each one of us, and which we call ego, as "I" or as "they"? What is our pride or shame but the pride or shame of the unseen in that which they have made? And what is our conscience but the inherited sum of countless dead experiences with varying good or evil? Nor can we hastily reject the Shintō thought that all the dead become gods, while we respect the convictions of those strong souls of today, who proclaim the divinity of man.

IV

Shintō ancestor worship, no doubt, like all ancestor worship, was developed out of funeral rites, according to that general law

---

borrowed from the Chinese to distinguish the ancient faith from Buddhism; and that the old name for the ancient religion is Kami no michi, "the Way of the Gods."

[i] Author's Footnote: Satow, "The Revival of Pure Shintō."

of religious evolution traced so fully by Herbert Spencer. There is reason to believe that the early forms of Shintō public worship may have been evolved out of a yet older family worship, much after the way in which M. Fustel de Coulanges,[40] in his wonderful book, *La Cité Antique*, has shown the religious public institutions among the Greeks and Romans to have been developed from the religion of the hearth. Indeed, the word *ujigami*, now used to signify a Shintō parish temple, and also its deity, means "family god," and in its present form is a corruption or contraction of *uchi no kami*, meaning the "god of the interior" or "the god of the house." Shintō scholars have, it is true, attempted to interpret the term otherwise; and Hirata, as quoted by Mr. Ernest Satow, declared the name should be applied only to the common ancestor, or ancestors, or to one so entitled to the gratitude of a community as to merit equal honors. Undoubtedly, such was the correct use of the term in his time, and long before it; however, the etymology of the word would certainly seem to indicate its origin in family worship, and to confirm modern scientific beliefs in regard to the evolution of religious institutions.

Just as among the Greeks and Romans, the family cult always continued to exist through all the development and expansion of the public religion, so the Shintō family worship has continued concurrently with the communal worship at the famed *Oho-ya-shiro*[i] of various provinces or districts, and with national worship at the great shrines of Ise and Kitzuki. Many objects connected with the family cult are certainly of foreign or modern origin; but its simple rites and its unconscious poetry retain their archaic charm. To the student of Japanese life, by far the most interesting aspect of Shintō is offered in this home worship, which like the home worship of the antique West, exists in a dual form.

V

In nearly all Izumo houses, there is a *kamidana*,[ii] or "Shelf of the Gods." On this is usually placed a small Shintō shrine (*miya*)

---

[i] The Great Shrine.
[ii] Author's Footnote: From *kami*, "the Powers Above," or the gods, and *tana*, "a shelf." The letter "t" of the latter word changes into a "d" in the

containing tablets bearing the names of gods, (at least one tablet of which is furnished by the neighboring Shintō parish temple), and various *ofuda*, holy texts or charms, which most often are written promises in the name of some *kami* to protect his worshiper. If there is no *miya*, the tablets or *ofuda* are simply placed on the shelf in a certain order, the most sacred having the middle place. Very rarely are images to be seen on a *kamidana*; for archaic Shintōism excluded images as rigidly as Jewish or Islamic law; and all Shintō iconography belongs to a comparatively modern era, especially to the period of the Ryōbu-Shintō,[41] and must be considered of Buddhist origin. If there are any images, they will probably be have been made only within recent years at Kitzuki: those small twin figures of Oho-kuni-nushi-no-kami and of Koto-shiro-nushi-no-kami, described in a former paper on the Kitzuki-no-oho-yashiro. Shintō *kakemono*,[42] which are also of recent origin, representing incidents from the *Kojiki*, are much more common than Shintō icons. These usually occupy the *toko*, or alcove, in the same room in which the *kamidana* is placed; but they will not be seen in the houses of the more cultivated classes.

---

compound word, just like that of *tokkuri*, "a jar" or "bottle," becomes *dokkuri* in the compound word *o-mikidokkuri*.

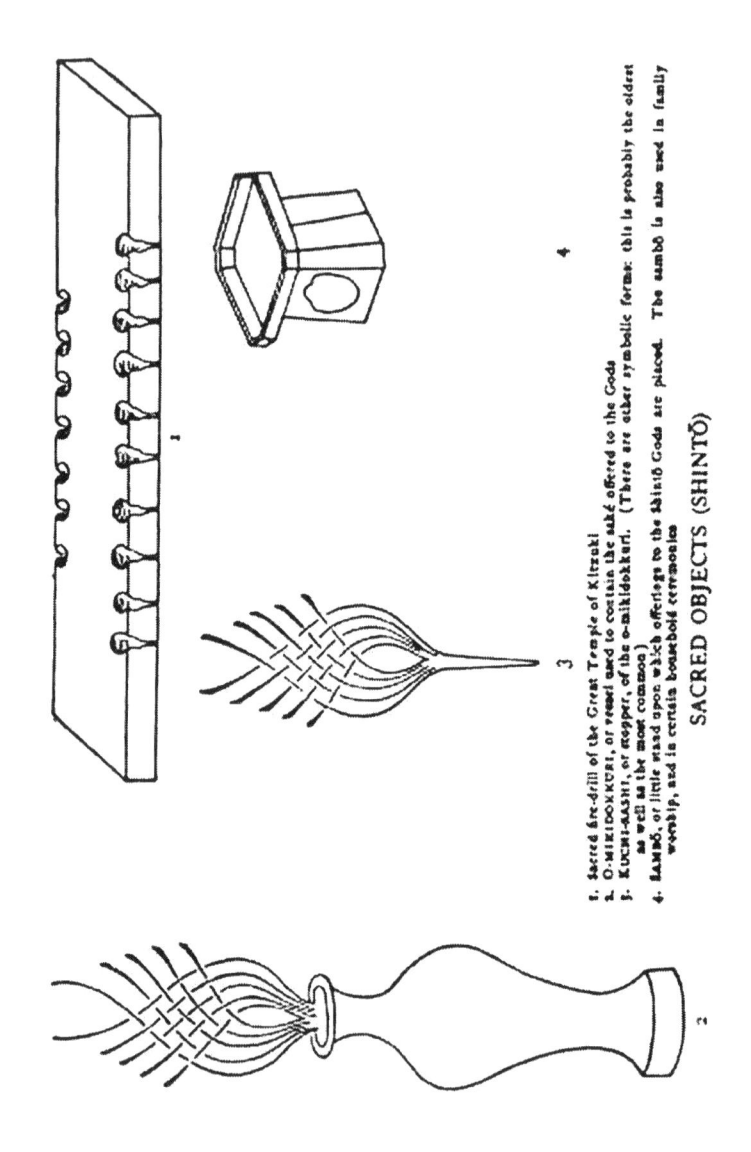

1. Sacred fire-drill of the Great Temple of Kitzuki
2. O-MIKIDOKKURI, or vessel used to contain the saké offered to the Gods
3. KUCHI-SASHI, or stopper, of the o-mikidokkuri. (There are other symbolic forms: this is probably the oldest as well as the most common).
4. SAMBŌ, or little stand upon which offerings to the Shintō Gods are placed. The sambō is also used in family worship, and is certain household ceremonies

SACRED OBJECTS (SHINTŌ)

Ordinarily, nothing will be found on the *kamidana* but the simple *miya* containing some *ofuda*. Very, very seldom will a mirror[1] be seen, or *gohei*,[43] except the *gohei* attached to the small *shimenawa* either hung just above the *kamidana* or attached to the box-like frame in which the *miya* sometimes is placed. The *shimenawa* and the paper *gohei* are the true emblems of Shintō; even the *ofuda* and the *mamori*[44] are quite modern. The *shimenawa* is suspended not only in front of the household shrine, but also above the front door of almost every home in Izumo. It is ordinarily a thin rope of rice straw; but in front of the homes of high Shintō officials, such as the Taisha-Guji of Kitzuki, its size and weight are enormous. One of the first curious facts that the traveler to Izumo cannot fail to be impressed by is the universal presence of this symbolic rope of straw, which may sometimes even be seen around a rice field. But the grand displays of the sacred symbol are on the great festivals of the new year, the accession of Jimmu Tennō[45] to the throne of Japan, and the Emperor's birthday. Then, all the miles of streets are decorated with *shimenawa* as thick as ship cables.

---

[1] Author's Footnote: The mirror, as an emblem of female deities, is kept in the secret, innermost shrine of various Shintō temples. But the mirror of metal, commonly placed before the public view in a Shintō shrine is not really of Shintō origin, but was introduced into Japan as a Buddhist symbol of the Shingon sect. As the mirror is the symbol in Shintō of female deities, the sword is the emblem of male deities. The real symbols of the god or goddess are not, however, exposed to human view under any circumstances.

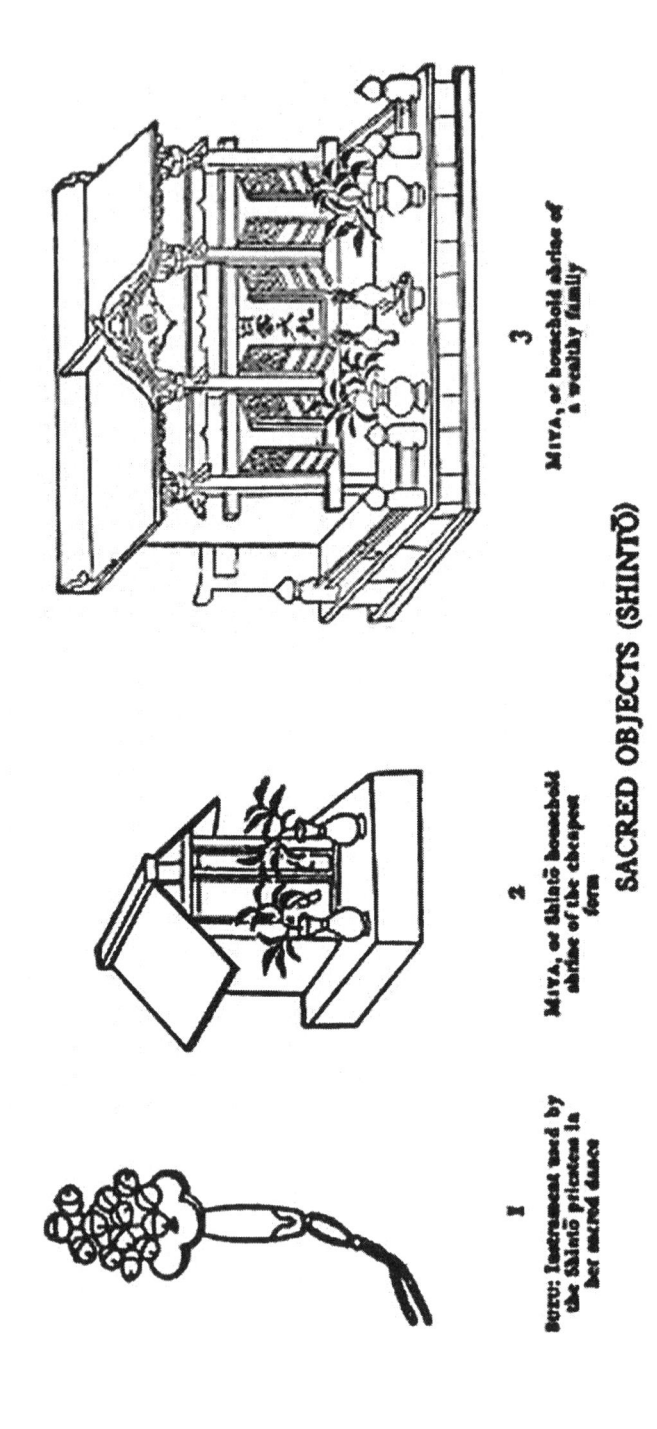

SUZU: Instrument used by the Shintō priestess in her sacred dance

MIYA, or Shintō household shrine of the cheapest form

MIYA, or household shrine of a wealthy family

SACRED OBJECTS (SHINTŌ)

VI

A particular feature of Matsué are the *miya* shops — establishments not indeed unique to the old Izumo town, but much more interesting than those to be found in larger cities of other provinces. There are *miya* of a hundred varieties and sizes, from the child's toy *miya* which sells for less than one *sen*,[i] to the large shrine destined for some rich home, and costing ten *yen*[ii] or more. Beside these household shrines of Shintō may occasionally be seen massive shrines of precious wood, lacquered and gilded, worth from three hundred to fifteen hundred *yen*. These are not household shrines, but festival shrines, and are made only for rich merchants. They are displayed on Shintō holidays and twice a year are carried through the streets in procession, to shouts of "*Chosaya! Chosaya!*"[iii] Each temple parish also possesses a large portable *miya* which is paraded on these occasions with much chanting and beating of drums. The majority of household *miya* are cheap constructions. A very fine one can be purchased for about two *yen*; but, those little shrines one sees in the houses of the common people cost, as a rule, considerably less than half a *yen*. Elaborate or costly household shrines are contrary to the spirit of pure Shintō. The true *miya* should be made of spotless white *hinoki*[iv] wood, and be put together without nails. Most of those I have seen in the shops had their parts joined only with rice paste, but the skill of the maker made this sufficient. Pure Shintō requires that a *miya* should be without gilding or ornamentation. The beautiful miniature temples in some rich homes may justly excite admiration by their artistic structure and decoration; but the ten or thirteen cent *miya*, in the house of a

---

[i] Valued at about one 1/100 of a *yen*.

[ii] The *yen* was then worth about fifty cents to the American dollar.

[iii] Author's Footnote: Anciently, the two great Shintō festivals on which the *miya* were thus carried in procession were the *Yoshigami no matsuri*, or Festival of the God of the New Year, and the anniversary of Jimmu Tennō ascending to the throne. The second of these is still observed. The celebration of the Emperor's birthday is the only other occasion when the *miya* are paraded. On both days, the streets are beautifully decorated with lanterns and *shimenawa*, the fringed ropes of rice straw that are the emblems of Shintō. Nobody now knows exactly what the words chanted on these days (*Chosaya! Chosaya!*) mean. One theory is that they are a corruption of Sagicho, the name of a great military festival, which was celebrated nearly at the same time as the Yoshigami no matsuri: both holidays now being obsolete.

[iv] Author's Footnote: *Thuya obtusa*.

laborer or a *kurumaya*,[1] of plain white wood, truly represents that spirit of simplicity characterizing the ancient religion.

VII

The *kamidana* or "God-shelf," upon which the *miya* and other sacred objects of Shintō are placed, is usually fastened at a height of about six or seven feet above the floor. As a rule, it should not be placed higher than the hand can reach with ease; but in houses having lofty rooms, the *miya* is sometimes put up at such a height that the sacred offerings cannot be made without the aid of a box or other object to stand on. It is not commonly a part of the house structure, but a plain shelf attached with brackets, either to the wall itself, at one side of the room, or as is much more usual, to the *kamoi*, or horizontal grooved beam, in which the screens of opaque paper (*fusuma*),[46] which divide room from room, slide to and fro. Occasionally, it is painted or lacquered; however, the ordinary *kamidana* is of white wood and is made larger or smaller in proportion to the size of the *miya*, or the number of the *ofuda* and other sacred objects to be placed on it. In some houses, notably those of innkeepers and small merchants, the *kamidana* is made long enough to support a number of small shrines dedicated to different Shintō deities, particularly those believed to preside over wealth and commercial prosperity. In the houses of the poor, it is nearly always placed in the room facing the street. Matsué shopkeepers usually erect it in their shops, so that the passerby or the customer can tell at a glance in what deities the occupant puts his trust.

There are many regulations concerning it. It may be placed to face south or east, but should not face west; and under no possible circumstances should it be allowed to face north or northwest. One explanation of this is the influence of Chinese philosophy on Shintō; according to which there is some imagined relationship between south and east and the Male Principle, and between west or north and the Female Principle. The popular notion on the subject is that because a dead person is buried with the head turned north, it would be very wrong to place a *miyai* so that it faces north; since everything relating to

---

[1] A *kurumaya* is a *jinrikisha* driver.

death is impure. The regulation about the west is not strictly observed.

Most *kamidana* of Izumo, however, face south or east. In the dwellings of the poorest, often consisting of but one room, there is little choice as to rooms; however, it is a rule, observed in the houses of the middle classes, that the *kamidana* must not be placed either in the guest room (*zashiki*) nor in the kitchen. In *shizoku* houses,[i] its place is usually in one of the smaller family rooms. Respect must be shown to it. For example, one must not sleep or even lie down to rest, with his feet turned towards it. One must not pray before it, or even stand before it, while in a state of religious impurity; such as that involving having touched a corpse or having attended a Buddhist funeral, or even during the period of mourning for relatives buried according to the Buddhist rite. Should any member of the family be thus buried, then during fifty days,[ii] the *kamidana* must be entirely closed from view with pure white paper, and even the Shintō *ofuda*, or pious invocations fastened on the door of the house, must have white paper pasted over them. During the same mourning period, the fire in the house is considered unclean; and at the close of the period, all the ashes of the braziers and of the kitchen must be thrown away, and a new fire kindled with flint and steel. Nor, according to the laws, are funerals the only source uncleanliness. Shintō, as the religion of purity and purification, has quite an extensive *Deuteronomy*.[47] During certain periods, women must not even pray before the *miya*, much less make offerings or touch the sacred vessels, or kindle the lights of the *kami*.

VIII

In front of the *miya* or whatever holy object of Shintō worship is placed on the *kamidana*, are set two quaintly shaped jars for the offerings of *saké*; two small vases, to contain sprays of the sacred plant *sakaki*,[48] or offerings of flowers; and a small lamp, shaped like a tiny saucer, where a wick of rush-pith floats

---

[i] The word *shizoku* refers to members of the warrior or samurai class.
[ii] Author's Footnote: Such at least is the mourning period under such circumstances in certain samurai families. Others say twenty days is sufficient. The Buddhist code of mourning is extremely varied and complicated, and it would require much space here to expand on that.

in rapeseed oil. Strictly speaking, all these utensils, except the flower vases, should be made of unglazed red earthenware, such as we find described in the early chapters of the *Kojiki*; and still at Shintō festivals in Izumo, when *saké* is drunk in honor of the gods, it is drunk out of cups of red, baked, unglazed clay, shaped like shallow round dishes. In recent years, it has become the fashion to make all the utensils of a fine *kamidana* of brass or bronze: even the *hanaiké* or flower vases. Among the poor, the most archaic paraphernalia are still used to a great extent, especially in the more remote country districts; the lamp being a simple saucer or *kawaraké* of red clay, and the flower vases most often bamboo cups, made by simply cutting a section of bamboo immediately below a joint and about five inches above it.

The brass lamp is a much more complicated object than the *kawaraké*, which costs but one *rin*.[1] The brass lamp costs about twenty-five *sen* at least, and consists of two parts. The lower part, shaped like a very shallow, broad wineglass, with a very thick stem, has an interior as well as an exterior rim, and the bottom of an equally broad and shallow brass cup, which is the upper part and contains the oil, fits exactly into this inner rim. This kind of lamp is always equipped with a small brass object in the shape of a flat ring, with a stem set at right angles to the surface of the ring. It is used for moving the floating wick and keeping it at any position required; and the little perpendicular stem is long enough to prevent the fingers from touching the oil.

---

[1] A *rin* was valued at 1/1000 of a *yen*.

The most curious objects to be seen on any ordinary *kamidana* are the stoppers of the *saké* vessels or *o-mikidokkuri* ("honorable *saké* jars"). These stoppers (*o-mikidokkuri-no-kuchi-sashi*) may be made of brass or of fine thin slips of wood, jointed and bent into the unique form required. Properly speaking, the thing is not a real stopper in spite of its name. Its lower part does not fill the mouth of the jar at all: it simply hangs in the opening like a leaf put there stem downwards. I found it difficult to learn its history; but, though there are many designs, the finer ones being brass, the shape of all of them seems to hint at a Buddhist origin. Possibly the shape was borrowed from a Buddhist symbol, the *Hoshi-no-tama*, that mystic gem whose radiant glow (suggested in *kanji* as a dancing flame) is the emblem of pure essence; and thus, the object would be both typical of the purity of the wine offering and the purity of the heart of the giver.

The little lamp may not be lit every evening in all homes, since there are families too poor to afford even this infinitesimal nightly expenditure of oil. But on the first, fifteenth, and twenty-eighth of each month, the light is always lit; for these are Shintō holidays of obligation, when offerings must be made to the gods, and when all *ujiko*, or parishioners of a Shintō temple, are supposed to visit their *ujigami*. In every home, on these days, *saké* is poured as an offering into the *o-mikidokkuri*, and sprays of the holy *sakaki*, or sprigs of pine, or fresh flowers are placed in the vases of the *kamidana*. On the first day of the new year, the *kamidana* is always decked with *sakaki*, *moromoki* (ferns), and pine sprigs, and also with *shimenawa*; and large double-sized rice cakes are placed on it as offerings to the gods.

IX

Only the ancient gods of Shintō are worshiped in front of the *kamidana*. The family ancestors or family dead are worshiped either in a separate room (called the *mitayama*, or "Spirit Chamber"), or if worshiped according to the Buddhist rites, in front of the *butsuma* or *butsudan*.[49]

The Buddhist family worship coexists in the vast majority of Izumo homes with the Shintō family worship; and whether the dead are honored in the *mitayama* or in front of the *butsudan* totally depends on the religious traditions of the household. Moreover, there are families in Izumo, particularly in Kitzuki, whose members do not profess Buddhism in any form, and a very few, belonging to the Shinshū or Nichiren-shū,[1,50] whose members do not practice Shintō. But, the domestic cult of the dead is maintained, whether the family is Shintō or Buddhist. The *ihai* or tablets of the Buddhist family dead (*hotoke*) are never placed in a special room or shrine, but in the Buddhist household shrine[II] along with the images or pictures of Buddhist deities enclosed there; or, at least, this is always the case when the honors paid to them are given according to the Buddhist instead of the Shintō rite. The form of the *butsudan* or *butsuma*, the character of its holy images, its *ofuda*, or its pictures, and even the prayers said before it, differ according to the fifteen different *shū* or sects; and a very large volume would have to be written in order to treat the subject of the *butsuma* completely. Therefore, I must satisfy myself with stating that there are Buddhist household shrines of all dimensions, prices, and degrees of

---

[I] Author's Footnote: In spite of the supposed rigidity of the Nichiren sect in such matters, most followers of its doctrine in Izumo are equally fervent Shintōists. I have not been able to observe whether the same is true of Izumo Shin-shū families as a rule; but, I know that some Shin-shū believers in Matsué worship at Shintō shrines. Adoring only that form of Buddha called Amida, the Shin sect might be termed a Buddhist "Unitarianism." It seems never to have been able to secure a strong footing in Izumo because of its doctrinal hostility to Shintō. Elsewhere throughout Japan, it is the most vigorous and prosperous of all Buddhist sects.

[II] Author's Footnote: Mr. Morse, in his *Japanese Homes*, published on hearsay, a very strange error when he stated, "The Buddhist household shrines rest on the floor – at least so I was informed." They never rest on the floor under any circumstances. In the better class of houses, special architectural arrangements are made for the *butsudan*; an alcove, recess, or other means, often so arranged as to be concealed from view by a sliding panel or a little door. In smaller houses, it may be put on a shelf, for lack of a better place, and in the homes of the poor, on top of the *tansu*, or clothes chest. It is never placed as high as the *kamidana*, but rarely at a less height than three feet above the floor. In Mr. Morse's own illustration of a Buddhist household shrine (p. 226) it does not rest on the floor at all, but on the upper shelf of a cupboard, which must not be confused with the *butsudan*: a very small one. The sketch in question seems to have been made during the Festival of the Dead, for the offerings in the picture are those of the Bon-matsuri. At that time, the household *butsudan* is always exposed to view, and often moved from its usual place in order to obtain room for the offerings to be set in front of it. To place any holy object on the floor is considered by the Japanese, very disrespectful. As for Shintō objects, to place even a *mamori* on the floor is deemed a sin.

magnificence; and that the *butsudan* of the Shin-shū, although to me the least interesting of all, is popularly considered to be the most beautiful in design and finish. The *butsudan* of a very poor household may be worth a few cents, but in Kyōto the rich devotee might purchase a shrine worth as many thousands of *yen* as he could pay.

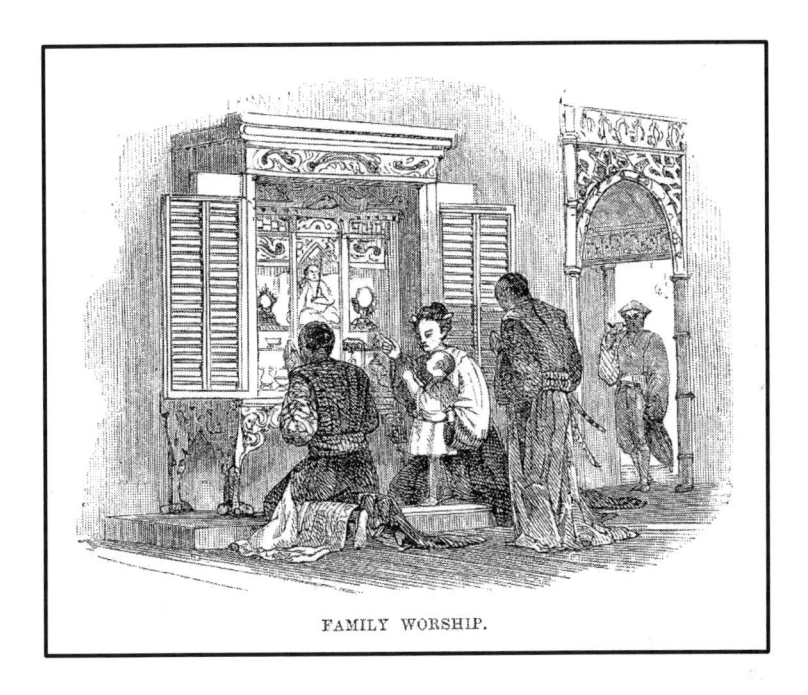

FAMILY WORSHIP.

Though the forms of the *butsuma* and the character of its contents may greatly vary, the form of the ancestral or mortuary tablet is generally that represented in Figure 4 of the illustrations of *ihai* given in this book.[1] There are some much more elaborate shapes, costly and rare, and simpler shapes of the cheapest and plainest description; but the form illustrated here is the common

---

[1] Author's Footnote: Two *ihai* are always made for each Buddhist dead. One usually larger than that placed in the family shrine, is kept in the temple of which the deceased was a parishioner, together with a cup in which tea or water is daily poured out as an offering. In almost any large temple, thousands of such *ihai* may be seen, arranged in rows, tier above tier; each with its cup in front of it; for, even the souls of the dead are supposed to drink tea. Sometimes, I fear, the offering is forgotten, because I have seen rows of cups containing only dust: the fault perhaps of some lazy acolyte.

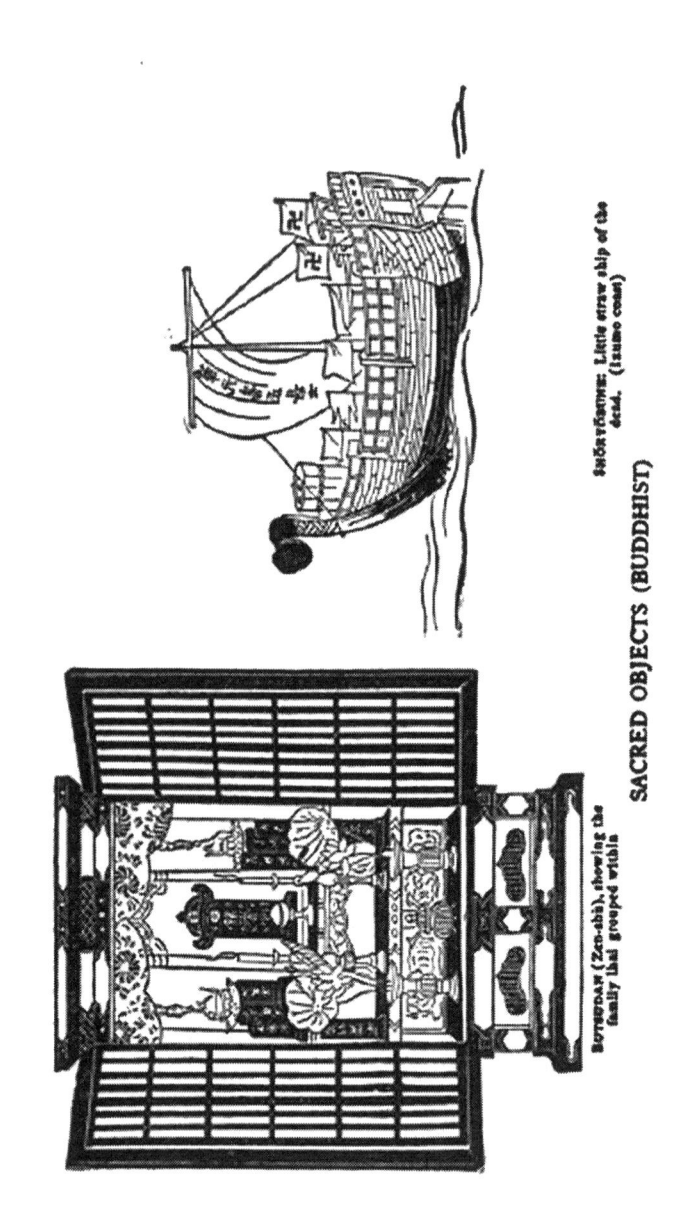

BUTSUDAN (Zen-shū), showing the family ihai grouped within

ShōRyō'BUNE: Little straw ship of the dead. (Izumo coast)

SACRED OBJECTS (BUDDHIST)

one in Izumo and the entire San-indo[51] country. There are differences, however, of size; the *ihai* of a man is larger than that of a woman, and has a headpiece also, which the tablet of a female does not; while a child's *ihai* is always very small. The average height of the *ihai* made for a male adult is a little more than a foot, and its thickness about an inch. It has a top, or headpiece, surmounted by the symbol of the Hoshi-no-tama or Mystic Jewel, and is ordinarily decorated with a cloud design of some kind, and the pedestal is a lotus flower rising out of the clouds. As a general rule, all this is richly lacquered and gilded; the tablet itself being lacquered in black and bearing the posthumous name, or *kaimyō*,[52] in letters of gold: *ken-mu-ji-shō-shin-ji*, or other syllables indicating the supposed virtues of the departed. The poorest people, unable to afford such handsome tablets, have *ihai* made of plain wood, and the *kaimyō* is sometimes simply written on these in black *kanji*; but more commonly it is written on a strip of white paper, which is then pasted on the *ihai* with rice paste. The living name is perhaps inscribed on the back of the tablet. Such tablets accumulate, of course, with the passing of generations; and in certain homes, great numbers of them are preserved.

A beautiful and touching custom still exists in Izumo, and perhaps throughout Japan, although much less common than it used to be. So far as I can learn, however, it was always confined to the cultivated classes. When a husband dies, two *ihai* are made, in case the wife resolves never to marry again. On one of these, the *kaimyō* of the dead man is painted in characters of gold, and on the other, that of the living widow; but, in the case of the living widow, the first *kanji* of the *kaimyō* is painted in red, and the other characters in gold. These two tablets are then placed in the household *butsuma*. Two larger ones, similarly inscribed, are then placed in the parish temple; but no cup is set before the *ihai* of the wife. The solitary crimson *kanji* signifies a solemn pledge to remain faithful to the memory of the dead; furthermore, the wife loses her living name among all her friends and relatives, and is thereafter addressed only by a fragment of her *kaimyō*; as for example, Shin-toku-in-san, an abbreviation of the much longer and more resonant posthumous name, Shin-toku-in-den-jōyo-teisō-daishi.[i] Thus, to be called by one's *kaimyō*

---

[i] Author's Footnote: This is a fine example of a samurai *kaimyō*. The *kaimyō* of *kwasoku* or samurai are different from those of humbler dead; and a Japanese,

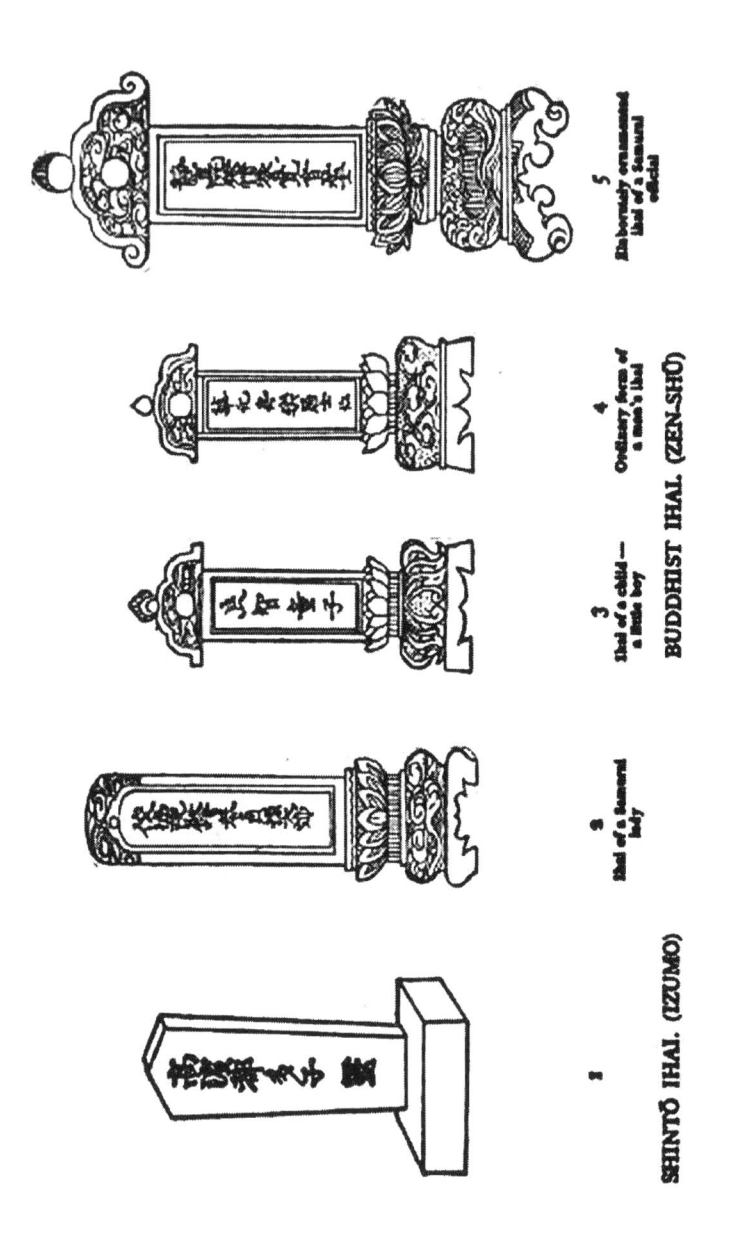

by a single glance at an *ihai*, can tell at once to what class of society the deceased belonged, by the Buddhist words used.

is both an honor to the memory of the husband and the loyalty of the bereaved wife. A similar pledge is taken by a man after the loss of a wife to whom he was passionately attached; and one crimson letter on his *ihai* registers the vow, not only in the home but also in the place of public worship; but, the widower is never called by his *kaimyō*, as is the widow.

The first religious duty of the morning in a Buddhist household is to set a little cup of tea, made with the first hot water prepared, *O-Hotoke-san-ni-o-cha-to-ageru*[i] in front of the tablets of the dead. Daily offerings of boiled rice are also made, and fresh flowers are put in the shrine vases. Incense, although not allowed by Shintō, is burned in front of the tablets. At night, and also during the day on certain festivals, both candles and a small oil lamp are lighted in the *butsuma*: a lamp somewhat differently shaped from the lamp in the *miya* and called *rintō*.

The Hearn family butsuma in the author's Tōkyō study.

---

[i] Author's Footnote: "Presenting the honorable tea to the august Buddhas;" for, by Buddhist faith, it is hoped, if not believed, that the dead become Buddhas and escape the sorrows of further reincarnation. Thus, the expression "Is dead" is often rendered in Japanese by the phrase "is become a Buddha."

73

On the day of each month corresponding to the date of death, a little meal is served in front of the tablets, consisting of *shōjin-ryōri* only, the vegetarian food of the Buddhists. But as Shintō family worship has its special annual festival, which lasts from the first to the third day of the new year, so Buddhist ancestor worship has its yearly Bonku, or Bon Matsuri,[53] lasting from the thirteenth to the sixteenth day of the seventh month. Then the *butsuma* is decorated to the fullest, special offerings of food and flowers are made, and all the house is made beautiful to welcome the coming of the ghostly visitors.

Shintō, like Buddhism, has its *ihai*, but these are of the most simple possible shape and material: mere slips of plain white wood. The average height is only about eight inches. These tablets are either placed in a special *miya* kept in a different room from that in which the shrine of the *kami* is erected, or else simply arranged on a small shelf the people call Mitama-san-no-tana, "the Shelf of the August Spirits." The shelf or the shrine of the ancestors and household dead is always placed at a considerable height in the *mitayama* or *soreisha* (as the Spirit Chamber is sometimes called), just as is the *miya* of the *kami* in the other room. Sometimes no tablets are used, the name being simply painted on the woodwork of the Spirit Shrine. But Shintō has no *kaimyō*: the living name of the dead is written on the *ihai*, with the sole addition of the word *mitama* (spirit). Monthly, on the day corresponding to the date of death, offerings of fish, wine, and other food are made to the spirits, accompanied by special prayer.[1] The *mitama-san* also have their own particular lamps and flower vases; and, although to a lesser degree, are honored with rites like those of the *kami*.

The prayers spoken before the *ihai* of either faith begin with the respective religious traditions of Shintō or Buddhism. The

---

[1] Author's Footnote: The idea underlying this offering of food and drink to the dead, or to the gods, is not so irrational as unthinking critics have declared it to be. The dead are not supposed to consume any of the visible substance of the food set before them, for they are thought to be in an ethereal state, requiring only the most ethereal kind of nutrition. The idea is that they absorb only the invisible essence of the food. And as fruits and other such offerings lose something of their flavor after having been exposed to the air for several hours, this slight change would have been taken in other days as evidence that the spirits had feasted on them. Scientific education necessarily dissipates these consoling illusions, and with them a host of tender and beautiful ideas as to the relation between the living and the dead.

Shintōist, clapping his hands three or four times,[i] first says the sacramental *Harai-tamai*.[ii] The Buddhist, according to his sect, murmurs *Namu-myō-hō-ren-ge-kyō*, or *Namu Amida Butsu*,[iii] or some other holy words of prayer or of praise to the Buddha, before commencing his prayer to the ancestors. The words said to them are seldom spoken aloud, either by the Shintōist or Buddhist: they are either whispered very low under the breath, or formed only within the heart.

---

[i] Author's Footnote: I find that the number of clappings differs somewhat in different provinces. In Kyūshū the clapping is very long, especially before the Prayer of the Rising Sun.
[ii] *Harai tamai kiyome tamai to Kami imi tami.*
[iii] *Namu Amida Butsu means* "Homage to Amida Buddha."

X

At nightfall in Izumo homes, the lamps of the gods and to the ancestors are lit, either by a trusted servant or by some member of the family. Orthodox Shintō regulations require that the lamps should be filled with pure vegetable oil only, *tomoshiabura*, and oil of rapeseed is customarily used. However, there is a definite inclination among the poorer people to substitute a microscopic kerosene lamp for the older lamps; however, this is held to be very wrong by the strictly orthodox, and even to light the lamps with a match is somewhat heretical. It is not believed that matches are always made with pure substances, and the lights of the *kami* should be kindled only with the purest fire: that holy, natural fire which lies hidden within all things. Therefore, in some little closet in the home of any strictly orthodox Shintō family, there is always a small box containing the ancient instruments used for the lighting of holy fire. These consist of the *hi-uchi-ishi*, or "fire-strike-stone;" the *hi-uchi-gane*, or steel; the *hokuchi*, or tinder, made of dried moss; and the *tsukegi*, fine slivers of resinous pine. A little tinder is laid on the flint, set smoldering with a few strokes of the steel, and blown on until it flames. A slip of pine is then ignited by this flame; and with it the lamps of the ancestors and the gods are lit. If several great deities are represented in the *miya* or on the *kamidana* by several *ofuda*, then a separate lamp is sometimes lighted for each; and if there is a *butsuma* in the house, its candles or lamp are lit at the same time.

Although the use of flint and steel for lighting the lamps of the gods will probably have become obsolete within another generation, it still prevails in Izumo, especially in the country districts. Even where the safety match has entirely supplanted the orthodox tools, the orthodox sentiment shows itself in the matter of the choice of matches to be used. Foreign matches are inadmissible: the native match maker quite successfully characterized foreign matches as containing phosphorus "made from the bones of dead animals," and that to kindle the lights of the *kami* with such unholy fire would be sacrilege. In other parts of Japan, the match makers stamped the words "*Saikyō go honzon yo*" (fit for the use of the August High Temple of Saikyō[1]) on their

---

[1] Author's Footnote: Another name for Kyōto, the Sacred City of Japanese Buddhism.

boxes. But Shintō sentiment in Izumo was too strong to be affected much by any such declaration; indeed, the recommendation of the matches as suitable for use in a Shin-shū temple was of itself sufficient to prejudice Shintōists against them. Accordingly, special precautions had to be taken before safety matches could be satisfactorily introduced into the Province of the Gods. Izumo matchboxes now bear the inscriptions: "Pure, and fit to use for kindling the lamps of the *kami*, or of the *hotoke*!"

The inevitable danger to all things in Japan is fire. It is the traditional rule that when a house catches fire, the first objects to be saved, if possible, are the household gods and the tablets of the ancestors. It is even said that if these are saved, most of the family valuables are certain to be saved, and that if these are lost, all is lost.

XI

The terms *soreisha* and *mitamaya*, as used in Izumo, may, I am told, signify either the small *miya* in which the Shintō *ihai* (usually made of cherry wood) is kept, or that part of the dwelling in which it is placed, and where the offerings are made. These, by all who can afford it, are served on the tables of plain white wood, and of the same, high, narrow form as the tables on which offerings are made in the temples and at public funeral ceremonies.

The most ordinary form of prayer addressed to the ancient ancestors in the household cult of Shintō is not uttered aloud. After pronouncing the initial beginning of all popular Shintō prayer, "*Harai-tamai*," etc., the worshiper says, with his heart only:

> *Spirits august of our far-off ancestors, ye forefathers of the generations, and of our families and of our kindred, unto you, the founders of our homes, we this day utter the gladness of our thanks.*

In the family cult of Buddhists, a distinction is made between the household *hotoke*, the souls of those long dead, and the souls of those who are recently deceased. These last are called *shin-botoke*, "new Buddhas," or more strictly, "the newly dead."

"Shrine Altar at Usa Hachiman," by Gekko Zuihitsu (1892).

No direct request for any supernatural favor is made to a *shin-botoke*; for, though respectfully called *hotoke*, the freshly departed soul is not really deemed to have reached Buddhahood: it is only on the long road there, and is perhaps in need of aid, rather than being capable of giving aid. Indeed, among the deeply pious, its condition is a matter of affectionate concern. This is especially the case when a little child dies; for, it is thought that the soul of an infant is feeble and exposed to many dangers. Therefore, a mother, speaking to the departed soul of her child, will advise it, admonish it, command it tenderly, as if addressing a living son or daughter. The ordinary words said in Izumo homes to any *shin-botoke* take the form of entreaty or counsel rather than of prayer, such as these:

"Jōbutsu seyō," or *"Jōbutsu shimasare."* (Do become a Buddha.)

"Mayō na yo." (Go not astray; or, Be never deluded.)

"Miren-wo-nokorasu." (Allow no regret (for this world) to linger with you.)

These prayers are never spoken aloud. Much more in accordance with the Western idea of prayer is the following, spoken by Shin-shū believers on behalf of a *shin-botoke*:

"O-mukai kudasare Amida-sama." (Vouchsafe, O Lord Amida, augustly to welcome (this soul.)

It is needless to say that ancestor worship, although adopted into Buddhism in China and Japan, is not of Buddhist origin. It is also needless to say that Buddhism rejects suicide. Yet in Japan, anxiety about the condition of the soul of the departed often caused suicide, or, at least justified it on the part of those who, though accepting Buddhist dogma, might adhere to ancient custom. Retainers killed themselves in the belief that by dying, they might give counsel, aid, and service to the soul of their lord or lady. Thus, in the novel *Hōgen no monogatari,*[i] a retainer says after the death of his young master:

> *Over the mountain of Shide, over the ghostly River of Sanzu, who will conduct him? If he be afraid, will he not call my name, as he was wont to do? Surely better that, by slaying myself, I go to serve him as of old, than to linger here, and mourn for him in vain.*

In Buddhist household worship, the prayers addressed to the family *hotoke*, the souls of those long dead, are very different from the addresses made to the *shin-hotoke*. The following are a few examples, always said under the breath:

> "*Kanai anzen.*" (Permit that our family may be preserved.)
>
> "*Enmei sakusai.*" (That we may enjoy long life without sorrow.)
>
> "*Shōbai hanjo.*" (That our business may prosper.) (Said by merchants and tradesmen.)
>
> "*Shison chōkin.*" (That the perpetuity of our descent may be assured.)
>
> "*Onteki taisan.*" (That our enemies be scattered.)
>
> "*Yakubyō shōmetsu.*" (That pestilence may not come to us.)

Some of the above are used also by Shintō worshipers. The old samurai still repeat the special prayers of their caste:

> "*Tenka taihei.*" (That long peace may prevail throughout the world.)

---

[i] A fictionalized story, a prose narrative, comparable to an Western epic, relating to the Hōgen Rebellion (保元の乱), the Japanese civil war fought in 1156 over Japanese imperial succession and control of the Fujiwara clan of regents. The rebellion succeeded in establishing the dominance of the samurai clans and eventually the first samurai lead government in the history of Japan.

"Bu-*un chōkyu.*" (That we may have eternal good fortune in war.)

"*Ka-si-mansoku.*" (That our house (family) may forever remain fortunate.)

Besides these silent prayers, any prayers prompted by the heart, whether of request or of gratitude, of course, may be repeated. Such prayers are said, or rather thought, in the speech of daily life. The following little prayer spoken by an Izumo mother to the ancestral spirit, sought on behalf of a sick child, is an example:

"*O-kage ni kodomo no byōki mo senkwai itashimashite, arigatō-gozaimasŭ!*" (By your august influence, the illness of my child has passed away; I thank you.)

"*O-kage nĭ*" literally means "in the august shadow of." There is a ghostly beauty in the original phrase that neither a free nor yet a precise translation can preserve.

XII

Thus, in this home worship of the Far East, by love the dead are made divine; and the foreknowledge of this tender deification must temper the natural melancholy of age with consolation. The dead in Japan are never so quickly forgotten as with us. By simple faith, they are deemed to still dwell among their beloved; and their place within the home remains ever holy. The aged patriarch about to pass away, knows that loving lips will nightly murmur the memory of him before the household shrine; that faithful hearts will entreat him in their own pain and bless him in their joy; that gentle hands will place in front of his *ihai*, pure offerings of fruits, flowers, and dainty meals of the things which he liked; and will pour for him the fragrant tea of guests or the amber rice wine into the little cup of ghosts and gods. Strange changes are coming to the land: old customs are vanishing; old beliefs are weakening; the thoughts of today will not be the thoughts of another age. But he happily knows nothing of this in his own quaint, simple, beautiful Izumo. He dreams that for him, as for his fathers, the little lamp will burn on through the generations. He sees, in softest dreams, the yet unborn: the children of his children's children; clapping their tiny hands in Shintō prayer, and making filial bows before the little, dusty tablet that bears his unforgotten name.

XVIII

OF WOMEN'S HAIR

I

THE HAIR OF THE YOUNGER DAUGHTER of the family is very long, and it is a spectacle of no small interest to see it styled. It is fashioned once every three days; and the operation, which costs four *sen*, is said to require one hour: as a matter of fact, it requires nearly two. The hairstylist (*kamiyui*) first sends her maiden apprentice, who cleans the hair, washes it, perfumes it, and combs it with extraordinary combs of at least five different kinds. So thoroughly is the hair cleansed that it remains immaculate beyond our Western conception of things, for three or four days. In the morning, during the dusting time, it is carefully covered with a handkerchief or a little blue towel; and the curious Japanese wooden pillow, which supports the neck not the head, renders it possible to sleep at ease without disheveling the marvelous structure.[i]

---

[i] Author's Footnote: Formerly, both sexes used the same pillow for the same reason. The long hair of a samurai youth, tied up in an elaborate knot, required much time to arrange. Since it has become the almost universal custom to wear the hair short, the men have adopted a pillow shaped like a small bolster.

After the apprentice has finished her part of the work, the hair stylist herself appears, and begins to build the coiffure. For this task, she uses, besides the extraordinary variety of combs, fine loops of gilded thread or colored paper twine, dainty bits of delightfully tinted crape-silk, delicate steel springs, and curious little basket-shaped things over which the hair is molded into the required forms before being fixed in place.

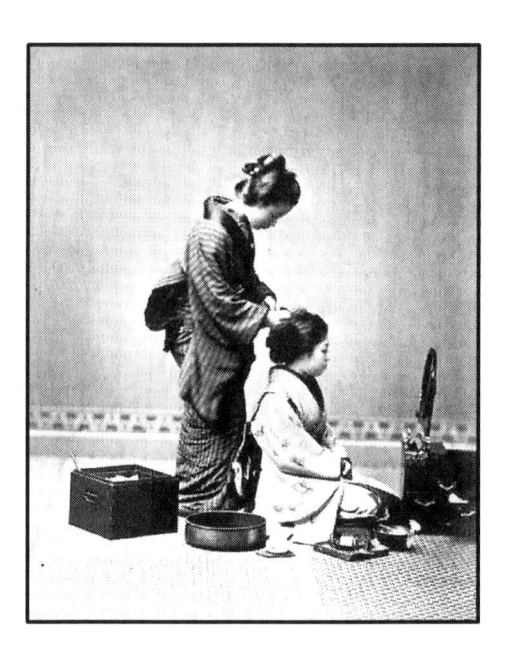

The *kamiyui* also brings razors with her; for, the Japanese girl is shaved: cheeks, ears, brows, chin, even nose! What is there to shave? Only that peachy down which is the velvet of the finest human skin, but which Japanese taste removes. There is, however, another use for the razor. All maidens bear the signs of their maidenhood in the form of a little round spot, about an inch in diameter, shaved clean on the very top of the head. This is only partially concealed by a band of hair brought back from the forehead across it, and fastened to the back hair. The girl-baby's head is totally shaved. When a few years old, the little creature's hair is allowed to grow, except at the top of the head, where a large tonsure is maintained. The size of the tonsure diminishes year by year, until it shrinks after childhood to the small spot described above; and this too, vanishes after marriage, when a still more complicated fashion of wearing the hair is adopted.

II

Such absolutely straight, dark hair as that of most Japanese women, might seem to Western ideas at least, ill-suited to the highest possibilities of the art of the *coiffeuse*.[i] But the skill of the *kamiyui* has made it obedient to every aesthetic whim. Indeed, ringlets are unknown as are curling irons, but what wonderful shapes the hair of the girl is made to assume: volutes, jets, whirls, eddyings, foliations, each passing into the other as smoothly as a linking of brush strokes in the writing of a Chinese master! Far beyond the skill of the Parisian *coiffeuse* is the art of the *kamiyui*. From the mythical era[ii] of the nation, Japanese ingenuity has exhausted itself in the invention and the improvement of pretty devices for the styling of women's hair; and probably there have never been so many beautiful styles of wearing it in any other country as there have been in Japan. These have changed through the centuries; sometimes becoming wondrously intricate in design, sometimes exquisitely simple; as in that gracious custom, recorded for us in so many quaint drawings, of allowing the long black tresses to flow unconfined below the waist.[iii] But every mode of which we have any pictorial record, has its own striking charm. Indian, Chinese, Malayan, and Kōrean ideas of beauty found their way to the Land of the Gods, and were appropriated and transfigured by the finer native concepts of beauty. Buddhism too, which so profoundly influenced all

---

[i] Author's Footnote: It is an error to suppose that all Japanese have blue-black hair. There are two distinct ethnic types. In one, the hair is a deep brown instead of pure black, and is also softer and finer. Rarely, but very rarely, one may see a Japanese head of hair having a natural tendency to wave. For curious reasons, which cannot be stated here, an Izumo woman is very much ashamed of having wavy hair: more ashamed than she would be of a natural deformity.

[ii] Author's Footnote: Even in the time of the writing of the *Kojiki*, the art of arranging the hair must have been somewhat developed. See Professor Chamberlain's introduction to translation, p. xxxi.; also vol. I., section ix.; vol. vii. Sections xii; vol. ix. Sections xviii., *et passim*.

[iii] Author's Footnote: An art expert can decide the age of an unsigned *kakemono* or other work of art in which human figures appear, by the style of the coiffure of the female personages.

Japanese art and thought, may possibly have influenced fashions of wearing the hair; for its female deities appear with the most beautiful coiffures. Notice the hair of a Kwannon or a Benten, and the tresses of the *Tennin*, those angel-maidens who float in azure on the ceilings of the great temples.

III

The particular attractiveness of the modern styles is the way in which the hair is made to serve as an elaborate halo for the features, giving delightful depth to whatever fairness or sweetness the young face may possess. Then, behind this charming black crown, is a riddle of graceful loopings and weavings, of which neither the beginning nor the ending can possibly be seen. Only the *kamiyui* knows the key to that riddle. The entirety is held in place with curious ornamental combs and pierced through with long, fine pins of gold, silver, nacre, transparent tortoise shell, or lacquered wood, with cleverly carved heads.[1]

---

[1] The principal and indispensable hairpin (*kanzsashi*), usually about seven inches long, is split, and its well-tempered double shaft can be used like a small pair of chopsticks for picking up small things. The head is topped by a

IV

Not less than fourteen different ways of styling the hair are practiced by the *coiffeuses* of Izumo; but without doubt in the capital, and in some of the larger cities of eastern Japan, the art is much more elaborately developed. The hairstylists (*kamiyui*) go from house to house to exercise their calling; visiting their clients on fixed days at certain regular hours. In Matsué, the hair of little girls from seven to eight years old is fashioned usually after the style called O-*tabako-bon*, unless it is simply "banged." In the O-*tabako-bon* (honorable smoking-box style), the hair is cut to the length of about four inches all around except above the forehead, where it is clipped a little shorter; and on the top of the head, it is allowed to grow longer and is gathered up in a peculiarly shaped knot, which gives reason for the curious name of the coiffure. As soon as the girl becomes old enough to go to a female public day-school, her hair is styled in the pretty, simple style called *katsu-rashita*, or perhaps in the new, ugly, semi-foreign "bundle-style" called *sokubatsu*, which has become the regulation style in boarding schools.

---

tiny, spoon-shaped projection, which has a special purpose in the Japanese toilette.

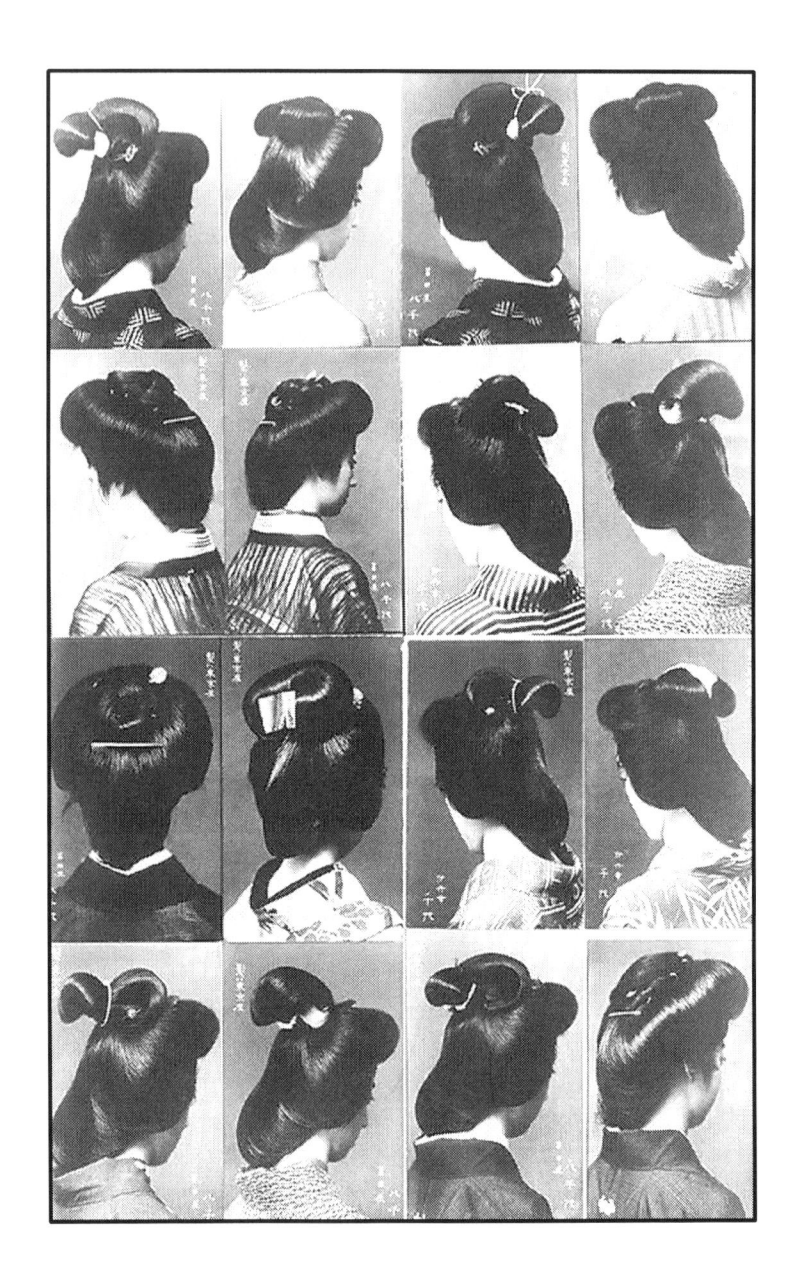

For the daughters of the poor, and even for most of those of the middle classes, the public school period is rather brief; their studies usually cease a few years before they are marriageable, and girls marry very early in Japan. The maiden's first elaborate coiffure is arranged for her when she reaches the age of fourteen or fifteen at the earliest. From twelve to fourteen, her hair is styled in the fashion called *Ōmoyedzuki*; then the style is changed to the beautiful coiffure called *jorōwage*. There are various forms of this style, more or less complex. A couple of years later, the *jorōwage* gives way to the *shinjōchō*[1] (new butterfly style), or the *shimada*, also called *takawage*. The *shinjōchō* style is common, worn by women of various ages, and is not considered refined. The *shimada*, exquisitely elaborate, is; but the more respectable the family, the smaller the form of this coiffure; geisha and *jorō* wear a larger and loftier variety of it, which properly answers to the name *takawage*, or "high coiffure."

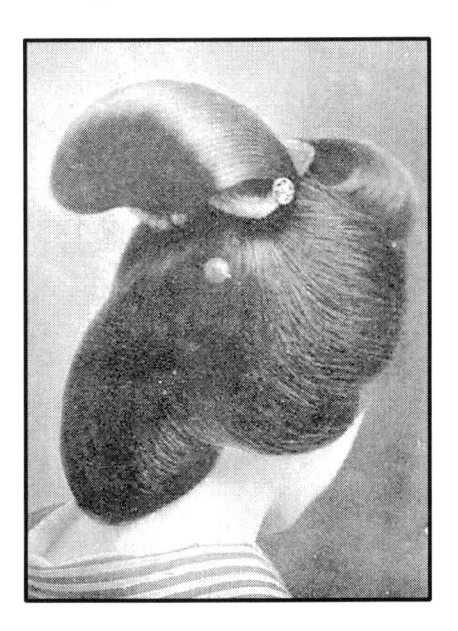

---

[1] Author's Footnote: The *shinjōchō* is also called *Ichōgaeshi* by old people, although the original *Ichōgaeshi* was somewhat different. The samurai girls used to wear their hair in the true *Ichōgaeshi* manner. The name is derived from the *ichō* tree (*Salisburia andiantifolia*), whose leaves have a strange shape, almost like that of a duck's foot. Certain bands of the hair in this coiffure bear a resemblance, in form, to *ichō* leaves.

90

Between eighteen and twenty years of age, the maiden again exchanges this style for another one termed *tenjingaeshi*; between twenty and twenty-four years of age she adopts the fashion called *mitsuwage*, or the "triple coiffure" of three loops; and a somewhat similar, but still more complicated coiffure, called *mitsuwakudzushi* is worn by young women of from twenty-five to twenty-eight. Up to that age, every change in the fashion of wearing the hair has been in the direction of elaborateness and complexity. But after twenty-eight, a Japanese woman is no longer considered young, and there is only one more coiffure for her; the *mochiriwage* or *bobai*, the simple and rather ugly style adopted by old women.

The girl who marries wears her hair in a fashion quite different from any of the preceding. The most beautiful, the most elaborate, and the most costly of all styles is the bride's coiffure, called *hanayome*, a word literally meaning "flower wife." The structure is as dainty as its name, and must be seen to be artistically appreciated. Afterwards, the wife wears her hair in the styles called *kumesa* or *maruwage*, another name for which is *katsuyama*. The *kumesa* style is not refined, and is the coiffure of the poor; the *maruwage* or *katsuyama* is refined. In former times, the samurai women wore their hair in two particular styles: the maiden's *coiffure* was *ichōgaeshi*, and that of the married folk, *katahajishi*. It is still possible to see a few *katahajishi* coiffures in Matsué.

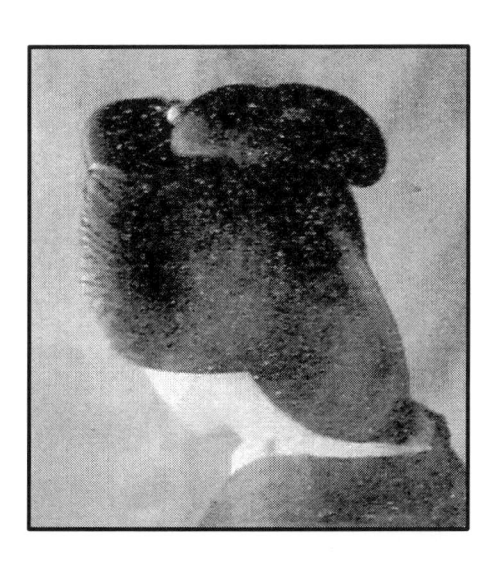

V

The family *kamiyui*, O-koto-san, the most skillful of her craft in Izumo, is a little woman of about thirty, still quite attractive. Around her neck there are three soft, pretty lines, forming what connoisseurs of beauty term "the necklace of Venus." This is a rare charm; but once nearly proved the ruin of Koto. The story is a curious one.

Koto had a rival at the beginning of her professional career; a woman of considerable skill as a *coiffeuse*, but of malignant disposition, named Jin. Jin gradually lost all her respectable customers, and little Koto became the fashionable hairstylist. But her old rival, filled with jealous hate, invented a wicked story about Koto, and the story found root in the rich soil of old Izumo superstition — and dreadfully grew. The idea of it had been suggested to Jin's cunning mind by those three soft lines about Koto's neck. She declared that Koto was a *nuke-kubi*.[54]

What is a *nuke-kubi*? "*Kubi*" signifies either the neck or head. "*Nakeru*" means to creep, to skulk, to prowl, or to slip away stealthily. To have a *nuke-kubi* is to have a head that detaches itself from the body and prowls around at night — by itself.

Koto has been twice married, and her second match was a happy one; but, her first husband caused her much trouble, and ran away from her at last, in company with some worthless woman. Nothing was ever heard of him afterward; so that Jin thought it quite safe to invent a nightmare story to account for his disappearance. She said that he abandoned Koto because, on awaking one night, he saw his young wife's head rise from the pillow , and her neck lengthen like a great white serpent, while the rest of her body remained motionless. He saw the head, supported by the ever lengthening neck, enter the next room and drink all the oil in the lamps, and then return to the pillow slowly: the neck simultaneously contracting. "Then he rose up and fled away from the house in great fear," said Jin.

As one story begets another, all sorts of strange rumors soon began to circulate about poor Koto. There was a tale that late at night, some police officer saw a woman's head without a body, nibbling on fruit from a tree overhanging some garden wall. Knowing it to be a *nuke-kubi*, he struck it with the flat of his sword. It retreated as swiftly as a bat flies, but not before he had been able to recognize the face of the *kamiyui*. "Oh! It is quite true!" declared Jin, the morning after the alleged occurrence, "And if you don't believe it, send word to Koto that you want to see her. She can't go out; her face is all swelled up."

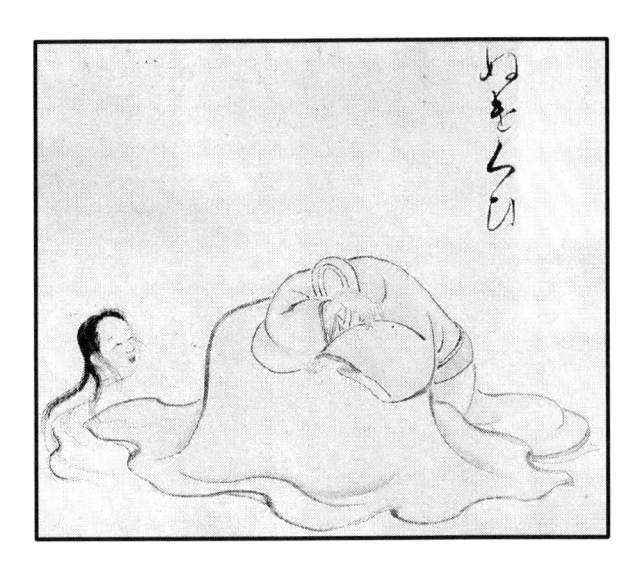

Now the last statement was fact; for, Koto had a very severe toothache at that time, and the fact helped the falsehood. The story found its way to the local newspaper, which published it, only as a strange example of popular gullibility; and Jin said, "Am I a teller of the truth? See, the paper printed it!"

So accordingly, crowds of curious people gathered in front of Koto's little house, and made her life such a burden to her, that her husband had to watch her constantly to keep her from killing herself. Fortunately, she had good friends in the family of the Governor, where she had been employed for years as *coiffeuse*. The Governor, hearing of the wickedness, wrote a public denunciation of it, set his name to it, and printed it. Now the people of Matsué reverenced their old samurai Governor as if he were a god, and believed his slightest word. Seeing what he had written, they became ashamed and also denounced the lie and the liar. The little hairdresser soon became more prosperous than before through popular sympathy.

Some of the most extraordinary beliefs of old days are kept alive in Izumo and elsewhere by what are called in America, traveling sideshows; and the inexperienced foreigner could never imagine the possibilities of a Japanese sideshow. On certain great holidays, the showmen make their appearance, put up their temporary theaters of rush mating and bamboo in some temple courtyard, satisfy expectations with the most incredible surprises, and then vanish as suddenly as they came. The "skeleton of a devil," the "claws of a goblin," and "a rat as large as a sheep," were some of the least extraordinary displays which I saw. The "goblin's claws" were remarkably fine shark's teeth; the devil's skeleton had belonged to an orangutan: all except the horns, ingeniously attached to the skull. The wondrous rat I discovered to be a tame kangaroo. What I could not fully understand was the exhibition of a *nuke-kubi*, in which a young woman stretched her neck, apparently, to a length of about two feet, making ghastly faces during the performances.

VI

There are also some strange old superstitions about women's hair. The myth of Medusa has many counterparts in Japanese folklore; the subject of such tales being always some wondrously beautiful girl, whose hair turns to snakes only at night, and who is discovered at last to be either a dragon or a dragon's daughter. But, in ancient times, it was believed that the hair of any young woman might, under certain trying circumstances, change into serpents; for instance, under the influence of long repressed jealousy.

94

There were many men of wealth who, in the days of Old Japan, kept their concubines (*mekaké* or *aishō*) under the same roof with their legitimate wives (*okusama*). It is told that, although the severest patriarchal discipline might compel the *mekaké* and the *okusama* to live together in perfect seeming harmony by day, their secret hate would reveal itself by night in the transformation of their hair. The long black tresses of each would uncoil, hiss, and try to devour those of the other. Even the mirrors of the sleepers would dash themselves together; for, says an ancient proverb, *kagami onna-no tamashii*, "a mirror is the soul of a woman."[i] There is a famous tradition of one Kato Sayemon Shigenji, who in the night, saw the hair of his wife and the hair of his concubine changed into vipers, writhing together and hissing and biting. Then Kato Sayemon grieved much for that secret bitterness of hatred which existed through his fault; and he shaved his head and became a priest of the great Buddhist monastery of Koya-san, where he dwelt until the day of his death under the name of Karukaya.

VII

The hair of dead women is arranged in the manner called *tabanegami*, somewhat resembling the *shimada* but extremely simplified, and without ornaments of any kind. The name *tabanegami* signifies hair tied into a bunch, like a bundle of rice. This style must also be worn by women during the period of mourning.

Ghosts, nevertheless, are represented with hair loose and long, falling weirdly over the face. No doubt because of the melancholy suggestiveness of its drooping branches, the willow is believed to be the favorite tree of ghosts; under which it is said, they mourn in the night, mingling their shadowy hair with the long, disheveled tresses of the tree.

---

[i] Author's Footnote: The old Japanese mirrors were made of metal, and were extremely beautiful. *Kagami ga kumoru to tamashii ga kumoru*, "When the mirror is dim, the soul is unclean" is another curious proverb relating to mirrors. Perhaps the most beautiful and touching story of a mirror in any language is that called *Matsuyama no kagami*, which has been translated by Mrs. James. (See Appendix A).

Tradition says that Ōkyo Maruyama[55] was the first Japanese artist who drew a ghost. The Shōgun, having invited him to his palace, said, "Make a picture of a ghost for me." Ōkyo promised to do so; but he was puzzled how to execute the order satisfactorily. A few days later, hearing that one of his aunts was very ill, he visited her. She was so emaciated that she looked like one already long dead. As he watched by her bedside, a ghastly inspiration came to him. He drew the fleshless face and long disheveled hair, and created from that hasty sketch, a ghost that surpassed all the Shōgun's expectations. Afterwards, Ōkyo became very famous as a painter of ghosts.

Japanese ghosts are always represented as almost transparent, and unusually tall, only the upper part of the figure being distinctly outlined, and the lower part fading utterly away. As the Japanese say, "a ghost has no feet," its appearance is like an exhalation, which becomes visible only at a certain distance above the ground; and it wavers, lengthens, and undulates in the conceptions of the artists, like a vapor moved by the wind. Occasionally, phantom women figure in picture books as the likeness of living women, but these are not true ghosts. They are fox-women or other goblins, and their supernatural character is suggested by a peculiar expression of the eyes and a certain, impossible elfish grace.

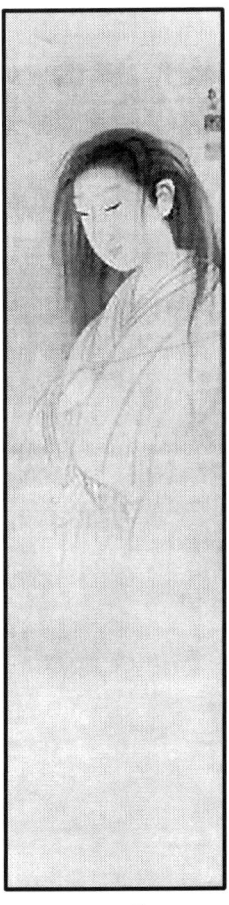

"The Ghost of Oyuki," by Ōkyo Maruyama (1750).

Little children in Japan, like little children in all countries, keenly enjoy the pleasure of fear; and they have many games in which such pleasure forms the chief attraction. Among these is *O-bake-goto*, or "ghost-play." Some nurse-girl or elder sister loosens her hair in front, so as to let it fall over her face, and pursues the little folk with moans and weird gestures, miming all the attitudes of the ghosts of the picture books.

VIII

As the hair of the Japanese woman is her richest ornament, it is, of all her possessions, that which she would most hate to lose. In other days, the man too manly to kill an erring wife, considered it vengeance enough to turn her away with all her hair cut off. Only the greatest faith or the deepest love can prompt a woman to the voluntary sacrifice of her entire *chevelure*[1], though partial sacrifices, offerings of one or two long thick cuttings, may be seen suspended in front of many an Izumo shrine.

What faith can do in the way of such sacrifice, he best knows who has seen the great cables, woven from women's hair, that hang in the vast Honganji temple of Kyōto. And love is stronger than faith, though much less demonstrative. According to an ancient custom, a bereaved wife sacrifices a portion of her hair to be placed in the coffin of her husband, and buried with him. The quantity is not fixed, but in the majority of cases, it is very small, so that the appearance of the *coiffure* is thereby no way affected. But, she who resolves to remain forever loyal to the memory of the lost, yields up all. With her own hand, she cuts off her hair, and lays the whole glossy sacrifice, emblem of her youth and beauty, on the knees of the dead.

It is never allowed to grow again.

---

[1] French for "head of hair."

XIX

FROM THE DIARY OF AN ENGLISH TEACHER

I

MATSUÉ, September 2, 1890

I am under contract to serve as English teacher in the Jinjō Chūgakkō, or Ordinary Middle School, and also in the Shihan-Gakkō, or Normal School, of Matsué, Izumo, for the term of one year.

The Jinjō Chūgakkō is an immense, two-story, wooden building in European style, painted a dark gray-blue. It has accommodations for nearly three hundred day scholars. It is situated in one corner of a great square of ground, bordered on two sides by canals, and on the other two by very quiet streets. This site is very near the ancient castle.

The Normal School is a much larger building occupying the opposite corner of the square. It is also much more handsome, is painted snowy white, and has a little cupola on its top. There are only about one hundred and fifty students in the Shihan-Gakkō, but they are boarders.

Between these two schools are other educational buildings, which I shall later learn more about.

It is my first day at the schools. Nishida Sentarō,[56] the Japanese teacher of English, has taken me through the buildings, introduced me to the Directors, and to all my future colleagues, given me all necessary instructions about hours and about text books, and furnished my desk with all things necessary. Before teaching begins, however, I must be introduced to the Governor of the province, Koteda Yasusada, with whom my contract has been made, through the medium of his secretary. So, Nishida leads the way to the Kenchō, or Prefectural Office, situated in another foreign-looking building across the street.

We enter it, climb a wide stairway, and enter a spacious room carpeted in European fashion: a room with bay windows and cushioned chairs. One person is seated at a small round table, and a dozen others are standing around him. All are in full Japanese costume, ceremonial costume; splendid silk *hakama*[57] or Chinese trousers, silk robes, silk *haori*[58] or jacket, marked with their *mon* or family crests: rich and dignified attire which makes me ashamed of my commonplace Western garb. These are officials of the Kenchō, and teachers: the person seated is the Governor. He rises to greet me, gives me the handshake of a giant; and as I look into his eyes, I feel I shall love that man to the day of my death. A face as fresh and as frank as a boy's, expressing much placid force and large-hearted kindness: all the calm of a Buddha. Beside him, the other officials look very small; indeed, the first impression of him is that of a man of another race. While I am wondering whether the old Japanese heroes were cast in a similar mold, he signals me to take a seat, and questions my guide in a mellow bass voice. There is a charm in the fluent depth of the voice, pleasantly confirming the idea suggested by the face. An attendant brings tea.

"The Governor asks," interprets Nishida, "if you know the old history of Izumo."

I reply that I have read the *Kojiki*, translated by Professor Chamberlain, and have therefore some knowledge of the story of Japan's most ancient province.

Some conversation in Japanese follows. Nishida tells the Governor that I came to Japan to study the ancient religion and customs, and that I am particularly interested in Shintō and the traditions of Izumo. The Governor suggests that I make visits to the celebrated shrines of Kitzuki, Yaegaki, and Kumano, and then asks, "Does he know the tradition of the origin of the clapping of hands before a Shintō shrine?"

I reply in the negative; and the Governor says the tradition is given in a commentary on the *Kojiki*.

"It is in the thirty-second section of the fourteenth volume, where it is written that Ya-he-Koto-Shiro-nushi-no-kami clapped his hands."

I think the Governor for his kind suggestions and his citation. After a brief silence, I am graciously dismissed with another genuine hand grasp; and we return to the school.

II

I have been teaching for three hours in the Middle School, and teaching Japanese boys turns out to be a much more agreeable task than I had imagined. Each class has been so well prepared for me beforehand by Nishida, that my utter ignorance of Japanese creates no difficulty in regard to teaching; moreover, although the lads cannot always understand my words when I speak, they can understand whatever I write on the blackboard with chalk. Most of them have already been studying English from childhood with Japanese teachers. All are wonderfully docile and patient. According to old custom, when the teacher enters, the whole class rises and bows to him. He returns the bow, and calls the roll.

Nishida is very kind. He helps me in every way he possibly can, and is constantly regretting that he cannot help me more. There are, of course, some difficulties to overcome. For instance, it will take me a very, very long time to learn the names of the boys, most of which names I cannot even pronounce, with the class roll in front of me. Although the names of the different classes have been painted on the doors of their respective rooms in English letters for the benefit of the foreign teacher, it will take me some weeks at least to become quite familiar with them. For the time being, Nishida always guides me to the rooms. He also shows me the way, through long corridors, to the Normal School, and introduces me to the teacher, Nakayama, who is to act as my guide there.

I have been engaged to teach only four times a week at the Normal School; but there I am also given a handsome desk in the teachers' room, and am made to feel at home almost immediately. Nakayama shows me everything of interest in the building before introducing me to my future pupils. The introduction is pleasant and novel as a school experience. I am guided along a corridor, and ushered into a large, bright, white painted room, full of young men in dark, blue military uniforms. Each sits at a very small desk, supported by a single leg, with three feet. At the end of the room is a platform with a high desk and a chair for the teacher. As I take my place at the desk, a voice rings out in English, "Stand up!" And all rise with a springy movement as if moved by machinery. "Bow down!" the same voice again commands; the voice of a young student wearing a captain's stripes on his sleeve: and all salute me. I bow in return; we take our seats; and the lesson begins.

All teachers at the Normal School are saluted in the same military fashion at the beginning of each class hour: only the command is given in Japanese. For my sake only, it is given in English.

III

September 22, 1890

The Normal School is a State institution. Students are admitted upon examination and production of testimony as to good character; but the number is, of course, limited. The young men pay no fees, no boarding money, nothing even for books, school clothes or other wearing apparel. They are lodged, clothed, fed, and educated by the State; however, they are required in return, after their graduation, to serve the State as teachers for the term of five years. Admission, however, by no means assures graduation. There are three or four examinations each year; and the students who fail to obtain a certain high average of examination marks, must leave the school; however exemplary their conduct or earnest their study. No leniency can be shown where the educational needs of the State are concerned, and these call for natural ability and a high standard of its proof.

The discipline is military and severe. Indeed, it is so thorough that the graduate of a Normal School is exempted by military law from more than a year's service in the army: he leaves college a trained soldier. Deportment is also a requirement. Special marks are given for it and however gawky a freshman may prove at the time of his admission, he cannot remain so. A spirit of manliness is cultivated, which excludes roughness but develops self-reliance and self-control. The student is required, when speaking, to look his teacher in the face, and to speak his words not only distinctly but resonantly.

Demeanor in class is partly enforced by the classroom fittings themselves. The tiny tables are too narrow to permit being used as supports for the elbows; the seats have no backs against which to lean; and the student must hold himself rigidly erect as he studies. He must also keep himself faultlessly neat and clean. Whenever and wherever he encounters one of his teachers, he must halt, bring his feet together, draw himself erect, and give the military salute: this is done with a swift grace difficult to describe.

The behavior of a class during study hours is, if anything, too faultless. Never a whisper is heard; never is a head raised from the book without permission. But when the teacher addresses a student by name, the youth rises instantly, and replies in a tone of such vigor that would seem to unaccustomed ears, almost startling by contrast with the stillness and self-repression of the others.

The female department of the Normal School, where about fifty young women are being trained as teachers, is a separate two-story quadrangle of buildings; large, airy, and so situated together with its gardens, as to be totally isolated from all the other buildings and invisible from the street. The girls are not only taught European sciences by the most advanced methods, but are trained in Japanese arts as well: the arts of embroidery, of decoration, of painting, and of arranging flowers. European drawing is also taught, and beautifully taught, not only here but in all the schools. It is taught, however, in combination with Japanese methods; and the results of this blending may certainly be expected to have some charming influence on future art production. The average capacity of the Japanese student in drawing is, I think, at least fifty per cent higher than that of European students. The soul of the nation is essentially artistic, and the extremely difficult art of learning to write *kanji*, in which all are trained from early childhood, has already disciplined the hand and the eye to a marvelous degree: a degree undreamed of in the West, long before the drawing master begins his lessons on perspective.

Attached to the great Normal School, and also connected by a corridor with the Jinjō Chūgakkō, is a large elementary school for little boys and girls. Its teachers are male and female students of the graduating classes, who are thus practically trained for their profession before entering the service of the State. Nothing could be more interesting as an educational spectacle to any sympathetic foreigner, than some of this elementary teaching. In the first room which I visited, a class of very little girls and boys, some as quaintly pretty as their own dolls, are bending at their desks over sheets of coal-black paper, which you would think they were trying to make still blacker by energetic use of writing brushes and what we call India ink. They are really learning to write Chinese and Japanese characters, stroke by stroke. Until one stroke has been well learned, they are not allowed to attempt another, much less a combination. Long before the first lesson is thoroughly mastered, the white paper has become all evenly black under the massive amount of brush strokes. But the same sheet is still used; for the wet ink makes a yet blacker mark on the dry, so that it can be easily seen.

In an adjoining room, I see another children's class learning to use scissors. Japanese scissors, which, being made in one piece, shaped something like the letter U, are much less easy to manage than ours. The little folk are being taught to cut out patterns and shapes of special objects or symbols to be studied. Flower forms are the most ordinary patterns and sometimes certain *kanji* are given as subjects.

In another room, a third small class is learning to sing. The teacher writes the music notes (do, re, mi) with chalk on a blackboard and accompanies the song with an accordion. The little ones have learned the Japanese national anthem, Kimigayo, and two native songs set to Scottish tunes, one of which reminds me, even in this remote corner of the Orient, many a charming memory: *Auld Lang Syne.*

No uniform is worn in this elementary school. All are in Japanese clothes; the boys in dark blue kimono, the little girls in robes of all tints, as radiant as butterflies. But, in addition to their robes, the girls wear *hakama*,[i] and these are of a vivid, warm sky-blue.

Between the hours of teaching, ten minutes are allowed for play or rest. The little boys play at "Demon Shadows" or at "Blind Man's Bluff" or some other funny games. They laugh, leap, shout, race, and wrestle; but, unlike European children, never quarrel or fight.[ii] As for the little girls, they get by themselves and either play at handball or form into circles to play at some round game, accompanied by song. The chorus of those little voices, in the round, is indescribably soft and sweet.

> *Kango-kango shō-ya,*
> *Naka yoni shō-ya,*
> *Don-don to kunde*
> *Jizō-san no midzu wo*
> *Matsuba no midzu irete,*
> *Makkuri kaéso.*[iii]

I notice that the young men, as well as the young women who teach these little folk, are extremely tender to their charges. A child whose kimono is out of order, or dirtied by play, is taken aside and brushed and rearranged as carefully as by an elder brother.

Besides being trained for their future profession by teaching the children of the elementary school, the girl students of

---

[i] Author's Footnote" There is a legend that the Sun Goddess invented the first *hakama*, by tying together the skirts of her robe.

[ii] Author's Footnote: Since the above was written, I have had two years' experience as a teacher in various large Japanese schools; and I have never had personal knowledge of any serious quarrel between students, and have never even heard of a fight among my pupils. And I have taught some eight hundred boys and young men.

[iii] Author's Footnote: "Let us play the game called *kango-kango*. Plenteously the water of Jizō-san quickly draw, and pour on the pine leaves, and turn back again." Many of the games of Japanese children, like many of their toys, have a Buddhist origin, or at least a Buddhist significance.

Shihan-Gakkō are also trained to teach in the neighboring kindergarten. It is a delightful kindergarten, with big cheerful, sunny rooms, where a stock of the most ingenious educational toys is piled on shelves for daily use.

IV

October 1, 1890

    Nevertheless, I am destined to see very little of the Normal School. Strictly speaking, I do not belong to its staff: my services being only lent by the Middle School, to which I give most of my time. I see the Normal School students only in their class rooms, for they are not allowed to go out to visit their teachers' homes in the town. So, I can never hope to become familiar with them as with the students of the Chūgakkō, who are beginning to call me "Teacher" instead of "Sir," and to treat me as a sort of elder brother. (I objected to the word "master," for in Japan, the teacher has no need of being masterful.) I feel less at home in the large, bright, comfortable rooms of the Normal School teachers than in our dingy, chilly teacher's' room at the Chūgakkō, where my desk is next to that of Nishida.

On the walls there are maps crowded with Japanese *kanji*; a few large charts representing zoological facts in light of evolutional science; and an immense frame filled with little black lacquered wooden tablets, so neatly fitted together that the entire surface is as uniform as that of a blackboard. On these are written, or rather painted in white, names of teachers, subjects, classes, and order of teaching hours; and by the ingenious tablet arrangement, any change of hours can be represented by simply changing the places of the tablets. Since all this is written in *kanji*, it remains to me a mystery, except in so far as the general plan and purpose are concerned. I have learned only to recognize the letters of my own name, and the simpler form of numerals.

On every teacher's desk there is a small *hibachi*[59] of glazed blue-and-white ware, containing a few lumps of glowing charcoal in a bed of ashes. During the brief intervals between classes, each teacher smokes his tiny Japanese pipe of brass, iron, or silver. The *hibachi* and a cup of hot tea are our consolations for the fatigue of the classroom.

Nishida and one or two other teachers know a good deal of English, and we chat together sometimes between classes. But more often, no one speaks. All are tired after the teaching hour, and prefer to smoke in silence. At such times the only sounds within the room are the ticking of the clock, and the sharp clang of little pipes being rapped on the edges of the *hibachi* to empty out the ashes.

V

October 15, 1890

Today I witnessed the annual athletic contests (*undō-kwai*) of all the schools in Shimane Ken.[1] These games were celebrated in the broad castle grounds of Ninomaru (Matsué Castle). Yesterday, a circular racetrack had been paced off, hurdles erected for leaping, thousands of wooden seats prepared for invited or privileged spectators, and a grand lodge built for the Governor, all before sunset. The place looked like a vast circus, with its tiers of plank seats rising one above the other, and the Governor's lodge magnificent with wreaths and flags. School children from

---

[1] Shimane Prefecture

all the villages and towns within twenty-five miles had arrived in surprising number. Nearly six thousand boys and girls were entered to take part in the contests. Their parents, relatives and teachers made an imposing assembly on the benches and within the gates. On the ramparts overlooking the huge enclosure, a much larger crowed had gathered, representing perhaps one third of the population of the city.

The signal to begin or to end a contest was a pistol shot. Four different kinds of games were performed in different parts of the grounds at the same time, as there was room enough for an army; and prizes were awarded to the winners of each contest by the hand of the Governor himself.

There were races between the best runners in each class of the different schools; and the best runner of all proved to be Sakane, of our own fifth-grade class, who came in first by nearly forty yards without seeming to even make an effort. He is our champion athlete, and as good as he is strong, so that it made me very happy to see him with his arms full of prize books. He also won a fencing contest decided by the breaking of a little earthenware saucer tied to the left arm of each combatant, and he also won a leaping match between our older boys.

There were many hundreds of other winners too, and many hundreds of prizes were given away. There were races in which the runners were tied together in pairs, the left leg of one to the right leg of the other. There were equally funny races, the winning of which depended on the runner's ability not only to run, but to crawl, climb, vault, and jump alternately. There were races also for the little girls, who seemed as pretty as butterflies in their sky-blue *hakama* and many colored robes; races in which the contestants each, as they ran, had to pick up three balls of different colors out of a number scattered over the ground. Besides this, the little girls had what is called a flag race, and a contest with rackets and shuttlecocks.[60]

Then came the tug-of-war. A magnificent tug-of-war too: one hundred students at one end of a rope, and another hundred at the other. But the most wonderful spectacles of the day were the dumbbell exercises. Six thousand boys and girls, massed in ranks about five hundred deep; six thousand pairs of arms rising and falling exactly together; six thousand pairs of sandaled feet advancing or retreating together at the signal of the masters of gymnastics, directing it all from the tops of various little wooden towers; six thousand voices chanting the "one, two, three," of the dumbbell drill, "*Ichi, ni, – san, shi, – go, roku, – shichi, hachi:*" all in unison.

Last came the curious game called "Taking the Castle." Two models of Japanese castles, about fifteen feet high, made with paper stretched over a framework of bamboo, were set up: one at each end of the field. Inside the castles an inflammable liquid has been placed in open containers, so that if the vessels were overturned, the whole thing would catch fire. The boys, divided into two parties, bombarded the castles with wooden balls, which passed easily through the paper walls. In a short time, both models were making a glorious blaze; of course, the party whose castle was the first to burn lost the game.

The games began at eight o'clock in the morning, and came to an end at five in the evening. Then at a signal, fully ten thousand voices sang out the superb national anthem, *Kimigayo*, and concluded it with three cheers for their Imperial Majesties, the Emperor and Empress of Japan.

The Japanese do not shout or roar as we do when we cheer: they chant. Each long cry is like the opening tone of an immense musical chorus: A-a-a-a-a-a-a-a!

VI

It is no small surprise to observe how botany, geology, and other sciences are taught daily, even in this remotest part of old

Japan. Plant physiology and the nature of vegetable tissues are studied under excellent microscopes, and in their relation to chemistry. At regular intervals, the instructor leads his classes into the countryside to illustrate the lessons of the term by examples taken from the flora of their native place. Agriculture, taught by a graduate of the famous Agricultural School at Sapporo,[i] is practically illustrated on farms purchased and maintained by the schools for purely educational purposes. Each series of lessons in geology is supplemented by visits to the mountains around the lake, or to the tremendous cliffs of the coast, where the students are taught to familiarize themselves with forms of stratification and the visible history of rocks. The basin of the lake and the country around Matsué is geographically studied, after the plans of instruction laid down in Huxley's[61] excellent manual. Natural History is also taught, according to the latest and best methods and with the help of the microscope. The results of such teaching are sometimes surprising. I know of one student, a lad of only sixteen, who voluntarily collected and classified more than two hundred varieties of marine plants for a Tokyō professor. Another, a youth of seventeen, wrote down in my notebook for me, without a reference book in hand (and as I afterward discovered, almost without omission or error) a scientific list of all the butterflies to be found in the area of the city.

VII

Through the Minister of Public Instruction, His Imperial Majesty has sent to all the great public schools of the Empire, a letter bearing the date of the thirteenth day of the tenth month, of the twenty-third year of Meiji.[62] The students and teachers of the various schools assemble to hear the reading of the Imperial Words on Education.

At eight o'clock, we of the Middle School, are all waiting in our own assembly hall for the coming of the Governor, who will read the Emperor's letter in the various schools. We only wait a little while; then the Governor comes with all the officers of the

---

[i] The Sapporo Agricultural College, (札幌農学校, *Sapporo nōgakkō*), now known as the Hokkaido University, where the esteemed diplomat, educator and author of *Bushidō: The Soul of Japan*, Inazō Nitobe, was educated.

Kenchō and the chief men of the city. We rise to salute him and then the national anthem is sung.

Then the Governor, ascending the platform, produces the Imperial epistle; a scroll in *kanji* manuscript, sheathed in silk. He removes it slowly from its woven envelope, lifts it reverentially to his forehead, unrolls it, lifts it again to his forehead, and after a moment's dignified pause, begins in that clear, deep voice of his, to read the melodious syllables in the ancient style, which is like a chant:

CHO-KU-GU. Chin omommiru ni waga kōso koso hani wo...

We consider that the Founder of Our Empire and the ancestors of Our Imperial House placed the foundation of the country on a grand and permanent basis, and established their authority on the principles of profound humanity and benevolence.

That Our subjects have throughout the ages deserved well of the State by their loyalty and piety and by their harmonious cooperation is in accordance with the essential character of Our nation; and on these very same principles Our education has been founded.

You, Our subjects, be therefore filial to your parents; be affectionate to your brothers; be harmonious as husbands and wives; and be faithful to your friends; conduct yourselves with propriety and carefulness; extend generosity and benevolence towards your neighbors; attend to your studies and follow your pursuits; cultivate your intellects and elevate your morals; advance public benefits and promote social interests; be always found in the good observance of the laws and constitution of the land; display your personal courage and public spirit for the sake of the country whenever required; and thus support the Imperial prerogative, which is coexistent with the Heavens and the Earth.

Such conduct on your part will not only strengthen the character of Our good and loyal subjects, but conduce also to the maintenance of the fame of your worthy forefathers.

This is the instruction bequeathed by Our ancestors and to be followed by Our subjects; for it is the truth which has guided and guides them in their own affairs and in their dealings towards aliens.

> *We hope, therefore, We and Our subjects will regard these sacred precepts with one and the same heart in order to attain the same ends.*[1]

Then the Governor and the Headmaster speak a few words; dwelling on the full significance of His Imperial Majesty's august commands, and exhorting all to remember and to obey them to the utmost; after which, the students have a holiday, to enable them to better recollect what they have heard.

VIII

All teaching in the modern Japanese system of education is conducted with the utmost kindness and gentleness. The teacher is a teacher only: he is not, in the English sense of mastery, a master. He stands in the relation of an elder brother to his pupils. He never tries to impose his will on them; he never scolds, seldom criticizes, and he scarcely ever punishes. No Japanese teacher ever strikes a pupil: such an act would cost him his post at once. He never loses his temper: to do so would disgrace him in the eyes of his boys and in the judgment of his colleagues. Practically speaking, there is no punishment in Japanese schools. Sometimes, very mischievous lads are kept in the schoolhouse during recreation time; yet, even this light penalty is not inflicted directly by the teacher, but by the director of the school on complaint of the teacher. The purpose in such cases is not to inflict pain by deprivation of enjoyment, but to give public illustration of a fault; and in the great majority of instances, consciousness of the fault thus brought home to the lad before his comrades, is quite enough to prevent its repetition.

No such cruel punishment like that of forcing a dull pupil to learn an additional task, or of sentencing him to strain his eyes

---

[1] Author's Footnote: I take the above translation from a Tōkyō educational journal, entitled *The Museum*. The original document, however, was impressive to a degree that perhaps no translation could give. The Chinese [Confucian] words by which the Emperor refers to himself and his will are far more impressive than our Western "We" or "Our;" and the words relating to duties, virtues, wisdom, and other matters are words that evoke in a Japanese mind ideas which only those who know Japanese life perfectly can appreciate, and which though variant from our own, are neither less beautiful nor less sacred.

copying four or five hundred lines, is ever dreamed of. Nor would such forms of punishment, in the present state of things, be long tolerated by the pupils themselves. The general policy of the educational authorities everywhere throughout the Empire is to get rid of students who cannot be perfectly well managed without punishment; and expulsions, nevertheless, are rare.

I often see a pretty spectacle on my way home from the school, when I take the shortcut through the castle grounds. A class of about thirty bareheaded little boys, in kimono and sandals, being taught to march and to sing by a handsome young teacher, also in Japanese clothes. While they sing, they are drawn up in line; and keep time with their little bare feet. The teacher, who has a pleasant, high, clear tenor voice, stands at one end of the rank and sings a single line of the song. Then all the children sing it after him. Then, he sings a second line, and they repeat it. If any mistakes are made, they have to sing the verse again. It is the *Song of Kusunoki Masashigé*,[63] noblest of Japanese heroes and patriots.

IX

I have said that severity on the part of teachers would scarcely be tolerated by the students themselves: a fact which may sound quite strange to English or American ears. Tom Brown's school[64] does not exist in Japan. The ordinary public school much more resembles the ideal Italian institution so charmingly painted for us in the *Cuoré* of De Amicis.[65] Furthermore, Japanese students claim and enjoy an independence which is contrary to all Western ideas of disciplinary necessity. In the West, the master expels the pupil. In Japan, it happens quite as often that the pupil expels the master.

Each public school is an earnest, spirited little republic, to which director and teachers are like President and Cabinet. They are indeed appointed by the prefectural government on recommendation of the Educational Bureau at the capital; however in actual practice, they maintain their positions by virtue of their capacity and personal character as estimated by their students, and are likely to be deposed by a revolutionary movement whenever found wanting. It has been alleged that students frequently abuse their power; but this allegation has been made by European residents, strongly prejudiced in favor of masterful English ways of discipline. (I recall that an English Yokohama paper, in this connection, advocated the introduction of the birch.[i])

My own observations have convinced me, as larger experience has convinced some others, that in most instances of pupils rebelling against a teacher, reason is on their side. They will rarely insult a teacher whom they dislike, or cause any disturbance in his class: they will simply refuse to attend school until he is removed. Personal feelings may often be a secondary reason, but it is seldom, so far as I have been able to learn, the primary cause for such a demand. A teacher whose manners are unsympathetic, or even positively disagreeable, nevertheless will be obeyed and revered while his students remain convinced of his capacity as a teacher and his sense of justice; and they are as keen to discern ability as they are to detect partiality. On the other hand, an amiable disposition alone will never atone for want of knowledge or skill to impart it. I knew of one case, in a neighboring public school, regarding a demand by the students for the removal of their professor of chemistry. In making their complaint, they frankly declared, "We like him. He is kind to all

---

[i] Birching is a form of corporal punishment utilizing a birch rod, twig, or bundle of twigs from a birch tree, typically applied to the recipient's bare buttocks, although the back and/or shoulders were often targets of this form of punishment as well. It was common practice in schools during the 18th and 19th centuries in both the UK and the United States.

of us; he does the best he can. But he does not know enough to teach us as we wish to be taught. He cannot answer our questions. He cannot explain the experiments which he shows us. We must have another teacher." Investigation proved that the lads were quite right. The young teacher had graduated at the university; he had come well recommended; however, he had no thorough knowledge of the science which he undertook to impart, and no experience as a teacher. The instructor's success in Japan is not guaranteed by a degree, but by his practical knowledge and his capacity to communicate it simply and thoroughly.

X

November 3, 1890

Today is the birthday of His Majesty the Emperor. It is a public holiday throughout Japan; and there will be no teaching this morning; but at eight o'clock, all the students and instructors enter the great assembly hall of the Jinjō Chūgakkō to honor the anniversary of His Majesty's august birth.

On the platform of the assembly hall, a table covered with dark silk has been placed; and on this table the portraits of Their Imperial Majesties, the Emperor and the Empress of Japan, stand side by side upright, framed in gold. The alcove above this platform has been decorated with flags and wreaths.

Before long the Governor enters, looking like a French general in his gold-embroidered uniform of office, followed by the Mayor, the Chief Military Officer, the Chief of Police, and all the officials of the provincial government. These take their places in silence to left and right of the platform. Then the school organ suddenly rolls out the slow, solemn, beautiful national anthem; and all present chant those ancient words, made sacred by the reverential love of a century of generations:

Ki-mi ga-a yo-o wa
Chi-yo ni-i-i ya-chi-yo ni sa-za-ré
I-shi no
I-wa o to na-ri-te
Ko-ke no
Mu-u su-u ma-a-a-dé.[1]

The anthem ceases. The Governor advances with a slow, dignified step from the right side of the room to the center of the open space in front of the platform and the portraits of Their Majesties; turns his face to them, and bows profoundly. Then he takes three steps forward toward the platform and halts, and bows again. Then he takes three more steps forward, and bows still more profoundly. The he retires, walking backward six steps and bows once more. Then he returns to his place.

After this, the teachers by parties of six, perform the same beautiful ceremony. When all have saluted the portrait of His Imperial Majesty, the Governor ascends the platform and makes a few eloquent remarks to the students about their duty to their Emperor, to their country, and to their teachers. Then the anthem is sung again; and all disperse to amuse themselves for the rest of the day.

XI

March 1, 1891

---

[1] Author's footnote. *Kimi ga yo wa chiyo ni yachiyo ni sasaré ishi no iwa o to narite koke no musu madé.* Freely translated: "May Our Gracious Sovereign reign a thousand years — reign ten thousand thousand years — reign till the little stone grows into a mighty rock, thick-velveted with ancient moss!"

The majority of the students of the Jinjō Chūgakkō are day-scholars only (*externes*, as we would say in France): they go to school in the morning, take their noon meal at home, and return at one o'clock to attend the brief afternoon classes. All the city students live with their own families; however, there are many boys from remote country districts who have no city relatives, and for them the school provides boarding houses, where a wholesome moral discipline is maintained by special masters. They are free, however, if they have sufficient means, to choose another boarding house (provided it is a respectable one), or to find quarters in some good family; but few adopt either course.

I doubt whether in any other country the cost of education — education of the most excellent and advanced kind — costs as little as in Japan. The Izumo student is able to live at a figure so far below the Western idea of necessary expenditure, that the mere statement of it can scarcely fail to surprise the reader. A sum equal to about twenty dollars in American money supplies him with board and lodging for one year. The whole of his expenses, including school fees, are about seven dollars a month. For his room and three ample meals a day, he pays every four weeks only one *yen*, eighty-five *sen*: not much more than a dollar and a half in American currency. If very, very poor, he will not be obliged to wear a uniform; but nearly all students of the higher classes do wear uniforms, as the cost of a complete uniform, including cap and leather shoes, is only about three and a half *yen* for the cheaper quality. Those who do not wear leather shoes, however, are required while in the school, to exchange their noisy wooden *geta* for *zori* or light straw sandals.

XII

But the mental education so admirably imparted in an ordinary middle school is not, after all, so cheaply acquired by the student as might be imagined from the cost of living and the low rate of school fees; for, nature exacts a heavier school fee, and rigidly collects her debt — in human life.

To understand why, one should remember that the modern knowledge which the modern Izumo student must acquire on a diet of boiled rice and *tōfu* was discovered, developed, and synthesized by minds strengthened on a costly diet of flesh. National underfeeding offers the most cruel problem which the educators of Japan must solve in order that she may become fully able to assimilate the civilization we have thrust upon her. As Herbert Spencer has pointed out, the degree of human energy, physical or intellectual, must depend on the nutritional value of food; and history shows that the well-fed races have been the energetic and the dominant. Perhaps mind will rule in the future of nations; but mind is a mode of force, and must be fed: through the stomach. The thoughts that have shaken the world were never framed on bread and water. They were created by beefsteak and mutton chops, by ham and eggs, by pork and puddings, and were stimulated by generous wines, strong ales, and strong coffee. Science also teaches us that the growing child or youth requires an even more nutritious diet than the adult, and that the student especially needs strong nourishment to repair the wear involved in brain exertion.

And what is the wear on the Japanese schoolboy's system from study? It is certainly greater than that which the system of the European or American student must suffer at the same period of life. Seven years of study are required to give the Japanese youth merely the necessary knowledge of his own triple system of ideographs [*kanji*]; or in less accurate or plainer speech, the enormous alphabet of his native literature. He also must study the literature and the art of two forms of his language: the written and the spoken. Likewise of course, he must learn native history and native morals. Besides these Asian studies, his course includes foreign history, geography, arithmetic, astronomy, physics, geometry, natural history, agriculture, chemistry, drawing, and mathematics. Worst of all, he must learn English; a language of which the difficulty to the Japanese cannot be even faintly imagined by anyone familiar with the construction of the native tongue; a language so different from his own that the very simplest Japanese phrase cannot be intelligibly rendered into English by a literal translation of the words, or even the form of the thought. He must learn all this on a diet no English boy could live on; always thinly clad in his poor cotton clothes without even a fire in his schoolroom during the terrible winter; only a *hibachi* containing a few lumps of glowing charcoal in a bed of ashes.[1] Is it to be wondered that even those Japanese students who pass successfully through all the educational courses the Empire can open to them, can only in rare instances, show results of their long training as large as those shown by students of the West? Better conditions are coming; but at present, under the new strain, young bodies and young minds too often give way. Those who break down are not the dullards, but the pride of schools, the captains of classes.

XIII

Yet, so far as the finances of the schools allow, everything possible is done to make the students both healthy and happy: to provide them with ample opportunities both for physical exercise and for mental enjoyment. Though the course of study is severe, the hours are not long. One of the daily five is devoted to military drill, made more interesting to the lads by the use of real rifles and bayonets, furnished by the government. There is a fine gymnastic ground near the school, equipped with trapezes, parallel bars, vaulting horses, etc.; and there are two masters of gymnastics attached to the Middle School alone. There are rowboats in which the boys can take their pleasure on the

---

[1] Author's Footnote: Stoves, however, are being introduced. In the higher government schools, and in the Normal Schools, the students who are boarders obtain a better diet than most poor boys can get at home. Their rooms are also well warmed.

beautiful lake whenever the weather permits. There is an excellent fencing [Kendō] school conducted by the Governor himself, who although so heavy a man, is considered one of the best fencers of his own generation. The style taught is the old one, requiring the use of both hands to wield the sword. Thrusting is rarely tried: it is nearly all heavy slashing. The foils [*shinai*] are made of long splinters of bamboo tied together so as to form something resembling a sword; masks and padded coats protect the head and body; for, the blows struck are heavy. This sort of fencing requires considerable agility and gives more active exercise than our more severe Western styles. Yet another form of healthy exercise consists of long journeys on foot to famous places. Special holidays are allowed for these. The students march out of town in military order, accompanied by some of their favorite teachers, and perhaps a servant to cook for them. Thus they may travel for a hundred or even a hundred and fifty miles and back. But if the journey is to be a very long one, only the strong lads are allowed to go. They walk in *waraji*, the true straw sandal, closely tied to the naked foot, which it leaves perfectly supple and free, without blistering or producing corns. They sleep at night in Buddhist temples; and their cooking is done in the open fields, like that of soldiers in camp.

For those little inclined to such sturdy exercise, there is a school library which is growing every year. There is also a monthly school magazine, edited and published by the boys. There is also a Students' Society, at whose regular meetings debates are held on all conceivable subjects of interest to the students.

XIV

April 4, 1891

Once a week, the students of the third, fourth, and fifth year classes write for me brief English compositions on easy themes which I select for them. As a rule the themes are Japanese. Considering the immense difficulty of the English language to Japanese students, the ability of some of my boys to express their thoughts in it is astonishing. Their compositions have also another interest for me as revelations, not of individual character, but of national sentiment or of aggregate sentiment of some sort or other. What seems to me most surprising in the compositions of the average Japanese student is that they have no personal distinction at all. Even the handwriting of twenty English compositions will be found to have a curious family resemblance; and striking exceptions are too few to affect the rule. Here is one of the best compositions on my table, by a student at the head of his class. Only a few idiomatic errors have been corrected.

The Moon

The Moon appears melancholy to those who are sad, and joyous to those who are happy. The Moon makes memories of home come to those who travel, and creates homesickness. So when the Emperor Godaigo, having been banished to Oki by the traitor Hojō, beheld the moonlight upon the seashore, he cried out, "The Moon is heartless!"

The sight of the Moon makes an immeasurable feeling in our hearts when we look up at it through the clear air of a beauteous night.

Our hearts ought to be pure and calm like the light of the Moon.

Poets often compare the Moon to a Japanese (metal) mirror (kagami); and indeed its shape is the same when it is full.

The refined man amuses himself with the Moon. He seeks some house looking out upon water, to watch the Moon, and to make verses about it.

The best places from which to see the Moon are Tsukigashi, and the mountain Obasute.

The light of the Moon shines alike upon foul and pure, upon high and low. That beautiful Lamp is nether yours nor mine, but everybody's.

When we look at the Moon we should remember that its waxing and its waning are the signs of the truth that the culmination of all things is likewise the beginning of their decline.

Any person totally unfamiliar with Japanese educational methods might presume that the foregoing composition shows some original power of thought and imagination. But this is not the case. I found the same thoughts and comparisons in thirty other compositions on the same subject. Indeed, the compositions of any number of middle school students upon the same subject are certain to be very much alike in idea and sentiment: though they are none the less charming for that. As a rule, the Japanese student shows little originality in the line of imagination. His imagination was made for him long centuries ago; partly in China, partly in his native land. From childhood he is trained to see and to feel nature exactly in the manner of those wondrous artists who, with a few swift brush strokes, fling down on a sheet of paper, the color sensation of a chilly dawn, a blazing noon, or an autumn evening. Through all his boyhood he is taught to commit to memory the most beautiful thoughts and comparisons to be found in his ancient, native literature. Every boy has thus learned that the vision of Fuji against the blue resembles a white, half-opened fan, hanging inverted in the sky. Every boy knows that cherry trees in full blossom look as if the most delicate of flushed summer clouds were caught in their branches. Every boy knows the comparison between the falling of certain leaves on snow and the casting down of texts on a sheet of white paper with a brush. Every boy and girl knows the verses comparing the print of cats' feet on snow to plum flowers,[1] and that comparing the impression of *bokkuri*[ii] on snow to the Japanese character for the number two.[iii] These were thoughts of old, old poets, and it would be very hard to invent prettier ones. Artistic power in composition is chiefly shown by the correct memorizing and clever combination of these old thoughts.

The students have been equally well trained to discover a moral in almost everything: animate or inanimate. I have tested them with a hundred subjects — Japanese subjects — for composition. I have never found them to fail at discovering a moral when the theme was a native one. If I suggested fireflies, they at once approved the topic, and wrote the story of that Chinese student who, being too poor to pay for a lamp, imprisoned many fireflies in a paper lantern, and thus was able to obtain light enough to study after dark, and to eventually become a great scholar. If I said frogs, they wrote the legend of Ono no Tofu,[66] who was persuaded to become a learned celebrity by witnessing the tireless perseverance of a frog trying to leap up to a willow branch. I have included just a few specimens of the moral ideas

---

[i] Author's Footnote: *Hachi yuki ya, Neko no ashii ato, Ume no hana.*
[ii] *Bokkuri* are a girl's lacquered wooden clogs.
[iii] Author's Footnote: *Ni no ji fumi dasu, Bokkuri kana.*

"Ryu Shoten, Mt. Fuji and Dragon," by Ogata Gekko (1896).

which I thus evoked. I have corrected some common mistakes in the originals, but have allowed a few differences to stand:

The Botan

The botan (Japanese peony) is large and beautiful to see; but it has a disagreeable smell. This should make us remember that what is only outwardly beautiful in human society should not attract us. To be attracted by beauty only may lead us into fearful and fatal misfortune. The best place to see the botan is the island of Daikonshima in the lake Nakaumi. There in the season of its flowering all the island is red with its blossoms.

The Dragon

When the Dragon tries to ride the clouds and come into heaven there happens immediately a furious storm. When the Dragon dwells on the ground it is supposed to take the form of a stone or other object; but when it wants to rise it calls a cloud. Its body is composed of parts of many animals. It has the eyes of a tiger and the horns of a deer and the body of a crocodile and the claws of an eagle and two trunks like the trunk of an elephant. It has a moral. We should try to be like the dragon, and find out and adopt all the good qualities of others.

At the close of this essay on the dragon is a note to the teacher, saying, "I believe not there is any Dragon. But, there are many stories and curious pictures about Dragon."

Mosquitoes

On summer nights we hear the sound of faint voices; and little things come and sting our bodies very violently. We call them ka, in English "mosquitoes." I think the sting is useful for us, because if we begin to sleep, the ka shall come and sting us, uttering a small voice; — then we shall be bringed back to study by the sting.

The following, by a lad of sixteen, is submitted only as a characteristic expression of half-formed ideas about a less familiar subject.

European and Japanese Customs

Europeans wear very narrow clothes and they wear shoes always in the house. Japanese wear clothes which are very lenient and they do not shoe except when they walk out-of-the-door.

What we think very strange is that in Europe every wife loves her husband more than her parents. In Nippon there is no wife who more loves not her parents than her husband.

And Europeans walk out in the road with their wives, which we utterly refuse to, except on the festival of Hachiman.

The Japanese woman is treated by man as a servant, while the European woman is respected as a master. I think these customs are both bad.

We think it is very much trouble to treat European ladies; and we do not know why ladies are so much respected by Europeans.

Conversation in the classroom about foreign subjects is often equally amusing and suggestive:

"Teacher, I have been told that if a European and his father and his wife were all to fall into the sea together, and that he only could swim, he would try to save his wife first. Would he really?"

"Probably," I reply.

"But why?"

"One reason is that Europeans consider it a man's duty to help the weaker first: especially women and children."

"And does a European love his wife more than his father and mother?"

"Not always; but generally, perhaps he does."

"Why, Teacher? According to our ideas that is very immoral."

"Teacher, how do European women carry their babies?"

"In their arms."

"Very tiring! And how far can a woman walk carrying a baby in her arms?"

"A strong woman can walk many miles with a child in her arms."

"But she cannot use her hands while she is carrying a baby that way, can she?"

"Not very well."

"Then it is a very bad way to carry babies," etc.

XV

May 1, 1891

My favorite students often visit me on afternoons. They first send me their cards, to announce their presence. On being told to come in, they leave their footgear on the doorstep, enter my little study, prostrate themselves; and we all sit down together on the floor, which is in all Japanese houses like a soft mattress. The servant brings *zabuton* or small cushions to kneel upon, and cakes and tea.

To sit as the Japanese do requires practice; and some Europeans can never acquire the habit. To acquire it, indeed, one must become accustomed to wearing Japanese clothes. But once the habit of sitting that way has been formed, one finds it the most natural and easy position, and assumes it by preference, for eating, reading, smoking, or chatting. It is not to be recommended, perhaps, for writing with a European pen, as the motion in our Western style of writing is from the supported wrist; however, it is the best posture for writing with the Japanese *fude*,[1] in which the whole arm is unsupported and the motion is from the elbow. After having become used to Japanese habits for more than a year, I must confess that I find it now somewhat annoying to use a chair.

---

[1] A *fude* is a Japanese writing or calligraphy brush which is periodically dipped in a trough of black, India ink when writing.

When we have all greeted each other, and taken our places on the kneeling cushions, a little polite silence ensues, which I am the first to break. Some of the lads speak a good deal of English. They understand me well when I pronounce every word slowly and distinctly, using simple phrases, and avoiding idioms. When a word with which they are not familiar must be used, we refer to a good English-Japanese dictionary, which gives each common meaning, both in the *kana*[67] and in *kanji* characters.

Usually my young visitors stay a long time and their stay is rarely tiresome. Their conversation and their thoughts are of the simplest and frankest. They do not come to learn: they know that to ask their teacher to teach out of school would be unjust. They speak chiefly of things which they think have some particular interest for me. Sometimes, they scarcely speak at all, but appear to sink into a sort of happy trance. What they come for really is the quiet pleasure of sympathy. Not an intellectual sympathy, but the sympathy of pure goodwill: the simple pleasure of being quite comfortable with a friend. They peep at my books and pictures; and sometimes they bring books and pictures to show me — delightfully strange things — family heirlooms which I much regret that I cannot buy. They also like to look at my garden and enjoy all that is in it: even more than I. Often, they bring me gifts of flowers. Never by any possible chance are they troublesome, impolite, curious, or talkative. Courtesy in its utmost possible exquisiteness: an exquisiteness of which even the French have no concept, seems as natural to the Izumo boy as the color of his hair or the tint of his skin. Nor is he less kind than courteous. To contrive pleasurable surprises for me is one of the particular delights of my boys; and they either bring or cause to be brought to the house, all sorts of strange things.

Of all the strange or beautiful things which I am thus privileged to examine, none gives me so much pleasure as a certain wonderful *kakemono* of Amida Nyorai.[68] It is a rather large picture and has been borrowed from a priest so that I may see it. The Buddha stands in the attitude of exhortation, with one hand uplifted. Behind his head, a huge moon makes a halo, and across the face of that moon streams winding lines of the thinnest clouds. Beneath his feet, like a rolling of smoke, curl heavier and darker clouds. Merely as a work of color and design, the thing is a marvel. But the real wonder of it is not in color or design at all. Minute examination reveals the astonishing fact that every shadow and cloud is formed by a faint text of *kanji* characters, so minute that only a keen eye can discern them. This text is the entire text of two famed *sutras*: the *Kwammu-ryō-ju-kyō* and the *Amida-kyō* — "text no larger than the limbs of fleas." All the strong, dark lines of the figure, such as the seams of the Buddha's robe, are formed by the characters of the holy invocation of the Shin-shū sect, repeated thousands of times: *Namu Amida Butsu!* Infinite patience, tireless silent labor of loving faith, in some dim temple, long ago.

A GROUP OF GRADUATES OF THE MIDDLE SCHOOL
1 Mr. Hearn   2 Mr. Nishida   3 The old teacher of Chinese Classics

Another day, one of my boys persuades his father to let him bring to my house a wonderful statue of Kōshi (Confucius), made, I am told, in China, toward the close of the period of the Ming dynasty. I am also assured it is the first time the statue has ever been removed from the family residence to be shown to anyone. Previously, whoever desired to pay it reverence had to visit the house. It is truly a beautiful bronze. The figure of a smiling, bearded old man, with fingers uplifted and lips apart as if speaking. He wears quaint Chinese shoes, and his flowing robes are adorned with the figure of the mystic phoenix. The microscopic finish of detail seems indeed to reveal the wonderful skill of a Chinese hand: each tooth, each hair, looks as though it had been made the subject of a special study.

Another student conducts me to the home of one of his relatives, so that I may see a cat made of wood, said to have been chiseled by the famed Hidari Jingorō:[69] a cat crouching and watching and so lifelike that real cats "have been known to put up their backs and spit at it."

XVI

Nevertheless, I have a private conviction that some old artists, even now living in Matsué, could make a still more wonderful cat. Among these is the venerable Arakawa Junosuke, who made many rare things for the Daimyō of Izumo in the Tempō era,[i] and whose acquaintance I have made through my school friends. One evening he brings to my house something very odd to show me, concealed in his sleeve. It is a doll; just a small carved, painted head without a body: the body being represented by only a tiny robe, attached to the neck. Yet, as Arakawa Junosuke manipulates it, it seems to become alive. The back of its head is like the back of a very old man's head, but its face is the face of an amused child and there is scarcely any forehead nor any evidence of a thinking disposition. Whatever way the head is turned, it looks so funny that one cannot help laughing at it. It represents a *kirakubo*; what we might call in English "a jolly old boy," one who is naturally too hearty and too innocent to feel trouble of any kind. It is not an original, but a model of a very famous original whose history is recorded in a faded scroll which Arakawa takes out of his other sleeve, and which a friend translates for me. This little history throws a curious light on the simple hearted ways of Japanese life and thought in other centuries:

> *Two hundred and sixty years ago this doll was made by a famous maker of Noh masks in the city of Kyōto for Emperor Gomidzunō-O. The Emperor used to have it placed beside his pillow each night before he slept, and was very fond of it. He composed the following poem concerning it:*
>
> *Yo no naka wo*
> *Kiraku ni kurase*
> *Nani goto mo*

---

[i] The *Tempō* Era extended from 1830 to 1844.

Omoeba omou
Omowaneba koso.[i]

On the death of the Emperor, this doll became the property of Prince Konoye, in whose family it is said to still be preserved.

About one hundred and seven years ago, the then Ex-Empress, whose posthumous name is Sei-Kwa-Mon-Yin, borrowed the doll from Prince Konoye and ordered a copy of it to be made. She always kept this copy beside her and was very fond of it.

After the death of the good Empress, this doll was given to a lady of the court, whose family name is not recorded. Afterwards this lady, for reasons which are not known, cut off her hair and became a Buddhist nun, taking the name of Shingyō-in.

And one who knew the nun Shingyō-in, a man whose name was Kondo-ju-haku-in-Hokyō, had the honor of receiving the doll as a gift.

Now I, who write this document, at one time fell sick; and my sickness was caused by despondency. And my friend Kondo-ju-haku-in-Hokyō, coming to see me, said, "I have in my house something which will make you well." And he went home and, presently returning, brought to me this doll, and lent it to me: putting it by my pillow that I might see it and laugh at it.

Afterward, I myself, having called upon the nun Shingyō-in, whom I now also have the honor to know, wrote down the history of the doll, and made a poem thereupon.

(Dated about ninety years ago: no signature.)

XVII

June 1, 1891

I find among the students, a healthy tone of skepticism in regard to certain forms of popular belief. Scientific education is rapidly destroying innocence in old superstitions still held among the uneducated and especially among the peasants; as for instance, faith in *mamori* and *ofuda*. The outward forms of

---

[i] Author's Footnote: This little poem signifies that whoever in this world thinks much, must have care, and that not to think about things is to pass one's life in untroubled bliss.

Buddhism and its images, relics, and its more common practices, little affect the average student. He is not, like a foreigner may be, interested in iconography, or religious folklore, or the comparative study of religions. In nine cases out of ten, he is rather ashamed of the signs and tokens of popular faith all around him. But the deeper religious sense, which underlies all symbolism, remains with him and the monistic idea in Buddhism[1] is being strengthened and expanded, rather than weakened by the new education. What is true of the effect of the public schools on the lower Buddhism is equally true of its effect on the lower Shintō. The students are all sincerely Shintō, or very nearly all; yet, not as fervent worshipers of certain *kami*, but as rigid observers of what the higher Shintō signifies: loyalty, filial piety, and obedience to parents, teachers and superiors, and respect to ancestors. For Shintō means more than faith.

When I stood for the first time in front of the shrine of the Great Deity of Kitzuki, as the first Westerner to whom that great privilege had been given,[ii] not without a sense of awe, there came to me the thought, "This is the shrine of the father of a race; this is the symbolic center of a nation's reverence for its past." I too, paid reverence to the memory of the founder of this people.

As I then felt, so the intelligent student feels about the Meiji era, which education has lifted above the common plane of popular beliefs. Shintō also means for him, whether he thinks on the question or not, all the ethics of the family and all that spirit of loyalty which has become so innate that, at the call of duty, life itself ceases to have value except as an instrument for duty's accomplishment. As yet, this Japan little needs to reason about the origin of its loftier ethics. Imagine the musical sense in our own race, so developed that a child could play a complicated instrument, as soon as the little fingers gained sufficient force and flexibility to strike the notes. By some such comparison only can one obtain a just idea of what inherent religion and instructtive duty signify in Izumo.

I find no trace among my students of the rude and aggressive form of skepticism so common in the West, which is

---

[i] The doctrine that there is only one ultimate substance or principle, whether mind (idealism), matter (materialism), or some third thing that is the basis of both.
[ii] Refer to Chapter VIII of *The Annotated Glimpses of Unfamiliar Japan, Volume I.*

the natural reaction after sudden emancipation from superstitious belief. But such sentiment may be found elsewhere, especially in Tōkyō among the university students; one of whom, upon hearing the tones of a magnificent temple bell exclaimed to a friend of mine, "Is it not a shame that in this nineteenth century, we must still hear such a sound?"

For the benefit of curious travelers, however, I may here take occasion to observe that to talk Buddhism to Japanese gentlemen of the new school is in just as bad taste as to talk Christianity at home to men of that class, whom knowledge has placed above creeds and forms. There are, of course, Japanese scholars willing to aid researches by foreign scholars in religion or in folklore; but these specialists do not attempt to gratify idle curiosity of the "globetrotting" kind. I may also say that the foreigner who desires to learn the religious ideas or superstitions of the common people, must obtain them from the people themselves, not from the educated classes.

XVIII

Among all my favorite students, two or three from each class, I cannot decide whom I like the best. Each student has a particular merit of his own, but I think the names and faces of those of whom I am about to speak, will remain in my memories the longest: Ishihara, Otani Masanobu,[70] Adzukizawa, Yokogi, Shida.

Ishihara is a samurai, a very influential lad in his class because of his uncommon force of character. Compared with others, he has a somewhat brusque, independent manner, pleasing however, by its honest manliness. He says everything he thinks, and precisely in the tone that he thinks it; even to the degree of being a little embarrassing sometimes. He does not hesitate, for example, to find fault with a teacher's method of explanation, and to insist on a more lucid one. He has criticized me more than once; but I never found that he was wrong. We like each other very much. He often brings me flowers.

One day that he had brought two beautiful sprays of plum blossoms, he said to me, "I saw you bow before our Emperor's picture at the ceremony on the birthday of His Majesty. You are not like a former English teacher we had."

"How?"

"He said we were savages."

"Why?"

"He said there is nothing respectable except God, his God, and that only vulgar and ignorant people respect anything else."

"Where did he come from?"

"He was a Christian clergyman, and said he was an English subject."

"But if he was an English subject, he was bond to respect Her Majesty the Queen. He could not even enter the office of a British consul without removing his hat."

"I don't know what he did in the country he came from. But that was what he said. Now we think we should love and honor our Emperor. We think it is a duty. We think it is a joy. We think it is happiness to be able to give our lives for our Emperor.[1] But he said we were only savages: ignorant savages. What do you think of that?"

"I think, my dear lad, that he himself was a savage: a vulgar, ignorant, savage bigot. I think it is your highest social duty to honor your Emperor, to obey his laws, and to be ready to give your blood whenever he may require it of you for the sake of Japan. I think it is your duty to respect the gods of your fathers, the religion of your country; even if you yourself cannot believe all that others believe. I think also, that it is your duty, for your Emperor's sake and for your country's sake, to resent any such wicked and vulgar language as that you have told me of, no matter by whom it is spoken."

Masanobu seldom visits me and always comes alone. A slender, handsome lad, with rather feminine features, reserved, perfectly self-possessed in manner, and refined. He is somewhat serious, does not smile often; and I have never heard him laugh. He has risen to the head of his class, and appears to remain there

---

[1] Author's Footnote: Having asked in various classes for written answers to the question, "What is your dearest wish?" I found about twenty percent of the replies expressed, with little variation of words, the simple desire to die "for His Sacred Majesty, Our Beloved Emperor." But a considerable proportion of the remainder contained the same aspiration, less directly stated in the wish to emulate the glory of [Lord] Nelson, or to make Japan first among nations by heroism and sacrifice. While this splendid spirit lives in the hearts of her youth, Japan should have little to fear for the future.

without any extraordinary effort. He devotes much of his leisure time to botany: collecting and classifying plants. He is a musician, like all the male members of his family. He plays a variety of instruments never seen or heard of in the West, including flutes of marble, flutes of ivory, flutes of bamboo in wonderful shapes and tones, and that shrill Chinese instrument called *shō*:[71] a sort of mouth organ consisting of seventeen tubes of different lengths fixed in a silver frame. He first explained to me the use in temple music of the *taiko*[72] and *shōko*[73] which are drums; of the flutes called *fei* or *teki* or the flageolet called *hichiriki*;[74] and of the *kakko*, which is a little drum shaped like a spool with a very narrow waist. On great Buddhist festivals, Masanobu, his father and brothers are the musicians in the temple services, and they play the strange music called *ojō* and *batto*; music which at first no Western ear can feel pleasure in, but which, when often heard, becomes understandable, and is found to possess a weird charm of its own. When Masanobu comes to the house, it is usually in order to invite me to attend some Buddhist or Shintō festival (*matsuri*), which he knows will interest me.

Adzukizawa bears so little resemblance to Masanobu that one might think the two belonged to very different races. Adzukizawa is large, raw-boned, heavy looking, with a face distinctly like that of a North American Indian. His people are not rich; he can afford few pleasures which cost money, except one: buying books. Even to be able to do this he works in his leisure hours to earn money. He is a perfect bookworm, a natural-born researcher, a collector of curious documents, a haunter of all the queer second-hand stores in Teramachi and other streets were old manuscripts or prints are on sale as waste paper. He is an omnivorous reader, and a perpetual borrower of volumes; which he always returns in perfect condition after having copied what he deemed of the most value to him. But his special delight is philosophy and the history of philosophers in all countries. He has read various volumes of the history of philosophy in Asia and everything of modern philosophy which has been translated into Japanese: including Spencer's *First Principles*.[75] I have been able to introduce him to Lewes[76] and John Fiske,[77] both of which he appreciates, although the strain of studying philosophy in English is no small one.

Happily he is so strong that no amount of study is likely to injure his health, and his nerves are as tough as wires. He is also quite frugal. As it is the Japanese custom to set cakes and tea before visitors, I always have both in readiness and an especially fine quality of *kwashi*,[1] made at Kitzuki, of which the students are very fond. Only Adzukizawa refuses to taste cakes or confections of any kind saying, "As I am the youngest brother, I must begin to earn my own living soon. I shall have to endure much hardship. And if I allow myself to like sweets now, I shall only suffer more later on." Adzukizawa has seen much of human life and character. He is naturally observant and he has managed, in some extraordinary way, to learn the history of everybody in Matsué. He has brought me old tattered prints to prove that the opinions now held by our director are diametrically opposed to the opinions he advocated fourteen years ago in a public address. I ask the director about it. He laughed and said, "Of course that is Adzukizawa! But he is right. I was very young then." Moreover, I wonder if Adzukizawa was ever young.

Yokogi, Adzukizawa's dearest friend, is a very rare visitor; for he is always studying at home. He is always first in his class,

---

[1] *Kwashi* is a Japanese confection.

the third year class, while Adzukizawa is fourth. Adzukizawa's account of the beginning of their acquaintance is this: "I watched him when he came and saw that he spoke very little, walked very quickly, and looked straight into everybody's eyes. So I knew he had a particular character. I like to know people with a particular character." Adzukizawa was perfectly right: under a very gentle exterior, Yokogi has an extremely strong character. He is the son of a carpenter, and his parents could not afford to send him to the Middle School. But, he had shown such exceptional qualities while in the Elementary School that a wealthy man became interested in him and offered to pay for his education.[1] He is now the pride of the school.

He has a remarkably placid face, with peculiarly long eyes and a beautiful smile. In class, he is always asking intelligent questions: questions so original that I am sometimes puzzled as to how to answer them. He never ceases to ask until the explanation is quite satisfactory to him. He never cares about the opinion of his comrades if he thinks he is right. On one occasion, when the whole class refused to attend the lectures of a new teacher of physics, Yokogi alone refused to act with them, arguing that although the teacher was not all that could be desired, there was no immediate possibility of his removal, and no just reason for making a man unhappy who, though unskilled, was sincerely doing his best. Adzukizawa finally stood by him. These two alone attended the lectures until the remainder of the students, two weeks later, found that Yokogi's views were rational. On another occasion, when a Christian missionary attempted some vulgar proselytism, Yokogi went boldly to the proselytizer's house, argued with him on the morality of his effort, and reduced him to silence. Some of his comrades praised his cleverness in the argument.

"I am not clever," he answered, "it does not require cleverness to argue against what is morally wrong; it requires only the knowledge that one is morally right." At least that is about the translation of what he said as told to me by Adzukizawa.

Shida, another visitor, is a very delicate, sensitive boy, whose soul is full of art. He is very skillful at drawing and painting, and he has a wonderful set of picture books by the old Japanese masters. The last time he came, he brought some prints to show

---

[1] Author's Footnote: Beautiful generosities of this kind are not uncommon in Japan.

me, rare ones: fairy maidens and ghosts. As I looked at his beautiful, pale face and weirdly frail fingers, I could not help fearing for him: fearing that he might soon become a little ghost.

I have not seen him now for more than two months. He has become very, very ill; and his lungs are so weak that the doctor has forbidden him to converse. But Adzukizawa has been to visit him and brings me this translation of a Japanese letter which the sick boy wrote and pasted on the wall above his bed:

> *Thou, my Lord-Soul, dost govern me. Thou knowest that I cannot now govern myself. Deign, I pray thee, to let me be cured speedily. Do not suffer me to speak much. Make me to obey in all things the command of the physician.*
> *This ninth day of the eleventh month of the twenty-fourth year of Meiji.*
> *From the sick body of Shida to his Soul.*

XIX

September 4, 1891

The long summer vacation is over; a new school year begins.

There have been many changes. Some of the boys I taught are dead. Others have graduated and gone away from Matsué forever. Some teachers have also left the school, their places have been filled, and there is a new director.

The dear, good Governor has gone: transferred to cold Niigata[1] in the northwest. It was a promotion, but he had ruled Izumo for seven years and everybody loved him; especially perhaps, the students, who looked on him as a father. The entire city's population crowded to the river to bid him farewell. The streets through which he passed on his way to take the steamer, the bridge, the wharves, even the rooftops, were thronged with a multitude eager to see his face for the last time. Thousands were weeping, and as the steamer glided from the wharf, such a cry arose — "A-a-a-a-a-a-a-a-a-a!" It was intended for a cheer, but it seemed to me the cry of a whole city in sorrow: so plaintive that I hope never to hear such a cry again.

---

[1] Niigata City (Niigata-shi (新潟市), the capital of Niigata Prefecture is located farther north from Matsué, along the western coast of Honshū.

The names and the faces of the younger classes are all strange to me. Without doubt, this is why the sensation of my first day's teaching in the school came back to me with extraordinary vividness when I entered the classroom of First Division A this morning.

The first sensation of a Japanese class is strangely pleasant, as you look over the range of young faces in front of you. There is nothing in them which is familiar to inexperienced Western eyes; yet, there is an indescribably pleasant something common to them all. Those traits have nothing incisive, nothing distinctive. Compared with Western faces, they seem only "half-sketched," so soft are their outlines — indicating neither aggressiveness nor shyness; neither eccentricity nor sympathy; neither curiosity nor indifference. Some, although faces of youths well grown, have an indescribable childish freshness and frankness; some are as uninteresting as others are attractive; a few are beautifully feminine. But all are equally characterized by a singular serenity — expressing neither love nor hate nor anything except perfect calm and gentleness — like the dreamy serenity of Buddhist images. Later, you will no longer recognize this aspect of passionless composure. With growing familiarity, each face will become more and more individualized for you by characteristics that were imperceptible before. However, the recollection of that first impression will remain with you; and the time will come when you will find, by many varied experiences, how strangely it foreshadowed something in Japanese character to be fully learned only after years of familiarity. You will recognize in the memory of that first impression, one glimpse of the soul of the nation, with its impersonal lovableness and its impersonal weakness — one glimpse of the nature of a life in which the Westerner, living alone, feels a psychic comfort, only comparable to the nervous relief of suddenly emerging from some stifling atmosphere into thin, clear, free-living air.

XX

Was it not the eccentric Fourier[78] who wrote about the horrible faces of "the *civilizés*?"[i] Whoever it was, would have found apparent confirmation of his physiognomic[ii] theory if he had known the effect produced by the first sight of European faces in the most eastern East. What we are taught at home to consider handsome, interesting, or characteristic in physiognomy, does not produce the same impressions in China or Japan. Variations of facial expressions that are as familiar to us as the letters of our own alphabet are not perceived at all in Western features by Asians at first meeting. What they immediately discern are the racial characteristics, not the individuality. The evolutionary meaning of the deep-set Western eye, protruding brow, large nose, ponderous jaw — symbols of aggressive force and habit — was revealed to the gentler race by the same sort of intuition through which a tame animal immediately comprehends the dangerous nature of the first predatory enemy which it sees. To Europeans, the smooth-featured, slender, low-statured Japanese seemed like boys; and "boy" is the term by which the native attendant of a Yokohama merchant is still called. To Japanese, the first red-haired, rowdy, drunken European sailors seemed fiends, *shōjō*, demons of the sea; and foreigners are still called "foreign devils" by the Chinese. The tall stature, massive strength, and fierce gait of foreigners in Japan enhanced the strange impression created by their faces. Children cried in fear on seeing them pass through the streets. In more remote districts, Japanese children are still apt to cry at the first sight of a European or American face.

---

[i] Literally, from the French, "civilized."

[ii] Also called **anthroposcopy**. The art of determining character or personal characteristics from the form or features of the body, especially of the face.

"Americans," by Yoshiiku Utagawa (1833 – 1904).

A lady of Matsué related in my presence this curious memory of her childhood:

"When I was a very little girl," she said, "our *daimyō* hired a foreigner to teach the military arts. My father and a great many samurai went to receive the foreigner, and all the people lined the streets to see; for, no foreigner had ever come to Izumo before. We all went to look. The foreigner came by ship: there were no steamboats then. He was very tall and walked quickly with long steps and the children began to cry at the sight of him because his face was not like that faces of the people of Nippon. My little brother cried out loud, and hid his face in Mother's robe; and Mother reproved him and said, "This foreigner is a very good man who has come here to serve our prince, and it is very disrespectful to cry at seeing him." But he still cried.

"I was not afraid and I looked up at the foreigner's face as he came and smiled. He had a great beard, and I thought his face was good, though it seemed to me a very strange face and stern. Then he stopped and smiled too, and put something in my hand, and touched my head and face very softly with his great fingers, and said something I could not understand, and went away. After he had gone, I looked at what he put into my hand and found that it was a pretty little glass to look through. If you put a fly under that glass, it looks quite big. At that time, I thought the glass was a very wonderful thing. I still have it."

She took a tiny, dainty pocket microscope from a drawer in the room and placed it before me.

The hero of this little incident was a French military officer. His services were necessarily curtailed with the abolition of the feudal system. Memories of him still linger in Matsué, and old people remember a popular bit about him; a sort of rapidly screeched nonsense, supposed to be an imitation of his foreign speech.

Tōjin no negoto niwa kinkarakuri medagashō,
Saiboji ga shimpeishite harishite keisan,
Hanryō na Sacr-r-r-r-é-na-nom-da-Jiu.

XXI

November 2, 1891

Shida will never come to school again. He sleeps under the shadow of the cedars, in the old cemetery of Tōkōji. Yokogi, at the memorial service, read a beautiful address (*saibun*) to the soul of his dead comrade.

But Yokogi himself is now down, and I am very much afraid for him. He is suffering from some condition of the brain, brought on, the doctor says, by studying a great deal too hard. Even if he gets well, he will always have to be careful. Some of us hope much; for, the boy is strongly built and so young. Strong Sakane burst a blood vessel last month and is now well. So, we trust that Yokogi will rally. Adzukizawa brings news of his friend daily.

However, the rally never comes. Some mysterious spring in the mechanism of the young life has been broken. The mind lives only in brief intervals between long hours of unconsciousness. Parents and friends watch for these living moments to whisper caressing things, or to ask, "Is there anything that you wish?"

And one night the answer comes: "Yes, I want to go to the school. I want to see the school."

Then they wonder if the fine brain has not wholly given way, while they answer, "It is past midnight and there is no moon. And the night is cold."

"No, I can see by the stars. I want to see the school again."

They make the kindliest protests in vain, but the dying boy only repeats, with the plaintive persistence of a last wish: "I want to see the school again. I want to see it now."

So there is a murmured consultation in the neighboring room and *tansu* drawers are unlocked, warm garments prepared. Then Fusaichi, the strong servant, enters with lantern lit, and cries out in his kind rough voice, "Master Tomi will go to the school on my back: 'tis but a little way. He shall see the school again."

Carefully they wrap up the lad in wadded robes; then he puts his arms around Fusaichi's shoulders like a child; and the strong servant bears him lightly through the wintery street. The father hurries beside Fusaichi bearing the lantern. It is not far to the school: just over the little bridge.

The huge dark gray building looks almost black in the night; but Yokogi can see. He looks at the windows of his own classroom; at the roofed side-door where each morning, for four happy years, he used to exchange his *getas* for soundless sandals of straw; at the lodge of the slumbering Kodzukai;[i] at the silhouette of the bell hanging black in its little turret against the stars.

Then he murmurs: —

"I can remember all now. I had forgotten — so sick I was. I remember everything again. Oh, Fusaichi, you are very good. I am so glad to have seen the school again."

And they hasten back through the long, empty streets.

XXII

November 26, 1891

Yokogi will be buried tomorrow evening beside his comrade Shida.

When a poor person is about to die, friends and neighbors come to the house and do all they can to help the family. Some bear the tidings to distant relatives; others prepare all necessary things; others, when the death has been announced, summon the Buddhist priests.[ii]

It is said that the priests always know of a parishioner's death at night, before any messenger is sent to them; for the soul of the dead knocks heavily, once, on the door of the family temple. Then the priests arise and robe themselves, and when the messenger comes, answer, "We know: we are ready."

Meanwhile, the body is carried out in front of the family *butsudan* and laid on the floor. No pillow is placed under the head. A naked sword is laid across the limbs to keep evil spirits

---

[i] Author's Footnote: The college porter.

[ii] Author's Footnote: Except in those comparatively rare instances where the family is exclusively Shintō in its faith, or, although belonging to both faiths, prefers to bury its dead according to Shintō rites. In Matsué, as a rule, high officials only have Shintō funerals.

away. The doors of the *butsudan* are opened, candles are lit in front of the tablets of the ancestors, and incense is burned. All friends send gifts of incense; although a gift of incense, however rare and precious, given on any other occasion, is held to be unlucky.

The Shintō household shrine must be hidden from view with white paper and the Shintō *ofuda* fastened on the house door must be covered up during the entire period of mourning.[1] In all that time, no member of the family may approach a Shintō shrine or pray to the *kami*, or even pass beneath a *torii*.

A screen (*biōbu*) is extended between the body and the main entrance to the death room and the *kaimyō*, inscribed on a strip of white paper, is fastened on the screen. If the dead is young, the screen must be turned upside-down; however, this is not done in the case of old people.

Friends pray beside the corpse. There, a little box is placed, containing one thousand peas to be used for counting during the recital of those one thousand pious invocations, which it is believed, will improve the condition of the soul on its unfamiliar journey.

The priests come and recite the *sutras* and then the body is prepared for burial. It is washed in warm water and robed all in white; but the kimono of the dead is lapped over to the left side, although it is considered unlucky at any other time to fasten one's kimono in that fashion, even by accident.

When the body has been put into that strange square coffin which looks something like a wooden palanquin, each relative also puts some of his or her hair or nail parings into the coffin, symbolizing their blood. And six *rin* are also placed in the coffin,

---

[1] Author's Footnote: Unless the dead is buried according to the Shintō rite. In Matsué, the mourning period is usually fifty days. On the fifty-first day, after the death, all members of the family go to Enjōji-nada (the lakeshore at the foot of the hill on which the great temple of Enjōji stands) to perform the ceremony of purification. At Enjōji-nada, on the beach, stands a tall stone statute of Jizō. The mourners pray in front of it, and then wash their mouths and hands with the water of the lake. Afterwards, they go to a friend's house for breakfast, the purification always being performed at daybreak, if possible. During the mourning period, no member of the family can eat at a friend's house; but if the burial has been according to the Shintō rite, all these ceremonial observances may be dispensed with.

for the six Jizō who stand at the heads of the ways of the Six Shadowy Worlds.

The funeral procession forms at the family residence. A priest leads it, ringing a little bell; a boy bears the *ihai* of the newly dead. The front of the procession is totally composed of men: relatives and friends. Some carry *hata*, small white symbolic banners; some bear flowers, and all carry paper lanterns; for in Izumo, the adult dead are buried after dark: only children are buried by day. Next comes the *kwan* or coffin, borne palanquin-style on the shoulders of men of that parish caste whose position it is to dig graves and assist at funerals. Last, come the women mourners.

They are all white-hooded and white-robed from head to foot, like phantoms.[1] Nothing more ghostly than this sheeted train of an Izumo funeral procession, illuminated only by the glow of paper lanterns, can be imagined. It is a weirdness that, once seen, will often return in dreams.

At the temple, the *kwan* is laid on the pavement in front of the entrance and another service is performed, with plaintive music and the recitation of *sutras*. Then, the procession forms again, winds once around the temple courtyard, and then makes its way to the cemetery; however, the body is not buried until twenty-four hours later, in case the supposed dead should awake in the grave.

Corpses are seldom burned in Izumo. In this, as in other matters, the predominance of Shintō sentiment is manifest.

XXIII

For the last time, I see his face again, as he lies on his deathbed; white-robed from neck to feet; white-girdled for his shadowy journey; but smiling with closed eyes in almost the same, strange, gentle way he would smile in class on learning the explanation of some seeming riddle in our difficult English tongue. Only, I think, the smile is sweeter now, as with the sudden larger knowledge of more mysterious things. So smiles,

---

[1] Author's Footnote: But at samurai funerals in the olden time, the women were robed in black.

through a dusk of incense in the great temple of Tōkōji,[79] the golden face of Buddha.

XXIV

December 23, 1891

The great bell of Tōkōji is booming for the memorial service, for the *tsuito-kwai* of Yokogi — as slowly and regularly as a minute-gun.[1] Gong after gong of its rich bronze thunder vibrates over the lake, surges over the roofs of the town, and breaks in deep sobs of sound against the green circle of the hills.

It is a touching service, this *tsuito-kwai*, with quaint ceremonies which, although long since adopted into Japanese Buddhism, are Chinese in origin: and are beautiful. It is also a costly ceremony and the parents of Yokogi are very poor; however, all the expenses have been paid by voluntary donation of students and teachers. Priests from every great temple of the Zen sect in Izumo have assembled at Tōkōji. All the teachers of the city and all the students have entered the *hondo*[ii] of the huge temple and taken their places to the right and to the left of the grand altar; kneeling on the matted floor and leaving, on the long broad steps outside, a thousand shoes and sandals.

A new *butsudan* has been placed in front of the main entrance and facing the high altar; within whose open doors the *ihai* of the dead boy glimmers in lacquer and gilding. An incense vessel with bundles of *senko* [incense] sticks and offerings of fruit, confections, rice, and flowers have been placed on a small stand in front of the *butsudan*. Tall, beautiful flower vases on each side of the *butsudan* are filled with blossoming sprays, exquisitely arranged. In front of the *honzon*,[iii] candles burn in massive candelabra, whose stems of polished brass are writhing monsters: the Dragon Ascending and the Dragon Descending. Incense curls up from vessels shaped like the sacred deer, like

---

[i] A gun fired at one-minute intervals as a sign of distress or mourning
[ii] In Buddhism, a *hondo* is a formal hall for rituals and ceremonies.
[iii] *Honzon* or *gohonzon* (ご本尊 or 御本尊) is the object of devotion in many forms of Japanese Buddhism. In Japanese, *go* is often added to the word as an honorific prefix indicating respect. *Honzon* means object of fundamental respect, veneration, or devotion; generally, *honzon* can refer to any such object of devotion, whether a statue or set of statues, a painted scroll of some sort, or some other object.

the symbolic tortoise, like the meditative stork of Buddhist legend. Beyond these, in the twilight of the vast alcove, the Buddha smiles the smile of Perfect Rest.

A little table has been placed between the *butsudan* and the *honzon*, and on either side of it, the priests kneel in ranks, facing each other: rows of polished heads and splendors of vermilion silks and gold-embroidered vestments.

The great bell ceases to gong; the *segaki* prayer (the prayer uttered when offerings of food are made to the spirits of the dead) is recited; and a sudden resonant, measured tapping accompanied by a plaintive chant, begins the musical service. The tapping is the tapping of the *mokugyo*, a large wooden fish head like the head of a dolphin but grotesquely idealized, lacquered and gilded — marking the time; and the chant is the chant of the Chapter of Kwannon in the *Hokkekyō* [the *Lotus Sutra*], with its magnificent invocation:

> *O Thou whose eyes are clear, whose eyes are kind, whose eyes are full of pity and of sweetness — O thou Lovely one, with thy beautiful face, with thy beautiful eyes —*
>
> *O Thou Pure One, whose luminosity is without spot, whose knowledge is without shadow — O Thou forever shining like the sun whose glory no power may repel — Thou sun-like in the course of Thy mercy, pourest light upon the world!*

While the voices of the leaders chant clear and high, in vibrant unison, the multitude of the priestly choir recite in the profoundest undertone, the mighty verses; and the sound of their recitation is like the muttering of the surf.

The *mokugyo* ceases its dull echoing, the impressive chant ends, and the leading officiants, one by one, high priests of famed temples, approach the *ihai*. Each bows low, ignites an incense stick, and sets it upright in the little vase of bronze. Each recites a holy verse of which the initial sound is the sound of a letter in the *kaimyō* of the dead boy. These verses, spoken in the order of the characters on the *ihai*, form the sacred acronym, whose name is The Words of Perfume.

Then, the priests retire to their places, and after a little silence, begin the reading of the *saibun*: the reading of the addresses to the soul of the dead. The students speak first: one from each class, chosen by election. The elected rises, approaches the little table in front of the high altar, bows to the *honzon*, draws from his bosom a paper, and reads it in those melodious, chanting, and plaintive tones which belong to the reading of Chinese texts. So, each one tells the affection of the living to the dead, in words of loving grief and loving hope. And last, among the students, a gentle girl rises, a pupil of the Normal School, to speak in tones as soft as a bird's. As each *saibun* is finished, the reader lays the written paper on the table before the *honzon*, bows, and retires.

It is now the turn of the teachers; and an old man takes his place at the little table, old Katayama, the teacher of Chinese, famed as a poet, adored as an instructor. Because the students all love him as a father, there is a strange intensity to the silence as he begins:

Kō-Shimane-ken-Jinjō-Chūgakkō-yo nensei...

Here upon the twenty-third day of the twelfth month of the twenty-fourth year of Meiji, I, Katayama Shōkei, teacher of the Jinjō Chūgakkō of Shimane-ken, attending in great sorrow the holy service of the dead (tsui-fuku), do speak unto the soul of Yokogi Tomisaburo, my pupil.

Having been, as thou knowest, for twice five years, at different periods, a teacher of the school, I have indeed met with not a few most excellent students. But very, very rarely in any school may the teacher find one such as thou — so patient and so earnest, so diligent and so careful in all things — so distinguished among thy comrades by thy blameless conduct, observing every precept, never breaking a rule.

Of old, in the land of Kihoku, famed for its horses, whenever a horse of rarest breed could not be obtained, men were want to say: "There is no horse." Still there are fine lads among our students — many ryume, fine young steeds; but we have lost the best.

To die at the age of seventeen — the best period of life for study — even when of the Ten Steps thou hadst already ascended six! Sad is the thought; but sadder still to know that thy last illness was caused only by thine own tireless zeal of study. Even yet more sad our conviction that with those rare gifts, and with that rare character of thine, thou wouldst surely, in that career to which thou wast destined, have achieved good and great things, honoring the names of thine ancestors, couldst thou have lived to manhood.

I see thee lifting thy hand to ask some question; then, bending above thy little desk to make note of all thy poor old teacher was able to tell thee. Again I see thee in the ranks — thy rifle upon thy shoulder — so bravely erect during the military exercises. Even now, thy face is before me, with its smile, as plainly as if thou wert present in the body — thy voice I think I hear distinctly as though thou hadst but this instant finished speaking — yet I know that, except in memory, these never will be seen and heard again. O Heaven, why didst thou take away that dawning life from the world, and leave such a one as I — old Shōkei, feeble, decrepit, and of no more use?

To thee my relation was indeed only that of teacher to pupil. Yet, what is my distress! I have a son of twenty-four years; he is now far from me, in Yokohama. I know he is only a worthless youth,[1] *yet never for so much as the space of one hour does the*

---

[1] Author's Footnote: Said only in courteous self-depreciation. In the same way a son, writing to his parent, would never, according to Japanese ideas of true

thought of him leave his old father's heart. Then how must the father and mother, the brothers and sisters of this gentle and gifted youth feel now that he is gone! Only to think of it forces the tears from my eyes: I cannot speak, so full my heart is.

Aa! Aa! — Thou hast gone from us; thou hast gone from us! Yet, though thou hast died, thy earnestness, thy goodness, will long be honored and told of as examples to students of our school.

Here, therefore, do we, thy teachers and thy schoolmates, hold this service in behalf of thy spirit — with prayer and offerings. Deign thou, O gentle Soul, to honor our love by the acceptance of our humble gifts.

Then a sound of sobbing is suddenly overwhelmed by the resonant booming of the great fish's head, as the high-pitched voices of the leaders of the chant begin the grand *Nehan-gyō*, the *Sutra of Nirvana*, the song of passage triumphant over the Sea of Death and Birth; and deep below those high tones and the hollow echoing of the *mokugyo*, the surging bass of a century of voices reciting the resonant words, sounds like the breaking of a sea.

Shō-gyō mu-jō, je-sho meppō...

Transient are all.
They, being born, must die.
And being born, are dead.
And being dead, are glad to be at rest.

---

courtesy and duty, sign himself, "Your affectionate son," but "Your ungrateful, or unloving son."

XX

TWO STRANGE FESTIVALS

I

THE OUTWARD SIGNS of any Japanese *matsuri* are the most puzzling of enigmas to the stranger who sees them for the first time. They are many and varied, quite unlike anything in the way of holiday decoration ever seen in the West. They each have a meaning founded on some belief or some tradition; a meaning known to every Japanese but utterly impossible for any foreigner to guess. Yet, whoever wishes to know something of Japanese popular life and feeling must learn the significance of at least the most common festival symbols and emblems. Such knowledge is especially necessary to the student of Japanese art. Without it, not only the delicate humor and charm of countless designs will escape him, but in many instances, the designs themselves will remain incomprehensible to him.

For hundreds of years the Japanese have utilized the emblems of festivity in graceful decorative ways. They figure in metal work, on porcelain, on the red or black lacquer of the most humble household utensils, on little brass pipes, and on the clasps of tobacco pouches. It may even be said that the majority of common decorative design is symbolic. The very figures of

153

which the meaning seems most obvious, those matchless studies[1] of animal or vegetable life with which the Western curio buyer is most familiar, have usually some ethical significance which is not perceived at all. Or take the commonest design dashed with a brush on the *fusuma* (sliding door) of a cheap hotel: a lobster, sprigs of pine, tortoises waddling in a swirl of water, a pair of storks, a spray of bamboo. It is rare that a foreign tourist thinks of asking why such designs are used instead of others, even when he has seen them repeated with slight variations, at twenty different places along his route. They have become conventional simply because they are emblems of which the meaning is known to all Japanese, however ignorant, but is never even remotely suspected by the stranger.

II

The first is the Festival of the New Year, which lasts for three days. In Matsué, its celebration is particularly interesting, as the old city still preserves many *matsuri* customs, which have either become, or are rapidly becoming, obsolete elsewhere. The streets are at that time profusely decorated and all the shops are closed. *Shimenawa* or *shimekazari*, the straw ropes which have been sacred symbols of Shintō from the Mythical Age, are hung along the facades of the buildings, and so connected that you see to right or left, what seems to be a single, mile-long *shimenawa*, with its straw pendants and white, fluttering paper *gohei*,

---

[1] Author's Footnote: As it has become, among a certain sect of Western Philistines and self-constituted art critics, the fashion to sneer at any writer who becomes enthusiastic about the truth to nature of Japanese art, I may cite here the words of England's most celebrated living naturalist on this very subject. Mr. Wallace's authority will scarcely, I presume, be questioned, even by the Philistines referred to:

"Dr. Mohnike possesses a large collection of colored sketches of the plants of Japan made by a Japanese lady, which are the most masterly things I have ever seen. Every stem, twig, and leaf is produced by single touches of the brush, the character and perspective of very complicated plants being admirably given, and the articulations of stem and leaves shown in a most scientific manner." (*Malay Archipelago*, Chapter XX.)

Now this was written in 1857, before European methods of drawing had been introduced. The same art of painting leaves, etc., with single strokes of the brush is still common in Japan, even among the poorest class of decorators.

extending along either side of the street, as far as the eye can see. Japanese flags, bearing the great crimson disk which is the emblem of the Land of the Rising Sun, on a white background, flutter above the gateways; and the same national emblem glows on countless paper lanterns, strung in rows along the eaves or across the streets and temple avenues. In front of every gate or doorway, a *kadomatsu* ("gate pine tree") has been erected; so that all the streets are lined with green and full of bright color.

The *kadomatsu* is more than its name implies. It is a young pine, or part of a pine, combined with plum branches and bamboo cuttings.[1] Pine, plum, and bamboo are growths of symbolic significance. Historically, the pine was only used, but from the era of Ō-ei,[80] the bamboo was added; and within more recent times the plum tree.

---

[1] Author's Footnote: There is a Buddhist saying about the *kadomatsu*:

Kadomatsu
Meido no tabi ne
Ichi-ri-zuka.

The meaning is that each *kadomatsu* is a milestone on the journey to the Meido; or in other words, that each New Year's festival signals only the completion of another state on the ceaseless journey to death.

The pine has many meanings, but the auspicious one most generally accepted is that of endurance and successful energy in time of misfortune. As the pine tree keeps its green needles when others lose their foliage, so the true man keeps his courage and his strength in adversity. The pine, as I have said, is also elsewhere, a symbol of vigorous old age.

No European could possibly guess the riddle of the bamboo. It represents a sort of pun in symbolism. There are two *kanji* both pronounced "*setsu*": one signifying the node or joint of the bamboo, and the other virtue, fidelity, constancy. Therefore, the bamboo is used as a lucky sign. The name "Setsu," be it known, is often given to Japanese maidens; just as the names "Faith," "Fidelia," and "Constance" are given to English girls.

The plum tree, however, whose symbolic meaning I said something in relation to in a former paper about Japanese gardens,[1] is not always used. Sometimes *sakaki*, the sacred plant of Shintō, is substituted for it and sometimes only pine and bamboo form the *kadomatsu*.

---

[1] See Chapter XVI, "In A Japanese Garden," in this volume.

156

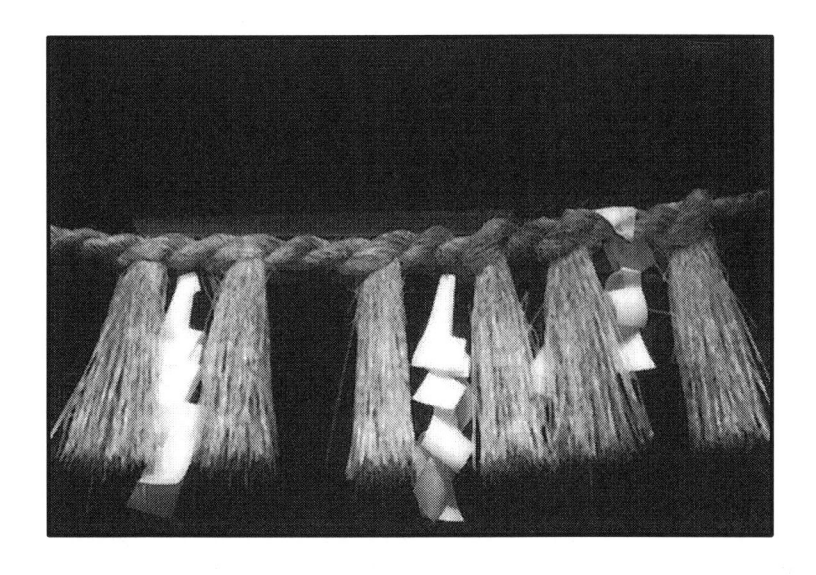

Every decoration used in the New Year's festival has a curious and unfamiliar meaning; and the most common of all, the straw rope, possesses the most complicated symbolism. In the first place, it is scarcely necessary to explain that its origin belongs to that most ancient legend of the Sun Goddess being tempted to come out of a cavern into which she had hidden, and being prevented from leaving by a deity who stretched a rope of straw across the entrance: all of which is written in the *Kojiki*. Next note that, although the *shimenawa* may be of any thickness, it must be twisted so that the direction of the twist is to the left; for, in ancient Japanese philosophy, the left is the pure or fortunate side; owing perhaps to the old belief, common among the uneducated of Europe to this day, that the heart lies to the left. Thirdly, note that the pendant straws, which hang down from the rope at regular intervals in tufts, like fringe, must be of different numbers according to the placement of the tufts; beginning with the number three so that the first tuft has three straws, the second five, the third seven, and the fourth again three, the fifth five, and the sixth seven, and so on for the length of the rope. The origin of the pendent paper cuttings (*gohei*), which alternate with the straw tufts, is likewise to be found in the legend of the Sun Goddess, but the *gohei* also represent offerings of cloth, historically made to the gods according to a long obsolete custom.

Besides the *gohei*, there are many other things attached to the *shimenawa*, the significance of which you could not imagine.

Among these are fern leaves, bitter oranges, *yuzuri* leaves, and little bundles of charcoal.

Why fern leaves (*moromoki* or *urajiro*)? Because the fern leaf is the symbol of the hope of exuberant posterity; even as it branches and re-branches, so may the happy family increase and multiply through the generations.

Why bitter oranges (*daidai*)? Because there is a Chinese word, *daidai*, signifying "from generation to generation." Therefore, the fruit called *daidai* has become a fruit of good fortune.

But why charcoal (*sumi*)? It signifies "prosperous changelessness." Here the idea is particularly curious. Even as the color of charcoal cannot be changed, so may the fortunes of those we love remain forever unchanged in all that gives happiness! The significance of the *yuzuri* leaf I explained in a previous paper.[i]

In addition to the great *shimenawa* in front of the house, *shimenawa* or *shimekazari*[ii] are suspended above the *toko*, or alcoves, in each room; and over the back gate, or over the entrance to the veranda of the second story (if there is a second story), a *wajime* is hung, which is a very small *shimekazari* twisted into a sort of wreath and decorated with fern leaves, *gohei*, and *yuzuri* leaves.

But the great domestic display of the festival is the decoration of the *kamidana*, the Shelf of the Gods. Great, double rice cakes are placed in front of the household *miya*, and the shrine is beautified with flowers, a tiny *shimekazari*, and sprays of *sakaki*. There are also placed, a string of cash, *kabu* (turnips), *daikon* (radishes), a *tai* fish (which is the "king of fishes"), dried slices of salted cuttlefish, *jinbaso* or "the Seaweed of the Horse of the God;"[iii] also the seaweed *kombu*, which is a symbol of pleasure and joy, because its name is deemed to be a homonym for gladness; and *mochibana*, artificial blossoms formed of rice flour and straw.

---

[i] See Chapter XVI, "In A Japanese Garden," in this volume.

[ii] Author's Footnote: The difference between the *shimenawa* and *shimekazari* is that the latter is a strictly decorative straw rope, to which many curious symbols are attached.

[iii] Author's Footnote: It belongs to the *sargassum* family, and is full of air sacs. Various kinds of edible seaweed form a considerable part of the Japanese diet.

The *sambō* is a curiously shaped little table on which offerings are made to the Shintō gods, and almost every well-to-do household in Izumo has its own *sambō*: such a family *sambō* being smaller however than *sambō* used in the temples. At the beginning of the New Year's Festival, bitter oranges, rice, and rice flour cakes, native sardines (*iwashi*), *chikara-iwai* ("strength-rice-bread"), black peas, dried chestnuts, and a fine lobster, are all tastefully arranged on the family *sambō*. The *sambō* is set in front of each visitor; and the visitor, by saluting it with a bow, expresses not only his heartfelt wish that all the good fortune symbolized by the objects on it may come to the family, but also his reverence for the household gods. The black peas (*mame*) signify bodily strength and health, because a word that is pronounced similarly, although written with a different *kanji*, means "robust."

But why a lobster? Here we have another curious concept. The lobster stands as a symbol of extreme old age; and in artistic design, signifies the wish that our friends may live so long that they will become bent like lobsters: under the weight of years.

The dried chestnuts (*kachiguri*) are emblems of success, because the first character of their name in Japanese is the homonym of *kachi*, which means "victory" or "conquest."

There are at least a hundred other unique customs and symbols belonging to the New Year's Festival that would require a large volume to describe. I have mentioned only a few that immediately appeal to even casual observation.

III

The other festival I wish to refer to is that of Setsubun, which according to the ancient calendar, corresponded with the beginning of the natural year: the period when winter first softens into spring. It is what we might term, according to Professor Chamberlain, a sort of movable feast, and it is chiefly famous for the curious ceremony of the casting out of devils: *Oni-yarai*. On the eve of the Setsubun, a little after dark, the Yaku-otoshi, or "caster-out of devils," wanders through the streets from house to house, rattling his *shakujō*,[1] uttering his strange, professional cry: "*Oni wa soto! Fuku wa uchi!*" (Devils out! Good fortune in!)

For an insignificant fee, he performs his little exorcism in any house to which he is called. This simply consists of the recitation of certain parts of a Buddhist *kyō*, or *sutra*, and the rattling of the *shakujō*. Afterwards, dried peas (*shiro-mame*) are thrown about the house in four directions. For some mysterious

---

[1] Author's Footnote: This is a curiously shaped staff with which the deity Jizō is commonly represented. It is still carried by Buddhist mendicants, and there are several sizes. That carried by the Yaku-otoshi is usually very short. There is a tradition that the *shakujō* was first invented as a manner of giving warning to insects or other little creatures in the path of a Buddhist pilgrim, so that they might not be unknowingly walked on.

reason, devils do not like dried peas and flee. The scattered peas are later swept up and carefully preserved until the first clap of spring thunder is heard; when it is the custom to cook and eat some of them. But just why, I cannot find out. Neither can I discover the origin of the dislike by devils of dried peas. On the subject of this dislike, however, I confess my sympathy with devils.

After the devils have been properly cast out, a small charm is placed above all the entrances of the building to keep them from coming back again. This consists of a little stick about the length and thickness of a skewer, a single holly leaf, and the head of a dried *iwashi*: a fish resembling a sardine. The stick is stuck through the middle of the holly leaf and the fish's head is fastened into a split made in one end of the stick; the other end being slipped into some joint of the woodwork immediately above a door. Why the devils are afraid of the holly leaf and the fish's head, nobody seems to know. Among the people, the origin of all these curious customs appears to be quite forgotten. The families of the upper classes who still maintain such customs, believe in the superstitions relating to the festival just as little as Englishmen today believe in the magical virtues of mistletoe or ivy.

This ancient and merry annual custom of casting out devils has been, for generations, a source of inspiration to Japanese artists. It is only after a long acquaintance with popular customs and ideas, that the foreigner can learn to appreciate the delicious humor of many creations of art, which he may indeed wish to buy, just because they are so oddly attractive in themselves; however, which must really remain enigmas to them, so far as their inner meaning is concerned: unless he knows Japanese life. The other day, a friend gave me a little card case of perfumed leather. On one side was stamped in relief the face of a devil, through whose open mouth could be seen the laughing, chubby face of Otafuku, joyful Goddess of Good Luck, painted on the silk lining of the interior. In itself, the thing was very curious and pretty; but the real merit of its design was this comic symbolism of good wishes for the New Year: *Oni wa soto! Fuku wa uchi.*

IV

Since I have spoken of the custom of eating some of the Setsubun peas at the time of the first spring thunder, I will here take the opportunity to say a few words about superstitions concerning thunder, which have not yet ceased to prevail among the peasants.

When a thunderstorm comes, the big brown mosquito nets are hung, and the women and children, perhaps the whole family, squat down under the curtains until the storm is over. From ancient days, it has been believed that lightning cannot kill anybody under a mosquito net. The Raijū or "Thunder Animal," cannot pass through a mosquito net. Only the other day, an old peasant who came to the house with vegetables to sell, told us that he and his whole family, while crouching under their mosquito netting during a thunderstorm, actually saw the lightning rushing up and down the pillar of the balcony opposite their room, furiously clawing at the woodwork but unable to enter because of the mosquito netting. His house had been badly damaged by a flash, but he supposed the claws of the Thunder Animal had done the mischief.

They say that the Thunder Animal springs from tree to tree during a storm; therefore, to stand under trees during a time of thunder and lightning is very dangerous because the Thunder Animal might step on one's head or shoulders. The Thunder Animal is also alleged to be fond of eating the human navel; for which reason, people should be careful to keep their navels well covered during storms and to lie down on their stomachs if possible. Incense is always burned during storms because the Thunder Animal hates the smell of incense. A tree struck by lightning is thought to have been torn and scarred by the claws of the Thunder Animal, and fragments of its bark and wood are carefully collected and preserved by people living in the vicinity; for, the wood of a blasted tree is supposed to have the unique virtue of curing toothaches.

There are many stories of the Raijū having been caught and caged. Once, it is said, the Thunder Animal fell into a well, and was entangled in the ropes and buckets; thus, it was captured alive. Old Izumo folk say they remember that the Thunder Animal was once exhibited in the courtyard of the temple of Tenjin in Matsué, enclosed in a cage of brass; and that people paid one *sen* each to look at it. It resembled a badger. When the weather was clear, it would sleep contentedly in its cage; but when there was thunder in the air, it would become excited and seem to obtain great strength, and its eyes would flash dazzlingly.

V

There is one very evil spirit, however, who is not in the least afraid of dried peas, and who cannot be so easily gotten rid of as the common devils are: that is the Binbogami. However, in Izumo, people know a certain household charm by which the Binbogami may sometimes be cast out.

"Binbogami." (Attributed to Kunisada Utagawa, c. 1885).

Before any cooking is done in a Japanese kitchen, the little charcoal fire is first blown to a bright red heat with that most useful and simple household utensil called a *hifukidake*. The *hifukidake* ("fire-blow-bamboo") is a bamboo tube, usually about three feet long and about two inches in diameter. At one end, the end that is to be turned toward the fire, only a very small opening is left. The woman who prepares the meal places the other end to her lips and blows through the tube on the lit charcoal. Thus, a quick fire may be obtained in a few minutes.

In the course of time, the *hifukidake* becomes scorched, cracked, and useless. A new "fire-blow-tube" is then made and the old one is used as a charm against Binbogami. One little copper coin (*rin*) is put into it, some magical words are spoken, and then the old utensil, with the *rin* inside, is either simply thrown out through the front gate into the street, or else flung into some neighboring stream. This, I do not know why, is deemed equivalent to pitching Binbogami out of doors and rendering it impossible for him to return for a considerable time.

It may be asked, how is the invisible presence of Binbogami to be detected? The little insect that makes that weird ticking noise at night, in England called the "Death Watch," has a Japanese relative, called the *binbomushi* or the "poverty insect." It is said to be the servant of Binbogami, the God of Poverty; and its ticking in a house is believed to signal the presence of that most unwelcome deity.

VI

One more feature of the Setsubun festival is worthy of mention: the sale of the *hitogata* ("people shapes"). These are little figures, made of white paper, which represent men, women, and children. They are cut out with a few clever scissor strokes and the difference in sex is indicated by variations in the shape of the sleeves and the little paper *obi*. They are sold in the Shintō shrines. The purchaser buys one for every member of the family: the priest writing on each one, the age and sex of the person for whom it is intended. These *hitogata* are then taken home and distributed. Each person slightly rubs his body or her body with the paper and says a little Shintō prayer. The next day, the *hitogata* are returned to the *kannushi*,[i] who after having recited certain prayers over them, burns them with holy fire.[ii] It is by this ceremony that it is hoped all physical misfortunes will be averted from the family during a year.

---

[i] A Shintō priest.
[ii] Author's Footnote: I may make mention here of another matter, in no way relating to the Setsubun. There lingers in Izumo, a wholesome — and I do not doubt formerly a most valuable — superstition about the sacredness of writing. Paper on which anything has been written, or even printed, must not be crumpled up, stepped on, dirtied, or put to any vulgar use. If it is necessary to destroy a document, the paper should be burned. I have gently been reprimanded in a little hotel at which I had stopped, for tearing up and crumpling some paper covered with my own writing.

XXI

By the Sea of Japan

I

IT IS THE FIFTEENTH DAY of the seventh month, and I am in Hōki. The faded road winds along a coast of low cliffs: the coast of the Japanese Sea. Always on the left, over a narrow strip of stony land or a heaping of dunes, its vast expanse appears; wrinkled blue to that pale horizon beyond which Korea lies under the same sun. Sometimes, through a sudden gap in the cliff's edge, there flashes the running surf. Always on the right there is another sea; a silent sea of green, reaching to far misty ranges of wooded hills with huge pale peaks behind them and a vast plain of rice fields, over whose surface soundless waves keep chasing each other under the same great breath that moves the blue today from Chōsen to Japan.

Although for a week the sky remained unclouded, for several days the sea has been growing angrier, and now the muttering of its surf sounds far into the land. They say that it always roughens so during the period of the Festival of the Dead; the three days of the Bon, which are the thirteenth, fourteenth, and fifteenth of the seventh month according to the ancient calendar. On the sixteenth day, after the *shōryōbune*, which are the Ships of Souls, have been launched, no one dares to enter it. No boats can be

167

hired and all the fishermen remain at home. For on that day, the sea is the highway of the dead, who must pass back over its waters to their mysterious home; therefore, that day it is called Hotoke-umi, the Buddha Flood — the Tide of the Returning Ghosts. Always on the night of the sixteenth day, whether the sea is calm or tumultuous, its entire surface shimmers with faint lights gliding out to the open sea, the dim fires of the dead; and there is heard a murmuring of voices, like the murmur of a far off city: the indistinguishable speech of souls.

II

But it may happen that some vessel, delayed despite efforts to reach port, may find herself far out at sea on the night of the sixteenth day. Then the dead will rise high around the ship, reach out long hands, and murmur, "*Tago, tago o-kure! Tago o-kure!*"[1] Never may they be refused; however, before the bucket is given, the bottom of it must be knocked out. Woe to all on board if an entire *tago* be allowed to fall, even by accident, into the sea! For, the dead would at once use it to fill and sink the ship.

Nor are the dead the only invisible powers which are dreaded at the time of the Hotoke-umi. There are the most

---

[1] Author's Footnote: "A bucket honorably condescend (to give)."

powerful *ma* and the *kappa*.[i] At all times the swimmer fears the *kappa*, the Ape of the Waters, hideous and obscene, who reaches up from the depths to draw men down and to devour their entrails. Only their entrails.

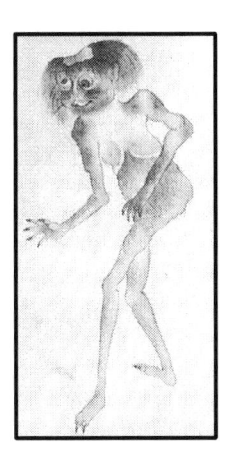

---

[i] Author's Footnote: The *kappa* is not really a sea goblin, but a river goblin, and haunts the sea only in the area of the mouths of rivers.

About a mile and a half from Matsué, at the little village of Kawachimura, on the river called Kawachi, stands a little temple called Kawako-no-miya, or the Miya of the Kappa. (In Izumo, among the common people, the word *kappa* is not used, but the term *kawake*, or "The Child of the River.") A document said to have been signed by a *kappa* is preserved in this little shrine. The story goes that in ancient times, the *kappa* living in the Kawachi used to seize and destroy many of the inhabitants of the village and many domestic animals. One day, however, while trying to seize a horse that had entered the river to drink, the *kappa* got its head twisted in some way under the belly-band of the horse, and the terrified animal, rushing out of the water, dragged the *kappa* into a field. There, the owner of the horse and a number of peasants seized and bound the *kappa*. All the villagers gathered to see the monster, which bowed its head to the ground and audibly begged for mercy. The peasants wanted to kill the goblin at once; however, the owner of the horse, who happened to be the head man of the *mura* (village), said, "It is better to make it swear never again to touch any person or animal belonging to Kawachimura." A written form of oath was prepared and read to the *kappa*. It said that it could not write, but that it would sign the paper by dipping its hand in ink, and pressing the imprint at the bottom of the document. This having been agreed to and done, the *kappa* was set free. From that time forward, no inhabitant or animal of Kawachimura was ever assaulted by the goblin.

The corpse of a person who has been seized by the *kappa* may be cast onshore after many days. Unless it was battered for a long while against the rocks by heavy surf, or nibbled by fish, it will show no outward wound; however it will be light and hollow: empty like a long-dried gourd.

III

Sometimes as we journey on, the monotony of undulating blue on the left, or the monotony of billowing green on the right, is broken by the gray apparition of a cemetery. A cemetery so long that our *jinrikisha* men, at full run, take a quarter of an hour to pass the huge congregation of its perpendicular stones. Such visions always indicate the approach of villages, but the villages prove to be as surprisingly small as the cemeteries are surprisingly large. The silent populations of the *hakaba*[1] outnumber the folk of the hamlets to which they belong, by hundreds of thousands; tiny thatched settlements sprinkled along the miles of coast and sheltered from the wind only by rows of somber pines. Legions and legions of stones, a host of sinister witnesses to the cost of the present to the past, and old, old, old! There are hundreds in place for so long that they have been worn into shapelessness merely by the blowing of sand from the

---

[1] A hakaba is a cemetery or graveyard.

dunes and their inscriptions totally erased. It is as if one were passing through the burial ground of all who ever lived on this windblown shore since the beginning of the land.

In all these *hakaba*, for it is the Bon, there are new lanterns in front of the newer tombs: the white lanterns that are the lanterns of the graves. Tonight, the cemeteries will be all aglow with lights like the fires of a city. But there are also countless tombs before which there are no lanterns; elder thousands, each the memory of an extinct family, or of which the absent descendants have forgotten even the name. Dim generations whose ghosts have no one to call them back, no local memories to love: all things related to their lives were so long ago obliterated.

IV

Many of these villages are only fishing settlements, and in them stand old thatched homes of men who sailed away on some eve of tempest and never came back. Yet, each drowned sailor has his tomb in the neighboring *hakaba*, and beneath it, something of him has been buried. But what?

Among these people of the west, something is always preserved which in other lands is cast away without a thought: the *hozo-no-o*, the flower stalk of a life, the umbilical cord of the newly born. It is wrapped carefully in many wrappings and on its outermost covering are written the names of the father, the mother, and the infant, together with the date and hour of birth; and it is kept in the family *o-mamori-bukuro* [a special bag or pouch]. The daughter, becoming a bride, bears it with her to her new home; and for the son, it is preserved by his parents. It is buried with the dead, and should one die in a foreign land, or perish at sea, it is entombed in lieu of the body.

V

Concerning those that go down to the sea in ships, and stay there, strange beliefs prevail on this far coast: beliefs assuredly more primitive than the gentle faith which hangs white lanterns in front of the tombs. Some hold that the drowned never journey to the Meido. They quiver forever in the currents; they billow in the swaying of tides; they toil in the wake of the junks; they shout in the plunging of breakers. It is their white hands that toss in the leap of the surf; their clutch that clatters the rocks or seizes the swimmer's feet in the pull of the undertow. The seamen speak euphemistically of the *O-baké*, the honorable ghosts, and fear them with a great fear. Therefore, cats are kept onboard!

A cat, they attest, has power to keep the *O-baké* away. How or why, I have not yet found anyone to tell me. I know only that cats are deemed to have power over the dead. If a cat is left alone with a corpse, will not the corpse rise and dance? Moreover, of all cats, a *mike-neko*, or cat of three colors, is most prized by sailors for this reason. But if they cannot obtain one (and cats of three colors are rare), they will take another kind of cat. Nearly every trading junk has a cat, and when the junk comes into port, its cat may usually be seen peeping through some little window in the vessel's side, or squatting in the open where the great rudder works; that is, if the weather is fair and the sea is still.

VI

These primitive and ghastly beliefs do not affect the beautiful practices of Buddhist faith in the time of the Bon, and from all those little villages, the *shōryōbune* are launched on the sixteenth day. They are much more elaborately and expensively constructed on this coast than in some other parts of Japan; for, although made of only straw, woven over a skeleton framework, they are charming models of junks, complete in every detail. Some are between three and four feet long. On the white paper sails is written the *kaimyō* or soul-name of the dead. There is a small water container onboard, filled with fresh water, and an incense cup. Along the gunwales flutter little paper banners bearing the mystic *manji*, which is the Sanskrit *svastika*.[i]

The form of the *shōryōbune* and the customs in regard to the time and manner of launching them differ much in different provinces. In most places they are launched in general for the family dead, wherever buried. In some places they are launched only at night with small lanterns on board. I am told also that it is the custom at certain sea villages to launch the lanterns all by themselves, in lieu of the *shōryōbune:* lanterns of a particular kind being manufactured only for that purpose.

On the Izumo coast, and elsewhere along this western shore, the soul boats are launched only for those who have been drowned at sea and the launching takes place in the morning instead of at night. Once every year, for ten years after death, a *shōryōbune* is launched: in the eleventh year the ceremony ceases. Several *shōryōbune* which I saw at Inasa were really beautiful and must have cost a rather large sum for poor fisher-folk to pay, but the ship carpenter who made them said that all the relatives of a drowned man contribute to purchase the little vessel: year after year.

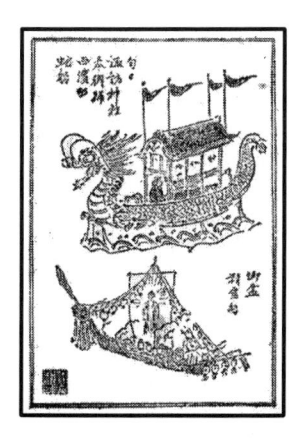

---

[i] Author's Footnote: The Buddhist symbol 卍.

VII

Near a sleepy little village called Kami-ichi, I make a brief stop in order to visit a famous sacred tree. It is in a grove close to the public highway but on a low hill. Entering the grove, I find myself in a sort of miniature glen surrounded on three sides by very low cliffs, above which enormous pines are growing — incalculably old. Their vast coiled roots have forced their way through the face of the cliffs, splitting rocks, and their mingling tops make a green twilight in the hollow. One pushes out three huge roots of a very unique shape, and the ends of these have been wrapped with long white papers bearing written prayers as well as offerings of seaweed. It is the shape of these roots, rather than any tradition, that seems to have made the tree sacred in popular belief. It is the object of a special cult and a little *torii* has been erected in front of it, bearing a votive proclamation of the most simple and curious kind. I cannot attempt to offer a translation of it; although for the anthropologist and folklorist, it certainly possesses peculiar interest. The worship of the tree, or at least of the *kami* which is supposed to live there, is one rare survivor of a phallic cult, probably common to most primitive races, and formerly widespread in Japan. Indeed, the government suppressed it scarcely more than a generation ago.

On the opposite side of the little hollow, carefully posed on a great, loose rock, I see something equally simple and almost equally curious, a *kitōja-no-mono*, or votive offering. It is two straw figures joined together and reclining side by side: a straw man and a straw woman. The workmanship is childishly clumsy but still the woman can be distinguished from the man by the ingenious attempt to imitate the female coiffure with a wisp of straw. Because the man is represented by a *mage*[81] now worn only by aged survivors of the feudal era, I suspect that this *kitōja-no-mono* was made after some ancient and strictly conventional model.

This queer votive offering tells its own story. Two people who loved each other were separated through the fault of the man; the charm of some *jorō*[1] perhaps having been the temptation of infidelity. Then, the wronged one came here and prayed to the *kami* to dispel the delusion of passion and touch the errant heart. The prayer has been heard; the pair has been reunited; and

---

[1] *Jorō* was used as a general term for prostitutes.

she, therefore, has made these two quaint effigies with her own hands and brought them to the *kami* of the pine — tokens of her innocent faith and her grateful heart.

VIII

Night falls as we reach the pretty hamlet of Hamamura, our last resting place by the sea, for tomorrow our way lies inland. The inn at which we stay is very small but very clean and cozy; and there is a delightful bath of natural hot water; for the *yadoya*[1] is situated close to a natural hot spring. This spring, so strangely close to the sea, I am told, provides the baths of all the houses in the village.

The best room is placed at our disposal but I linger awhile to examine a fine *shōryōbune*, waiting, on a bench near the street entrance, to be launched tomorrow. It seems to have been finished just a short time ago; for, fresh clippings of straw lie scattered around it and the *kaimyō* has not yet been written on its sail. I am surprised to hear that it belongs to a poor widow and her son, both of whom are employed by the hotel.

SHŌRYŌBUNE: Little straw ship of the dead. (Izumo coast)

---

[1] A *yodoya* is a very basic type of Japanese inn which provides, with few trappings, basic sleeping accomodations and food as required.

I was hoping to see the *Bon-odori* at Hamamura, but I am disappointed. At all the villages, the police have prohibited the dance: Fear of cholera has resulted in stringent sanitary regulations. In Hamamura, the people have been ordered to use no water for drinking, cooking, or washing except the hot water of their own volcanic springs.

A little, middle-aged woman, with a remarkably sweet voice, comes to wait on us at supper time. Her teeth are blackened and her eyebrows are shaved after the fashion of married women twenty years ago;[82] nevertheless, her face is still a pleasant one, and in her youth, she must have been uncommonly pretty. Though acting as a servant, it appears that she is related to the family that owns the inn, and that she is treated with the consideration due to a relative. She tells us that the *shōryōbune* is to be launched for her husband and brother, both fishermen of the village, who perished in sight of their own home eight years ago. The priest of the neighboring Zen temple is to come in the morning to write the *kaimyō* on the sail, as no one in the household are skilled at writing *kanji*.

I give her the customary little gift[i] and, through my attendant,[ii] ask her various questions about her history. She was married to a man much older than herself, with whom she lived very happily; and her brother, a youth of eighteen, lived with them. They had a good boat, a little piece of land, and she was skillful at the loom; so they managed to live well. In summer, the fishermen fish at night. When all the fleet is out, it is pretty to see the line of torch fires burning, two or three miles away, like a string of stars. They do not go out when the weather threatens; but in certain months, the great storms (*taifu*) come so quickly that the boats are overtaken almost before they have time to hoist sail. The sea was as still as a temple pond on the night when her husband and brother last sailed away: the *taifu*[iii] rose before daybreak. What followed, she tells with a simple pathos that I cannot reproduce in our more complicated language.

---

[i] While the Western custom of tipping was not acceptable in Japan, it was, on occasion, acceptable for a guest at an inn to provide their maid or attendant with a small gift of what was commonly referred to as "tea money."

[ii] Setsuko Koizumi (Mrs. Hearn). Hearn did not normally speak of his wife and preferred to keep many parts of his private life just that: private, even from his readers.

[iii] The word *taifu* relates to a sudden, intense squall or storm, and is the root word of "typhoon."

"All the boats had come back except for my husband's: for my husband and brother had gone out farther than the others, so they were not able to return as quickly. All the people were looking and waiting. Every minute the waves seemed to be growing higher and the wind more terrible; and the other boats had to be dragged far up on the shore to save them. Then suddenly, we saw my husband's boat coming very, very quickly. We were so glad! It came quite near, so that I could see the face of my husband and the face of my brother. But suddenly, a great wave struck it on one side, and it turned over into the water; and it did not come up again. And then we saw my husband and my brother swimming; but, we could see them only when the waves lifted them up. Tall, like hills, the waves were, and the head of my husband and the head of my brother would go up, up, up, and then down. Each time they rose to the top of a wave so that we could see them, they would cry out, '*Tasukete*! *Tasukete*!'[i] But the strong men were afraid; the sea was too terrible; I was only a woman! Then, my brother could not be seen any more. My husband was old, but very strong and he swam a long time; so near that I could see his face was like the face of one in fear, and he called '*Tasukete*!' But none could help him, and he also went down at last. Yet, I could see his face before he went down.

---

[i] Author's Footnote: "Help! Help!"

"And for a long time after, every night, I used to see his face as I saw it then; so that I could not rest, but only weep. I prayed and prayed to the Buddhas and to the *kami-sama* that I might not dream that dream. Now it never comes; but I can still see his face, even while I speak. In that time, my son was only a little child."

She cannot conclude her simple account without sobs. Then, suddenly bowing her head to the matting, and wiping away her tears with her sleeve, she humbly asks our pardon for this little exhibition of emotion, and laughs she soft low laugh required by Japanese politeness. This, I must confess, touches me still more than the story itself. At a fitting moment, my Japanese attendant delicately changes the theme and begins a light chat about our journey, and the *danna-sama's*[i] interest in the old customs and legends of the coast. Moreover, he succeeds in amusing her by some tales of our wanderings in Izumo.

She asks where we are going and my attendant answers, probably as far as Tottori.[83]

"*Ah! Tottori! Sō degozarimasu ka?* (Oh, you don't say!)…Now, there is an old story, the "Story of the Futon of Tottori." But the *danna-sama* knows that story?"

Indeed, the *danna-sama* does not, and eagerly begs to hear it. And the story is written down, as I learn it through the lips of my interpreter.

IX

Many years ago, a very small *yadoya* in Tottori town received its first guest: an itinerant merchant. He was received with more than common kindness, for the landlord desired to make a good name for his little inn. It was a new inn, but as its owner was very poor, most of its *dōgu* (furniture and utensils) had been purchased from the *furuteya*.[ii] Nevertheless, everything was clean, comforting, and pretty. The guest ate heartily and drank plenty of good, warm *saké*; after which his bed was prepared on the soft floor, and he laid himself down to sleep.

---

[i] *Danna-sama* may be translated literally as "Mr. Master," an honorific. Here it also here means "my husband."

[ii] Author's Footnote: *Furuteya*, the establishment of a dealer in second-hand wares, — *furude*.

But here I must interrupt the story for a few minutes, to say a word about Japanese beds. Never, unless some resident happens to be sick, do you ever see a bed in any Japanese house by day; even though you visit all the rooms and peer into all the corners. In fact, no bed exits, in the Western meaning of the word. That which the Japanese call "bed" has no bed frame, no spring, no mattress, no sheets, no blankets. It consists only of thick quilts, stuffed or rather padded, with cotton, which are called *futon*. A certain number of *futon* are laid down on the *tatami* (the floor mats), and a certain number of others are used for coverings. The wealthy can lie on five or six quilts, and cover themselves with as many as they please; while, poor folk must satisfy themselves with two or three. Of course, there are many kinds; from the servant's cotton *futon* which is no larger than a Western hearth rug and not much thicker, to the heavy and superb silk *futon*, eight feet long by seven wide, which only the *kanemochi* (rich men) can afford. Besides these, there is the *yogi*, a massive quilt made with wide sleeves like a kimono, in which you can find much comfort when the weather is extremely cold. All such things are neatly folded up and stowed out of sight by day in closets built into the wall and closed with *fusuma*: pretty sliding screen doors covered with opaque paper, usually decorated with elegant designs. There are also kept those curious wooden pillows,[84] invented to preserve the Japanese coiffure from becoming disarranged during sleep.

The pillow has a certain sacredness; but I have not been able to learn the origin and the precise nature of the beliefs concerning it. I know only this; that to touch it with the foot is considered very wrong and that if it is kicked or so moved, even by accident, the clumsiness must be atoned for by lifting the pillow to the forehead with the hands, and respectfully replacing it in its original position: with the word "*gomen*," meaning, "I pray to be excused."

Now, as a rule, one sleeps soundly after having drunk plenty of warm *saké*, especially if the night is cool and the bed very snug. But the guest, having slept but a very little while, was aroused by the sound of voices in his room; voices of children, always asking each other the same questions:

"*Ani-san samukarō?*"

"*Omae samukarō?*"

The presence of children in his room might annoy the guest, but could not surprise him, for in these Japanese hotels, there are no doors, but only papered sliding screens between rooms. So it seemed to him that some children must have wandered into his room by mistake in the dark. He uttered some gentle reprimand. For only a moment there was silence, then a sweet, thin plaintive voice, close to his ear, asked, "*Ani-san samukarō?*" (Elder Brother probably is cold?). And another sweet voice answering caressingly, "*Omae samukarō?* (Nay, you probably are cold?).

He arose and re-lit the candle in the *andon*,[1] and looked around the room. There was no one. The *shōji* were all closed. He examined the cupboards: they were empty. Wondering, he lay down again, leaving the light still burning, and immediately the voices spoke again, complainingly, close to his pillow:

"*Ani-san samukarō?*"

"*Omae samukarō?*"

Then, for the first time, he felt a chill creep over him, which was not the chill of the night. Again and again he heard; and each time he became more afraid; for, he knew that the voices were in the *futon*! It was the covering of the bed that spoke.

---

[1] *Andon*, a paper lantern of peculiar construction, used as a night light. Some forms of the *andon* are remarkably beautiful.

He hurriedly gathered together the few articles belonging to him and, descending the stairs, woke the landlord and told him what had happened. Then the host, much angered, replied, "That to make pleased the honorable guest, everything has been done, the truth is; but the honorable guest too much august *saké* having drunk, bad dreams has seen." Nevertheless, the guest insisted on paying at once that which he owed, and on seeking lodging elsewhere.

The next evening, another guest came, who asked for a room for the night. At a late hour, the landlord was awakened by his lodger with the same story. This lodger, strange to say, had not drunk any *saké*. Suspecting some spiteful plot to ruin his business, the landlord answered passionately, "You to please all things honorably have been done. Nevertheless, ill-omend and vexatious words you spoke. And that my inn, my means of livelihood is: that you also know. For which reason you have no right to say such things! Then the guest, getting into a rage, loudly said things much more evil, and the two parted in hot anger.

However, after the guest was gone, the landlord, thinking all this very strange, climbed to the empty room to examine the *futon*. While there, he heard the voices and discovered that the guests had said only the truth. It was one covering, only one that cried out. The rest were silent. He took the covering into his own room, and for the remainder of the night lay beneath it. The voices continued until the hour of dawn: "*Ani-san samukarō?*" "*Omae samukarō?*" So he could not sleep.

At daybreak, he got up and went out to find the owner of the *furuteya* at which the *futon* had been purchased. The dealer knew nothing. He had bought the *futon* from a smaller shop, and the keeper of that shop had purchased it from a still poorer dealer living in the farthest suburb of the city. And so the innkeeper went from one to the other, asking questions.

Then, at last it was found that the *futon* had belonged to a poor family and had been bought from the landlord of a little house in which the family had lived in the area of the town. The story of the *futon* was this:

The rent of the little house was only sixty *sen* a month, but even this was a great deal for the poor folks to pay. The father could earn only two or three *yen* a month, and the mother was ill and could not work. There were two children; a boy of six years and a boy of eight. They were strangers in Tottori.

One winter's day the father became ill, and after a week of suffering he died, and was buried. Then the long-sick mother followed him and the children were left alone. They knew no one who they could ask for aid; and in order to live they began to sell what there was to sell.

That was not much; the clothes of the dead father and mother, and most of their own, some cotton quilts, a few poor household utensils: *hibachi*, bowls, cups, and other bits. Every day they sold something until there was nothing left but one futon. And a day came when they had nothing to eat and the rent was not paid.

The terrible *Dai-kan*, the season of greatest cold, had arrived, and the snow had drifted too high that day for them to wander far from the little house; so they could only lie down under their one *futon* and shiver together, and comfort each other in their own childish way.

"*Ani-san samukarō?*"

"*Omae samukarō?*"

They had no fire, nor anything with which to make a fire. The darkness came and the icy wind screamed into the little house.

They were afraid of the wind but they were more afraid of the owner of the house, who roughly woke them to demand his rent. He was a hard man with an evil face. Finding there was no one to pay him, he turned the children out into the snow and took their one *futon* away from them, and locked up the house.

They had only one, thin, blue kimono each, for all their other clothes had been sold to buy food: and they had nowhere to go. There was a temple of Kwannon not far away, but the snow was too high for them to reach it. So when the landlord was gone, they crept back behind the house. There, the drowsiness of cold fell on them, and they slept, embracing each other to keep warm. While they slept, the gods covered them with a new *futon*, ghostly white and very beautiful: they did not feel the cold anymore. For many days they slept there; then, somebody found them, and a bed was made for them in the *hakaba* of the Temple of Kwannon of the Thousand Arms.[85]

The innkeeper, having heard these things, gave the *futon* to the priests of the temple, and the *kyō*[i] was recited for the little souls. And from then on, the *futon* ceased to speak.

X

One legend recalls another, and tonight I hear many strange ones. The most remarkable is a tale that my attendant suddenly remembers: a legend of Izumo.

Once, in the Izumo village called Mochida-no-ura, there lived a peasant who was so poor that he was afraid to have children. Each time that his wife bore him a child, he cast it into the river and pretended that it had been born dead. Sometimes it was a son, sometimes a daughter; but always the infant was thrown into the river at night. Six were thus murdered.

But as the years passed, the peasant found himself more prosperous. He had been able to save money and to purchase land. At last his wife bore him a seventh child: a boy.

Then the man said, "Now we can support a child and we will need a son to aid us when we are old. And this boy is beautiful, so we will raise him."

The infant thrived and each day the hard peasant wondered more at his own heart; for each day, he knew that he loved his son more.

One summer's night he walked out into his garden, carrying his child in his arms. The little one was five months old. The night was so beautiful, with its great moon, that the peasant cried out, "*Aa! Kon ya medzurashii e yo da!*" ("Ah! Tonight truly a wondrously beautiful night is!")

Then the infant, looking up into this face and speaking the speech of a man said, "Why, father! The last time you threw me away, the night was just like this, and the moon looked just the same, did it not?"[ii]

And from then on, the child remained like other children of the same age, and spoke not a word.

---

[i] *Kyō* literally means *sutra*, the voice or teaching of Buddha.
[ii] Author's Footnote: "*Ototsan! Washi wo shimai ni shitesashita toki mo, chōde kon ya ne yona tsuki yo data ne?*" – Izumo dialect.

The peasant became a monk.

XI

After supper and a bath, feeling too warm to sleep, I wander out alone to visit the village *hakaba*, a long cemetery on a sand hill, or rather a large dune, thinly covered with soil at its summit, but revealing, through its crumbling sides, the story of its creation by ancient tides, mightier than tides of today.

I wade up to my knees in sand in order to reach the cemetery. It is a warm, moonlight night, with a great breeze. There are many *bon* lanterns (*bondōrō*), but the sea wind has blown out most of them and only a few here and there still shed a soft, white glow: pretty shrine-shaped cases of wood with openings of symbolic outlines, covered with white paper. There are no visitors beside myself, for it is late. Much gentle work has been done here today; for all the bamboo vases have been provided with fresh flowers or sprays, the water basins filled with fresh water, and the monuments cleaned and beautified. In the farthest nook of the cemetery, I find in front of one very humble tomb, a pretty, small *zen* or lacquered dining tray, covered with dishes and bowls containing a perfect, dainty little Japanese meal. There is also a pair of new chopsticks and a little cup of tea: some of the dishes are still warm. A loving woman's work: the prints of her little sandals are fresh on the path.

XII

There is an Irish folk saying that any dream may be remembered, if the dreamer, after awakening, first scratches his head in an effort to recall it; but should he forget this precaution, the dream can never be brought back to memory, just as though one tries to reform the curling of smoke blown away.

Indeed, nine hundred and ninety-nine out of a thousand dreams hopelessly evaporate; however, certain rare dreams, which come when thought has been strangely impressed by unfamiliar experiences — dreams particularly apt to occur at a time of travel — remain in memory, imaged with all the vividness of real events. Of such was the dream I dreamed at Hamamura, after having seen and heard those things previously written down.

Some pale, broad, paved place, perhaps the thought of a temple courtyard, tinted by a faint sun; and before me a woman, neither young nor old, seated at the base of a great, gray pedestal that supported I know not what, for I could look only at the woman's face. For a while, I thought that I remembered her: a woman of Izumo. Then she seemed a weirdness. Her lips were moving, but her eyes remained closed and I could not choose but to look at her.

In a voice that seemed to come thinly through the distance of years, she began a soft, wailing chant. And as I listened, vague memories came to me of a Celtic lullaby. As she sang, with one hand she loosened her long black hair until it fell coiling on the stones, and having fallen, it was no longer black but blue, pale day-blue, and was moving sinuously, crawling with swift blue rippling to and fro. Then, suddenly, I became aware that the rippling was far, very far away, and that the woman was gone. There was only the sea; blue, billowing to the verge of heaven, with long, slow flashes of soundless surf.

Awaking, I heard in the night, the muttering of the real sea: the vast, husky speech of the Hotoke-Ume, the Tide of the Returning Ghosts.

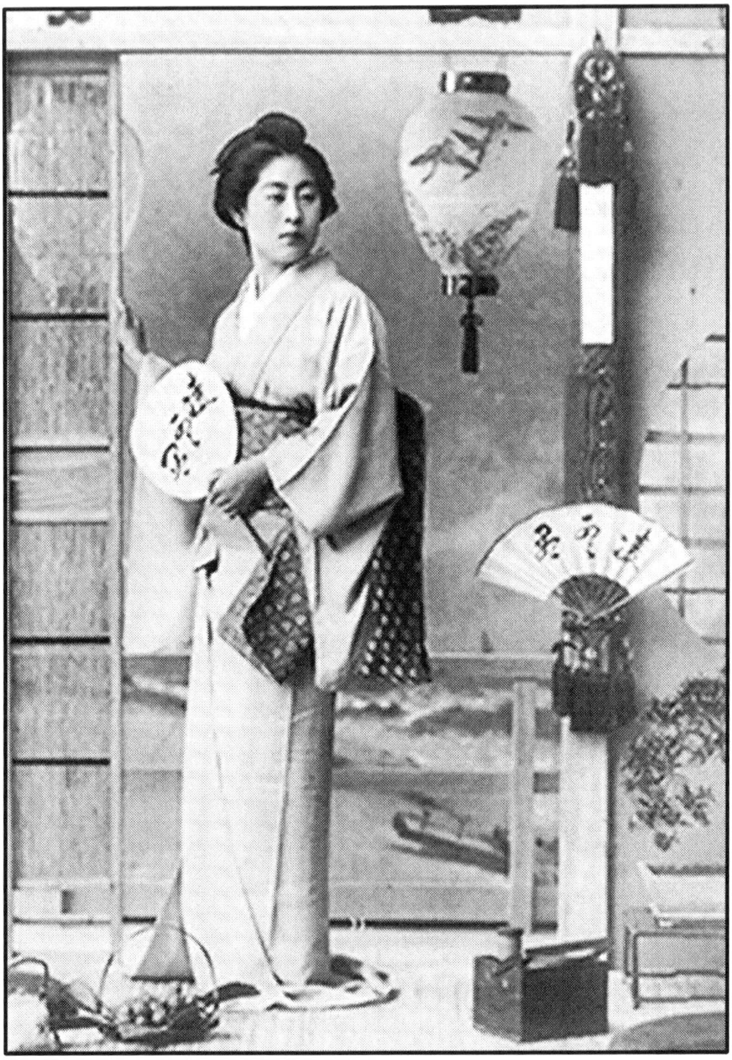

XXII

OF A DANCING GIRL

NOTHING IS MORE SILENT than the beginning of a Japanese banquet and no one, except a native, who observes the opening scene could possibly imagine the tumultuous ending.

The robed guests take their places, quite noiselessly and without speech, on the kneeling cushions. Maidens whose bare feet make no sound lay the lacquered services on the matting in front of them. For a while, there is only smiling and flitting, as in dreams. You are not likely to hear any voices from outside, as a banquet house is usually secluded from the street by spacious gardens. At last, the master of ceremonies, host or provider, breaks the hush with the consecrated words, "*O-somatsu degozarimasu ga! — Dōzo o-hashi!*" at which all present bow silently, take up their *hashi* (chopsticks), and begin to eat. But *hashi*, deftly used, cannot be heard at all. The maidens pour warm *saké* into the cup of each guest, without making the least sound, and it is not until several dishes have been emptied, and several cups of *saké* absorbed, that tongues are loosened.

Then, all at once, with a little burst of laughter, a number of young girls enter, make the customary bow of greeting, glide into the open space between the lines of the guests, and begin to serve the wine with a grace and dexterity of which no common maid is capable. They are pretty, clad in very costly kimono of silk, girdled like queens, and the beautifully styled hair of each is decked with mock flowers, wonderful combs and pins, and with curious ornaments of gold. They greet the stranger as if they had always known him; they jest, laugh, and utter funny little cries. These are the geisha,[i] or dancing girls, hired for the banquet.

Samisen[ii] tinkle. The dancers withdraw to a clear space at the far end of the banquet hall, always big enough to admit more guests than ever assemble on common occasions. Some form the orchestra, under the direction of a woman of uncertain age: there are several *samisen* and a tiny drum played by a child. Others, singly or in pairs, perform the dance. It may be swift and merry, consisting totally of graceful posing; two girls dancing together with such coordination of step and gesture as only years of training could make possible. More frequently, it is rather like acting than like what we foreigners would call dancing; acting accompanied with extraordinary waving of sleeves and fans, and with a play of eyes and features: sweet, subtle, subdued, totally Oriental. There are more voluptuous dances known to geisha, but on ordinary occasions and in front of refined audiences, they

---

[i] Author's Footnote: The Kyōto word is *maiko*. [Maiko are actually apprentice geisha (*geiko* in Kyōto.]
[ii] Author's Footnote: Guitars of three strings.

portray beautiful old Japanese traditions, like the legend of the fisherman Urashima, beloved by the Sea God's daughter. At intervals, they sing ancient Chinese poems, expressing a natural emotion with delicious vividness in a few exquisite words. And always they pour the wine — that warm, pale yellow, drowsy wine which fills the veins with soft contentment, making a faint sense of ecstasy through which, as through some opiate sleep, the commonplace becomes wondrous and blissful, and the geisha Maids of Paradise, and the world much sweeter than, in the natural order of things, it could ever possibly be.

The banquet, at first so silent, slowly changes to a merry commotion. The company breaks ranks, form groups, and the girls pass from group to group, laughing, chatting, and still pouring *saké* into the cups which are being exchanged and emptied with low bows.[1] Men begin to sing old samurai songs and old Chinese poems. One or two even dance. A geisha tucks her robe will up to her knees, and the *samisen* strike up the quick melody, "*Kompira funé funé.*" As the music plays, she begins to run lightly and swiftly in a figure-eight, and a young man carrying a

---

[1] Author's Footnote: It is sometimes customary for guests to exchange cups, after duly rincing them. It is always a compliment to ask for your friend's cup.

saké bottle and cup, also runs in the same figure-eight. If the two meet on a line, the one through whose error the meeting happens must drink a cup of *saké*. The music becomes quicker and quicker and the runners run faster and faster; for they must keep time to the melody: the geisha wins.

In another part of the room, guests and geisha are playing *ken*.[1] They sing as they play, facing each other, clap their hands, and fling out their fingers at intervals with little cries: the *samisen* keep time.

> *Choito, – don-don!*
> *Otagaidané;*
> *Choito, – don-don!*
> *Oidemashitané;*
> *Choito, – don-don!*
> *Shimaimashitané.*

Now, to play *ken* with a geisha requires a perfectly cool head, a quick eye, and much practice. Having been trained from childhood to play all kinds of *ken* (and there are many), she generally only loses for politeness, when she loses at all. The signs of the most common *ken* are a Man, a Fox, and a Gun. If the geisha makes the sign of the Gun, you must instantly, and in exact time to the music, make the sign of the Fox, who cannot use the Gun. For if you make the sign of the Man, then she will answer with the sign of the Fox, who can deceive the Man, and you lose. And if she makes the sign of the Fox first, then you should make the sign of the Gun, which can kill the Fox. But all the while, you must watch her bright eyes and supple hands. These are pretty; and if you allow yourself, just for one fraction of a second, to think how pretty they are, you are bewitched and conquered.

Notwithstanding all this apparent comradeship, a certain rigid decorum between guest and geisha is always preserved at a Japanese banquet. However flushed with wine a guest may have become, you will never see him attempt to caress a girl; he never forgets that she appears at the festivities only as a human flower, to be looked at, not to be touched. The familiarity which foreign

---

[1] "Ken," actully called *Jan-ken-pon* (じゃんけんぽん), or more commonly called *janken* (じゃんけん) is a game very similar to the Western game of "Rock, Paper, Scissors." The word "*ken*" itself means "fist."

tourists in Japan frequently permit themselves with geisha or with waitresses, though endured with smiling patience, is really much disliked and considered by native observers as evidence of extreme vulgarity.

For a time the merriment grows; but as midnight draws near, the guests begin to slip away, one by one, unnoticed. Then, the noise gradually dies down, the music stops; and at last the geisha, having escorted the latest of the feasters to the door, with laughing cries of "*Sayōnara,*" can sit down alone to break their long fast in the deserted hall.

Such is the geisha's part. But what is her mystery? What are her thoughts, emotions, her secret self? What is her true existence beyond the night circle of the banquet lights; far from the illusion formed around her by the mist of wine? Is she always as mischievous as she seems while her voice ripples out with mocking sweetness the words of the ancient song?

Kimi to neyaru ka, go sengoku toruka?
Nanno gosengoku kimi to neyo?[i]

Or might we think her capable of keeping that passionate promise she utters so deliciously?

Omae shindara tera ewa yaranu!
Yaete konishite sake de nomu.[ii]

"Why, as for that," a friend tells me, "there was O-Kama of Ōsaka who realized the song only last year. For she, having collected from the funeral pile the ashes of her lover, mingled

---

[i] Author's Footnote: "Once more to rest beside her, or keep five thousand *koku*? What care I for *koku*? Let me be with her!"
There lived in ancient times a *hatamoto* called Fuji-eda Geki, a vassal of the Shōgun. He had an income of five thousand *koku* of rice: a great income in those days. But he fell in love with an inmate of the Yoshiwara [the pleasure district of Edo], named Ayaginu, and wished to marry her. When his master told the vassal to choose between his fortune and his passion, the lovers fled secretly to a farmer's house, and there committed suicide together. And the above song was made about them. It is still sung.

[ii] Author's Footnote: "Dear, shouldst thou die, grave shall hold thee never! I thy body's ashes, mixed with wine will drink."

them with *saké*, and at a banquet, drank them, in the presence of many guests." In the presence of many guests! Alas for romance!

In the house in which geisha live, there is always a strange image placed in the alcove. Sometimes it is made of clay, rarely of gold, most commonly of porcelain. It is revered; offerings are made to it of sweets, rice bread and wine; incense smolders in front of it; and a lamp is burned before it. It is the image of an erect kitten with one paw outstretched, as if inviting; thus its name, the Beckoning Kitten.[i] It is the *genius loci*:[ii] it brings good fortune, the patronage of the rich, the favor of banquet-givers. Now, they who know the soul of the geisha state that the likeness of the image is the likeness of herself — playful and pretty, soft and young, lithe and caressing, and as cruel as a devouring fire.

Worse still than this they have said of her: that in her shadow walks the God of Poverty, that the fox-women are her sisters, that she is the ruin of youth, the waster of fortunes, the

---

[i] Author's Footnote: *Maneki-neko*.
[ii] A *genius loci* (Latin) in classical Roman religion was the protective spirit of a place. It was often depicted in religious iconography as a figure holding a Cornucopia, patera and/or a snake.

destroyer of families, that she knows love only as the source of the follies which are her gain, and grows rich on the substance of men whose graves she has made. They say that she is the most consummate of pretty hypocrites, the most dangerous of schemers, the most insatiable of mercenaries, and the most pitiless of mistresses. This cannot all be true. Yet, much is true; that, like the kitten, the geisha is by profession a creature of prey. There are many really lovable kittens. Even so, there must be really delightful dancing girls.

The geisha is only what she has been made in answer to foolish human desire for the illusion of love mixed with youth and grace; however, without regrets or responsibilities. Thus she has been taught, besides *ken*, to play at hearts. The eternal law is that people may play with impunity at any game in this unhappy world except for three, which are called life, love, and death. Those the gods have reserved for themselves, because nobody else can learn to play them without doing mischief. Therefore, to play with a geisha any game more serious than *ken*, or at least *go*,[i] is displeasing to the gods.

The girl begins her career as a slave: a pretty child bought from miserably poor parents under a contract, according to which the purchasers may claim her services for eighteen, twenty, or even twenty-five years. She is fed, clothed, and trained in a house occupied only by geisha,[ii] and passes the rest of her childhood under severe discipline. She is taught etiquette, grace and polite speech. She has daily lessons in dancing and she is obliged to learn by heart a multitude of songs and their ambience. In addition, she must learn games, the serving of banquets and weddings, and the art of dressing and looking beautiful. Whatever physical gifts she may have are carefully cultivated. Afterwards, she is taught to handle musical instruments: first the little drum (*tsudzumi*), which cannot be played at all without considerable practice; then she learns to play the *samisen* a little, with a plectrum of tortoise shell or ivory. At eight or nine years of age, she attends banquets, chiefly as a drum player. She is then the most charming little creature imaginable, and already knows how to fill your wine cup exactly full, with a single tip of the bottle and without spilling a drop, between two taps of her drum.

---

[i] Go (碁) is the Japanese equivalent of chess.
[ii] An *okiya* (置屋).

Later, her discipline becomes crueler. Her voice may be flexible enough, but lacks the requisite strength. In the coldest hours of winter nights, she must climb to the roof of her house and there sing and play until the blood oozes from her fingers and the voice dies in her throat. The desired result is an atrocious cold. After a period of hoarse whispering, her voice changes its tone and strengthens. She is ready to become a public singer and dancer.

She usually makes her first appearance in this capacity at the age of twelve or thirteen. If pretty and skillful, her services will be much in demand, and her time paid for at the rate of twenty to twenty-five *sen* per hour. Only then do her purchasers begin to reimburse themselves for the time, expense, and trouble of her training; and they are not likely to be generous. For many years more, all that she earns must pass into their hands. She can own nothing, not even her clothes.

At seventeen or eighteen, she has made her artistic reputation. She has attended many hundreds of events, and knows by sight all the important people of her city: the character of each, the history of all. Her life has been chiefly a night life and rarely has she seen the sun rise since she became a dancer. She has learned to drink wine without ever losing her head, and to fast for seven or eight hours without ever feeling the worse. She has had many lovers.[86] To a certain extent, she is free to smile on whom she pleases; however, she has been well taught, above all else, to use her power to charm for her own advantage. She hopes to find somebody able and willing to buy her freedom. Later, that somebody would almost certainly discover many new and excellent meanings to those Buddhist texts that tell about foolishness of love, and the impermanency of all human relationships.

At this point of her career, we may leave the geisha; subsequently, her story is likely to prove unpleasant, unless she dies young. Should that happen, she will have the funeral ceremony of her class, and many curious rites will preserve her memory.

Sometime perhaps, while wandering through Japanese streets at night, you hear sounds of music, a tinkling of *samisen* music floating through the great gateway of a Buddhist temple, together with the shrill voices of singing girls; which may seem to you a strange thing. The deep courtyard is filled with people looking and listening. Then, making your way through the crowd to the temple steps, you see two geisha seated on the matting inside, playing and singing, and a third dancing in front of a little table. On the table is an *ihai*, or mortuary tablet; in front of the tablet burns a little lamp and incense in a cup of bronze; a small meal has been placed there (fruit and sweets), like a meal it is customary to offer the dead on the occasion of festivals. You learn that the *kaimyō* on the tablet is that of a geisha and that the comrades of the dead girl gather in the temple on certain days to gladden her spirit with songs and dances. Then, whoever pleases, may attend the ceremony free of charge.

But the dancing girls of ancient times were not like the geisha of today. Some of them were called *shirabyōshi*[87] and their hearts were not extremely hard. They were beautiful and wore queerly shaped caps decorated with gold. They were clad in splendid attire and danced with swords in the dwellings of princes. There is an old story about one of them which I think it is worthwhile to tell.

I

It was formerly, indeed it still is, a custom with young Japanese artists to travel on foot through various parts of the Empire in order to see and sketch the most celebrated scenery, as well as to study famous art objects preserved in Buddhist temples; many of which occupy sites that are extraordinarily picturesque. It is mainly to such wanderings that we owe those beautiful books of landscape views and life studies which are now so curious and rare, and which teach better than anything else, that only the Japanese can paint Japanese scenery. After you have become acquainted with their methods of interpreting their own nature, foreign attempts along the same line will seem to you strangely flat and without soul. The foreign artist will give you realistic reflections of what he sees, but he will give you nothing more. The Japanese artist gives you what he feels: the mood of a season, the precise sensation of an hour and place. His work is qualified by a power of suggestiveness rarely found in the art of the West. The Western painter renders minute detail: he satisfies the imagination he evokes. But his Japanese brother either suppresses or idealizes detail: steeps his distances in mist, bands his landscapes with clouds, makes his experience a memory in which only the strange and beautiful survive, with their sensations. He surpasses imagination; excites it, leaves it hungry with the hunger of charm seen only in glimpses. Nevertheless, in such glimpses he is able to convey the feeling of a time, the character of a place, in a way that seems magical. He is a painter of recollections and of sensations, rather than of clear-cut realities; and in this lies the secret of his amazing power: a power not to be appreciated by those who have never witnessed the scenes of his inspiration. Above all things, he is impersonal. His human figures are devoid of individuality; yet, they have inimitable merit as types embodying the characteristics of a class: the childish curiosity of the peasant, the shyness of the maiden, the fascination of the *jurō*, the self-consciousness of the samurai, the funny, placid prettiness of the child, the resigned gentleness of age. Travel and observation were the influences that developed this art. It was never a growth of studios.

A great many years ago, a young art student was traveling on foot from Kyōto to Edo, over the mountains. The roads then were few and bad, and travel was so difficult, compared to what it is now, that a current proverb was, *Kawai ko wa tabi wo sasé*, (A pet child should be made to travel). But, the land was what it is today. There were the same forests of cedar and pine, the same groves of bamboo, the same peaked villages with thatched roofs, the same terraced rice fields dotted with the great yellow straw hats of peasants bending in the slime. From the roadside, the same statues of Jizō smiled on the same pilgrim figures passing to the same temples; and then, as now, on summer days one might see naked, brown children laughing in all the shallow rivers, and all the rivers laughing in the sun.

The young art student, however, was no *kawai ko*:[i] he had already traveled a great deal, was used to bad food and rough lodging, and accustomed to make the best of every situation. On this journey, one evening after sunset, he found himself in a region where it did not seem possible to obtain either food or lodging of any kind: everywhere the land was cultivated. While attempting a shortcut over a range of hills to find some village, he had lost his way.

There was no moon, and pine shadows made blackness all around him. The district into which he had wandered seemed

---

[i] Cute (naïve) child.

"Comparison of Beauties and Flowers – Willow," by Gekko Ogata (1898).

utterly wild; there were no sounds but the humming of the wind in the pine needles, and an infinite tinkling of bell insects.[i] He stumbled on, hoping to reach some riverbank, which he could follow to a settlement. At last a stream abruptly crossed his path, but it proved to be a swift torrent, pouring into a gorge between cliffs. Forced to retrace his steps, he decided to climb to the nearest peak, from where he might be able to see some sign of human life; however, on reaching it, he could only see more hills around him.

He had almost resigned himself to passing the night under the stars when he saw, at some distance down the farthest slope of the hill he had just climbed, a single, thin, yellow ray of light, evidently coming from some dwelling. He made his way towards it and soon saw a small cottage: apparently a peasant's home. The light he had seen still streamed from it through a crack in the closed storm doors. He hurried forward and knocked at the entrance.

"Full Moon at Kozuka," by Hiroaki (Shotei) Takahashi, c. 1937.

---

[i] Simply put, a cricket.

II

Not until he had knocked and called several times did he hear any stirring inside. Then, a woman's voice asked what he wanted. The voice was remarkably sweet and the speech of the unseen questioner surprised him; for, she spoke in the cultivated speech of the capital. He responded that he was a student who had lost his way in the mountains; that he wished, if possible, to obtain food and lodging for the night; and that if this could not be given, he would be very grateful for information as to how to reach the nearest village: adding that he had means enough to pay for the services of a guide. The voice, in return, asked several other questions, indicating extreme surprise that anyone could have reached the dwelling from the direction he had taken, but his answers evidently allayed suspicion; for the resident exclaimed, "I will come in a moment. It would be difficult for you to reach any village tonight and the path is dangerous."

After a brief delay, the storm doors were pushed open and a woman appeared with a paper lantern, which she held so as to illuminate the stranger's face, while her own remained in shadow. She scrutinized him in silence, then said briefly, "Wait. I will bring water." She fetched a washbasin, set it on the doorstep, and offered the guest a towel. He removed his sandals, washed the dust of travel from his feet, and then was shown into a neat room which appeared to occupy the whole interior, except a small, boarded space at the rear, used as a kitchen. A cotton *zabuton* was laid for him to kneel on and a brazier set before him.

It was only then that he had a good opportunity to observe his hostess and he was startled by the delicacy and beauty of her features. She might have been three or four years older than he, but was still in the bloom of youth. Certainly, she was not a peasant girl. In the same unique, sweet voice, she said to him, "I am alone and I never receive guests here. Nevertheless, I am sure it would be dangerous for you to travel farther tonight. There are some peasants in the neighborhood, but you cannot find your way to them in the dark without a guide. So I can let you stay here until morning. You will not be comfortable, but I can give you a bed, and I suppose you are hungry. There is only some *shōjin-ryōri*,[i] not at all good, but you are welcome to it."

The traveler was quite hungry and only too glad for the offer. The young woman kindled a little fire, prepared a few dishes in silence, stewed leaves of *na*, some *aburagé*, some *kampyō*,[ii] and a bowl of coarse rice, and quickly set the meal in front of him, apologizing for its quality. But during his meal, she hardly spoke at all and her reserved manner embarrassed him. As she answered the few questions he asked merely by a bow or by a solitary word, he soon refrained from pressing the conversation.

Meanwhile, he had observed that the small house was spotlessly clean and the utensils in which his food was served were immaculate. The few cheap objects in the room were pretty. The *fusuma* of the *oshiire* and *zendana*[iii] were only of white paper, but decorated with large *kanji* exquisitely written; characters suggesting, according to the law of such decoration, the favorite themes of the poet and artist: spring flowers, mountain and sea, summer rain, sky and stars, autumn moon, river water, autumn breeze. At one side of the room stood a kind of low altar, supporting a *butsudan*, whose tiny lacquered doors, left open, showed a mortuary tablet inside, in front of which a lamp was burning between offerings of wild flowers. Above this household shrine hung a picture of more than common merit, representing the Goddess of Mercy, wearing the moon for her halo.

As the student finished his little meal, the young woman observed, "I cannot offer you a good bed, and there is only a paper mosquito curtain. The bed and the curtain are mine, but tonight I have many things to do, and will have no time to sleep; therefore, I beg you to try to rest, though I am not able to make you comfortable."

He then understood that she was, for some strange reason, entirely alone, and was voluntarily giving up her only bed to him

---

[i] Author's Footnote: Buddhist food, containing no animal substance. Some kinds of *shōjin-ryōri* are quite appetizing.

[ii] *Aburagé* is a deep-fried *tofu*. *Kampyō* are long strips of gourd, often used for sushi.

[iii] Author's Footnotge: The terms *oshiire* and *zendana* might be partly translated by "wardrobe" and "cupboard." The *fusuma* are sliding screens serving as doors.

on a kindly pretext. He protested honestly against such an overindulgence of hospitality and assured her that he could sleep quite soundly anywhere on the floor, and did not care about the mosquitoes. But she replied, in the tone of an elder sister, that he must obey her wishes. She really had something to do, and she wanted to be left by herself as soon as possible; therefore, understanding him to be a gentleman, she expected he would allow her to arrange matters in her way. To this end, he could offer no objection as there was only one room. She spread the mattress on the floor, fetched a wooden pillow, suspended her paper mosquito curtain, unfolded a large screen on the side of the bed toward the *butsudan*, and then bid him goodnight in a manner that assured him she wished him to retire at once; which he did, but not without some reluctance at the thought of all the trouble he had unintentionally caused her.

III

Unwilling as the young traveler felt to accept a kindness involving the sacrifice of another's rest; he found the bed more than comfortable. He was very tired and had scarcely laid his head on the wooden pillow before he forgot everything in sleep.

Yet, only a little while seemed to have passed when he was awakened by the sound of feet, but not of feet walking softly. It seemed instead the sound of feet in rapid motion, as if excited. Then it occurred to him that robbers might have entered the house. As for himself, he had little to fear because he had little to lose. His anxiety was chiefly for the kind person who had granted him hospitality. Into each side of the paper mosquito curtain a small square of brown netting had been fitted, like a little window, and he tried to look through one of these, but the high screen stood between him and whatever was going on. He thought of calling, but this impulse was stopped by the thought that in case of real danger, it would be both useless and imprudent to announce his presence before understanding the situation. The sounds that had made him uneasy continued and were more and more mysterious. He decided to prepare for the worst and to risk his life if necessary, in order to defend his young hostess. Quickly tightening his robes, he slipped noiselessly from under the paper curtain, crept to the edge of the screen and peered out. What he saw was astonishing.

The young woman, magnificently attired, was dancing all alone in front of her illuminated *butsudan*. He recognized her costume as that of a *shirabyōshi*, although much richer than any he had ever seen worn by a professional dancer. Her beauty, marvelously enhanced by it in that lonely time and place, appeared almost supernatural, but what seemed even more wonderful was her dancing. For an instant he felt the tingling of a weird doubt. The superstitions of peasants, the legends of fox-women, flashed before his imagination; but the sight of the Buddhist shrine and the sacred picture, dissipated the thought and shamed him for the folly of it. At the same time, he became conscious that he was watching something she had not wished him to see, and that it was his duty as her guest, to return at once behind the screen. But the spectacle fascinated him. He felt, with no less pleasure than amazement, that he was looking on the most accomplished dancer he had ever seen, and the more he watched, the more the allure of her grace grew on him. Suddenly she paused, panting. She unfastened her *obi*,[i] turned in the act of removing her upper robe, and jumped violently as her eyes encountered his own.

He tried immediately to excuse himself. He said he had been suddenly awakened by the sound of quick feet, which had caused him some uneasiness, mainly for her sake, because of the lateness of the hour and the lonesomeness of the place. Then, he confessed his surprise at what he had seen, and spoke of the way in which it had attracted him. "I beg you," he continued, "to forgive my curiosity, for I cannot help wondering who you are and how you could have become so marvelous a dancer. I have seen all the dancers of Saikyō;[ii] yet, I have never seen among the most celebrated of them, a girl who could dance like you. Once I had begun to watch you, I could not take my eyes away."

At first, she seemed angry, but before he had ceased to speak, her expression changed. She smiled and seated herself in front of him. "No, I am not angry with you," she said. "I am only sorry that you watched me, for I am sure you must have thought me mad when you saw me dancing that way, all by myself; and now I must tell you the meaning of what you have seen.

---

[i] An *obi* (帯, おび) is the sash worn with traditional Japanese clothing such as *keikogi* worn in Japanese martial arts and as part of the kimono and *yukata*.
[ii] Saikyo means "West Capital" or Kyōto.

So she told her story. Her name he remembered hearing as a boy, her professional name, the name of the most famous of *shirabyōshi*, the darling of the capital who, in the zenith of her fame and beauty, had suddenly vanished from public life: no one knew where or why. She had fled from wealth and fortune with a youth who loved her. He was poor, but between them they possessed enough means to live simply and happily in the country.

They built a little house in the mountains and there, for a number of years, they existed only for each other. He adored her. One of his greatest pleasures was to see her dance. Each evening he would play some favorite melody and she would dance for him. But one long, cold winter he fell sick, and in spite of her tender nursing, died. Since then, she had lived alone with the memory of him, performing all those small rites of love and homage with which the dead are honored. Daily, in front of his tablet, she placed the customary offerings and nightly danced to please him, as before.

This was the explanation of what the young traveler had seen. It was indeed rude, she continued, to have awakened her tired guest; but she had waited until she thought he was sleeping soundly, and then she tried to dance very, very lightly. So she hoped he would pardon her for having unintentionally disturbed him.

When she had told him everything, she made a little tea, which they drank together. Then she begged him so plaintively to please her by trying to sleep again, that he found himself obliged to go back, with many sincere apologies, under the paper mosquito curtain.

He slept well and long, and the sun was high before he awoke. On rising, he found a meal, as simple as that of the evening before, prepared for him, and he felt hungry. Nevertheless, he ate sparingly, fearing the young woman might have stinted herself in providing for him. Then he prepared to leave, but when he wanted to pay her for what he had received and for all the trouble he had caused her, she refused to take anything from him, saying, "What I had to give was not worth money, and what I did was done for kindness alone. So I ask that you will try to forget the discomfort you suffered here and will remember only the goodwill of one who had nothing to offer."

He still tried to induce her to accept something; but at last, finding that his insistence only caused her pain, he took leave of her with such words as he could find to express his gratitude; and not without some regret, for her beauty and her gentleness had charmed him more than he would have liked to acknowledge to anyone but her. She showed him the path to follow and watched him descend the mountain until he passed out of sight. An hour later, he found himself on a familiar highway. Then a sudden remorse touched him: he had forgotten to tell her his name. For an instant he hesitated, and then said to himself, "What does it matter? I will always be poor." And he continued on.

IV

Many years passed by and many fashions with them; and the painter became old. But before becoming old, he had become famous. Princes, charmed by the wonder of his work, had competed with one another in giving him patronage; so that he grew rich and possessed a beautiful house of his own in the City of the Emperors. Young artists from many provinces were his pupils and lived with him; serving him in all things while receiving his instruction. His name was known throughout the land.

Now, an old woman came to his house one day, who asked to speak with him. The servants, seeing that she was poorly dressed and looked miserable, took her to be some common beggar and questioned her roughly. But when she answered, "I can tell no one except your master why I have come," they thought she was mad and deceived her, saying, "He is not now in Saikyō, nor do we know how soon he will return."

But the old woman came again and again — day after day and week after week — each time being told something that was not true: "Today he is ill," or, "Today he is very busy," or, "Today he has much company and therefore cannot see you." Nevertheless, she continued to come, always at the same hour each day, and always carrying a bundle wrapped in a ragged covering. The servants at last thought it was best to speak to their master about her, so they said to him, "There is a very old woman, whom we believe to be a beggar, at our lord's gate. More than fifty times she has come, asking to see our lord, and refusing to tell us why, saying that she can tell her wishes only to our lord. We have tried to discourage her, as she seemed to be mad, but she always comes. Therefore, we have decided to mention the matter to our lord, in order that we may learn what is to be done from now on."

Then the Master answered sharply, "Why did none of you tell me this before?" and went out himself to the gate where he spoke very kindly to the woman, remembering how he also had been poor. He asked her if she wanted alms from him.

But she answered that she had no need of money or food, and wished that he would paint a picture for her. He wondered at her wish and invited her to enter his house. So she entered into the vestibule, and kneeling there, began to untie the knots of the bundle she had brought with her. When she had unwrapped it, the painter saw curious, rich, quaint garments of silk, embroidered with designs in gold, yet very frayed and discolored by wear and time: the wreck of a wonderful costume of other days — the attire of a *shirabyōshi*.

While the old woman unfolded the garments one by one and tried to smooth them with her trembling fingers, a memory stirred in the Master's brain, flickered dimly there in a little space, and then suddenly it lit up. In that soft shock of recollection, he saw again the lonely mountain dwelling in which he had received uncompensated hospitality, the tiny room prepared for his rest; the paper mosquito curtain, the faintly burning lamp in front of the Buddhist shrine, the strange beauty of one dancing there alone in the dead of night. Then, to the astonishment of the aged visitor, he, favored of princes, bowed low before her and said, "Pardon my rudeness in having forgotten your face for a moment; but it was more than forty years since we last saw each other. Now I remember you well. You gave to me the only bed you had. I saw you dance, and you told me all of your story. You had been a *shirabyōshi*, and I have not forgotten your name.

He spoke it. She, astonished and confused, could not at first reply to him, for she was old, had suffered much, and her memory had begun to fail. But he spoke more and more kindly to her and reminded her of many things that she had told him, describing the house in which she had lived alone, so that at last, she also remembered. She answered with tears of pleasure, "Surely the Divine One who looks down from above the sound of prayer has guided me. But when my unworthy home was honored by the visit of the august Master, I was not as I am now. And it seems to me like a miracle of our Lord Buddha that the Master should remember me."

Then she told the rest of her simple story. In the course of years, she had become, through poverty, obliged to part with her little house and in her old age, she had returned alone to the great city in which her name had long been forgotten. It had caused her much pain to lose her home, but it grieved her even more that, in becoming weak and old, she could no longer dance each evening in front of the *butsudan*, to please the spirit of the dead whom she had loved. Therefore, she wanted to have a picture of herself painted, in the costume and the attitude of the dance, so that she might hang it before the *butsudan*. She had sincerely prayed to Kwannon for this, and had sought out the Master because of his fame as a painter, since she desired an uncommon work for the sake of the dead — a picture painted with great skill; and she had brought her dancing attire, hoping that the Master might be willing to paint her in it.

He listened to everything with a kindly smile, and answered her: "It will be a pleasure for me to paint the picture which you want. Today I have something to finish which cannot be delayed, but if you will come here tomorrow, I will paint you exactly as you wish, and as well as I am able."

But she said: "I have not yet told the Master the thing which troubles me, and it is this; that I can offer nothing in return for so great a favor except these dancer's clothes. They are of no value in themselves, although they were once costly. Still, I hoped the Master might be willing to take them, seeing they have become curiosities; for, there are no more *shirabyōshi*, and the *maiko* of these times wear no such robes."

"You must not think at all of that matter!" the good painter exclaimed. "No; I am glad to have this chance to repay a small part of my old debt to you. So tomorrow, I will paint you just as you wish."

She bowed three times in front of him, saying thanks, and then said, "Let my lord pardon, though I have yet something more to say; for, I do not wish that he should paint me as I am now, but only as I used to be when I was young, as my lord knew me."

He said, "I remember well. You were very beautiful."

"The Actor Segawa Kikunojo II as Shirabyoshi Renri,"
by Torii Kyomitsu (1735 - 1785).

Her wrinkled features lightened up with pleasure as she bowed her thanks to him for those words and she exclaimed: "Then indeed all that I hoped and prayed for may be done! Since he remembers my poor youth, I ask my lord to paint me, not as I am now, but as he saw me when I was not old and, as it has pleased him to say generously, not unattractive. Oh Master, make me young again! Make me seem beautiful so that I may still seem beautiful to the soul of him, for whose sake I, the unworthy, ask this! He will see the Master's work and he will forgive that I can no longer dance."

Once more the Master asked her not to be concerned and said: "Come tomorrow, and I will paint you. I will make a picture of you, just as you were when I saw you: a young and beautiful *shirabyōshi*. I will paint it as carefully and as skillfully as if I were painting the picture of the richest person in the land. Never doubt, but come."

V

So the old dancer came at the appointed hour and the artist painted a picture of her on soft, white silk; yet, not a picture of her as she seemed to the Master's pupils, but the memory of her as she had been in the days of her youth: bright-eyed as a bird, lithe as a bamboo, dazzling as a *tennin*[1] in her costume of silk and gold. Under the magic of the Master's brush, the vanished grace returned and the faded beauty bloomed again. When the *kakemono* had been finished and stamped with his seal, he mounted it elegantly on silk cloth and attached rollers of cedar with ivory weights to it, and a silk cord by which to hang it. Then he placed it in a little box of white wood and gave it to the *shirabyōshi*. He would also have presented her with a gift of money, but although he earnestly pressed her, he could not persuade her to accept his help.

"No," she answered with tears, "indeed I need nothing. I only wanted the picture. For that I prayed and now my prayer has been answered; and I know that I never can wish for anything more in this life; and that if I die, desiring nothing, then to enter on the way of Buddha will not be difficult. One thought alone causes me sorrow: that I have nothing to offer to the

---

[1] Author's Footnote: *Tennin*, a "Sky maiden," or Buddhist angel.

Master but this dancer's apparel, which is indeed of little value, although I implore him to accept it. I will pray each day that his future life may be a life of happiness, because of the wondrous kindness which he has done me."

"No," protested the painter, smiling. "What is it that I have done? Truly nothing. As for the dancer's garments, I will accept them if that will make you happier. They will bring back pleasant memories of the night I passed in your home, when you gave up all your comforts for my unworthy sake; and yet, would not allow me to pay for that which I used. For that kindness I hold myself to still be in your debt. But now, tell me where you live, so that I may see the picture in its place." For, he had decided to place her beyond the reach of want.

But she excused herself with humble words and would not tell him, saying that her dwelling place was too meager to be looked at by someone such as he. Then with many bows, she thanked him again and again, and then went away with her treasure, weeping for joy.

Then the Master called to one of his pupils: "Go quickly after that woman, but so that she does not know she is followed, and bring me word of where she lives." So the young man followed her, unseen.

He was gone a long while, and when he returned, he laughed in the manner of one obligated to say something which was unpleasant to hear, and said, "I followed that woman, oh Master, out of the city to the dry bed of the river, near the place where criminals are executed. There I saw a hut like an *eta*[88] might live in, and that is where she lives: a forsaken and filthy place."

"Nevertheless," the painter replied, "tomorrow you will take me to that forsaken and filthy place. While I live, she shall not want for food, clothing, or comfort." And since all wondered, he told them the story of the *shirabyōshi*, after which, his words no longer seemed strange to them.

VI

On the morning of the following day, an hour after sunrise, the master and his pupil made their way to the dry bed of the river, beyond the edge of the city, to the place of outcasts.

They found the entrance of the little house closed by a single shutter, on which the master tapped many times without getting a response. Then, finding the shutter unlocked from the inside, he pushed it aside slightly and called through the opening. No one answered so he decided to enter. At the same time, with extraordinary vividness, there came back to him the sensations of the very instant when, as a tired lad, he stood pleading for admission to the lonesome little cottage among the hills.

Quietly entering alone, he saw that the woman was lying there, wrapped in a single, thin and tattered futon, seemingly asleep. On a crude shelf, he recognized the *butsudan* from forty years earlier, with its tablet. Now, as then, a tiny lamp was burning in front of the *kaimyō*. The *kakemono* of the Goddess of Mercy, with her lunar halo, was gone, but hanging on the wall facing the shrine, he saw his own elegant gift, and an *ofuda* hanging beneath it: an *ofuda* of Hito-koto-Kwannon;[1] that Kwannon to whom it is unlawful to pray to more than once, because she answers but a single prayer. There was little else in the desolate house; only the clothes of a female pilgrim and a mendicant's staff and bowl.

But the Master did not pause to look at these things, for he wanted to awaken and to gladden the sleeper. He called her name cheerily twice and then a third time.

Then suddenly, he saw that she was dead. He wondered as he gazed on her face, for it seemed less old. A vague sweetness, like a ghost of youth, had returned to it; the lines of sorrow had been softened, the wrinkles strangely smoothed, by the hand of a phantom master, mightier than he.

---

[1] Author's Footnote: Her shrine is at Nara, not far from the temple of the giant Buddha.

"One Hundred Dances - Wisteria Maiden," by Gekko Ogata (c. 1891).

XXIII

FROM HŌKI TO OKI

I

I DECIDED TO GO TO OKI.[89] Not even a missionary had ever been to Oki, and its shores had never been seen by European eyes, except on those rare occasions when men-of-war steamed by them, cruising about the Japanese Sea. This alone would have been sufficient reason for going there, but a stronger one was provided for me by the ignorance of the Japanese themselves about Oki. Except for the far away Riu-Kiu,[90] or Loo-Choo Islands, inhabited by a somewhat different race with a different language, the least-known portion of the Japanese Empire is perhaps Oki.

Since it belongs to the same prefectural district as Izumo, each new governor of Shimane-ken is supposed to pay one visit to Oki after his inauguration, and the Chief of Police of the province sometimes goes there on an inspection tour. There are also some mercantile houses in Matsué, and in other cities, which send a commercial traveler to Oki once a year. Furthermore, there is quite a large trade with Oki; almost all carried on by small sailing vessels, but such official and commercial communications have not been of a nature to make Oki much better known today than in the medieval period of Japanese history.

Among the common people of the west coast, there still exist extraordinary stories of Oki, much like those about the fabulous Isle of Women, which figures so largely in the imaginative literature of various Asian races. According to these old legends, the moral ideals of the people of Oki were extremely fantastic: the most rigid ascetic could not dwell there and maintain his indifference to earthly pleasures; plus, however wealthy on his arrival, the visiting stranger must soon return to his native land, naked and poor, because of the seductions of women.

I had quite sufficient travel experience in strange countries to feel certain that all these marvelous stories signified nothing beyond the bare fact that Oki was a *terra incognita*;[91] and I even felt inclined to believe that the average morals of the people of Oki, judging by those of the common folk of the western provinces, must be very much better than the morals of our ignorant classes at home: which I subsequently determined to be the case.

For some time I could find no one among my Japanese acquaintances to give me any information about Oki, beyond the fact that in ancient times, it had been a place of banishment for the Emperors Go-Daigo and Go-Toba, dethroned by military dictators, and this I already knew. But at last, quite unexpectedly, I found a friend, a former fellow teacher, who had not only been to Oki, but was going there again in a few days about some business matter. We agreed to go together. His accounts of Oki differed substantially from those of the people who had never been there. The Oki folks, he said, were almost as much civilized as the Izumo folks: they had nice towns and good public schools. They were very simple, honest beyond belief, and extremely kind to strangers. Their only boast was that of having kept their race unchanged since the time that the Japanese had first come to Japan; or, in more romantic terms, since the Age of the Gods. They were all Shintōists, members of the Izumo Taisha faith, but Buddhism was also maintained among them, chiefly through the generous subscription of private individuals. And, there were very comfortable hotels, so that I would feel quite at home.

He also gave me a little book about Oki, printed for the use of the Oki schools, from which I obtained the following brief summary of facts.

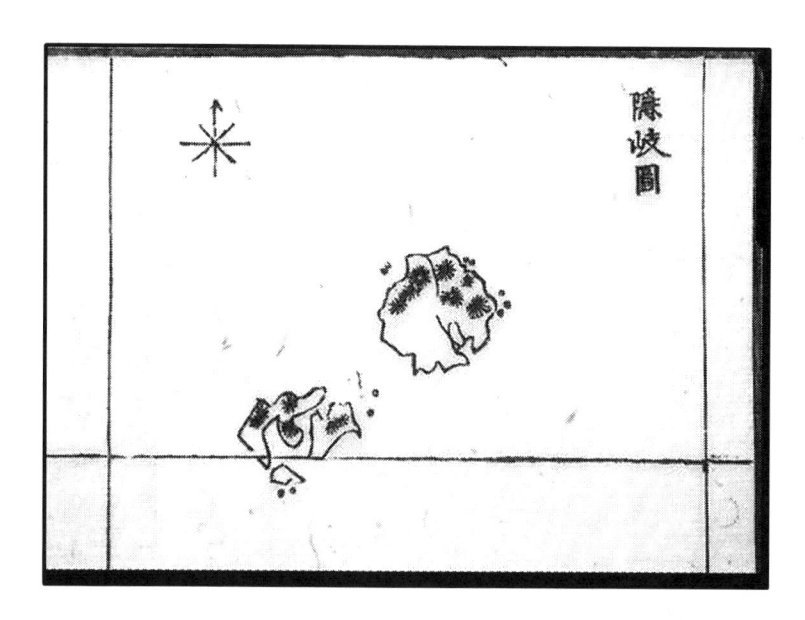

II

Oki-no-Kuni, or the Land of Oki, consists of two groups of small islands in the Sea of Japan, about one hundred miles from the coast of Izumo. Dōzen, as the nearer group are called, comprises, besides various islets, three islands lying close together: Chiburishima, or the Island of Chiburi (sometimes called Higashinoshima, or Eastern Island); Nishinoshima, or the Western Island, and Nakanoshima, or the Middle Island. Much larger than any of these is the principal island of Dōgo, which together with various islets, mostly uninhabited, form the remaining group. It is sometimes called Oki, although the name Oki is more generally used for the whole archipelago.[1]

Officially, Oki is divided into four *kōri* or counties. Chiburi and Nishinoshima together form Chiburigōri; Nakanoshima, with an islet, makes Amagōri, and Dōgo is divided into Ochigōri and Sukigōri.

All these islands are very mountainous, and only a small portion of their area has ever been cultivated. Their chief sources of revenue are their fisheries, in which nearly the whole population has always been engaged from the most ancient times.

---

[1] Author's Footnote: The names Dōzen or Tōzen, and Dōgo or Tōgo, signify "the Before Islands" and "the Behind Islands."

215

During the winter months, the sea between Oki and the west coast is highly dangerous for small vessels; and in that season the islands have little communication with the mainland. Only one passenger steamer runs to Oki from Sakai in Hōki.[92] In a direct line, the distance from Sakai in Hōki to Saigo, the chief port of Oki, is said to be thirty-nine *ri*; however, the steamer stops at the other islands on her way there.

There are quite a number of little towns, or rather villages, in Oki, of which forty-five belong to Dōgo. The villages are nearly all situated on the coast. There are large schools in the principal towns. The population of the islands is stated to be 30,196, but the respective populations of towns and villages is not given.

III

From Matsué in Izumo to Sakai in Hōki is a trip of barely two hours by steamer. Sakai is the chief seaport of Shimane-ken. It is an ugly little town full of unpleasant smells. It exists only as a port, has no industries, scarcely any shops, and only one Shintō temple of small dimensions and smaller interest. Its principal buildings are warehouses, pleasure resorts for sailors, and a few dingy hotels, which are always overcrowded with guests waiting for steamers to Ōsaka, to Bakkean, to Hamada, to Niigata, and various other ports. No steamers run regularly anywhere on this coast; their owners attach no business value whatever to punctuality, and guests usually have to wait for a much longer time than they could possibly have expected, and the hotels are glad for it.

But the harbor is beautiful: a long bay between the high land of Izumo and the low coast of Hōki. It is perfectly sheltered from storms and deep enough to admit all but the largest steamers. The ships can lie close to the houses, and the harbor is nearly always crowded with all sorts of craft, from junks to steam ferryboats of the latest construction.

My friend and I are lucky enough to secure back rooms at the best hotel. Back rooms are the best in nearly all Japanese

---

[1] A *ri* is a traditional Japanese unit of distance, sometimes called the "Japanese league" because it is of similar length to the European league. The *ri* equals 2160 *ken* or 12 960 *shaku* (the *shaku* being the Japanese equivalent of the foot), about 3927 meters or 2.44 statute miles.

buildings. At Sakai, they have the additional advantage of overlooking the busy wharves and the whole, luminous bay, beyond which the Izumo hills undulate in huge green billows against the sky. There was much to see and to be amused with. Steamers and sailing craft of all sorts were laying two and three deep in front of the hotel, and the naked dock laborers were loading and unloading in their own unique way. These men are recruited from among the strongest peasants of Hōki and Izumo: some were fine men, over whose brown backs the muscles rippled at every movement. They were assisted by boys of fifteen or sixteen apparently, apprentices learning the work, but not yet strong enough to bear heavy burdens. I noticed that nearly all had bands of blue cloth bound around the calves to keep the veins from bursting, and all sang as they worked. There was one curious alternating chorus, in which the men in the hold gave the signal by chanting "*Dokoe, dokoe!*" (Haul away!) and those at the hatch responded by improvisations on the appearance of each package as it ascended:

Dokoe, dokoe!

Onnago ne ko da.

Dokoe, dokoe!

Oya da yo, oya da yo.

Dokoe, dokoe!

Choi-choi da, choi-choi da.

Dokoe, dokoe!

Matsué da, Matsué da.

Dokoe, dokoe!

Koetsumo Yonago da,[i] *etc.*

---

[i] Author's Footnote: "*Dokoe, dokoe!*" "This is only a woman's baby" (a very small package). "*Dokoe, dokoe!*" "This is the daddy, this is the daddy" (a big package)." "*Dokoe, dokoe!*" "This very small, very small!" "*Dokoe, dokoe!*" "This is for Matsué, this is for Matsué!" "*Dokoe, dokoe!*" "This is for Koetsumo of Yonago," etc.

But this chant is for light, quick work. A very different chant accompanied the more painful and slower labor of loading heavy sacks and barrels onto the shoulders of the stronger men:

> *Yan-yui!*
>
> *Yan-yui!*
>
> *Yan-yui!*
>
> *Yan-yui!*
>
> *Yoi-ya-sa-a-a-no-do-koe-shi!*[1]

Three men always lifted the weight. At the first "*yan-yui*" all stooped; at the second, all took hold; the third signified ready; at the fourth, the weight rose from the ground; and with the long cry of "*yoiyasa no dokoeshi*," it was dropped on the brawny shoulder waiting to receive it.

Among the workers was a naked, laughing boy, with a fine contralto that rang out so merrily through all the noise, so as to create something of a sensation in the hotel. A young woman, one of the guests, came out onto the balcony to look and exclaimed, "That boy's voice is RED" —— at which everybody smiled. Under the circumstances, I thought the observation very expressive, although it recalled a certain famous story about scarlet and the sound of a trumpet, which does not seem nearly as funny now as it did at a time when we knew less about the nature of light and sound.

The Oki steamer arrived the same afternoon, but she could not approach the wharf, and I could only get a momentary glimpse of her stern through a telescope, with which I read the name, in English letters of gold: OKI-SAIGO. Before I could get any idea of her dimensions, a huge black steamer from Nagasaki glided between and moored right in the way.

I watched the loading and unloading, and listened to the song of the boy with the "red" voice until sunset, when everyone quit working. After that, I watched the Nagasaki steamer. She had made her way to our wharf as the other vessels moved out, and lay directly under the balcony. The captain and crew did not

---

[1] Author's Footnote: These words seem to have no more meaning than our "yo-heave-ho." *Yan-yui* is a cry used by all Izumo and Hōki sailors.

appear to be in a hurry about anything. They all squatted down together on the foredeck, where a feast was spread for them by lantern light. Dancing girls climbed on board and feasted with them, sang to the sound of the *samisen*, and played the game of *ken* with them. Late into the night, the feasting and fun continued; and although an alarming quantity of *saké* was consumed, there was no roughness or boisterousness. However, *saké* is the most sleep-inducing of wines, and by midnight only three of the men remained on deck. One of these had not drunk any *saké* at all, but still wanted to eat. Happily for him, there climbed on board, a night-walking *mochiya*[i] with a box of *mochi*, which are cakes of rice flour sweetened with native sugar. The hungry one bought everything and reprimanded the *mochiya* because there was no more; nevertheless, he offered to share the *mochi* with his comrades, at which point, the first to whom the offer was made answered like this:

"I, your servant, *mochi* for this world in no use have. *Saké* alone, this life in if there be, nothing beside desirable is."

"For me, your servant," spoke the other, "women this fleeting life in the supreme thing is; *mochi* or *saké* for earthly use have I none."

But, having made all the *mochi* disappear, the hungry one turned to the *mochiya* and said:

"O *Mochiya-san*, I, your servant, women or *saké* for earthly requirement have none. *Mochi* than things better this life of sorrow in existence have not!"[93]

IV

Early in the morning we were notified that the *Oki-Saigo* would leave at precisely eight o'clock, and that we had better purchase our tickets at once. The hotel servant, according to Japanese custom, relieved us of all anxiety about baggage, etc., and bought our tickets: first-class fare, eighty *sen*. After a hearty breakfast, the hotel boat came under the window to take us away.

---

[i] A roving vendor of *mochi*, who travels through the streets at night selling his wares.

Warned by experience of the discomforts of European dress on Shimane steamers, I adopted Japanese clothes and exchanged my shoes for sandals. Our boatmen sculled swiftly through the confusion of ships and junks, and as we cleared the wharf, I saw, far out in midstream, the *joki* waiting for us. *Joki* is a Japanese name for steam vessel. The word had not yet impressed me as being capable of a sinister interpretation. She seemed nearly as long as a harbor tug, although much more stout; and she so resembled the Lilliputian steamers of Lake Shinji,[1] that I felt somewhat afraid of her: even for a trip of one hundred miles. But an exterior inspection gave no clue to the mystery of her interior.

We reached her and climbed onto her starboard side through a small square hole. Immediately I found myself cramped in a heavily roofed gangway, four feet high and two feet wide, and in the middle of a frightful squeeze — passengers stifling in the effort to pull baggage three feet in diameter through the two-foot opening. It was impossible to advance or retreat, and behind me the engine room gratings were pouring wonderful heat into this infernal corridor. I had to wait with the back of my head pressed against the roof until, in some unimaginable way, all the baggage and passengers had squashed and squeezed through. Then, stepping into a doorway, I fell over a heap of

---

[1] Lake Shinji (宍道湖, Shinji-ko) is a lake in the northeast area of the Shimane Prefecture in Japan. The lake is the seventh largest in Japan, with a circumference of 48 km. It is enclosed by the Shimane peninsula (Shimane-hanto) to the north, and the Izumo and Matsué plains to the west and east.

sandals and *geta*, into the first-class cabin. It was pretty, with its polished woodwork and mirrors, surrounded by couches five inches wide; and in the center it was nearly six feet high. Such height would have been a cause for comparative happiness, except that, from various polished bars of brass that extended across the ceiling, all kinds of small baggage, including two cages of singing crickets (*chongisu*), had been carefully suspended. Furthermore, the cabin was already extremely full; with everybody, of course, on the floor, and nearly everybody lying at full length. The heat struck me as being supernatural. Now, they that go down to the sea in ships,[94] out of Izumo and such places, for the purpose of doing business in great waters, are never supposed to stand up, but to squat in the ancient, patient manner. The view from coast or lake steamers is constructed so that only this posture is possible.

Seeing an open door in the port side of the cabin, I picked my way over a tangle of bodies and limbs, among them a pair of fairy legs belong to a dancing girl, and found myself immediately in another gangway, also roofed, and choked up to the roof with baskets of squirming eels. There was no exit, so I climbed back over all the legs and tried the starboard gangway a second time. Even during that short time, it had been half-filled with baskets of unhappy chickens; but I made a reckless dash over them in spite of the frantic cackling, which hurt my soul, and succeeded in finding a way to the cabin roof. It was totally occupied by watermelons, except for one corner, where there was a big coil of rope. I put melons inside of the rope and sat on them in the sun. It was not comfortable, but I thought that there I might have some chance for my life in case of a catastrophe, and I was sure that even the gods could not give any help to those below.

During the squeeze, I had become separated from my companion, but I was afraid to make any attempt to find him. Forward, I saw the roof of the second cabin, crowded with third-class passengers squatting around a *hibachi*. To pass through them seemed impossible, and to retreat would have involved the murder of either eels or chickens; therefore, I sat on the melons.

The boat started with a stunning scream. In another moment, her funnel began to rain soot on me; for, the so-called first-class cabin was well astern. Then came small cinders mixed with the soot: the cinders were occasionally red-hot. I sat burning on the watermelons for some time, trying to imagine a way of changing my position without committing another assault on the chickens. Finally, I made a desperate try to get to leeward of the volcano. It was then that I began to learn for the first time, the peculiarities of the *joki*. What I tried to sit on turned upside down, and what I tried to hold onto, instantly gave way: always in the direction of overboard. Things seemingly clamped or rigidly braced to outward proved, on cautious examination, to be dangerously mobile; and things that, according to Western ideas ought to have been movable, were fixed like the rocks of the perpetual hills. In whatever direction a rope or stay could possibly have been stretched so as to make somebody unhappy, it was there. In the middle of these trials, the frightful little craft began to swing, the watermelons began to roll to and fro, and I came to the conclusion that this *joki* had been planned and constructed by demons.

Which I stated to my friend. He had not only rejoined me quite unexpectedly, but had brought along with him one of the ship's boys to spread an awning above us and the watermelons, to block cinders and sun.

"Oh, no!" he answered reproachfully. "She was designed and built at Hyōgo,[1] and really, she might have been made much worse."

"I beg your pardon," I interrupted. "I don't agree with you at all."

"Well, you will see for yourself," he persisted. Her hull is good steel, and her little engine is wonderful. She can make her hundred miles in five hours. She is not very comfortable, but she is very swift and strong.

"I would rather be in a *sampan*,[ii]" I protested, "if there were rough weather."

---

[i] Hyōgo refers both to Hyōgo Prefecture (兵庫県, Hyōgo-ken) located in the Kansai region on Honshū, the capital of which is Kobé, and Hyōgo (city) or Hyōgo-ku (兵庫区), one of Kobé's nine wards.

[ii] A sampan is a relatively flat bottomed Chinese wooden boat from 3.5 to 4.5 meters long. Some sampans include a small shelter on board, and may be used as a permanent habitation on inland waters. Sampans are generally used for transportation in coastal areas or rivers, and are often used as fishing boats. It is unusual for a sampan to sail far from land, as they do not have the means to survive rough weather.

"But she never goes to sea in rough weather. If it only looks as if there might possibly be some rough weather, she stays in port. Sometimes she waits a whole month. She never runs any risks."

I could not feel sure about it, but I soon forgot all discomforts, even the discomfort of sitting on watermelons, in the delight of the divine day and the magnificent view that opened wider and wider before us, as we rushed from the long bay into the Sea of Japan, following the Izumo coast. There was not a spot in the soft, blue vastness above, not one flutter on the metallic smoothness of the all-reflecting sea. If our little steamer rocked, it was no doubt because she had been overloaded. To port, the Izumo hills were flying by; a long procession of broken shapes, somber green, separating at intervals to form mysterious little bays, with fishing hamlets hiding in them. Miles away to starboard, the Hōki shore receded into the naked, white horizon, an ever-diminishing streak of warm blue, edged with a threadline of white: the gleam of a sand beach. Beyond it, in the center, a vast, shadowy pyramid loomed up into heaven: the ghostly peak of Daisen.[95]

My companion touched my arm to call my attention to a group of pine trees on the summit of a peak to port, and laughed and sang a Japanese song. I then, for the first time understood how swiftly we had been traveling; for I recognized the four famous pines of Mionoseki,[1] on the windy heights above the shrine of Koto-shiro-nushi-no-kami. There used to be five trees: one was uprooted by a storm and some Izumo poet wrote about the remaining four, the words which my friend had sung:

Seki no gohan matsu

Ippun kirya, shihon;

Ato wa kirarenu

Miyōto matsu.

Which means: "Of the five pines of Seki, one has been cut, and four remain; and of these, no one must now be cut: they are wedded pairs." In Mionoseki, beautiful little *saké* cups and *saké* bottles are sold, on which are pictures of the four pines, and above the pictures, in spidery text of gold, the verses, "*Seki no gohan matsu.*" These are for keepsakes, and there are many other curious and pretty souvenirs to buy in those pretty shops: porcelains bearing the picture of the Mionoseki temple; metal clasps for tobacco pouches representing Koto-shiro-nushi-no-kami trying to put a big *tai* fish into a basket too small for it; and funny masks of glazed earthenware, representing the laughing face of the god. For Ebisu, or Koto-shiro-nushi-no kami, is a jovial god, patron of honest labor and especially of fishermen, although less of a laughter lover than his father, the great deity of Kitzuki, about who it is said: "Whenever the happy laugh, the god rejoices."

We passed the cape, the Miho of the *Kojiki* |Cape Miho in Izumo|, and the harbor of Mionoseki opened before us, showing its island shrine of Benten in the middle, and the crescent of quaint houses with their feet in the water, and the great *torii* and granite lions of the far-famed temple. Immediately, a number of passengers rose to their feet, and turning their faces toward the *torii*, began to clap their hands together in Shintō prayer.

---

[1] Refer to *The Annotated Glimpses of Unfamiliar Japan, Volume I, Chapter X,* "At Mionoseki."

I said to my friend, "There are fifty baskets of chickens in the gangway; and yet, these people are praying to Koto-shiro-nushi-no-kami that nothing horrible may happen to this boat."

"More likely," he answered, "they are praying for good fortune, although there is a saying: 'The gods only laugh when men pray to them for wealth.' But of the great deity of Mionoseki, there is a good story told. Once there was a very lazy man who went to Mionoseki and prayed to become rich. And the same night, he saw the god in a dream; and the god laughed and took off one of his own divine sandals, and told him to examine it. And the man saw that it was made of solid brass, but had a big hole worn through its sole. Then the god said, 'You want to have money without working for it. I am a god, but I am never lazy. See! My sandals are of brass; yet, I have worked and walked so much that they are quite worn out.'"

V

The beautiful bay of Mionoseki opens between two headlands: Cape Mio (or Miho, according to the archaic spelling) and the Cape of Jizō (Jizōzaki), now most inappropriately called by the people "The Nose of Jizō" (*Jizō no hana*). This "Nose of Jizō" is one of the most dangerous points on the coast in times of surf, and the great terror of small ships returning from Oki. There is nearly always a heavy swell there, even in fair weather. Yet, as we passed the ragged promontory, I was surprised to see the water as still as glass. I felt suspicious of that noiseless sea: its soundlessness recalled the beautiful, treacherous sleep of waves and winds, which precede a tropical hurricane. However, my friend said, "It may remain like this for weeks. In the sixth month and in the beginning of the seventh, it is usually very quiet and is not likely to become dangerous before the *Bon*. But there was a little squall last week at Mionoseki, and the people said that it was caused by the anger of the god."

"Eggs?" I asked.[i]

---

[i] The God of Mionoseki hates eggs: hen's eggs. Likewise, he hates hens and chickens, and abhors the cock above all living creatures. In Mionoseki, there are no cocks, hens, chickens, or eggs. You could not buy a hen's egg in that place even for twenty times its weight in gold. No boat, junk, or steamer could be hired to convey so much as the feather of a chicken, much less an

"No, a *kudan*."

"What is a *kudan*?"

"Is it possible you have never heard of the *kudan*? The *kudan* has the face of a man and the body of a bull. Sometimes it is born of a cow, and that is a sign of things that are going to happen. The *kudan* always tells the truth. Therefore, in Japanese letters and documents, it is customary to use the phrase, *Kudan no gotoshi*, 'Like the kudan,' or 'On the truth of the *kudan*.'"[1]

"But why is the God of Mionoseki angry about the *kudan*?"

"People said it was a stuffed *kudan*. I did not see it, so I cannot tell you how it was made. There were some traveling showmen from Ōsaka at Sakai. They had a tiger, many curious animals, and the stuffed *kudan*, and they took the *Izumo Maru* for Mionoseki. As the steamer entered the port, a sudden squall came and the priests of the temple said the god was angry because impure things, bones and parts of dead animals, had been brought to the town. The show people were not even allowed to land: they had to go back to Sakai on the same steamer. As soon as they had gone away, the sky became clear again, and the wind stopped blowing: so that some people thought what the priests had said was true."

VI

Evidently, there was much more moisture in the air than I had supposed. On really clear days, Daisen can be clearly seen even from Oki; but we had scarcely passed the "Nose of Jizō" when the huge peak began to wrap itself in vapor of the same color as the horizon, and in a few minutes it vanished, like a specter might vanish. The effect of this sudden disappearance was very extraordinary; for, only the peak passed out of sight and that which had veiled it could not be in any way distinguished from horizon and sky.

---

egg, to Mionoseki. Indeed, it is even held that if you have eaten eggs in the morning, you must not dare visit Mionoseki until the following day; for, the great deity of Mionoseki is the patron of mariners and the ruler of storms; and woe to the vessel which bears to his shrine even the odor of an egg.

[1] Author's Footnote: This curious meaning is not given in Japanese-English dictionaries, where the idiom is translated merely by the phrase "as aforesaid."

Meanwhile, the *Oki-Saigo*, having reached the farthest outlying point of the coast on her route, began to race in a straight line across the Japanese Sea. The green hills of Izumo fled away and turned blue, and the spectral shores of Hōki began to melt into the horizon, like bands of clouds. Then I was obliged to confess my surprise at the speed of the horrid little steamer. She moved with scarcely any sound, so smooth was the working of her wonderful little engine; but she began to swing heavily, with deep, slow swings. To the eye, the sea looked as level as oil, but there were long, invisible swells, ocean pulses that made themselves felt beneath the surface. Hōki evaporated; the Izumo hills turned gray, and their gray steadily paled as I watched them. They grew more and more colorless, seeming to become transparent: and then they were not. Only blue sky and blue sea, welded together in the white horizon.

It was just as lonesome as if we had been a thousand leagues from land. In that weirdness, we were told some very lonesome things, by an ancient mariner who found leisure time to join us among the watermelons. He talked of the *hotoke-umi*, and the ill luck of being at sea on the sixteenth day of the seventh month. He told us that even the great steamers never went to sea during Bon: no crew would venture to take a ship out then. He related the following stories with such simple sincerity that I think he must have believed what he said:

"The first time I was very young. From Hokkaidō we had sailed, the voyage was long, and the winds turned against us. In addition, the night of the sixteenth fell, as we were working on over this very sea.

"All at once, in the darkness, we saw behind us a great junk — all white — that we had not noticed till she was quite close to us. It made us feel queer, because she seemed to have come from nowhere. She was so near us that we could hear voices; and her hull towered up high above us. She seemed to be sailing very fast, but she came no closer. We shouted to her, but we got no answer. And, while we were watching her, all of us became afraid, because she did not move like a real ship. The sea was terrible and we were lurching and plunging; but that great junk never rolled. Just at the same moment that we began to feel afraid, she vanished so quickly that we could scarcely believe we had really seen her at all.

"That as the first time. But four years ago I saw something still more strange. We were bound for Oki, in a junk, and the

227

wind again delayed us, so that we were at sea on the sixteenth day. It was in the morning, a little before midday; the sky was dark and the sea very ugly. All at once, we saw a steamer running in our track, very quickly. She got so close to us that we could hear her engines, *katakata, katakata*: but we saw no one on deck. Then she began to follow us, keeping exactly at the same distance, and whenever we tried to get out of her way, she would turn after us and keep exactly in our wake. Then we suspected what she was, but we were not sure until she vanished. She vanished like a bubble, without making the least sound. None of us could say exactly when she disappeared. None of us saw her vanish. The strangest thing was that after she was gone, we could still hear her engines working behind us: *katakata, katakata, katakata*!

"That is all I saw, but I know others, sailors like myself, who have seen more. Sometimes, many ships will follow you, though never at the same time. One will come close and vanish, then another, and then another. As long as they come behind you, you need never be afraid. But, if you see a ship of that sort running before you, against the wind, that is very bad! It means that all onboard will be drowned."

VII

The luminous blankness circling us continued to remain empty for less than an hour. Then, out of the horizon toward which we steamed, a small, gray vagueness began to grow. It lengthened fast and seemed to be a cloud. And a cloud it proved to be; but slowly, beneath it, blue, filmy shapes began to define against the whiteness, and sharpened into a chain of mountains. They grew taller and bluer, a little sierra, with one paler shape towering in the middle, three times the height of the rest and covered by clouds— Takuhizan, the sacred mountain of Oki, on the island Nishinoshima.

Takuhizan has legends, which I learned from my friend. On its summit stands an ancient shrine of the deity Gongen-sama. It is said that on the thirty-first night of the twelfth month, three ghostly fires rise from the sea, ascend to the shrine, and enter the stone lanterns which stand in front of it: there they remain burning like lamps. These lights do not arise at once, but separately from the sea, and rise to the top of the peak one by one. The people go out in boats to see the lights rise from the water, but only those whose hearts are pure can see them: those who have evil thoughts or desires look for the holy fires in vain.

In front of us, as we steamed on, the surface of the sea suddenly appeared to become speckled with strange craft that were previously invisible: light, long fishing boats with immense square sails of a beautiful yellow color. I could not help remarking to my comrade how pretty those sails were. He laughed and told me they were made of old *tatami*.[1] I examined them through a telescope and found that they were exactly what he had said: woven straw coverings of old floor mats. Nevertheless, that first tender yellow sprinkling of Oki sails over the soft blue water was a charming sight.

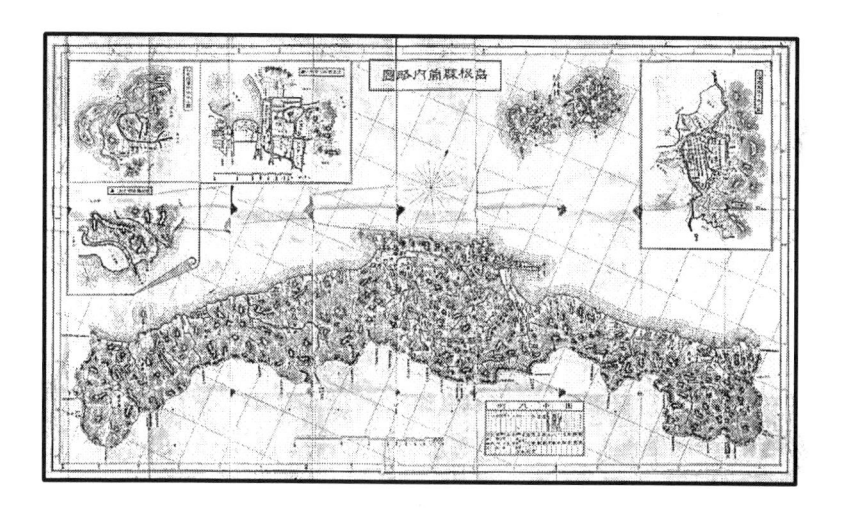

---

[1] Author's Footnote: The floor of a Japanese dwelling might be compared to an immense, but very shallow wooden tray, divided into compartments corresponding to the various rooms. These divisions are formed by grooved, polished woodwork, several inches above the level, and made for the accommodation of the *fusuma*, or sliding screens, separating room from room. The compartments are filled up, level with the partitions, with *tatami*, or mats about the thickness of light mattresses, covered with beautifully woven rice straw. The squared edges of the mats fit exactly together, and as the mats are not made for the house, but the house for the mats, all tatami are exactly the same size. The fully finished floor of each room is thus like a great, soft bed. No shoes, of course, can be worn in a Japanese house. As soon as the mats become in the least soiled, they are replaced by new ones.

They sailed by, like yellow butterflies passing, and then the sea was empty again. Gradually, a little to port, a point in the approaching line of blue cliffs shaped itself and changed color, dull-green above reddish-gray below. It sharpened into a huge rock, with a dark patch on its face, but the rest of the land remained blue. The dark patch blackened as we came nearer: a great gap full of shadow. Then, the blue cliffs beyond also turned green, and their bases reddish-gray. We passed to the right of the huge rock, which proved to be a detached and uninhabited island, Hakashima. In another moment, we were steaming into the archipelago of Oki, between the lofty islands of Chiburishima and Nakashima.

VIII

The first impression was almost uncanny. Rising sheer from the water on either side, the tall, green, silent hills stretched away before us, changing tint through the summer vapor to form a fantastic vista of blue cliffs, peaks, and promontories. There was not one sign of human life. Above their pale bases of naked rock, the mountains sloped up beneath a somber wildness of dwarf vegetation. There was absolutely no sound, except the sound of the steamer's tiny engine: *poum-poum, poum! Poum-poum, poum*! like the faint tapping of a geisha's drum. This savage silence continued for miles: only the absence of tall timber gave evidence that human feet had ever walked those peaked hills. But all at once, to the left, in a mountain wrinkle, a little gray hamlet appeared, and the steamer screamed and stopped, while the hills repeated the scream seven times.

This settlement was Chiburimura, of Chiburishima (Nakashima being the island to starboard): evidently nothing more than a fishing station. First a wharf of uncemented stone, rising from the cove like a wall; then great trees through which one caught sight of a *torii* in front of some Shintō shrine, and of a dozen houses, climbing the hollow hill one behind the other, roof beyond roof. Above these were some terraced patches of tilled ground in the middle of desolation: that as all. The boat halted to deliver mail, and then continued on.

But then, contrary to expectation, the scenery became more beautiful. The shores on either side at once receded and rose: we were traversing an island sea bounded by three lofty islands. At first, the way in front of us had seemed barred by vapory hills, but these, drawing nearer, turned green and suddenly opened magnificent chasms between them on both sides: mountain gates revealing league-long, wondrous vistas of peaks, cliffs and capes of a hundred blues, ranging away from velvety indigo into far tones of exquisite and spectral delicacy. A tinted haze made all remoteness dreamy, and veiled the rugged nudities of rock with illusions of color.

The beauty of the scenery of Western and Central Japan is not like the beauty of scenery in other lands. It has a peculiar character of its own. Occasionally the foreigner may find memories of former travel suddenly stirred to life by some view of a mountain road, or stretch of coast seen through a fog or spray. However, this illusion of resemblance vanishes as swiftly as it comes: details immediately sharpen into strangeness, and you become aware that the remembrance was evoked by form only, never by color. Colors indeed there are which delight the eye, but not the colors of mountain greenery, not colors of the land. Cultivated plains, expanses of growing rice, may offer some approach to the warmth of green, but the whole general tone of this nature is dusky; the vast forests are somber; the tints of grasses are harsh or dull. Fiery greens, such as burn in tropical scenery do not exist, and the blossom bursts take on a more exquisite radiance by contrast with the heavy tones of the vegetation out of which they flame. Outside of parks, gardens, and cultivated fields, there is a unique absence of warmth and tenderness in the tints of green; and nowhere need you hope to find any such richness of green like that which makes the loveliness of an English lawn.

Ama divers, the Oki Islands, by Hokusai, c. 1835.

    Yet, these Asian landscapes possess charms of extraordinary color — phantom color, delicate, elfish, indescribable — created by the wonderful atmosphere. Vapors enchant the distances, bathing peaks in bewitchments of a hundred tones of blue and gray, transforming naked cliffs to amethyst; stretching spectral gauzes across the topazine morning; magnifying the splendor of noon by hiding the horizon; filling the evening with the smoke of gold, bronzing the waters, banding the sundown with ghostly purple and green of mother of pearl. The old Japanese artists who made those marvelous *ehon*, those picture books which have now become so rare, tried to fix the sensation of these enchantments in color; and they were successful in their backgrounds to an almost miraculous degree; for which very reason, some of their foregrounds have been a puzzle to foreigners unacquainted with certain features of Japanese agriculture. You will see blazing saffron-yellow fields, faint purple plains, crimson and snow-white trees, in those old picture books; and perhaps you will exclaim, "How absurd!" But if you knew Japan, you would cry out, "How deliciously real"; for, you would know those fields of burning yellow are fields of flowering rape, the purple expanses are fields of blossoming *miyako*, and the snow-white or crimson trees are not fanciful, but represent faithfully, certain phenomena of blooming peculiar to the plum trees and cherry trees of the country. But these chromatic extravaganzas can be witnessed only during very brief periods of particular seasons. Throughout the greater part of the year, the foreground of an inland landscape is apt to be dull in the matter of color.

It is the mists that make the magic of the backgrounds; yet, even without them, there is a strange, wild, dark beauty in Japanese landscapes: a beauty not easily defined in words. The secret of it must be sought in the extraordinary lines of the mountains, in the strangely abrupt crumpling and jagging of the ranges. No two masses closely resemble each other; every one has an eccentricity of its own. Where the chains reach to any considerable height, softly swelling lines are rare: the general characteristic is abruptness, and the charm is the charm of irregularity.

Without doubt, this weird nature first inspired the Japanese with their unique sense of the value of irregularity in decoration; taught them that single secret of composition which distinguishes their art from all other art, and of which Professor Chamberlain has said, it is their special mission to teach the West.[1] Certainly, whoever has once learned to feel the beauty and significance of the old Japanese decorative art, can subsequently find little pleasure in the corresponding art of the West. What he has really learned is that nature's greatest charm is irregularity. Perhaps something of no small value might be written on the question: whether the highest charm of human life and work is not also irregularity.

---

[1] Author's Footnote: See the article on art in his *Things Japanese*.

Ichikawa Danjuro IX as Mongaku Shonin from the series
"One Hundred Roles of Ichikawa Danjuro," by Toyohara Kunichika, 1898.

IX

From Chiburimura we made steam west for the port of Urago, which is on the island of *Nishinoshima*. As we approached it, Takuhizan came into imposing view. Far away, it had seemed like a soft, beautiful shape; but as its blue tones evaporated, its image became rough and even grim: an enormous, jagged bulk, all robed in somber green, through which, as through tatters, there poked here and there, naked rock of the wildest shapes. I remember one fragment as it caught the slanting sun on the irregularities of its summit and seemed an immense gray skull. At the base of this mountain, facing the shore of Nakashima, rises a pyramid-like mass of rock, covered with scraggy undergrowth, and several hundred feet in height: Mongakuzan. On its desolate summit stands a little shrine.

Takuhizan signifies "The Fire Burning Mountain," a name due perhaps either to the legend of its ghostly fires, or to some ancient memory of its volcanic period. Mongakuzan means "The Mountain of Mongaku": Mongaku Shōnin, the great monk.[96] It is said that Mongaku Shōnin fled to Oki and that he lived alone on the top of that mountain for many years, doing penance for his deadly sin. Whether he really ever visited Oki I am not able to say; there are traditions which state the contrary, but the peak has borne his name for hundreds of years.

Now this is the story of Mongaku Shōnin:

Many centuries ago, in the city of Kyōto, there was a captain of the garrison whose name was Endō Moritō. He saw and loved the wife of a noble samurai, and when she refused to listen to his desires, he vowed that he would destroy her family unless she consented to the plan that he submitted to her. The plan was that, on a certain night, she should allow him to enter her house and to kill her husband, after which, she was to become his wife.

She, pretending to consent, devised a noble strategy to save her honor; for, after having persuaded her husband to absent himself from the city, she wrote a letter to Endō, bidding him come on a certain night to the house. On that night, she dressed herself in her husband's robes and made her hair like the hair of a man, and laid down in her husband's place, pretending to sleep.

Endō came in the dead of night with his sword drawn, and with one blow cut off the head of the sleeper, seized it by the hair, lifted it up, and saw that it was the head of the woman he loved and wronged.

Then a great remorse came over him, and hurrying to a neighboring temple, he confessed his sin, did penance, cut off his hair, and became a monk, taking the name of Mongaku. In later years, he attained great holiness, so that people still pray to him, and his memory is venerated throughout the land.

Now at Asakusa, in Tōkyō, on one of the curious little streets which lead to the great temple of Kwannon the Merciful, there are always wonderful images to be seen; figures that seem alive although made only of wood; figures illustrating the ancient legends of Japan. There, you may see Endō standing: in his right hand the reeking sword and in his left, the head of a beautiful woman. The face of the woman you may soon forget because it is only beautiful, but you will not forget the face of Endō, because it is naked hell.

X

Urago is a strange little town, perhaps quite as large as Mionoseki, and built, like Mionoseki, on a narrow ledge at the base of a steep semicircle of hills. But it is much more primitive and colorless than Mionoseki, and its houses are still more closely cramped between cliffs and water, so that its streets, or rather alleys, are no wider than gangways. As we drop anchor, my attention was suddenly riveted by a strange spectacle: a white wilderness of long, fluttering, vague shapes, in a cemetery on the steep hillside, rising in terraces, high above the roofs of the town. The cemetery was full of gray *haka* and images of deities, and over every *haka*, there was a curious white paper banner fastened to a thin bamboo pole. Through a glass, one could see that these banners were inscribed with Buddhist texts: *Namu-myō-hō-renge-kyō*"; "*Namu Amida Butsu*"; "*Namu Daiji Dai-hi Kwan-ze-on Bosatsu*"; and other words. Upon asking, I learned that it was an Urago custom to place these banners every year above the graves during one whole month preceding the Festival of the Dead, together with various other ornamental and symbolic things.

The water was full of naked swimmers, who shouted laughing welcomes; and a host of light, swift boats, sculled by naked fishermen, darted out to look for passengers and freight. It was my first chance to observe the physique of Oki islanders, and I was much impressed by the vigorous appearance of both men and boys. The adults seemed to me of a taller, more powerful type than the men of the Izumo coast. Not a few of those brown backs and shoulders displayed, in the motion of sculling, what is comparatively rare in Japan, even among men picked for heavy labor: a magnificent development of muscles.

Because the steamer stopped for an hour at Urago, we had time to dine ashore in the main hotel. It was a very clean and pretty hotel, and the fare infinitely superior to that of the hotel at Sakai. Yet, the price charged was only seven *sen*, and the old landlord refused to accept the entire *chadai* gift[1] offered him, retaining less than half and putting back the rest, with gentle force, into the sleeve of my *yukata*.

XI

From Urago, we proceeded to Hishi-ura, which is on Naka-noshima, and the scenery grew more wonderful as we steamed between the islands. The channel was just wide enough to create

---

[1] A *chadai* is a kind tip or gratuity, more commonly referred to as "tea money."

the illusion of a grand river, flowing with the stillness of vast depth between mountains of a hundred forms. The long, lovely vision was everywhere walled in by peaks, blue through the sea haze; and on either side, the ruddy gray cliffs, sharply rising up from the depths, sharply mirrored their least harsh features in the water, with never a distortion, like on a sheet of steel. The horizon did not reappear until we reached Hishi-ura and even then, it was only visible between two high headlands, as if seen through the mouth of a river.

Hishi-ura is far prettier than Urago, but it is much less populous, and has the appearance of an agricultural town rather than a fishing village. It bends around a bay formed by low hills, which slope back gradually toward the mountainous interior, and which display a considerable extent of cultivation. The buildings are somewhat scattered, and in many cases, isolated by gardens, while those facing the water are quite handsome modern constructions. Urago boasts the best hotel in all of Oki and it has two new temples: one a Buddhist temple of the Zen sect, one a Shintō temple of the Izumo Taisha faith: each the gift of a single person. A rich widow, the owner of the hotel, built the Buddhist temple and the wealthiest of the merchants contributed the other: one of the handsomest *miya* for its size that I ever saw.

XII

Dōgo, the main island of the Oki archipelago, sometimes itself called Oki, lies at a distance of eight miles northeast of the Dōzen group, beyond a stretch of very dangerous sea. We made for it immediately after leaving Urago, passing to the open sea through a narrow and fantastic straight between Nakanoshima and Nishinoshima, where the cliffs take the form of enormous fortifications: bastions and ramparts rising by tiers. Three colossal rocks, anciently forming a single mass which would seem to have been divided by some tremendous shock, rise from deep water near the mouth of the channel, like shattered towers. The last promontory of Nishinoshima, which we pass to port, a huge red, naked rock, turns to the horizon a point so strangely shaped that it has been called by a name signifying "The Hat of the Shintō Priest."

As we glide out into the swell of the sea, other extraordinary shapes appear, rising from great depths. Komori, "The Bat," a ragged silhouette against the horizon, has a hole worn through it, which glares like an eye. Farther out, two masses, curved and pointed, and almost joined at the top, bear a grotesque resemblance to the uplifted pincers of a crab. There is also visible, a small dark mass that, until approached closely, seems like the figure of a man sculling a boat. Beyond these are two islands: Matsushima, uninhabited and inaccessible, where there is always a swell to beware of; and Omorishima, even loftier, which rises from the ocean in enormous, reddish precipices. There seemed to be some grim force in those sinister masses; some occult power which made our steamer reel and shiver as she passed them, but I saw a marvelous effect of color under those formidable cliffs of Omorishima. They were lit by a slanting sun, and where the glow of the bright rock fell on the water, each black-blue ripple flashed bronze: I thought of a sea of metallic, violet ink.

From Dōzen, the cliffs of Dōgo can clearly be seen when the weather is not foul. They are streaked here and there, with chalky white, which breaks through their blue, even in time of haze. Above them, a large mass is visible, a *point de repére*[1] for the mariners of Hōki: the mountain of Daimanji. Dōgo, indeed, is one great cluster of mountains.

Its cliffs rapidly turned green and we followed them eastward for perhaps half an hour. Then unexpectedly, they opened widely, revealing a superb bay, widening far into the land, surrounded by hills, and full of ships. Beyond a confusion of masts, there crept into view a long, gray line of house fronts, at the base of a crescent of cliffs, the city of Saigo, and in a little while we touched a wharf of stone. There I said farewell, for a month, to the *Oki-Saigo*.

XIII

Saigo was a great surprise. Instead of the big fishing village I had expected to see, I found a city much larger and handsomer, and in all respects, more modernized than Sakai; a city of long streets full of good shops; a city with excellent public buildings; a city of which the entire appearance indicated commercial prosperity. Most of the buildings were roomy, two-story houses of merchants and everything had a bright, new look. The unpainted

---

[1] French for "a point of reference."

woodwork of the houses had not yet darkened into gray and the blue tints of the tiling were still fresh. I learned that this was because the town had been recently rebuilt after a conflagration, and rebuilt on a larger and handsomer plan.

Still, Saigo seems larger than it really is. There are about one thousand houses, which number in any part of Western Japan means a population of at least five thousand, but must also mean considerably more in Saigo. These form three long streets, Nishimachi, Nakamachi, and Higashimachi (names respectively signifying the Western, Middle, and Eastern Streets), bisected by numerous cross streets and alleys. What makes the place seem disproportionately large is the strange way the streets twist about, following the irregularities of the shore, and even doubling on themselves, so as to create, from certain points of view, an impression of depth, which does not exist. For, Saigo is peculiarly, although admirably, situated. It fringes both banks of a river, the Yabigawa, near its mouth, and likewise extends around a large point within the splendid bay, besides stretching itself out on various tongues of land. But though smaller than it looks, to walk through its serpentine streets is a good afternoon's work.

Besides being divided by the Yabigawa, the town is intersected by various waterways, crossed by a number of bridges. On the hills behind it stand several large buildings, including a public school, with accommodations for three hundred students; a pretty Buddhist temple (quite new), the gift of a rich citizen; a prison; and a hospital, which deserves its reputation for being, for its size, the most handsome Japanese building not only in Oki, but in all Shimane-ken; and there are several small, but very pretty, gardens.

As for the harbor, you can count more than three hundred ships riding there on a summer's day. Grumblers, especially of the type who still use wooden anchors, complain of the depth, but the men-of-war do not.

XIV

Never, in any part of Western Japan, have I been more comfortable than in Saigo. My friend and I were the only guests at the hotel which had been recommended to us. The broad and lofty rooms of the upper floor which we occupied overlooked the main street on one side, and on the other, commanded a beautiful mountain landscape beyond the mouth of the Yabigawa, which flowed by our garden. The sea breeze never failed, by day or night, and made those pretty fans, which it is the Japanese custom to present to guests during the hot season, unnecessary. The food was astonishingly good and curiously varied. I was told that I could order *seyō-ryōri* (Western cooking) if I wished: beefsteak with fried potatoes, roast chicken, and so forth. I did not take advantage of the offer, because I make it a rule, while traveling, to escape trouble by keeping to a purely Japanese diet; but it was a great surprise to be offered, in Saigo, what is almost impossible to obtain in any other Japanese town of five thousand inhabitants. From a romantic point of view however, this discovery was a disappointment. Having made my way into the most primitive region of all Japan, I had imagined myself far beyond the range of all modernizing influences; and the suggestion of beefsteak with fried potatoes was disillusioning. Nor was I entirely consoled by the subsequent discovery that there were no newspapers or telegraphs.

There is one serious obstacle to the enjoyment of these comforts: an omnipresent, frightful, heavy, all-penetrating smell: the smell of decomposing fish used as fertilizer. Tons and tons of cuttlefish entrails are used on the fields beyond the Yabigawa, and the never sleeping sea wind blows the stench into every building. They keep incense burning in vain in most of the houses during the warm season. After having been in the city for three or four consecutive days, you become better able to endure this odor; but if you should leave town for even a few hours, you will be astonished, on returning, to discover how much your nose had been numbed by habit and refreshed by absence.

XV

On the morning of the day after my arrival at Saigo, a young physician called to see me, and requested me to dine with him at his house. He explained very frankly that, as I was the first foreigner who had ever stopped in Saigo, it would bring much pleasure both to his family and to himself to have a good chance to see me; however, the natural courtesy of the man overcame any hesitation that I might have felt to gratify the curiosity of strangers. I was not only treated delightfully at his beautiful home, but actually sent away with presents; most of which I attempted, in vain, to decline. In one matter, however, I remained obstinate, even at the risk of offending: the gift of a wonderful specimen of *bateiseki* (a substance which I shall speak of later). This I persisted in refusing to take, knowing it to be not only very costly, but very rare. My host at last yielded; but afterwards, secretly sent two smaller specimens to the hotel, which Japanese etiquette made it impossible to return. Before leaving Saigo, I experienced many other unexpected kindnesses from the same gentleman.

Not long after, one of the teachers of the Saigo public school paid me a visit. He had heard of my interest in Oki, and brought with him two fine maps of the islands made by him, a little book about Saigo, and as a gift, a collection of Oki butterflies and insects that he had made. It is only in Japan that one is likely to meet with these wonderful exhibitions of pure goodness on the part of perfect strangers.

A third visitor, who had called to see my friend, performed an action equally characteristic, but which also caused me not a little pain. We squatted down to smoke together. He drew from his *obi* a remarkably beautiful tobacco pouch and pipe case, containing a little silver pipe, which he began to smoke. The pipe case was made of a sort of black coral, curiously carved, and attached to the *tabako-iré*, or pouch, by a heavy cord of three colors of braided silk, passed through a ball of transparent agate.

Seeing me admire it, he suddenly drew a knife from his sleeve, and before I could stop him, severed the pipe case from the pouch and presented it to me. I felt almost as if he had cut one of his own nerves apart when he cut that wonderful cord; and nevertheless, once this had been done, to refuse the gift would have been rude in the extreme. I made him accept a present in return; but after that experience, I was careful never again, while in Oki, to admire anything in the presence of its owner.

XVI

Every province in Japan has its own peculiar dialect, and that of Oki, as might be expected in a country so isolated, is particularly distinct. In Saigo, however, the Izumo dialect is largely used. The townsfolk in their manners and customs, closely resemble Izumo country folk; indeed, there are many Izumo people among them, most of the large businesses being in the hands of strangers. The women did not impress me as being as attractive as those of Izumo: I saw several very pretty girls, but these proved to be strangers.

However, it is only in the country that one can properly study the physical characteristics of a population. Those of the Oki islanders may best be noted at the fishing villages, many of which I visited. Everywhere I saw fine, strong men and vigorous women, and it struck me that the extraordinary availability and cheapness of nutritious food had quite as much to do with this robustness as climate and constant exercise. Indeed, it is so easy to live in Oki that men of other coasts, who find existence difficult, emigrate to Oki if they can get a chance to work there, even at less pay.

An interesting spectacle to me were the vast processions of fishing boats which always, weather permitting, began to shoot out to sea a couple of hours before sundown. The surprising swiftness with which those light craft were propelled by their sinewy scullers, many of whom were women, spoke of a skill acquired only through the patient experience of generations. Another matter that amazed me was the number of boats. One night I was able to count three hundred and five torch fires, each one signifying a crew; and I knew that from almost any of the forty-five coast villages, I might see the same spectacle at the same time. The main part of the population, in fact, spends its summer nights at sea. It is also a revelation to travel from Izumo to Hamada by night on a swift steamer during the fishing season. The horizon, for a hundred miles, is lit with torch fires: the toil of a whole coast is revealed in that vast illumination.

Although the human population appears to have gained rather than lost vigor on this barren soil, the horses and cattle of the country seem to have degenerated. They are remarkably diminutive. I saw cows not much bigger than Izumo calves, with calves about the size of goats. The horses, or rather ponies, belong to a special breed of which Oki is rather proud: very small, but hardy. I was told that there were larger horses, but I saw none, and could not learn whether they were imported. It seemed a curious thing to me, when I saw Oki ponies for the first time, that Sasaki Takatsuna's[97] battle steed, not less famous in Japanese stories than the horse Kyrat in the ballads of Kurroglou [the Bandit-Minstrel of northern Persia], is declared by the islanders to have been a native of Oki. They have a legend that it once swam from Oki to Mionoseki.

XVII

Almost every district and town in Japan has its *meibutsu* or its *kembutsu*. The *meibutsu* of any place are its special products, whether natural or artificial. The *kembutsu* of a town or district are its sights, its places worth visiting for any reason: religious, traditional, historical, or pleasurable. Temples and gardens, remarkable trees, and curious rocks are *kembutsu*. So also are any locations from which beautiful scenery may be looked at, or locations where one can enjoy such charming spectacles as the blooming of cherry trees in spring, the flickering of fireflies in summer nights, the blushing of maple leaves in autumn, or even that long, snaky motion of moonlight on the water to which Chinese poets have given the delightful name of *Kinryō*, "the Golden Dragon."

The great *meibutsu* of Oki is the same as that of Hinomisaki, — dried cuttlefish; a type of food much in demand both in China and Japan. The cuttlefish of Oki, Hinomisaki, and Mionoseki are all called *ika* (a kind of squid); but those caught at Mionoseki are white, and average fifteen inches in length, while those of Oki and Hinomisaki rarely exceed twelve inches and have a reddish tinge. The fisheries of Mionoseki and Hinomisaki are scarcely known, but the fisheries of Oki are famed, not only throughout Japan, but also in Korea and China. It is only through the tilling of the sea that the islands have become prosperous and capable of supporting thirty thousand souls on a coast of which only a very small portion can be cultivated at all. Enormous quantities of cuttlefish are shipped to the mainland; but I have been told that the Chinese are the best customers of Oki for this product. Should the supply ever fail, the result would be disastrous beyond belief, but at present it seems inexhaustible, though the fishing has been going on for thousands of years. Hundreds of tons of cuttlefish are caught, cured, and prepared for exportation, month after month; and many hundreds of acres are fertilized with the entrails and other refuse.

A police officer told me several strange facts about this fishery. On the northeastern coast of Saigo, it is not uncommon for one fisherman to capture upwards of two thousand cuttlefish in a single night. Boats have been burst by the weight of a few hauls, and caution has to be observed in loading. Besides the squid, however, this coast swarms with another variety of mollusk that also furnishes a food staple: the formidable *tako*, or true octopus. *Tako* weighing fifteen *kwan* each, or nearly one hundred and twenty five pounds, are sometimes caught near the fishing settlement of Nakamura. I was surprised to learn that there was no record of any person having been injured by these monstrous creatures.

Another *meibutsu* of Oki is much less known than it deserves to be: the beautiful, jet-black stone called *bateiseki*, or "horse hoof stone."[i] It is found only in Dōgo, and never in large masses. It is about as heavy as flint, and chips like flint, but the shine which it takes is like that of agate. There are no veins or specks in it and the intense black color never varies. Artistic objects made of *bateiseki* including ink stones, wine cups, little boxes, small *dai*, or stands for vases or statues; even jewelry, the material being worked in the same manner as the beautiful agates of Yumachi in Izumo. These articles are comparatively costly, even in the place they are made.

There is an old legend about the origin of the *bateiseki*. It owes is name to some fancied resemblance to a horse's hoof, either in color or in the semicircular marks often seen on the stone in its natural state, and caused by its tendency to split in curved lines. But the story goes that the *bateiseki* was formed by the touch of the hoofs of a sacred steed, the wonderful mare of the great Minamoto warrior, Sasaki Takatsuna. She had a foal, which fell into a deep lake in Dōgo, and was drowned. She plunged into the lake herself, but could not find her foal, being deceived by the reflection of her own head in the water. For a long time she sought and mourned in vain; but even the hard rocks felt for her, and where her hoofs touched them, beneath the water, they became changed into *bateiseki*.[ii]

Scarcely less beautiful than *bateiseki*, and equally black, is another *Oki-meibutsu*, a sort of coral-like product called *umi-matsu* or "sea pine." Pipe cases, brush stands, and other small articles are manufactured from it, and these, when polished, seem to be covered with black lacquer. Objects of *umi-matsu* are rare and dear.

Mother-of-pearl wares, however, are very cheap in Oki and form another variety of *meibutsu*. The shells of the *awabi*[iii] or "sea ear," which reaches a surprising size in these western waters, are

---

[i] Author's Footnote: It seems to be a black obsidian.
[ii] Author's Footnote: There are several other versions of this legend. In one, it is the mare, and not the foal, which was drowned.
[iii] *Awabi* is the Japanese name for abalone.

converted by skillful polishing and cutting, into wonderful dishes, bowls, cups, and other articles, over whose surfaces the play of iridescence is like a flickering of fire of a hundred colors.

XVIII

Emperor Go-Toba.

According to a little book published in Matsué, the *kembutsu* of Oki-no-kuni are divided among three of the four principal islands: only Chiburishima has nothing of special interest. For many generations, the attractions of Dōgo have been the shrine of Agonashi Jizō, at Tsubamezato; the waterfall (Dangyō-taki) at Yuenimura; the mighty cedar tree (*sugi*) in front of the shrine of Tama-Wakusajinja at Shimomura, and the small lake called Sai-no-ike, where the *bateiseki* is said to be found. Nakanoshima possesses the tomb of the exiled Emperor Go-Toba, at Ama-mura, and the residence of the ancient Chōja, Shikekurō,[98] where he occasionally lived, and where relics of him are kept even to this day. Nishinoshima possess, at Beppu, a shrine in memory of the exiled Emperor Go-Daigo, and on the summit of Takuhizan, that shrine of Gongen-sama, from where a wonderful view of the whole archipelago is said to be had on cloudless days.

Though Chiburishima has no *kembutsu*, her poor little village of Chiburi, the same Chiburimura at which the Oki steamer always touches on her way to Saigo, is the scene of perhaps the most interesting of all the traditions of the archipelago.

Five hundred and sixty years ago, the exiled Emperor Go-Daigo managed to escape from the observation of his guards and to flee from Nishinoshima to Chiburi. The brown sailors of that little hamlet offered to serve him, even with their lives if need be. They were loading their boats with "dried fish," without doubt the same dried cuttlefish which their descendants still carry to Izumo and to Hōki. The Emperor promised to remember them should they succeed in landing him either in Hōki or in Izumo; and they put him in a boat.

But when they had sailed only a little way, they saw the pursuing vessels. Then they told the Emperor to lie down, and they piled the dried fish high on top of him. The pursuers came on board and searched the boat, but they did not even think of touching the strong-smelling cuttlefish. When the men of Chiburi were questioned, they invented a story and gave the enemies of the Emperor a false clue to follow. And so, by means of the cuttlefish, the good Emperor managed to escape from banishment.

XIX

I found there were various difficulties in the way of becoming acquainted with some of the *kembutsu*. There are no actual roads in all Oki, only mountain paths; consequently, there are no *jinrikisha*, with the exception of one, specially imported by the leading physician of Saigo, and available for use only in the streets. There are not even any *kago*,⁹⁹ or palanquins, except one for the use of the same physician. The paths are terribly rough according to the testimony of the strong peasants themselves, and the distances, particularly in the hottest period of the year, are disheartening. Ponies can be hired; but my experiences of a similar wild country in western Izumo persuaded me that neither pleasure nor profit was to be gained by a long and painful ride over pine-covered hills, through slippery gullies, and along stream beds, merely to look at a waterfall. I abandoned the idea of visiting Dangyō-taki, but decided, if possible, to see Agonashi-Jizō.

I first heard in Matsué of Agonashi-Jizō, while suffering from one of those toothaches in which the pain seems to be several hundred miles in depth: one of those toothaches which disturb your ideas of space and time. A friend who sympathized said, "People who have a toothache pray to Agonashi-Jizō. Agonashi-Jizō is in Oki, but Izumo people pray to him. When cured, they go to Lake Shinji, to the river, to the sea, or to any running stream, and drop twelve pears (*nashi*), one for each of the twelve months, into the water. They believe the currents will carry all these to Oki across the sea.

"Now, Agonashi-Jizō means 'Jizō who has no jaw;' for, it is said that in one of his former lives, Jizō had such a toothache in his lower jaw that he tore off his jaw, threw it away, and died. And he became a *bosatsu*.¹⁰⁰ The people of Oki made a statue of him, without a jaw, and all who suffer toothache pray to that Jizō of Oki."

This story interested me; for, more than once, I had felt a strong desire to do like Agonashi-Jizō, though lacking the necessary courage and indifference to earthy consequences. Moreover, the tradition suggested such a humane and profound comprehension of toothache, and so great a sympathy with its victims, that I felt myself somewhat consoled.

Nevertheless, I did not go to see Agonashi-Jizō, because I found out there was no longer any Agonashi-Jizō to see. The news was brought one evening by some friends, *shizoku*ⁱ of Matsué, who had settled in Oki: a young police officer and his

---

ⁱ *Shizoku* means residents or citizens.

wife. They had walked across the island to see us, starting before daylight and crossing no less than thirty-two streams on their way. The wife, only nineteen, quite slender and pretty, did not appear tired by that long, rough journey.

What we learned about the famous Jizō was this: The name Agonashi-Jizō was only a poor corruption of the true name, Agonaoshi-Jizō or "Jizō the Healer of Jaws." The little temple in which the statue stood had been burned, and the statue along with it, except a fragment of the lower part of the figure, now piously preserved by some old peasant woman. It was impossible to rebuild the temple because the disestablishment of Buddhism had entirely destroyed the resources of that faith in Oki; however, the peasants of Tsubamezato had built a little Shintō *miya* on the site of the temple, with a *torii* in front of it, and people still prayed there to Agonashi-Jizō.

This last curious fact reminded me of the little *torii* I had seen built in front of the images of Jizō in the Cave of the Children's Ghosts. Shintō, in these remote districts of the west, now appropriates the popular deities of Buddhism, just as old Buddhism used to absorb the deities of Shintō in other parts of Japan.

XX

I went to the Sai-no-ike and to Tama-Wakasu-jinja, because these two *kembutsu* can be reached by boat. The Sai-no-ike, however, much disappointed me. It can only be visited in very calm weather because the way to it lies along a frightfully dangerous coast: nearly all sheer cliffs. But the sea is beautifully clear, and the eye can distinguish forms at a great depth below the surface. After following the cliffs for about an hour, the boat reaches a sort of cove, where the beach is entirely composed of small, round boulders. They form a long ridge, the outer edge of which is always in motion; rolling to and from with a crash like a volley of musketry at the rush and ebb of every wave. To climb over this ridge of moving stone balls is quite disagreeable; however, after that, one has only about twenty yards to walk before the Sai-no-ike appears, surrounded on three sides by wooded hills. It is little more than a large freshwater pool, perhaps fifty yards wide: not in any way wonderful. You can see no rocks under the surface, only mud and pebbles. That any part of it was ever deep enough to drown a foal is hard to believe. I wanted to swim across to the farther side, to check the depth, but the mere proposal scandalized the boatmen. The pool was sacred to the gods and was guarded by invisible monsters; to enter it was impious and dangerous. I felt obliged to respect the local ideas on the subject, and contented myself with inquiring where the *bateiseki* was found. They pointed to the hill on the western side of the water; however, this did not tally with the legend. I could find no trace of any human labor on that savage hillside and there was certainly no habitation within miles of the place: it was the very abomination of desolation.[1]

It is never wise for the traveler in Japan to expect much on the strength of the reputation of *kembutsu*. The interest attached to the vast majority of *kembutsu* altogether depends on the exercise of imagination and the ability to exercise such imagination again depends on one's acquaintance with the history and mythology of the country. Knolls, rocks, and stumps of trees have been for hundreds of years objects of reverence for the peasants, solely for the reason of local traditions relating to them. Broken iron kettles, bronze mirrors covered with green patina, rusty pieces of sword blades, and fragments of red earthenware have drawn generations of pilgrims to the shrines in which they are preserved. At various small temples that I visited, the temple treasures consisted of trays full of small stones. The first time I saw those little stones, I thought that the priests had been studying geology or mineralogy; each stone being labeled in Japanese characters. On examination, the stones proved to be absolutely worthless in of themselves, even as specimens of neighboring rocks; but the stories which the priests or acolytes could tell about each and every stone were more than interesting. The stones, in fact, served as crude beads for the recital of a litany of Buddhist legends.

After the experience of the Sai-no-ike, I had little reason to expect to see anything extraordinary at Shimonishimura; but this time I was agreeably mistaken. Shimonishimura is a pretty fishing village within an hour's row from Saigo. The boat follows a wild but beautiful coast, passing one unique, truncated hill, Oshiroyama, on which a strong castle stood in ancient times. There is now only a small Shintō shrine there, surrounded by pines. From the hamlet of Shimonishimura to the Temple of

---

[1] Author's Footnote: There are two ponds not far from each other. The one I visited was called *O-ike*, or "The Male Pond," and the other, *Me-ike*, or "The Female Pond."

Tama-Wakasu-jinja is a walk of twenty minutes over very rough paths between rice fields and vegetable gardens. The location of the temple, surrounded by its sacred grove, in the heart of a landscape framed by mountain ranges of many colors, is charmingly impressive. The building seems to have once been a Buddhist temple: it is now the largest Shintō structure in Oki. In front of its gate stands the famous cedar, not remarkable in height, but wonderful for girth. Two yards above the soil, its circumference is forty-five feet. It has given its name to the holy place; the Oki peasantry scarcely ever speak of Tama-Wakasu-jinja, but only of "Ō-*sugi*," the Great Cedar.

Tradition says that a Buddhist nun planted this tree more than eight hundred years ago. It is also alleged that whoever eats with chopsticks made from the wood of that tree will never have a toothache, and will live to become exceedingly old.[1]

XXI

The shrine dedicated to the spirit of Emperor Go-Daigo is in Nishinoshima, at Beppu; a picturesque fishing village composed of one long street of thatched cottages fringing a bay, at the foot of a half-moon of hills. The simplicity of manners and the honest, healthy poverty of the place are quite wonderful, even for Oki. There is a kind of inn for visitors at which hot water is served instead of tea, and dried beans instead of *kwashi*, and millet instead of rice. The absence of tea, however, is much more significant than that of rice, but the people of Beppu do not suffer from a lack for proper nourishment, as their robust appearance bears witness. There are plenty of vegetables, all raised in tiny gardens, which the women and children till during the absence of the boats; and there is an abundance of fish. There is no Buddhist temple, but there is an *ujigami*.

The shrine of the Emperor is at the top of a hill called Kurokizan, at one end of the bay. The hill is covered with tall pines and the path is very steep; so that I thought it would be prudent to put on straw sandals, in which one never slips. I

---

[1] Author's Footnote: Speaking of the supposed power of certain trees to cure toothaches, I may mention a curious superstition about the *yanagi*, or willow tree. Sufferers from toothache sometimes stick needles into the tree, believing that the pain caused to the tree spirit will force it to exercise its power to cure. I could not, however, find any record of this practice in Oki.

found the shrine to be a small wooden *miya*, scarcely three feet high, and black with age. There were remains of other *miya*, much older, lying in some bushes nearby. Two large stones, uncut and without inscriptions of any sort, have been placed in front of the shrine. I looked into it and saw a crumbling metal mirror, dingy paper *gohei* attached to splints of bamboo, two little *o-mikidokkuri*, or Shintō *saké* bottles of red earthenware, and one *rin*. Indeed, there was nothing else to see except certain delightful glimpses of coast and peak, visible in the bursts of warm blue light which penetrated the consecrated shadows, between the trunks of the great pines.

Only this humble shrine commemorates the good emperor's life among the peasants of Oki. But there is now being erected, at the little village of Go-sen-goku-mura, near Yonago in Tottori, by voluntary subscription, a quite handsome monument of stone to the memory of his daughter, the princess Hinako-Nai-Shinnō, who died there while attempting to follow her august parent into exile. Near the place of her rest stands a famous chestnut tree, of which this story is told:

While the Emperor's daughter was ill, she asked for chestnuts, and some were given to her; although she took only one, bit it a little, and threw it away. It found root and became a grand tree. All the chestnuts of that tree bear marks like the marks of little teeth; for in Japanese legend, even the trees are loyal and strive to show their loyalty in all sorts of tender, dumb ways. That tree is called Hagata-guri-no-ki, which means "The Tree of the Tooth-marked Chestnuts."

XXII

Long before visiting Oki, I had heard that such a crime as theft was unknown in the little archipelago; that it had never been found necessary to lock things up there; and that, whenever weather permitted, the people slept with their houses open to the four winds of heaven.

After careful investigation, I found these surprising statements, to a great extent, true. In the Dōzen group, at least, there are no thieves and practically no crime. Ten policemen are sufficient to control the entirety of both Dōzen and Dōgo, with their population of thirty thousand, one hundred and ninety-six souls. Each policeman has a number of villages under his inspection, which he visits on regular days. His absence for any length of time from one of those never seems to be taken advantage of. His work is mostly confined to the enforcement of health regulations and to the writing of reports. It is very seldom that he finds it necessary to make an arrest, for the people scarcely ever quarrel.

"Taira Tadamori and the 'Oil Thief,'" by Utagawa Kuniyoshi (1852).

Only on the island of Dōgo are there petty thefts, and only in that part of Oki do people take any precautions against thieves. In the past there was no prison and thefts were never heard of. The people Dōgo still claim that the few persons arrested on their island for such offenses are not natives of Oki, but strangers from the mainland. What appears to be quite true is that, theft was unknown in Oki before the port of Saigo received its present importance. The whole trade of Western Japan has been increased by the rapid growth of steam travel to other parts of the empire; and the port of Saigo appears to have gained commercially, but to have lost morally, by the new conditions.

Yet, offenses against the law are still surprisingly few, even in Saigo. Saigo has a prison and there were people in it during my stay in the city; however, the inmates had been convicted only of such misdemeanors as gambling (which is strictly prohibited in every form by Japanese law), or the violation of lesser ordinances. When a serious offense is committed, the offender is not punished in Oki, but is sent to the great prison at Matsué, in Izumo.

The Dōzen islands however, perfectly maintain their ancient reputation for irreproachable honesty. There have been no thieves on those three islands within the memory of man; and there are no serious quarrels, no fighting, nothing to make life miserable for anybody. As wild and bleak as the land is, all can manage to live comfortably enough; food is cheap and plentiful, and manners and customs have retained their primitive simplicity.

XXIII

To foreign eyes, the defenses of even an Izumo dwelling against thieves seem ludicrous. *Chevaux de fries*[1] of bamboo stakes are used extensively in eastern cities of the empire, but in Izumo, these are not often seen and do not protect the really weak points of the buildings on which they are placed. As for outside walls and fences, they serve only as screens or for ornamental boundaries: anyone can climb over them. Anyone can also cut

---

[1] *Chevaux de frise* (French) is the plural form of *cheval de frise*, a Medieval defensive obstacle consisting of a portable frame (sometimes just a simple log) covered with many long iron or wooden spikes or even actual spears.

his way into an ordinary Japanese house with a pocketknife. The *amado* are thin sliding screens of soft wood, easy to break with a single blow; and in most Izumo homes, there is not a lock which could resist one vigorous pull. Indeed, the Japanese themselves are so aware of the futility of their wooden panels against burglars, that all who can afford it, build *kura*[1]: small, heavy, fireproof and (for Japan) almost burglar-proof structures with very thick earthen walls, a narrow, ponderous door fastened with a gigantic padlock, and one very small, iron-barred window, high up near the roof. The *kura* are whitewashed and look very neat. They cannot be used for dwellings, however, as they are moldy and dark, and serve only as storehouses for valuables. It is not easy to rob a *kura*.

But there is no trouble in "burglariously" entering an Izumo house unless there happen to be good watchdogs on the premises. The robber knows the only difficulties in the way of his enterprise are such that he is likely to encounter after having made entrance. In view of these difficulties, he usually carries a sword.

Nevertheless, he does not wish to find himself in any predicament requiring the use of a sword; and to avoid such an unpleasant possibility, he has recourse to magic.

He looks around the premises for a *tarai*, a kind of tub. If he finds one, he performs a nameless operation in a certain part of the yard, and covers the spot with the tub, turned upside down. He believes that if he can do this, that a magical sleep will fall on all the residents of the house, and that he will thus be able to carry away whatever he pleases, without being heard or seen.

But every Izumo household knows the countercharm. Each evening, before retiring, the careful wife sees that a *hōchō*, or kitchen knife, is laid on the kitchen floor and covered with a *kanadarai*, or brass washbasin, on the upturned bottom of which is placed a single straw sandal, of the noiseless kind called *zōri*, also turned upside down. She believes that this little bit of witchcraft will not only nullify the robber's spell, but also render it impossible for him, even if he succeeded in entering the house without being seen or heard, to carry anything away. Unless very

---

[1] *Kura* (倉 or 蔵) are traditional Japanese storehouses; commonly durable buildings built from timber, stone, or clay, used to safely store valuable commodities. Kura in rural communities are normally of simpler construction and are used for storing grain or rice.

tired, she will also see that the *tarai* is brought into the house before the *amadō* are closed for the night.

"Catching a Thief" - kabuki, by Kunisada Utagawa (1858).

If, through omission of these (precautions that the good wife might avow), or despite them, the house is robbed while the family is asleep, a search is made early in the morning for the footprints of the burglar and a *moxa*[i] is set burning on each footprint. By doing this, it is hoped or believed that the burglar's feet will be made so sore that he cannot run far, and that the police will easily overtake him.

---

[i] Author's Footnote: *Moxa*, a corruption of the native name of the mugwort plant: *moe-kusa*, or *mogusa*, "the burning weed." Small cones of its fiber are used for cauterizing, according to the old Chinese system of medicine: the little cones being placed on the patient's skin, lit, and left to smolder until wholly consumed. The result is a profound scar. The *moxa* is not only used therapeutically, but also as a punishment for very naughty children. See the interesting note on this subject in Professor Chamberlain's *Things Japanese*.

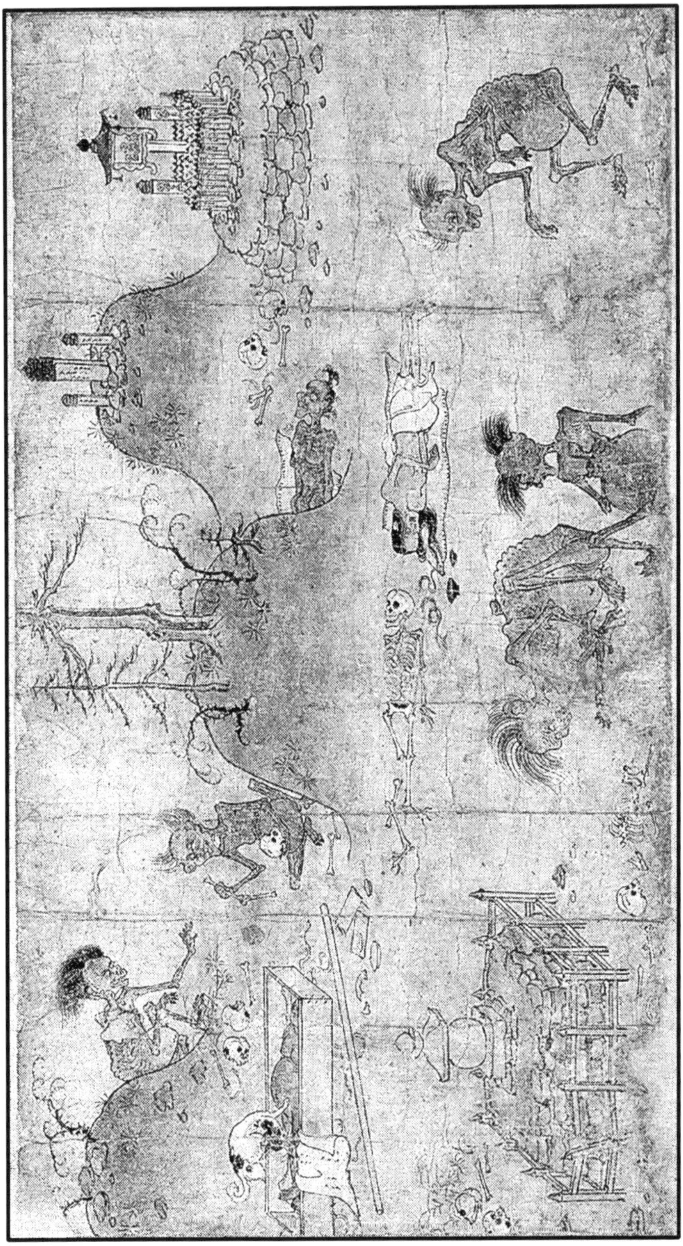

XXIV

It was in Oki that I first heard of an extraordinary superstition about the cause of *okori* (*ague*, or intermittent fever), mild forms of which prevail in certain districts at certain seasons. I have since learned that this quaint belief is an old one in Izumo and in many parts of the San-indō. It is a curious example of the manner in which Buddhism has been used to explain all mysteries.

Okori is said to be caused by the *gaki-botoke*, or hungry ghosts. Strictly speaking, the *gaki-botoke* are the *pretas* of Indian Buddhism; spirits condemned to travel in the Gakidō, the sphere of the penance of perpetual hunger and thirst.[1] In Japanese Buddhism, the name *gaki*, is also given to those souls who have no one among the living to remember them, and to prepare the customary offerings of food and tea for them.

These spirits suffer and try to obtain warmth and nutrition by entering into the bodies of the living. The person into whom a *gaki* enters, at first feels intense cold and shivers, because the

---
[1] A form of what would, in Western religions, be called Purgatory.

gaki is cold. But, a feeling of intense heat follows the chill, as the *gaki* becomes warm. Having warmed itself and absorbed some nourishment at the expense of its unwilling host, the *gaki* goes away, and the fever ceases for a time. But at exactly the same hour on another day, the *gaki* will return and the victim must shiver and burn until the haunter has become warm and has satisfied its hunger again. Some *gaki* visit their patients every day, others every alternate day or even less often. In brief, the periods of any form of intermittent fever are explained by the presence of the *gaki*, and the intervals between the episodes by its absence.

XXV

Of the world of *hotoke* (which becomes *botoke* in such compound words as *nure-botake*,[1] *gaki-botoke*), there is something curious to say.

Hotoke signifies a Buddha. *Hotoke* also signifies the Souls of the Dead, since faith holds that these, after a worthy life, either enter on the way to Buddhahood, or become Buddhas.

Hotoke, used as a synonym, has also come to mean a corpse; hence the verb *hotoke-zukuri*, "to look ghastly," or to have the resemblance of one long dead.

Hotoke-san is the name of the "Image of a Face" seen in the pupil of the eye, *Hotoke-san*, "The Lord Buddha." Not the supreme of the Hokkekyō, but the lesser Buddha who dwells in each of us: the spirit.[ii]

Sang Rosetti: "I looked and saw your heart in the shadow of your eyes."[iii] Exactly the opposite is the Asian thought. A Japanese lover would have said, "I looked and saw my own Buddha in the shadow of your eyes."

---

[i] Author's Footnote: *Nure-botak*i, "a wet god." This term is applied to the statue of a deity left exposed to the open air.

[ii] Author's Footnote: According to popular legend, in each eye of the child of a god or dragon, two Buddhas are visible. The statement, in some of the Japanese ballads, that the hero sung of had four buddhas in his eyes, is equivalent to the declaration that each of his eyes had a double pupil.

[iii] From "Three Shadows," by Dante Gabriel Rossetti.

What is the psychological theory connected with so unique a belief?[1] I think it might be this: the soul, within its own body, always remains invisible; yet, may reflect itself in the eyes of another, as in the mirror of a necromancer. Vainly you gaze into the eyes of the beloved to see her soul and you see there only your own soul's shadow, almost transparent: beyond is only mystery, reaching to the infinite.

Is this not true? The ego, as Schopenhauer wonderfully said, is the dark spot in consciousness, just as the point where the nerve of sight enters the eye is blind. We see ourselves only in others, and through others, we dimly guess what we are. In the deepest love of another being, do we not indeed love ourselves? What are our personalities and individualities but countless vibrations in the Universal Being? Are we not all one in the unknowable ultimate? One with the inconceivable past? One with the everlasting future?

XXVI

In Oki, as in Izumo, the public school is slowly but surely destroying many of the old superstitions. Even the fishermen of the new generation laugh at things in which their fathers believed. I was rather surprised to receive from an intelligent young sailor, who I had questioned through an interpreter, about the ghostly fire of Takuhizan, this scornful answer, "Oh, we used to believe those things when we were savages; but we are civilized now!"

Nevertheless, he was somewhat ahead of his time. In the village to which he belonged, I discovered that the superstition about foxes prevails to a degree scarcely equaled in any part of Izumo. The history of the village was quite curious. From time immemorial, it had been reputed to be a settlement of *kitsune-mochi*;[ii] in other words, all its inhabitants were commonly believed, and perhaps believed themselves, to be the owners of goblin foxes. Being all *kitsune-mochi*, they could eat and drink together, and marry, and give in marriage among themselves without affliction. They were dreaded with a ghostly fear by the

---

[i] Author's Footnote: The idea of the Atman will perhaps occur to many readers. [The word *Atman* (Sanskrit) refers to "self," however the terms "soul" and "ego" are sometimes substituted.]
[ii] See Volume I, Chapter XV.

neighboring peasants, who obeyed their demands both in reasonable matters and unreasonable. They were exceptionally prosperous, but some twenty years ago, an Izumo stranger settled among them. He was energetic, intelligent, and possessed some money. He bought land, made various shrewd investments, and in a surprisingly short time became the wealthiest citizen in the place. He built a very pretty Shintō temple and presented it to the community. There was only one obstacle in the way of his becoming a really popular person: he was not a *kitsune-mochi*, and he had even said that he hated foxes. This thing alone threatened to cause discord in the *mura* (village), especially because he married his children to strangers, and thus began, in the middle of the *kitsune-mochi*, to establish a sort of anti-fox colony

"Fox Fire at Oji," by Hiroshige Ando (1857).

Therefore, for a long time, the fox backers have been trying to force their extra goblins on him. Shadows glide about the gate of his home on moonless nights, muttering, "*Kaere! Kyō kara kokoye: kuruda!*" (Be off now! From now on, it is here that you must live: go!") Then, the upper *shoji* are violently pushed apart, and the voice of the enraged house owner is heard, "*Koko wa kiraida! Modori!*" (Detestable is that which you do! Leave!) And the shadows flee.[1]

XXVII

Because there were no cuttlefish at Hishi-ura, and no horrid smells, I enjoyed myself there more than I did anywhere else in Oki. But, in any event, Hishi-ura would have interested me more than Saigo. The life of the pretty little town is peculiarly old-fashioned and the ancient domestic industries, which the introduction of machinery has almost destroyed in Izumo and elsewhere, still exist in Hishi-ura. It was pleasant to watch the rosy girls weaving kimono of cotton and kimono of silk, relieving each other whenever the work became fatiguing. All this quaint, gentle life is open to inspection, and I loved to watch it. I had other pleasures also: the bay is a delightful place for swimming, and there were always boats ready to take me to anyplace of interest along the coast. At night, the sea breeze made the rooms which I occupied wonderfully cool; and from the balcony, I could watch the bay waves breaking in slow, cold fire on the steps of the wharves: a beautiful phosphorescence. I could hear Oki mothers singing their babies to sleep with one of the oldest lullabies in the world:

> *Nenneko,*
> *O-yama no*
> *Usagi no ko,*
> *Naze mata*
> *O-mimi ga*
> *Nagai e yara?*
> *Okkasan no*
> *O-naka ni*
> *Oru toku ni,*

---

[1] Author's Footnote: In 1892, a Japanese newspaper, published in Tōkyō, stated on the authority of a physician who had visited Shimane, that the people of Oki believe in ghostly dogs instead of ghostly foxes. This is a mistake caused by the literal rendering of a term often used in Shimane, especially in Iwami; namly, *inu-gami-mochi*. It is only a euphemism for *kitsune-mochi*; the *inu-gami* is only the *hito-kitsune*, which is supposed to make itself visible in various animal forms.

Biwa no ha,
Sasa no ha,
Tobeta sona;
Sore de
O-mimi ga
Nagai e sona.[1]

The melody was uniquely sweet and wistful, quite different from that to which the same words are sung in Izumo and in other parts of Japan.

One morning, I hired a boat to take me to Beppu, and was at the point of leaving the hotel for the day, when the elderly landlady, touching my arm, exclaimed, "Wait a little while. It is not good to cross a funeral." I looked around the corner and saw the procession coming along the shore. It was a Shintō funeral: a child's funeral. Young boys came first carrying Shintō emblems, little white flags and branches of the sacred *sakaki*; and behind the coffin walked the mother, a young peasant, crying very loud and wiping her eyes with the long sleeves of her coarse blue dress. Then the old woman at my side murmured, "She sorrows, but she is very young. Perhaps it will come back to her." For, she is a pious Buddhist, my good old landlady, and without doubt supposed the mother's belief to be like her own, although the funeral was conducted according to the Shintō rite.

XXVIII

In Buddhism there are certain weirdly beautiful consolations unknown to Western religion. The young mother who loses her first child may at least pray that it will come back to her out of the night of death; not only in dreams, but through reincarnation. Praying, she writes the first *kanji* of her lost darling's name on the inside of the hand of the little corpse.

Months pass and again she becomes a mother. Eagerly she examines the flower-soft hand of the infant. And look! The very

---

[1] Author's Footnote: Which words signify something like this: "*Sleep, baby, sleep! Why are the honorable ears of the child of the hare of the honorable mountain so long? It is because when he dwelt within her honored womb, his mama ate the leaves of the loquat, the leaves of the bamboo grass. This is why his honorable ears are so long.*"

same *kanji* is there; a rosy birthmark on the tender palm. The returned soul looks at her through the eyes of the newly born, with the gaze of other days.

XXIX

While on the subject of death, I will speak of a primitive but touching custom which exists both in Oki and Izumo: that of calling the name of the dead immediately after death. For, it is thought that the call may be heard by the fading soul, which might sometimes be thus induced to return. Therefore, when a mother dies, the children should first call her, and of all the children, first the youngest (for she loved that one the most); and then the husband and all those who loved the dead, in turn, cry to her.

It is also the custom to call loudly the name of one who faints or becomes senseless for any reason. There are curious beliefs underlying this custom.

It is said that of those who swoon especially from pain or grief, many approach very near to death: these always have the same experience. "You feel," said one to me in answer to my question about the belief: "as if you were suddenly somewhere else, and quite happy, only tired. And you know that you want to go to a Buddhist temple that is quite far away. At last you reach the gate of the temple courtyard and you see the temple inside, and it is wonderfully large and beautiful. And you pass the gate and enter the courtyard to go to the temple, but suddenly you hear voices of friends far behind you, calling your name very, very earnestly. So, you turn back, and all at once you come to yourself again. At least it is so if your heart cares to live. But one who is really tired of living will not listen to the voices, and walks on into the temple. What happens there no man knows, for they who enter that temple never return to their friends.

"That is why people call loudly into the ear of one who swoons.

"Now, it is said that all who die, before going to the Meido, make one pilgrimage to the great temple of Zenkōji,[101] which is in the country of Shinano, in Nagano-ken. And they say that whenever the priest of that temple preaches, he sees the souls gather there in the *hondō*[1] to hear him, all with white wrappings about their heads. So, Zenkōji might be the temple which is seen by those who swoon. But I do not know."

XXX

I went by boat from Hishi-ura to Amamura, in Naka-noshima, to visit the tomb of the exiled Emperor Go-Toba. The scenery along the way was beautiful, and of a softer outline than I had seen on my first trip through the archipelago. Small rocks, rising from the water, were covered with seagulls and cormorants, which hardly took notice of the boat, even when we came almost within an oar's length. This fearlessness of wild creatures is one of the most charming impressions of travel in these remote parts of Japan; still unvisited by tourists with shotguns. The early European and American hunters in Japan seem to have found no difficulty, and felt no compunction, in exterminating what they considered "game" over entire districts: destroying life merely for the wanton pleasure of destruction. Their example is being imitated now by "Young Japan," and the destruction of bird life is poorly controlled by game laws. Happily, the government does interfere sometimes to stop particular forms of the hunting vice. Some brutes, who had observed the habits of swallows to make their nests in Japanese houses, last year offered to purchase some thousands of swallow skins at a tempting price. The effect of the advertisement was cruel enough; but the police were promptly notified to stop the murdering, which they did. About the same time, in one of the Yokohama papers, there appeared a letter from some holy person, announcing, as a triumph of Christian sentiment, that a "converted" fisherman had been persuaded by foreign missionaries to kill a turtle, which his Buddhist comrades had vainly begged him to spare.

Amamura, a very small village, lies in a narrow plain of rice fields extending from the sea to a range of low hills. From the landing place to the village is about a quarter mile. The narrow path leading to it passes around the base of a small hill, covered with pines, on the outskirts of the village. There is quite a handsome Shintō shrine on the hill; small but admirably constructed, and approached by stone steps and a paved walk. There

---

[1] The term *hondō* refers to the main hall of the temple.

are the usual lions and lamps of stone, and the ordinary simple offerings of paper and women's hair in front of the shrine. However, I saw among the votive objects, a number of curious things which I had never seen in Izumo: tiny, miniature buckets, well-buckets, complete with rope and pole, neatly made out of bamboo. The boatman said that farmers bring these to the shrine when praying for rain. The deity was called Suwa-Dai-Myōjin.

It was at the neighboring village, of which Suwa-Dai-Myōjin seems to be the *ujigami*,[i] that the Emperor Go-Toba is said to have dwelt, in the house of the Chōja Shikekurō.[ii] The Shikekurō home remains, and still belongs to the Chōja's descendants, but they have become very poor. I asked permission to see the cups from which the exiled emperor drank, and other relics of his stay said to be preserved by the family, but due to illness in the house, I could not be received. So, I only had a glimpse of the garden where there is a celebrated pond: a *kembutsu*.

The pond is called Shikekurō's Pond or *Shikekurō no ike*. It is said that for seven hundred years the frogs of that pond have never been heard to croak; for, Emperor Go-Toba, having one night been kept awake by the croaking of the frogs in the pond, arose, went out, and commanded them saying, "Be silent!" From then on they have remained silent through the centuries, even to this day.

Near the pond there was, in that time, a great pine tree, of which the rustling on windy nights disturbed the emperor's rest. He spoke to the pine tree, saying to it, "Be still!" After that, the tree was never head to rustle, even during storms. However, that tree has ceased to exist. Nothing remains of it but a few fragments of its wood and bark, which are carefully preserved as relics by the aged residents of Oki. Such a fragment was shown to me in the *toko* of the guestroom of the house of a physician in Saigo: the same gentleman whose kindness I have related elsewhere.

The tomb of the Emperor lies on the slope of a low hill, about ten minutes' walk from the village. It is far less imposing than the poorest of the tombs of the Matsudaira at Matsué, in the grand old courtyards of Gesshōji; however, it was perhaps

---

[i] An *ujigami* is the resident Shintō deity or patron god.
[ii] The term "*chōja*" (長者) is a class of relatively rich people at the village level. Often *chōja* are leaders or headmen of the village.

the best which the poor little country of Oki could provide. This is not, however, the original place of the tomb, which was moved by imperial order in the sixth year of Meiji to its present site. A high fence, or rather stockade of heavy wooden posts, painted black, encloses a piece of ground perhaps one hundred and fifty feet long by about fifty feet wide, and graded into three levels or low terraces. Pines shade all the space within. The tomb is placed in the center of the last, and highest of the little terraces: a single, large slab of gray rock laid horizontally. A narrow, paved walk leads from the gate to the tomb, ascending each terrace by three or four steps. A little inside this gateway, which is opened to visitors only once a year, there is a *torii* facing the tomb, and in front of the highest terrace there are a pair of stone lamps. All this is severely simple but effective in a certain, touching way. The country stillness is only broken by the singing of the *semi* and the ringing sound of that strange little insect the *suzumushi*, whose call sounds just like the tinkling of the tiny bells which are shaken by the *miko* in her sacred dance.

XXXI

I remained almost eight days at Hishi-ura on the occasion of my second visit there, but only three at Urago. Urago proved a less pleasant place to stay in; not because it smells were any stronger than those of Saigo, but for other reasons that will presently appear.

More than one foreign man-of-war has stopped at Saigo, and English and Russian naval officers have been seen on the streets. They were tall, fair-haired, stalwart men; and the people of Oki still imagine that all foreigners from the West have the same stature and complexion. I was the first foreigner who ever stayed even one night in the town, and I stayed there two weeks; however, being small, dark, and dressed like a Japanese, I stirred up little attention among the common people: it seemed to them that I was only a curious-looking Japanese from some remote part of the empire. At Hishi-ura, the same impression prevailed for a time; and even after the fact of my being a foreigner had become generally know, the population caused me no annoyance whatever: they had already become accustomed to seeing me walking about the streets or swimming across the bay. But it was quite different at Urago.

The first time I landed there I had managed to escape notice, being in Japanese costume and wearing a very large Izumo-style hat, which partly concealed my face. After I left for Saigo, the people must have found out that a foreigner, the very first ever seen in Dōzen, had actually been there in Urago without their knowledge; for, my second visit made a sensation such as I had never caused anywhere else, except at Kaka-ura.

I barely had time to enter the hotel before the street became entirely blocked by an amazing crowd wanting to see. The hotel was unfortunately situated on a corner, so that it was soon besieged on two sides. I was shown to a large back room on the second floor, where I had no sooner squatted down on my mat, then the people began to come upstairs, quite noiselessly, all leaving their sandals at the foot of the stairs. They were too polite to enter the room; but four or five would put their heads through the doorway at a time, bow, smile, look, and leave to make way for those who filled the stairway behind them. It was no easy matter for the servant to bring me my dinner. Meanwhile, not only had the upper rooms of the houses across the way become packed with gawkers, but all the rooftops, north, east and south, which commanded a view of my apartment, had become occupied by a swarm of men and boys. Numbers of boys had also climbed (I never could imagine how) on the narrow eaves over the galleries below my windows; and all the openings of my room, on three sides, were full of faces. Then tiles gave way and boys fell, but nobody appeared to be hurt. The strangest fact was that during the performance of these extraordinary gymnastics, there was a silence of death. Had I not seen the throng, I might have supposed there was not a soul in the street.

The landlord began to scold; but, finding scolding of no use, he summoned a policeman. The policeman begged me to excuse the people, who had never seen a foreigner before, and asked me if I wished him to clear the street. He could have done that by merely lifting his little finger; but as the scene amused me, I begged him not to order the people away, but only to tell the boys not to climb on the awnings, some of which they had already damaged. He told them most efficiently, speaking in a very low voice. During all the rest of the time I was in Urago, no one dared to go near the awnings. A Japanese policeman never speaks more than once about anything new, and always speaks to the purpose.

The public curiosity, however, lasted, unabated, for three days, and would have lasted longer if I had not fled from Urago. Whenever I went out, I drew the population after me, with a pattering of *geta*, like the sound of surf moving stones. Yet, except for that peculiar sound, there was silence. No words were spoken. Whether this was because the entire mental faculty was so strained by the intensity of the desire to see that speech became impossible, I am not able to decide. There was no roughness in all that curiosity; there was never anything approaching rudeness, except in the matter of climbing to my room without permission; and that was done so gently that I did not want the intruders scolded. Nevertheless, three days of such experience proved trying. Despite the heat, I had to close the doors and windows at night to prevent myself from being watched while asleep. I had no anxiety about my possessions at all: thefts are never committed on the island; but that perpetual, silent crowding around me at last became more than embarrassing. It was innocent but it was weird. It made me feel like a ghost: a new arrival in the Meido, surrounded by shapes without voices.

XXXII

There is very little privacy of any sort in Japanese life. Indeed, among the people, what we term privacy in the West, does not exist. There are only walls of paper dividing the lives of men; there are only sliding screens instead of doors; there are neither locks nor bolts to be used by day; and whenever weather permits, the fronts and perhaps even the sides of the house, are literally removed: its interior opened wide to the air, light, and public gaze. Not even the rich man closes his front gate by day. Within a hotel, or even a common house, nobody knocks before entering your room: there is nothing to knock on except a *shōji* or *fusuma*, which cannot be knocked on without being broken. In this world of paper walls and sunshine, nobody is afraid or ashamed of their fellow men or fellow women. Whatever is done is done after a fashion, in public. Your personal habits, your idiosyncrasies (if you have any), your foibles, your likes and dislikes, your loves or your hates, must be known to everybody. Neither vices nor virtues can be hidden; there is absolutely nowhere to hide them, and this condition has lasted from the most ancient times. There has never been, for the common millions at least, even the idea of living unobserved.

Life can be comfortably and happily lived in Japan only on the condition that all matters relating to it are open to the inspection of the community; which implies exceptional moral conditions, such as do not exist in the West. It is perfectly comprehensible only to those who know by experience, the extraordinary charm of Japanese character, the infinite goodness of the common people, their instinctive politeness, and the absence among them of any tendencies to indulge in criticism, ridicule, irony, or sarcasm. No one endeavors to expand his own individuality by criticizing his colleague; no one tries to make himself appear a superior being: any such attempt would be vain in a community where the weaknesses of each are known to all; where nothing can be concealed or disguised, and where affectation could only be regarded as a mild form of insanity.

XXXIII

Some of the old samurai of Matsué are living in the Oki islands. When the great military caste was disestablished, a few shrewd men decided to try their fortunes in the little archipelago, where customs remained old-fashioned and land was cheap. Several succeeded; probably because of the wholehearted honesty and simplicity of manners in the islands; for, samurai have seldom elsewhere been able to succeed in businesses of any sort when forced to compete with experienced traders. Others failed, but were able to adopt various, humble occupations which gave them the means to live.

I learned that besides these aged survivors of the feudal period, there were in Oki, several children of once noble families, youths and maidens of illustrious extraction, bravely facing the new conditions of life in this remotest and poorest region of the empire. Daughters of men to whom the population of a town once bowed down to were learning the bitter toil of the rice fields. Youths, who might in another era have aspired to offices of state, had become the trusted servants of Oki *heimin*.[i] Others, again, had entered the police,[ii] and rightly regarded themselves as fortunate.

---

[i] Literally, the common people of Japan, when compared to the privileged samurai in former times.

[ii] Author's Footnote: The Japanese police are nearly all of the samurai class, now called *shizoku*. I think this force may be condidered the most perfect

No doubt that change of civilization forced on Japan by Christian bayonets, for the holy motive of gain, may yet save the empire from perils greater than those of the late social disintegration; but it was cruelly sudden. To imagine the consequence of depriving the English landed gentry of their revenues would not enable one to realize exactly what a similar deprivation meant to the Japanese samurai; for, the old warrior caste knew only the arts of courtesy and the arts of war.

Hearing of these things, I could not help thinking about a strange pageant at the last great Izumo festival of Rakuzan-jinja.

XXXIV

The hamlet of Rakuzan, known only for its bright yellow pottery and its little Shintō shrine, sleeps at the foot of a wooded hill about one *ri* from Matsué, beyond a wilderness of rice fields. The deity of Rakuzan-jinja is Naomasa, grandson of Tokugawa Ieyasu, and father of the *daimyō* of Matsué.

Some of the Matsudaira slumber in Buddhist ground, guarded by tortoises and lions of stone, in marvelous old courtyards of Gesshōji; but Naomasa, the founder of their long line, is enshrined at Rakuzan, and the Izumo peasants still clap their hands in prayer before his *miya*, and implore his love and protection.

Formerly, on each annual *matsuri*, or festival, of Rakuzan-jinja, it was customary to carry the *miya* of Naomasa-san from the village shrine to Matsué Castle. It was borne in solemn procession to those strange old family temples in the heart of the fortress grounds: Go-jō-nai-Inari-Daimyōjin and Kusunoki-Matsuhira-Inari-Daimyōjin, whose decaying courtyards, populated with lions and foxes of stone, are shadowed by enormous trees. After certain Shintō rites had been performed at both temples, the *miya* was carried back in procession to Rakuzan. This annual ceremony was called the *miyuki* or *togyō* — the "August Going," or "August Visit" of the ancestor to the ancestral home.

But the revolution has changed all things. The *daimyō* passed away; the castles fell to ruin; the samurai class was abolished and

---

police in the world; but whether it will retain those magnificent qualities which at present distinguish it, after the lapse of another generation, is doubtful. It is now the samurai blood that shows.

dispossessed; and the *miya* of Lord Naomasa made no "August Visit" to the home of the Matsudaira for more than thirty years.

It came to pass a short time ago, that certain old men of Matsué decided to once more revive the ancient customs of the Rakuzan *matsuri*, and there was a *miyuki*.

The *miya* of Lord Naomasa was placed on a barge, draped and decorated, and thus conveyed by river and canal to the eastern end of the old Matsubara Road, along whose pine-shaded way, the *daimyō* formerly departed to Edo on their annual visit, or returned. All those who rowed the barge were aged samurai who had, in their youth, rowed the barge of Matsudaira-Dewa-no-kami, the last lord of Izumo. They wore their ancient feudal costumes and they tried to sing their ancient boat song, *O-funa-uta*. But more than a generation had passed since the last time they had sung it. Some of them had lost their teeth, so that they could not pronounce the words well, and all, being old, lost their breath easily in the exertion of wielding the oars. Nevertheless, they rowed the barge to the appointed place.

From there, the shrine was carried to a spot by the side of the Matsubara Road, where had stood an august teahouse, *O-chaya*, at which the *daimyō*, returning from the Shōgun's capital, used to rest and receive their faithful retainers, who always came in procession to meet them. No teahouse stands there now; but, in keeping with the old custom, the shrine and its escort waited at the place, among the wildflowers and pines. Then, a strange sight was seen.

For, there came to meet the ghost of the great lord, a long procession of shapes that also seemed like ghosts: shapes risen out of the dust of cemeteries. Warriors in crested helmets and masks of iron, wearing breastplates of steel and two swords; and spearmen wearing *queues*[i] and retainers in *kamishimo*;[ii] and bearers of *hasami-bako*.[iii] Yet, these were not ghosts, but aged samurai of Matsué, who had carried arms in the service of the last of the *daimyō*. Among them appeared his surviving ministers, the venerable *karō*;[iv] and these, as the procession turned toward the city, took their old places of honor and marched valiantly in front of the shrine, although bent with years.

How that pageant might have impressed other strangers I do not know. For me, knowing something of the history of each of those aged men, the scene had a significance apart from its interest as a feudal procession. Today, each and every one of those old samurai are unspeakably poor. Their beautiful homes vanished long ago; their gardens have been turned into rice fields; their household treasures were cruelly bargained for and bought for almost nothing by curio dealers, to be resold at high prices to foreigners at the open ports. Yet, what they could have obtained considerable money for, and what had ceased to be of any service to them, they clung to fondly, through all their poverty and humiliation. Never could they be induced to part

---

[i] Magé, the common hairstyle of samurai during the Edo jidai.

[ii] A *kamishimo* (上下 or 裃), was the highly stylized ceremonial uniform or set of clothing worn by samurai and courtiers during the Edo period, which included a formal kimono, *hakama*, and a sleeveless jacket with exaggerated shoulders called a *kataginu*.

[iii] Highly decorated, chests, typically made in sets of two, used when travelling for carrying items, such as those to eat a picnic, to important papers and documents. A lacquered pole, inserted through raised metal loops on either side of each chest, would be carried on the shoulders of a servant.

[iv] *Karō* (家老, "house elder") were top-ranking samurai officials and advisors in service to the *daimyō*.

with their armor and their swords, even pressured by dire need, under the new and harder conditions of life.

The riverbanks, streets, balconies, and blue-tiled roofs were crowded with people; yet, there was a great quiet as the procession passed. Young people gazed in hushed wonder, feeling the rare value of that chance to look on what will belong, in the future, only to picture books and to the quaint Japanese stage. Old men wept silently, remembering their youth.

Well spoke the ancient thinker:

Everything is only for a day, both that which remembers, and that which is remembered.

XXXV

Once more, homeward bound, I sat on the cabin roof of the *Oki-Saigo* — this time happily unencumbered by watermelons — and tried to explain to myself the feeling of melancholy with which I watched those wild island coasts vanishing over the pale sea, into the white horizon. No doubt, it was inspired partly by the recollection of kindnesses received from many whom I shall never meet again; partly also, by my familiarity with the ancient soil itself, and remembrance of shapes and places: the long blue visions down channels between islands — the faint gray fishing hamlets hiding in stony bays — the elfish oddity of narrow streets in little primitive towns — the forms and tints of peak and valley made lovable by daily intimacy — the crooked, broken paths of shadowed shrines of gods with long, mysterious names — the butterfly-drifting of yellow sails out of the glow of an unknown horizon. Yet, I think it was due much more to a particular sensation in which every memory was steeped and toned, as a landscape is steeped in the light and toned in the colors of the morning: the sensation of conditions closer to nature's heart, and farther from the monstrous machine-world of Western life, than any into which I have ever entered north of the tropics. Then it seemed to me, that I loved Oki — in spite of the cuttlefish — chiefly because of having felt there, as nowhere else in Japan, the full joy of escape from the far-reaching influences of high-pressure civilization — the delight of knowing one's self, in Dōzen at least, well beyond the range of everything artificial in human existence.

"Tshushima," by Hiroshige Ando (1856).

XXIV

Of Souls

KINJURŌ, THE ANCIENT GARDENER, whose head shines like an ivory ball, sat himself down for a moment on the edge of the *ita-no-ma*[i] outside my study, to smoke his pipe at the *hibachi* always left there for him. As he smoked, he found reason to reprimand the boy who assists him. I did not know exactly what the boy had been doing, but I heard Kinjurō tell him to try to behave himself like a creature having more than one soul. Because those words interested me, I went out and sat down by him.

"O Kinjurō," I said, "whether I myself have one or more souls I am not sure; but it would please me very much to learn how many souls you have."

"I, the selfish one, have only four souls," answered Kinjurō, with unperturbed conviction.

"Four?" I asked, doubting that I had understood him.

"Four," he repeated. "But that boy I think can have only one soul, because he is so wanting in patience."

---

[i] *Ita-no-ma* refers to an area of wooden floor, intentionally not covered by *tatami* mats, as was the case in many Japanese homes; tatami being reserved for only special areas of the house.

"And in what manner," I asked, "did you come to learn that you have four souls?"

"There are wise men." he answered, while knocking the ashes out of his little silver pipe. "There are wise men who know these things, and there is an ancient book which speaks of them. According to the age of a man, the time of his birth, and the stars of heaven, the number of his souls may be determined. But, this is the knowledge of old men: the young folk of these times, who learn the things of the West, do not believe."

"And tell me O Kinjurō, do there now exist people who have more souls than you?"

"Assuredly. Some have five, some six, some seven, some eight souls. But no one is permitted by the gods to have more than nine souls."

Now, I could not believe this as a universal statement, remembering a woman on the other side of the world who possessed many generations of souls, and knew how to use them all. She wore her souls just as other women wear their dresses, and changed them several times a day. The multitude of dresses in the wardrobe of Queen Elizabeth was nothing compared to the number of this wonderful person's souls; for which reason, she never appeared the same on two different occasions; and she changed her thought, and her voice with her souls. Sometimes she was from the South, and her eyes were brown; and again she was from the North, and her eyes were gray. Sometimes she was of the thirteenth, and sometimes of the eighteenth century. Some people doubted their own senses when they saw these things and tried to find out the truth by begging photographs of her, and then comparing them. The photographers loved to photograph her because she was more than fair; but at the same time they were also confounded by the discovery that she was never the same subject twice. So the men who most admired her could not dare to fall in love with her, because that would have been absurd. She had altogether too many souls. Some of you who read what I have written will bear witness to its veracity.

"Concerning this Country of the Gods, O Kinjurō, what you say may be true, but there are other countries having only gods made of gold; and in those countries, matters are not so well arranged. The inhabitants there are plagued with a plague of souls; for, while some have but half a soul, or no soul at all, others have souls in multitude thrust upon them, for which neither nourishment nor employment can be found. Souls thus situated, exceedingly torment their owners; that is to say, Western souls. But tell me, what is the use of having more than one or two souls?"

"Master, if all had the same number and quality of souls, all would surely be of one mind. But that people are different from each other is apparent; and the differences among them are because of the difference in the quality and the number of their souls.

"And, it is better to have many souls rather than a few?"

"It is better."

"And, the man having but one soul is an imperfect being?"

"Very imperfect."

"Yet, a very imperfect man might have had a perfect ancestor?"

"That is true."

"So, a man of today, possessing but one soul, may have had an ancestor with nine souls?"

"Yes."

"Then, what has become of those other eight souls, which the ancestor possessed, but which the descendant does not have?"

"Ah! That is the work of the gods. The gods alone fix the number of souls for each of us. Many are given to the worthy, few to the unworthy."

"Then, the souls do not descend from the parents?"

"No! The souls are most ancient with incalculable years."

"I want to know, can a man separate his souls? Can he, for instance, have one soul in Kyōto and one in Tokyō and one in Matsué at the same time?"

"He cannot; they always remain together."

279

"How? One within the other, like the little lacquered boxes of an *inrō?*[1]"

"No. Only the gods know that."

"And the souls are never separated?"

"Sometimes they may be separated. But if the souls of a man are separated, then that man becomes mad. Mad people are those who have lost one of their souls."

"But after death, what becomes of the souls?"

"They still remain together. When a man dies, his souls ascend to the roof of the house, and they stay on the roof for the period of nine and forty days."

"On what part of the roof?"

"On the *yane-no-mune*, they stay on the ridge of the roof."

"Can they be seen?"

"No, they are like the air is. To and fro on the ridge of the roof they move, like a little wind."

"Why do they not stay on the roof for fifty days instead of forty-nine?"

"Seven weeks is the time allotted to them before they must depart: seven weeks make the measure of forty-nine days. But why this should be, I cannot tell."

I was not unaware of the ancient belief that the spirit of a dead man, for a time, haunts the roof of his house, because it is referred to quite impressively in many Japanese dramas; among others, in the play called *Kagaimi-yama*, which makes people weep. However, I had not heard before of triplex or quadruplex and other still more highly complex souls. I vainly questioned Kinjurō in the hope of learning the authority for his beliefs. They were the beliefs of his fathers: that was all he knew.[ii]

---

[i] An *inrō* (印籠) is a traditional Japanese case consisting of a stack of tiny, nested boxes, for holding small objects. Because traditional Japanese clothing lacked pockets, objects were often carried in *inrō* suspended from the obi, or sash. Most types of *inrō* were created for specialized contents, such as tobacco, pipes, writing brush and ink, but *inrō* were suited for carrying anything small.

[ii] Author's Footnote: Afterwards, I found that the old man had expressed to me only one popular form of belief, which would require a large book to fully

Like most Izumo folk, Kinjurō was a Buddhist as well as a Shintōist. As the former, he belonged to the *Zen-shū*, as the latter, to the *Izumo-Taisha*. Yet, his beliefs seemed to me not of either. Buddhism does not teach the doctrine of compound-multiple souls. There are old Shintō books not accessible to the multitude, who speak of a doctrine very remotely similar to Kinjurō's;

---

explain; a belief founded on Chinese astrology, but possibly modified by Buddhist and by Shintō ideas. This notion of compound souls cannot be explained at all, without a prior knowledge of the astrological relationships between the Chinese zodiac signs and the Ten Celestial Storms. Some understanding of these may be obtained from the curious article "Time," in Professor Chamberlain's admirable little book, *Things Japanese*. The relationships having been identified, it is further necessary to know that, under the Chinese astrological system, each year is under the influence of one or another of the Five Elements: wood, fire, earth, metal, water. According to the day and year of one's birth, one's temperament is celestially decided. A Japanese verse tells us the number of souls or natures corresponding to each of the Five Element Influences; namely, nine souls for wood, three for fire, one for earth, seven for metal, five for water:

> *Kiku karani*
> *Himitsu no yama ni*
> *Tsuchi hitotsu*
> *Namatsu kane to zo*
> *Go suiryō are.*

Multiplied into ten, by being each one divided into both "elder" and "younger," the Five Elements become the Ten Celestial Storms; and their influences are commingled with those of the rat, bull, tiger, hare, dragon, serpent, horse, goat, ape, cock, dog, and boar (the twelve zodiac signs), all of which have relationships to time, place, life, luck, misfortune, etc. But even these hints give no idea whatever, how enormously complicated the subject really is.

The book the old gardener referred to, once as widely known in Japan as any fortune telling book in any European country, was the *San-ze-sō*, copies of which may still be picked up. Contrary to Kinjurō's opinion, however, it is held, by those educated in such Chinese matters, that it is just as bad to have too many souls as to have too few. To have nine souls is to be too "many-minded," without fixed purpose; to have only one soul is to lack quick intelligence. According to the Chinese astrological ideas, the words "nature" or "characters" would perhaps be more accurate than the word "souls" in this case. There is a world of curious ideas, born out of these beliefs. For one example of hundreds, a person having a fire-nature must not marry one having a water-nature. Hence, the proverbial saying about two who cannot agree: "They are like fire and water."

but Kinjurō had never seen them. Those books say that each of us has two souls, the *ara-tama*, or "rough soul," which is vindictive; and the *nigi-tama*, or gentle soul, which is all-forgiving. Furthermore, we are all possessed by the spirit of Oho-maga-tsu-hi-no-kami, the Wondrous Deity of Exceeding Great Evils; and also by the spirit of Oho-naho-bi-no-kami, the Wondrous Great Rectifying Deity, a counteracting influence. These were not exactly the ideas of Kinjurō, but I remembered something Hirata wrote which reminded me of Kinjurō's words about a possible separation of souls. Hirata's teaching was that the *ara-tama* of a man may leave his body, assume his shape, and without his knowledge destroy a hated enemy. So I asked Kinjurō about it. He said he had never heard of a *nigi-tama* or an *ara-tama*; but he told me this:

"Master, when a man has been discovered by his wife to be secretly enamored of another, it sometimes happens that the guilty woman is seized with a sickness that no physician can cure; for, one of the souls of the wife, moved exceedingly by anger, passes into the body of that woman to destroy her. But the wife also sickens, or loses her mind awhile, because of the absence of her soul.

"And there is another and more wonderful thing known to us of Nippon, which you, being of the West, may never have heard. By the power of the gods, for a righteous purpose, sometimes a soul may be withdrawn a little while from its body, and be made to utter its most secret thought. But no suffering to the body is then caused. And the wonder is wrought in this way:

"A man loves a beautiful girl whom he is at liberty to marry; but he doubts whether he can hope to make her love him in return. He seeks the *kannushi* of a certain Shintō temple,[1] and tells of his doubt, and asks the aid of the gods to solve it. Then, the priests demand, not his name, but his age and the year, day, and hour of his birth, which they write down for the gods to know; and they bid the man return to the temple after the space of seven days.

"And during those seven days, the priests offer prayer to the gods that the doubt may be solved; and one of them, each morning, bathes all his body in cold, pure water, and at each meal, eats only food prepared over holy fire. And on the eighth

---

[1] Author's Footnote: Usually an Inari temple. Such things are never done at the great Shintō shrines.

day, the man returns to the temple, and enters an inner room where the priests receive him.

"A ceremony is performed, and certain prayers are said, after which all wait in silence. And then, the priest who has performed the rites of purification, suddenly begins to tremble violently in all his body, like one trembling with a great fever. And this is because, by the power of the gods, the soul of the girl whose love is doubted has entered, all fearfully, into the body of that priest. She does not know; for at that time, wherever she may be, she is in a deep sleep from which nothing can arouse her. But her soul, having been summoned into the body of the priest, cannot speak anything but the truth; and it is made to tell all its thoughts. And the priest speaks not with his own voice, but with the voice of the soul; and he speaks in the person of the soul, saying, 'I love,' or 'I hate,' according to what the truth may be, and in the language of women. If there is hate, then the reason of the hate is spoken; but if the answer is of love, there is little to say. And then the trembling of the priest stops, for the soul passes from him; and he falls forward upon his face, like one dead, and long so remains."

"Tell me, Kinjurō," I asked, after all these queer things had been related to me, "have you yourself ever known of a soul being removed by the power of the gods, and placed in the heart of a priest?"

"Yes, I myself have known it."

I remained silent and waited. The old man emptied his little pipe, threw it down beside the *hibachi*, folded his hands, and looked at the lotus flowers for some time before he spoke again. Then he smiled and said:

"Master, I married when I was very young. For many years we had no children; then, my wife at last gave me a son, and became a Buddha. But, my son lived and grew up handsome and strong. When the revolution came, he joined the armies of the Son of Heaven; and he died the death of a man in the great war of the South,[102] in Kyūshū. I loved him and I wept with joy when I heard that he had been able to die for our Sacred Emperor, since there is no more noble death for the son of a samurai. So, they buried my boy far away from me in Kyūshū, on a hill near Kumamoto, which is a famous city with a strong garrison. I went there to make his tomb beautiful, but his name is here also, in Ninomura, engraved on the monument to the men of Izumo

283

who fell in the good fight for loyalty and honor in our Emperor's holy cause. When I see his name there, my heart laughs, and I speak to him; then it seems as if he were walking bedside me again, under the great pines. But that is another matter.

"I sorrowed for my wife. All the years we had lived together, no unkind word had ever been uttered between us. When she died, I never thought to marry again. But after two more years had passed, my father and mother wanted a daughter in the house, and they told me of their wish; and of a girl who was beautiful and of good family, although poor. The family were of our kindred, and the girl was their only support: she wove garments of silk and cotton, and she received little money for this. Because she was loyal and attractive, and our relatives were not fortunate, my parents wanted me to marry her and help her people; for in those days, we had a small income of rice. Then, being accustomed to obeying my parents, I allowed them to do what they thought best. So the *nakōdo*[1] was summoned, and the arrangements for the wedding began.

"I was able to see the girl in the home of her parents twice, and I thought myself fortunate the first time I looked at her; for she was very pretty and young. However, the second time, I saw that she had been weeping, and that her eyes avoided mine. Then my heart sank; for I thought, "She dislikes me, and they are forcing her to do this thing." Then I decided to question the gods, and I delayed the marriage and went to the temple of Yanagi-no-Inari-sama, which is on Zaimokuchō Street.

"When the trembling came on him, the priest, speaking with the soul of that maid, said to me, 'My heart hates you, and the sight of your face gives me sickness, because I love another, and because this marriage is forced on me. Yet, though my heart hates you, I must marry you because my parents are poor and old, and I alone cannot long continue to support them, for my work is killing me. But although I may strive to be a dutiful wife, there never will be gladness in your house because of me; for my heart hates you with a great and lasting hate; and the sound of your voice makes a sickness in my breast (*koe kiite mo mune ga waruku naru*); and only to see your face makes me wish that I were dead (*kao miru to shinitaku naru*).'

---

[1] A *nakōdo* (仲人) or matchmaker serves in the role of a go-between between families in the marriage process.

"Thus knowing the truth, I told it to my parents; and I wrote a letter of kind words to the maid, praying pardon for the pain I had unknowingly caused her. I feigned long illness, so that the marriage might be broken off without gossip, and we made a gift to that family, and the maid was glad. For, she was enabled, at a later time, to marry the young man she loved. My parents never pressed me again to take a wife; and since their death, I have lived alone. O Master, look on the extreme wickedness of that boy!"

Taking advantage of our conversation, Kinjurō's young assistant had improvised a rod and line with a bamboo stick and a bit of string, and had fastened a pellet of tobacco stolen from the old man's pouch to the string's end. With this bait, he had been fishing in the lotus pond, and a frog had swallowed it, and was now suspended high above the pebbles, sprawling in rotary motion, kicking in frantic spasms of disgust and despair. "Kaji!" shouted the gardener.

The boy dropped his rod with a laugh, and ran to us unashamed; while the frog, having disgorged the tobacco, plopped back into the lotus pond. Evidently Kaji was not afraid of scoldings.

"*Goshō ga warui!*" declared the old man, shaking his ivory head. "O Kaji, I am very afraid that your next birth will be bad! Do I buy tobacco for frogs? Master, did I not rightly say that this boy has but one soul?"

7

A *noppera-bō* (のっぺら坊) or faceless ghost (Unidentified artist).

XXV

OF GHOSTS AND GOBLINS

I

THERE WAS A BUDDHA, according to the *Hokkekyō*, who "even assumed the shape of a goblin to preach to such as were to be converted by a goblin." In the same *sutra* this promise of the Teacher can be found:

> *While he is dwelling lonely in the wilderness, I will send thither goblins in great numbers to keep him company.*

The appalling character of this promise is indeed somewhat modified by the assurance that also gods are to be sent. But if I ever become a holy man, I will take heed not to live in the wilderness, because I have seen Japanese goblins, and I do not like them.

Kinjurō showed them to me last night. They had come to town for the *matsuri* of our own *ujigami*, or parish temple; and, as there were many curious things to be seen at the night festival, we started for the temple after dark: Kinjurō carrying a paper lantern painted with my crest.[1]

It had snowed heavily in the morning; but now the sky and the sharp, still air were as clear as diamond, and the crisp snow made a pleasant crunching sound under our feet as we walked; and it occurred to me to say, "O Kinjurō, is there a god of snow?"

"I cannot tell," replied Kinjurō. "There are many gods I do not know, and there is not any man who knows the names of all the gods. But there is the Yuki-onna, the Woman of the Snow."

"And what is the Yuki-onna?"

"She is the White One that makes the faces in the snow. She does no harm, only causes fear. By day, she lifts only her head, and frightens those who journey alone. But at night, she rises up

---

[1] An example of the author's crest may be seen on the title page of this volume: a heron.

sometimes, taller than the trees, and looks around a little while, and then falls back in a shower of snow."[i]

"What is her face like?"

"It is all white, white. It is an enormous face. And it is a lonesome face." (The word Kinjurō used was *samushii*. Its common meaning is "lonesome" but he used it, I think, in the sense of "weird.")

"Did you ever see her, Kinjurō?"

"Master, I never saw her. But my father told me that once, when he was a child, he wanted to go to a neighbor's house through the snow to play with another little boy, and that on the way he saw a great, white face rise up from the snow and look around lonesomely, so that he cried for fear and ran back. Then his people all went out and looked; but there was only snow. Then they knew that he had seen the Yuki-Onna."

"And in these days, Kinjurō, do people ever see her?"

"Yes. Those who make the pilgrimage to Yabumura, in the period called *Dai-Kan*, which is the Time of the Greatest Cold,[ii] they sometimes see her."

"What is there at Yabumura, Kinjurō?"

"There is the Yabu-jinja, which is an ancient and famous temple of Yabu-no-Tennō-san, the God of Colds, Kaze-no-kami. It is high on a hill, nearly nine *ri* from Matsué. The great *matsuri* of that temple is held on the tenth and eleventh days of the second month. On those days, strange things may be seen; for, one who gets a very bad cold prays to the deity of Yabu-jinja to cure it, and takes a vow to make a pilgrimage, naked, to the temple at the time of the *matsuri*.

"Naked?"

"Yes. The pilgrims wear only *waraji*,[iii] and a little cloth around their loins. A great many men and women go naked through the snow to the temple, though the snow is deep at that

---

[i] Author's Footnote: In other parts of Japan I have heard the Yuki-Onna described as a very beautiful phantom who lures young men to lonesome places for the purpose of sucking their blood.
[ii] Author's Footnote: In Izumo, the *Dai-Kan*, or Period of Greatest cold, falls in February.
[iii] *Waraji* (草鞋) are sandals made of straw rope.

time; and each man carries a bunch of *gohei* and a naked sword as gifts to the temple. Each woman carries a metal mirror. At the temple, the priests receive them, performing curious rites; for, the priests then, according to ancient custom, dress themselves like sick men, and lie down and groan, and drink potions made of herbs, prepared in the Chinese manner."

"But do not some of the pilgrims die of cold, Kinjurō?"

"No, our Izumo peasants are hardy. Besides, they run swiftly, so that they reach the temple all warm, and before returning, they put on thick warm robes. But sometimes, on the way, they see the Yuki-Onna.

II

Each side of the street leading to the *miya* was illuminated with a line of paper lanterns bearing holy symbols; and the immense courtyard of the temple had been transformed into a town of booths, shops and temporary theaters. In spite of the cold, the crowd was impressive. There seemed to be all the usual attractions of a *matsuri*, and a number of unusual ones. Among the familiar attractions, I only missed the maiden wearing an *obi* of living snakes; probably because it had become too cold for snakes. There were several fortune tellers and jugglers; there were acrobats and dancers; there was a man making pictures out of sand; and there was a menagerie containing an emu from Australia and a couple of enormous bats from the Loo Choo Islands — bats trained to do several things. I did reverence to the gods, bought some extraordinary toys, and then we went to look for goblins. They were living in a large permanent structure, rented to showmen on special occasions.

Gigantic characters, reading "*IKI-NINGYO,*" painted on the signboard at the entrance, partly hinted at the nature of the exhibition. *Iki-ningyō* ("living images")[i] somewhat corresponds to our Western wax figures; however, the equally realistic Japanese creations are made of much cheaper material. Having bought two wooden tickets for one *sen* each, we entered and passed behind a curtain to find ourselves in a long corridor lined with

---

[i] The word *iki* (息) literally means, breath or breathing; and *ningyō* (人形) literally means human shape or form; thus, breathing (or living) human forms).

booths, or rather matted compartments, about the size of small rooms. Each space, decorated with scenery appropriate to the subject, was occupied by a group of life-size figures. The group nearest the entrance, representing two men playing *samisen* and two geisha dancing, seemed to me without a reason for being there, until Kinjurō had translated a little placard in front of it, announcing that one of the figures was a living person. We watched in vain for a wink or tremor. Suddenly, one of the musicians laughed aloud, shook his head, and began to play and sing. The deception was perfect.

The remaining groups, twenty-four in number, were powerfully impressive in their peculiar way, representing mostly famous traditions or sacred myths. Feudal heroisms, the memory of which stirs every Japanese heart; legends of filial piety; Buddhist miracles, and stories of Emperors were among the subjects. Sometimes, however, the realism was brutal, as in one scene representing the body of a woman lying in a pool of blood, with brains scattered by a sword stroke. Nor was this unpleasantness altogether atoned for by her miraculous resuscitation in the adjoining compartment, where she reappeared, returning thanks in a Nichiren temple, and converting her slaughterer, who happened, by some extraordinary accident, to go there at the same time.

At the end of the corridor, there hung a black curtain, behind which screams could be heard. Above the black curtain was a placard inscribed with the promise of a gift to anybody able to traverse the mysteries beyond, without being frightened.

"Master," said Kinjurō, "the goblins are inside."

We lifted the curtain and found ourselves in a sort of lane between hedges, and behind the hedges we saw tombs: we were in a graveyard. There were real weeds and trees, and *sotoba* and *haka*: the effect was quite natural. Moreover, as the roof was very high, and kept invisible by a clever arrangement of lights, all seemed only darkness; and this gave one a sense of being out under the night, a feeling accentuated by the chill of the air. Here and there we could see sinister shapes, mostly of super-human stature, some seeming to wait in dim places, others floating above the graves. Quite near to us, towering above the hedge on our right was a Buddhist priest, with his back turned to us.

"A *yamabushi*, an exorcist?" I asked Kinjurō.

"No," said Kinjurō. "See how tall he is. I think that must be a *tanuki-bōzu*."

The *tanuki-bōzu* is the priestly form assumed by the goblin-badger (*tanuki*) for the purpose of waylaying late travelers to destruction. We went on, and looked up into his face. It was a nightmare — his face.

"In truth a *tanuki-Bōzu*," said Kinjurō. "What does the master honorably think about it?"

Instead of replying, I jumped back; for the monstrous thing had suddenly reached over the hedge and clutched at me, with a moan. Then it fell back, swaying and creaking. It was moved by invisible strings.

"I think, Kinjurō, that it is a nasty, horrid thing. But, I will not claim the gift."

We laughed and proceeded to consider a "Three-eyed Friar" (*Mitsu-me-Nyudō*). The "Three-eyed Friar" also watched for the unwary at night. His face is soft and as smiling as the face of a Buddha, but he has a hideous eye in the top of his shaved head, which can only be seen when seeing it does no good. The *Mitsu-me-Nyūdō* made a grab at Kinjurō, and startled him almost as much as the *tanuki-bōzu* had startled me.

"The Mountain Woman: Yamauba," by Totoya Hokkei (c. 1880).

Then we looked at the *Yama-Uba*, the "Mountain Nurse." She catches little children and nurses then for a while, and then devours them. She has no mouth in her face, but she has a mouth in the top of her head, under her hair. The *Yama-Uba* did not grab at us, because her hands were occupied with a nice little boy, whom she was just going to eat. The child had been made wonderfully pretty to heighten the effect.

Then I saw the specter of a woman hovering in the air above a tomb, at some distance, so that I felt safer observing it. It had no eyes, its long hair hung loose, and its white robe floated as lightly as smoke. I thought of a statement in a composition by one of my pupils about ghosts: "Their greatest peculiarity is that they have no feet." Then I jumped again, for the thing, quite soundlessly but very swiftly, came at me through the air.

The rest of our journey among the graves was little more than a succession of similar experiences; but it was made amusing by the screams of women and bursts of laughter from people who lingered only to watch the effect of what had scared themselves, on others.

III

Leaving the goblins, we visited a little open-air theater to see two girls dance. After they had danced awhile, one girl produced a sword and cut off the other girl's head, and put it on a table, where it opened its mouth and began to sing. All this was done prettily; but my mind was still haunted by the goblins. So I questioned Kinjurō.

"Kinjurō, those goblins of which we have seen, do people believe in the reality of it?"

"Not anymore," answered Kinjurō. "Not at least among the people of the city. Perhaps in the country it may not be so. We believe in the Lord Buddha, we believe in the ancient gods; and there are many who believe the dead sometimes return to avenge a cruelty or to compel an act of justice. But, we do not now believe all that was believed in ancient times…Master," he added, as we reached another strange exhibition, "it is only one *sen* to go to hell, if the master would like to go."

IV

We passed behind a curtain into a big room full of curious clicking and squeaking noises. These noises were made by unseen wheels and pulleys moving a multitude of *ningyō* on a broad shelf, about breast high, which surrounded the room on three sides. These *ningyō* were not *iki-ningyō*, but very small images: puppets. They represented all things in the Underworld.

The first thing I saw was Sozu-Baba, the Old woman of the River of Ghosts, who takes away the garments of souls. The garments were hanging on a tree behind her. She was tall and rolled her green eyes and gnashed her long teeth, while the shivering of the little white souls in front of her were like trembling butterflies. Farther on appeared Emma Dai-O, great King of Hell, nodding grimly. At his right hand, on their tripod, the heads of Kaguhana and Mirume, the Witnesses, whirled as though on a wheel. At his left, a devil was busy sawing a soul in two. I noticed that he used his saw like a Japanese carpenter: pulling it towards him instead of pushing it. Then, various exhibitions of the tortures of the damned: a liar bound to a post was having his tongue pulled out by a devil — slowly, with artistic jerks — it was already longer than the owner's body. Another devil was pounding another soul in a mortar, so vigorously that the sound of the screaming could be heard above the noise of the machinery. A little farther on was a man being eaten alive by two serpents that had women's faces: one serpent was white and one blue. The white had been his wife, the blue his concubine. Elsewhere, all the tortures known to medieval Japan were being deftly practiced by swarms of devils. After reviewing them, we visited the Sai-No-Kawara,[i] and saw Jizō with a child in his arms, and a circle of other children running swiftly around him, to escape from demons that brandished their clubs and ground their teeth.

Hell proved, however, to be extremely cold, and while meditating on the partial inappropriateness of the atmosphere, it occurred to me that in the common Buddhist picture books of the Jigoku,[ii] I had never noticed any illustrations of torment by cold. Indeed, Indian Buddhism teaches the existence of cold hells. There is one, for instance, where people's lips are frozen so that they can only say "*Ah-ta-ta!*" Therefore, the hell is called Atata. There is also the hell where tongues are frozen, and where people say only "*Ah-baba!*" and therefore, it is called Ababa. And there is the Pundarika, or Great White Lotus Hell, where the spectacle of the bones laid bare by the cold is "like a blossoming of white lotus flowers." Kinjurō thinks there are cold hells, according to Japanese Buddhism, but he is not sure. I am not sure that the idea of cold could be made very terrible to the Japanese. They confess a general liking for cold, and compose Chinese poems about the loveliness of ice and snow.

V

Out of Hell, we found our way to a magic lantern show being given in a larger, and even colder structure. A Japanese magic lantern show is nearly always interesting in more ways

---

[i] According to Buddhist legend, children who die prematurely are sent to the underworld as punishment for causing great sorrow to their parents. They are sent to Sai-no-Kawara, the Riverbed of Souls in Purgatory, where they pray for salvation by building small stone towers, piling pebble upon pebble, in the hopes of climbing out of limbo into paradise. But hell demons, answering to the command of the old hag Shozuka-no-Baba (Soza-Baba), soon arrive and scatter their stones and beat them with iron clubs. But no need to worry, for Jizō comes to the rescue.

[ii] *Jigoku* is the Japanese term for Hell.

than one; but perhaps especially for showing the native genius for adapting Western inventions to Eastern tastes. A Japanese magic lantern show is essentially dramatic. It is a play, of which the dialogue is spoken by invisible people; the actors and the scenery being only luminous shadows. Therefore, it is peculiarly well suited to goblins and weirdness of all kinds, and plays in which ghosts figure as the favorite subjects. Because the hall was bitterly cold, I stayed only long enough to see one performance; of which the following is a summary:

SCENE I. A beautiful peasant girl and her aged mother, squatting together at home. Mother weeps violently, gestures agonizingly. From her frantic speech, broken by wild sobs, we learn that the girl must be sent as a victim to the *kami-sama* of some lonesome temple in the mountains. That god is a bad god. Once a year, he shoots an arrow into the thatch of some farmer's house as a sign that he wants a girl — to eat! Unless the girl is sent to him at once, he destroys the crops and the cows. Exit mother, weeping and shrieking, and pulling out her gray hair. Exit girl, with downcast head, and air of sweet resignation.

SCENE II. Before a wayside inn; cherry trees in blossom. Enter coolies carrying, like a palanquin, a large box, in which the girl is supposed to be. Deposit the box; enter to eat; tell story to long-winded landlord. Enter noble samurai, with two swords. Asks about box. Hears the story of the coolies repeated by the long-winded landlord. Exhibits fierce indignation; vows that the *kami-sama* are good, do not eat girls. Declares that so-called *kami-sama* to be a devil. Observes that devils must be killed. Orders box opened. Sends girl home. Gets into box himself, and commands coolies, under pain of death, to bear him right quickly to that temple.

SCENE III. Enter coolies, approaching temple through forest at night. Coolies afraid. Drop box and run. Exit coolies. Box alone in the dark. Enter veiled figure, all white. Figure moans unpleasantly; utters horrid cries. Box remains impassive. Figure removes veil, showing its face: a skull with glowing eyes. (*Audience unanimously utters the sound "Aaaaaa!"*) Figure displays its hands: monstrous and apish, with claws. (*Audience utters a second "Ahhhhh!"*) Figure approaches the box, touches the box, opens the box! Up leaps noble samurai. A wrestle; drums sound the roll of battle. Noble samurai successfully practices noble art of *jūjutsu*. Casts demon down, tramples on him triumphantly, cuts off his head. Head suddenly enlarges, grows to the size of a house, tries to bite off head of samurai. Samurai slashes it with his sword. Head rolls backward, spitting fire, and vanishes. *Finis. Exeunt omnes.*

VI

The vision of the samurai and the goblin reminded Kinjurō of a queer tale, which he began to tell me as soon as the shadow play was over. Ghastly stories are apt to fall flat after such an exhibition; but Kinjurō's stories are always peculiar enough to justify the telling under almost any circumstances. Therefore, I listened eagerly, in spite of the cold:

"A long time ago, in the days when fox-women and goblins haunted this land, there came to the capital, with her parents, a samurai girl, so beautiful that all men who saw her fell in love with her. Hundreds of young samurai desired and hoped to marry her; making their desire known to her parents; for, it has always been the custom in Japan, that parents should arrange marriages. But, there are exceptions to all customs, and the case of this maiden was such an exception. Her parents declared that they intended to allow their daughter to choose her own husband, and that all who wished to win her, would be free to woo her.

"Many men of high rank and of great wealth were admitted to the house as suitors; and each one courted her as best he knew how; with gifts, fair words, with poems written in her honor, and with promises of eternal love. And to each one, she spoke sweetly and hopefully; but she made strange conditions. For, every suitor she obliged to bind himself by his word of honor as a samurai, to submit to a test of his love for her, and never to divulge to a living person, what that test might be. All agreed to this.

"But, even the most confident suitors suddenly ceased their persistent solicitations after having been put to the test; and all of them appeared to have been greatly terrified by something. Indeed, not a few even fled away from the city, and could not be persuaded by their friends to return. But no one ever so much as

297

hinted why. Therefore, it was whispered by those who knew nothing of the mystery, that the beautiful girl must either be a fox-woman or a goblin.

"Now, when all the wooers of high rank had abandoned their pursuit, there came a samurai who had no wealth except for his sword. He was a good man and true, and of pleasing appearance. The girl seemed to like him; however, she made him take the same pledge that the others had taken; and after he had taken it, she told him to return on a certain evening.

"When that evening came, he was received at the house by none other than the girl herself. With her own hands, she set before him the repast of hospitality, and waited on him, after which she told him that she wished him to go out with her, at a late hour. To this he gladly consented, and inquired as to what place she desired to go. But, she said nothing, and all at once became very silent and strange in her manner. After a while, she retired from the room, leaving him alone.

"Only long after midnight she returned, dressed in white, like a soul; and without speaking a word, signaled him to follow her. Out of the house they hastened, while the entire city slept. It was what is called an *oborozuki-yo*, a 'moon-clouded night.' Always, on such a night, it is said, ghosts wander. She swiftly led the way, and the dogs howled as she flitted by, passing beyond the edge of the city to a place of knolls shadowed by enormous trees, where an ancient cemetery was. She glided into it: — a white shadow into blackness. He followed, wondering; his hand on his sword. Then his eyes became accustomed to the darkness, and he saw.

"She paused by a newly made grave and signaled for him to wait. The tools of the gravedigger were still lying there. Seizing one, she began to dig furiously, with strange haste and strength. At last her spade struck a coffin lid and made it boom. Another moment and the fresh white wood of the *kwan* was bare. She tore off the lid, revealing a corpse inside: the body of a child. With goblin gestures, she twisted off an arm from the body, ripped it in two, and squatting down, began to devour the upper half. Then, flinging the other half to her lover, she yelled to him, 'Eat, if you love me! This is what I eat!'

"He did not hesitate, not even for a single instant. He squatted down on the other side of the grave and ate the half of the arm, and then said, '*Kekkō degozarimasu! Mo sukoshi chōdai;*'[i] for, that arm was made of the best *kwashi*[ii] that Kyōto could produce.

"Then the girl sprang to her feet with a burst of laughter, and cried, 'You only, of all my brave suitors, did not run away! And I wanted a husband who could not fear. I will marry you; I can love you: you are a man!'"

VII

"O Kinjurō," I said, as we made our way home, "I have heard and I have read many Japanese stories about the returning of the dead. Likewise, you yourself have told me it is still believed that the dead return, and why. But according to both that which I have read and that which you have told me, the coming back of the dead is never a thing to be desired. They

---

[i] Author's Footnote: "It is excellent: I pray you give me a little more."
[ii] Author's Footnote: *Kwashi*: a Japanese confection.

return because of hate, or because of envy, or because they cannot rest because of sorrow. But, where is it written about any who return for something which is not evil? Surely the common history of them is like that which we have seen tonight: much that is horrible and wicked, and nothing about that which is beautiful or true."

Now, I said this so that I might tempt him; and he answered as I wanted, telling the following story:

"Long ago, in the days of a *daimyō* whose name has been forgotten, there lived in this old city, a young man and a maid who loved each other very much. Their names are not remembered, but their story remains. From infancy, they had been betrothed; and as children, they played together, for their parents were neighbors. As they grew up, they became even fonder of each other.

"Before the youth had become a man, his parents died, but he was able to enter the service of a rich samurai, an officer of high rank, who had been a friend of his people. His protector soon took him into great favor, finding him to be courteous, intelligent, and skilled with arms. So the young man hoped to find himself shortly in a position that would make it possible for him to marry his betrothed. But war broke out in the north and east; and he was summoned, suddenly, to follow his master to the field. Before departing, however, he was able to see the girl; and they exchanged pledges in the presence of her parents. He promised that should he remain alive, to return within a year from that day to marry his betrothed.

"Much time passed after his leaving without news of him, for there was no mail in that time as now. The girl grieved so much for thinking of the chances of war, that she became all white, thin and weak. Then at last, she heard about him through a messenger sent from the army to bear news to the *daimyō*, and once again, another messenger brought a letter to her. Thereafter, there came no word. A year is a long time for one who waits. The year passed, and he did not return.

"Other seasons passed, and still he did not come. She thought he was dead, and sickened, lay down, died, and was buried. Then her old parents, who had no other child, grieved unspeakably, and came to hate their home because of its loneliness. After a time, they decided to sell all they had and to set out on a *sengaji*, the great pilgrimage to the thousand temples of the Nichiren-shū, which requires years to perform. So they sold their little house with all it contained, except for the ancestral tablets and holy things which must never be sold, and the *ihai* of their buried daughter; which were placed, according to the custom of those about to leave their native home, in the family temple. The family was of the Nichiren-shū, and their temple was Myōkōji.

"They had been gone only four days when the young man, who had been betrothed to their daughter, returned to the city. He had attempted, with the permission of his master, to fulfill his promise, but the provinces on his way were full of war, the roads and passes guarded by troops, and he had been delayed by many difficulties. When he heard of his misfortune, he became sick with grief, and for many days he remained, without knowing anything, like one about to die.

"But, when he began to recover his strength, all the pain of memory came back again, and he was sorry that he had not died. Then he decided to kill himself on the grave of his betrothed. As soon as he was able to go out unobserved, he took his sword and went to the cemetery where the girl was buried. It is a lonesome place, the cemetery of Myōkōji. There, he found her tomb and knelt in front of it, prayed and wept, and whispered to her that which he was about to do. Suddenly, he heard her voice cry out to him, '*Anata!*' ('You!') and felt her hand on his hand. He turned, and saw her kneeling beside him, smiling, and as beautiful as he remembered her, only a little pale. Then his heart leaped, so that he could not speak because of the wonder and doubt, and the joy of the moment. But she said, 'Do not doubt, it is really I. I am not dead. It was all a mistake. I was buried, because my people thought me dead: buried too soon. My own parents thought me dead, and went on a pilgrimage. Yet, you see, I am not dead: not a ghost. It is I. Do not doubt it! I have seen your heart, and that was worth all the waiting and the pain. But now, let us go away at once to another city, so that people may not know this thing, and trouble us; for, all still believe me dead.'

"And they went away, no one observing them. They went to the village of Minobu, which is in the province of Kai, for there is a famous temple of the Nichiren-shū in that place. The girl said, 'I know that in the course of their pilgrimage, my parents will surely visit Minobu; so that if we live here, they will find us, and we shall all be together again.' And when they came to

Minobu, she said, 'Let us open a little shop.' They opened a little food shop, on the wide way leading to the holy place, and there they sold cakes for children, toys, and food for pilgrims. For two years, they lived and prospered, and a son was born to them.

"When the child was a year and two months old, the parents of the wife came in the course of their pilgrimage to Minobu; and stopped at the little shop to buy food. Seeing their daughter's betrothed, they cried out and wept and asked questions. Then he brought them inside and bowed down before them, astonishing them saying, 'Truly as I speak it, your daughter is not dead. She is my wife, and we have a son. She is even now in the back room, lying down with the child. I want you to go in at once and bring joy to her; for her heart longs for the moment of seeing you again.'

"So, while he busied himself with making everything ready for their comfort, they entered the inner room very softly; the mother first.

"They found the child asleep, but the mother was not there. She seemed to have gone out for a little while, and her pillow was still warm. They waited a long while for her, and then began to look; but she was never seen again.

"Only when they found, underneath the blanket which covered the mother and child, something which they remembered having left years before in the temple of Myōkōji did they understand. It was the little mortuary tablet, the *ihai*, of their buried daughter."

I suppose I must have looked thoughtful after this tale; for the old man said, "Perhaps the Master honorably thinks, concerning the story, that it is foolish?"

"No, Kinjurō, the story is in my heart."

XXVI

The Japanese Smile

I

THOSE WHOSE IDEAS OF THE WORLD and its wonders have been formed chiefly by novels and romance, still indulge a vague belief that the East is more serious than the West. Those who judge things from a higher standpoint argue, on the contrary, that under present conditions, the West must be more serious than the East; and also that seriousness, or even something resembling its opposite, may exist only as a fashion. But the fact is that in this, as in all other questions, no rule susceptible of application to either half of humanity can be accurately framed. Scientifically, we can do no more just now, than study certain contrasts in a general way, without hope of a satisfactory explanation for the highly complex causes which produce them. One such contrast of particular interest is that provided by the English and the Japanese.

It is normal to say that the English are a serious people — not superficially serious, but serious all the way down to the bedrock of the national character. It is almost equally safe to say that the Japanese are not very serious; either above or below the surface, or even when compared with nations much less serious than our own. In the same proportion, at least, that they are less serious and are more happy: they still, perhaps, remain the happiest people in the civilized world. We serious folk of the West cannot call ourselves very happy. Indeed, we do not yet fully know how serious we are, and it would probably frighten us to learn how much more serious we are likely to become, under the ever-growing pressure of industrial life. It is, possibly, by living for a long while among a people less gravely disposed, that we can best learn our own temperament. This conviction came to me very strongly when, after having lived for nearly three years in the interior of Japan, I returned to English life for a few days at the open port of Kobé. To hear English once more spoken by Englishmen touched me more than I could have believed possible; however, this feeling lasted only for a moment. My object was to make some necessary purchases. Accompanying me was a Japanese friend,[1] to whom all that foreign life was utterly new and wonderful, and who asked me this curious question: "Why is it that the foreigners never smile? You smile and bow when you speak to them; but they never smile. Why?"

The fact was, I had altogether fallen into Japanese habits and ways and had gotten out of touch with Western life. My companion's question first made me aware that I had been acting somewhat curiously. It also seemed to me a fair

---

[1] The author's "friend" was his wife, Setsuko Koizumi.

304

illustration of the difficulty in mutual comprehension between the two races: each quite naturally, though quite erroneously, estimating the manners and motives of the other by its own. If the Japanese were puzzled by English seriousness, the English are, to say the least, equally puzzled by Japanese levity. The Japanese speak of the "angry faces" of foreigners. The foreigners speak with strong contempt for the Japanese smile: they suspect it signifies insincerity; indeed, some say it cannot possibly signify anything else. Only a few of the more observant have recognized it as an enigma worth studying.

One of my Yokohama friends, a thoroughly lovable man who had spent more than half his life in the open ports of the East,[i] said to me, just before my leaving for the interior: "Since you are going to study Japanese life, perhaps you will be able to find out something for me. I can't understand the Japanese smile. Let me tell you one experience of many. One day, as I was driving down from the bluff,[ii] I saw an empty *kuruma* coming up on the wrong side of the curve. I could not have pulled up in time if I had tried; but I didn't try, because I didn't think there was any particular danger. I only yelled to the man in Japanese to get to the other side of the road; instead of which, he simply backed his *kuruma* against a wall on the lower side of the curve, with the shafts outwards. At the rate I was going, there wasn't room even to swerve; and the next minute, one of the shafts of the *kuruma* was in my horse's shoulder. The man wasn't hurt at all. When I saw the way my horse was bleeding, I quite lost my temper, and struck the man over the head with the butt of my whip. He looked right into my face and smiled, and then bowed. I can see that smile now. I felt as if I had been knocked down. The smile utterly perplexed me: killed all my anger instantly. Mind you, it was a polite smile. But what did it mean? Why the devil did the man smile? I can't understand it?"

Neither, at that time, could I, but the meaning of much more mysterious smiles has since been revealed to me. A Japanese can smile in the teeth of death, and usually does. But he then smiles for the same reason that he smiles at other times. There is neither defiance nor hypocrisy in the smile; nor is it to be confused with that smile of sickly resignation, which we are likely to associate with a weakness of character. It is an elaborate and long cultivated etiquette. It is also a silent language; however, any effort to interpret it according to Western notions of physiognomical[iii] expression would be just about as successful as

---

[i] The "Yokohama friend" the author is speaking of was Mitchell McDonald, Hearn's closest "Western" friend in Japan. Refer to Note 1 in this volume.

[ii] The "bluff" is the high area south of downtown Yokohama. It begins south of Motomachi Street and Yamashita Park and is bounded by Honmoku-dori on the east, standing high above the surrounding area, and includes the International schools.

[iii] Physiognomy is the suposed "art," popular in 18th and 19th centuries whereby a person's features or characteristic expression are regarded as an indication of personality; the art of judging human character from facial features; divination based on facial features.

an attempt to interpret Chinese characters by their real or imagined resemblance to shapes of familiar things.

First impressions, being largely instinctive, are scientifically recognized as partly trustworthy, and the very first impression produced by the Japanese smile is not far from the truth. The stranger cannot fail to notice the generally happy and smiling character of the native faces; and this first impression is, in most cases, wonderfully pleasant. The Japanese smile at first charms. It is only at a later time, when one has observed the same smile under extraordinary circumstances; in moments of pain, shame disappointment, that one becomes suspicious of it. Its apparent inopportuness may even, on certain occasions, cause violent anger. Indeed, many of the difficulties between foreign residents and their native servants have occurred due to the smile. Any man who believes in the British tradition that a good servant must be solemn, is not likely to endure the smile of his "boy" with patience. At present, however, this particular phase of Western eccentricity is becoming more fully recognized by the Japanese. They are beginning to learn that the average English-speaking foreigner hates smiling, and is likely to consider it insulting; therefore, Japanese employees at the open ports have generally ceased to smile, and have assumed an attitude of sullenness.

At this moment, there comes to me the memory of a strange story told by a lady of Yokohama, about one of her Japanese servants: "My Japanese nurse came to me the other day, smiling as if something very pleasant had happened, and said that her husband was dead, and that she wanted permission to attend his funeral. I told her she could go. It seems they burned the man's body. Well, in the evening, she returned, and showed me a vase containing some ashes of bones (I saw a tooth among them); and she said, 'That is my husband.' And she actually laughed as she did it! Did you ever hear of such disgusting creatures?"

It would have been quite impossible to convince the narrator of this incident, that the behavior of her servant, instead of being heartless, might have been heroic, and capable of a very touching interpretation. Even one not a Philistine, might be deceived in such a case by appearances; however, quite a number of the foreign residents of the open ports are pure Philistines, and never try to look below the surface of the life around them, except as hostile critics. My Yokohama friend, who told me the story about the *kurumaya* was quite differently inclined: he recognized the error of judging by appearances.

II

Miscomprehension of the Japanese smile has more than once led to extremely unpleasant results, as happened in the case of "T", a Yokohama merchant of former days. "T" had employed, in some capacity (I think partly as a teacher of Japanese) a nice old samurai, who wore, according to the fashion of the era, a *magé* and two swords. The English and the Japanese do not understand each other very well now; but at the time in question, they understood each other much less. The Japanese servants in foreign employment, at first acted precisely as they would have acted in the service of distinguished Japanese;[i] and this innocent mistake provoked a good deal of abuse and cruelty. Finally, the discovery was made that, to treat Japanese like West Indian Negroes, might be very dangerous. A certain number of foreigners were killed, with good moral consequences.

But, I am digressing. "T" was rather pleased with his old samurai, though quite unable to understand his Japanese politeness, his bows, or the meaning of the small gifts which he presented occasionally, with an exquisite courtesy — entirely wasted on "T". One day, he came to ask a favor. (I think it was the eve of the Japanese New Year, when everybody needs money, for reasons not to be dwelt on here). The favor was that "T" would lend him a little money on one of his swords, the long one. It was a very beautiful weapon, and the merchant saw that it was also very valuable, and lent the money without hesitation. Some weeks later, the old man was able to redeem his sword.

What caused the beginning of the subsequent unpleasantness nobody now remembers. Perhaps "T's" nerves got out of order. Be that as it may, one day he became very angry with the old man, who submitted to the expression of his wrath with bows and smiles. This made him still more angry, and he used some extremely bad language; but the old man still bowed and smiled; accordingly, he was ordered to leave the house. But the old man

---

[i] Author's Footnote: The reader will find it well worth his while to consult the chapter entitled "Domestic Service," in Miss Bacon's *Japanese Girls and Women*, [*Japanese Girls and Women*, by Alice Mabel Bacon, Copyright 1892, Houghton, Mifflin and Company] for ain interesting and just presentation of the practical sides of the subject, as relating to servants of both sexes. The poetic side, however, is not treated, perhaps because intimately connected with religious beliefs which one, writing from the Christian standpoint, could not be expected to consider sympathetically. Domestic service in ancient Japan was both transfigured and regulated by religion; and the force of the religious sentiment concerning it may be discerned from the Buddhist saying, still current:

Oya-ko wa is-se,
Fūfu wa ni-se,
Shujū wa san-se.

The relation of parent and child endures for the space of one life only; that of husband and wife for the space of two lives; but the relation between master and servant continues for the period of three existences.

continued to smile, at which "T", losing all self-control, struck him. And then "T" suddenly became afraid, for the long sword instantly leaped from its sheath, and swirled above him. The old man ceased to seem old. Now, in the grasp of anyone who knows how to use it, the razor-edged blade of a Japanese sword, wielded with both hands, can take a head off with extreme ease. But, to "T's" astonishment, the old samurai, almost in the same moment, returned the blade to its sheath with the skill of a practiced swordsman, turned on his heel, and left.

Then "T" wondered, and sat down to think. He began to remember some nice things about the old man, the many kindnesses unasked and unpaid, the curious little gifts, the impeccable honesty. "T" began to feel ashamed. He tried to console himself with the thought, "Well, it was his own fault; he had no right to laugh at me when he knew I was angry." Indeed, "T" even resolved to make amends when an opportunity offered itself.

But no opportunity ever came, because on the same old man performed *hara-kiri*, after the manner of a samurai. He left a very beautiful written letter explaining his reasons. For a samurai to receive an unjust blow, without avenging it, was a shame not to be borne. He had received such a blow, and under any other circumstances, he might have avenged it; however, the circumstances were, in this case, of a very peculiar kind. His code of honor forbade him to use his sword on the man to whom he had pledged it once for money, in an hour of need. And thus, being unable to use his sword, there remained only the alternative of an honorable suicide for him.

In order to make this story less disagreeable, the reader may suppose that "T" was really very sorry and behaved generously to the family of the old man. What he must not suppose is that "T" was ever able to imagine why the old man had smiled the smile, which led to the outrage, and the tragedy.

III

To comprehend the Japanese smile, one must be able to enter a little into the ancient, natural, and popular life of Japan. From the modernized upper classes, nothing is to be learned. The deeper significance of racial differences is being daily, more and more, illustrated in the effects of higher education. Instead of creating any community of feeling, it appears only to widen the distance between the West and the East. Some foreign observers have declared that it does this by developing certain, latent peculiarities to an extreme; among others, an inherent materialism little perceptible among the common people. This explanation is one I cannot quite agree with; but it is at least undeniable that, the more highly he is cultivated, according to Western methods, the farther the Japanese is psychologically removed from us. Under the new education, his character seems to crystallize into something of singular hardness, and to Western observation at least, of unique opacity.

Emotionally, the Japanese child appears incomparably closer to us than the Japanese mathematician, the peasant than the statesman. Between the most elevated class of thoroughly modernized Japanese and the Western thinker, anything resembling intellectual sympathy is non-existent: it is replaced on the native side by a cold and faultless politeness. Those influences, which in other lands appear most potent to develop the higher emotions, seem here to have the extraordinary effect of suppressing them. Abroad, we are accustomed to associating emotional sensibility with intellectual expansion: it would be a grievous error to apply this rule in Japan. Even the foreign teacher, in an extraordinary school, can feel, year by year, his students drifting farther away from him, as they pass from class to class. In various higher educational institutions, the separation widens still more rapidly; so that, prior to graduation, pupils may become to their professor, little more than casual acquaintances.

The enigma is perhaps, to some extent, a physiological one, requiring scientific explanation; but its solution must first be sought in ancestral habits of life and imagination. It can be fully discussed only when its natural causes are understood; and these, we may be sure, are not simple. According to some observers, it is asserted that, because higher education in Japan has not yet had the effect of stimulating the higher emotions to the Western level, its developing power cannot have been exerted uniformly and wisely, but in special directions only, at the cost of character. Yet, this theory involves the unjustifiable assumption that character can be created by education; and it ignores the fact that the best results are obtained by affording opportunity for the exercise of preexisting inclination, rather than by any system of teaching.

The causes of the phenomenon must be looked for in the national character; and whatever higher education may accomplish in the remote future; it can scarcely be expected to transform nature. But, does it at present, atrophy certain finer tendencies? I think that it unavoidably does; for the simple reason that, under existing conditions, the moral and mental powers are overtasked by its requirements. All that wonderful national spirit of duty, of patience, of self-sacrifice, anciently directed to social, moral, or religious idealism, must, under the discipline of higher training, be concentrated upon an end which not only demands, but exhausts its fullest exercise. For that end, to be accomplished at all, must be accomplished in the face of difficulties that the Western student rarely encounters, and could scarcely be made even to understand. All those moral qualities that made the old Japanese character admirable are certainly the same that make the modern Japanese student the most indefatigable, the most docile, the most ambitious in the world. But they are also qualities which urge him to efforts in excess of his natural powers, with the frequent result of mental and moral exhaustion. The nation has entered into a period of intellectual overstrain. Consciously or unconsciously, in obedience to sudden necessity, Japan has undertaken nothing less than the tremendous task of forcing mental expansion to the highest existing standard: this means forcing the development of the nervous system. For the desired intellectual change, to be accomplished within a few generations, must involve a physiological change that cannot be produced without terrible cost. In other words, Japan has attempted too much.

Yet, under the circumstances, she could not have attempted less. Happily, even among the poorest of her poor, the educational policy of the government is seconded with an astonishing zeal. The entire nation has plunged into study with a fervor of which it is utterly impossible to convey any adequate conception in this little essay. Yet, I will cite a touching example. Immediately after the frightful earthquake of 1891, the children of the ruined cities of Gifu and Aichi, crouching among the ashes of their homes, cold and hungry and shelterless, surrounded by horror and unspeakable misery, still continued their studies, using tiles, from their own burnt houses instead of slates, and bits of lime for chalk, even while the earth still trembled beneath them.[1] Such a fact reveals what future miracles may justly be expected from the amazing power of such purpose.

It is true that as yet, the results of higher training have not been altogether happy. Among the Japanese of the old régime, one encounters a courtesy, an unselfishness, a grace of pure goodness, impossible to over-praise. Among the modernized of the new generation, these have almost disappeared. One meets a class of young men who ridicule the old times and the old ways, without having been able to elevate themselves above the vulgarity of imitation and the commonness of shallow skepticism. What has become of the noble and charming qualities they must have inherited from their fathers? Is it not possible that the best of those qualities have been transmuted into mere effort; an effort so excessive as to have exhausted character, leaving it without weight or balance?

It is to the still fluid, mobile, natural existence of the common people that one must look for the meaning of some apparent differences in the racial feeling and emotional expression of the West and the Far East. It is possible to enjoy common feelings with those gentle, kindly, sweet-hearted folk, who smile at life, love, and death alike; and by familiarity and sympathy, we can learn why they smile.

The Japanese child is born with this happy tendency, which is fostered through the entire period of home education. But it is cultivated with the same exquisiteness that is shown in the cultivation of the natural tendencies of a garden plant. The smile is taught like the bow; like the prostration; like that little hissing sucking in of the breath, which follows, as a token of pleasure, the salutation to a superior; like all the elaborate and beautiful etiquette of the old courtesy. Laugher is not encouraged, for

---

[1] Author's Footnote: The shocks continued, though with lessening frequency and violence, for more than six months after the cataclysm. [This was the Mino-Owari Earthquake (美濃尾張地震, Mino-Owari Jishin) that struck the former provinces of Mino and Owari in the Nōbi Plain area during the Meiji period. It is also referred to as the Nōbi Earthquake (濃尾地震, Nōbi Jishin) or the Great Nōbi Earthquake (濃尾大地震, Nōbi Daijishin) and is the largest known inland earthquake in central Japan. The earthquake struck on October 28, 1891, at 6:38am. Based on the scale of destruction, it has since been estimated to have had a magnitude of 8.0 on the Richter Scale.]

obvious reasons, but the smile is to be used on all pleasant occasions, when speaking to a superior or to an equal, and even on occasions that are not pleasant — it is part of manners.

The most agreeable face is the smiling face, and to always present the most agreeable face possible to parents, relatives, teachers, friends, and well-wishers, is like a rule of life. And furthermore, it is a rule of life to present to the outer world an appearance of happiness, to convey to others, as far as possible, a pleasant impression. Even though the heart is breaking, it is a social duty to smile bravely. On the other hand, to look serious or unhappy is rude, because this may cause anxiety or pain to those who love us; likewise, it is foolish, since it may excite unkindly curiosity on the part of those who don't love us. Cultivated from childhood as a duty, the smile soon becomes instinctive.

In the mind of the poorest peasant lives the conviction that, to exhibit the expression of one's personal sorrow, pain or anger is rarely useful, and always unkind. Hence, although natural grief must have, in Japan as elsewhere, its natural expression, an uncontrollable burst of tears in the presence of superiors or guests is an impoliteness. The first words of even the most uneducated country woman, after the nerves give way in such a circumstance, are invariably, "Pardon my selfishness in that I have been so rude!" It should also be observed that the reasons

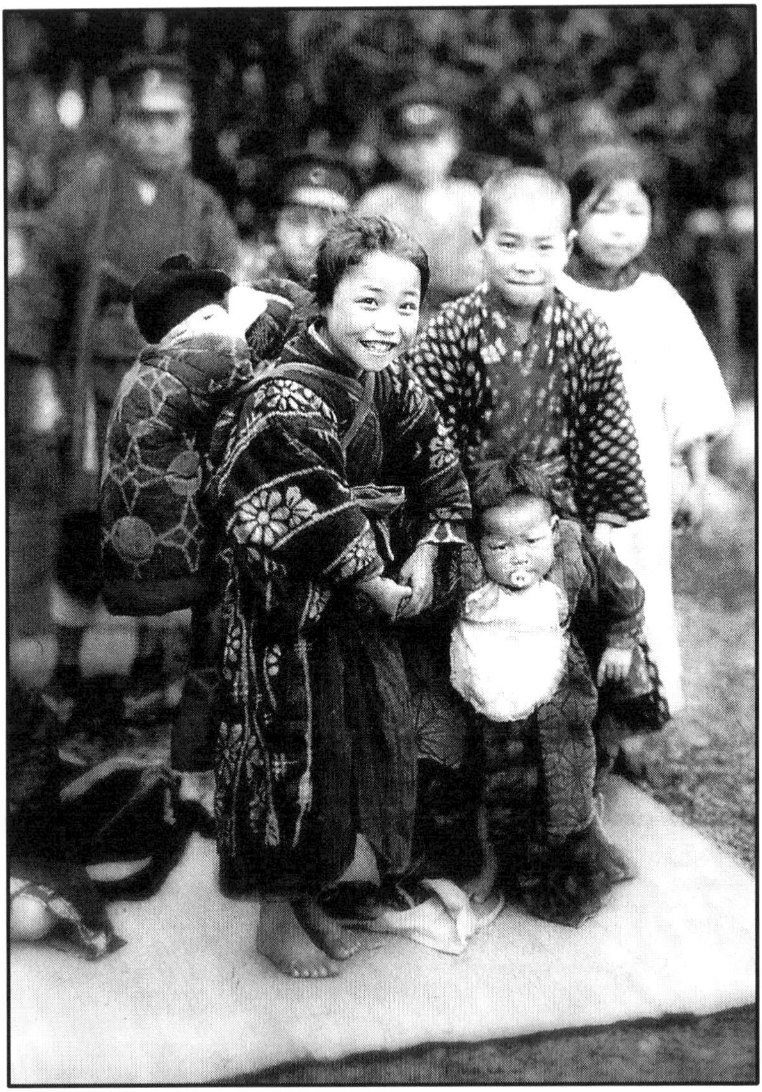

for the smile are not only moral; they are to some extent aesthetic; partly representing the same idea which regulated the expression of suffering in Greek art; however, they are much more moral than aesthetic, as we shall presently see.

From this primary etiquette of the smile, a secondary etiquette has developed; the observance of which has frequently caused foreigners to form the most cruel misjudgments as to Japanese sensibility. It is the native custom that, whenever a painful or shocking fact must be told, the announcement should be made, by the sufferer, with a smile.[1] The more grave the subject, the more accentuated the smile. When the matter is very unpleasant to the person speaking of it, the smile often changes to a low, soft laugh. However bitterly the mother who has lost her first-borne may have wept at the funeral, it is probable that, if in your service, she will tell of her bereavement with a smile: like the preacher, she holds that there is a time to weep and a time to laugh. It was a long while before I myself could understand how it was possible for those who I believed to have loved a person who recently died, to tell me of that death with a laugh. Yet, the laugh was politeness carried to the greatest point of self-denial. It meant, "This you might honorably think to be an unhappy event. Please do not allow your superiority to feel concern about so inferior a matter, and pardon the necessity which causes us to outrage politeness by speaking about such an affair at all."

The key to the mystery of the most unaccountable smiles is Japanese politeness. The servant sentenced to dismissal for a fault, prostrates himself, and asks pardon with a smile. That smile indicates the very reverse of callousness or insolence: "Be assured that I am satisfied with the great justice of your honorable sentence, and that I am now aware of the gravity of my fault. Yet, my sorrow and my necessity have caused me to indulge the unreasonable hope that I may be forgiven for my great rudeness in asking pardon." The youth or girl beyond the age of childish tears, when punished for some error, receives the punishment with a smile, which means: "No evil feeling arises in my heart; much worse than this my fault has deserved." And the *kurumaya* cut by the whip of my Yokohama friend, smiled for a similar reason, as my friend must have intuitively felt, since the smile at once disarmed him: "I was wrong, and you are right to

---

[1] Author's Footnote: Of course, the converse is the rule in condoling with the sufferers.

be angry. I deserve to be struck, and therefore feel no resentment."

But it should be understood that the poorest and humblest Japanese is rarely submissive under injustice. His apparent docility is chiefly due to his moral sense. The foreigner who strikes a native for sport may have reason to find that he has made a serious mistake. The Japanese are not to be trifled with, and brutal attempts to trifle with them have cost several worthless lives.

Even after the foregoing explanations, the incident of the Japanese nurse may still seem incomprehensible; but this, I feel quite sure, is because the narrator either suppressed or overlooked certain facts in the case. In the first half of the story, all is perfectly clear. When announcing her husband's death, the young servant smiled, in accordance with the native formality already referred to. What is quite incredible is that, of her own accord, she should have invited the attention of her mistress to the contents of the vase, or funeral urn. If she knew enough of Japanese politeness to smile in announcing her husband's death, she must certainly have known enough to prevent her from perpetrating such an error. She could have shown the vase and its contents only in obedience to some real or imagined command; and when so doing, it is more than possible she may have spoken the low, soft laugh that accompanies either the unavoidable performance of a painful duty, or the enforced utterance of a painful statement. My own opinion is that she was obliged to gratify an unjustifiable curiosity. Her smile or laugh would then have signified: "Do not permit your honorable feelings to be shocked on my unworthy account; it is indeed very rude of me, even at your honorable request, to mention so contemptible a thing as my sorrow.

IV

The Japanese smile must not be imagined as a kind of *sourire figé*,[1] perpetually worn as a mask for the soul. Like other matters of behavior, it is regulated by an etiquette, which varies in different classes of society. As a rule, the old samurai were not given to smiling on all occasions; they reserved their amiability

---

[1] French, literaly translated as a "fixed smile."

for superiors and friends, and would seem to have maintained, toward inferiors, an austere reserve. The dignity of the Shintō priesthood has become proverbial; and for centuries the gravity of the Confucian code was mirrored in the decorum of magistrates and officials. From ancient times, the nobility affected a still loftier reserve; and the solemnity of rank deepened through all the hierarchies, up to that awesome state surrounding the Tenshi-sama,[1] upon whose face no living man may look. But in private life, the behavior of even the highest had its amiable relaxation; and even today, with some hopelessly modernized exceptions, the noble, the judge, the high priest, the august minister, the military officer, will assume at home, in the break from duty, the charming habits of the antique courtesy.

---

[1] Tenshi-sama refers to the Emperor.

The smile, which illuminates conversation, is in itself, but a small detail of that courtesy; but the sentiment that it symbolizes certainly makes up the larger part. If you happen to have a cultivated Japanese friend, who in all things has remained truly Japanese; whose character has remained untouched by the new egotism and by foreign influences, you will almost certainly be able to study in him, the particular social traits of the whole people: traits in his case exquisitely accentuated and polished. You will observe that, as a rule, he never speaks of himself, and that, in reply to searching personal questions, he will answer as vaguely and briefly as possible, with a polite bow of thanks. But on the other hand, he will ask many questions about yourself: your opinions, your ideas, even trifling details of your daily life seem to have deep interest for him. You will probably have occasion to note that he never forgets anything which he has learned concerning you; yet, there are certain rigid limits to his kindly curiosity, and perhaps even to his observation: he will never refer to any disagreeable or painful matter, and he will seem to remain blind to eccentricities or small weaknesses, if you have any. To your face, he will never praise you; but he will never laugh at you or criticize you. Indeed, you will find that he never criticizes people, but only the results of their actions. As a private adviser, he will not even directly criticize a plan of which he disapproves, but is apt to suggest a new one, in some such guarded language as: "Perhaps it might be more to your immediate interest to do thus and so." When obliged to speak to others, he will refer to them in a curious, indirect fashion, by citing and combining a number of incidents sufficiently characteristic to form a picture. But in that event, the incidents narrated will almost certainly be of a nature to awaken interest, and to create a favorable impression. This indirect way of conveying information is essentially Confucian. "Even when you have no doubt," says the *Li-Ki*,[103] "do not let what you say appear as your own view."

It is quite probable that you will notice many other traits in your friend requiring some knowledge of Chinese classics to understand; but no such knowledge is necessary to convince you of his exquisite consideration for others, and his studied suppression of self. Among no other civilized people is the secret of happy living so thoroughly comprehended as among the Japanese. By no other race is the truth so widely understood that our pleasure in life must depend on the happiness of those around us, and consequently, on the cultivation in ourselves of unselfishness and patience. For which reason, in Japanese society, sarcasm, irony, and cruel wit are not indulged. I might almost say that they have no existence in refined life. A personal failing is not made the subject of ridicule or reproach; an eccentricity is not commented on; and involuntary mistake excites no laughter.

Stiffened somewhat by the Chinese conservatism of the old conditions, it is true that this ethical system was maintained to the extreme of giving strength to ideas, and at the cost of individuality. Yet, if regulated by a broader comprehension of social requirements, if expanded by scientific understanding of the freedom that is essential for intellectual evolution, the very same moral policy is that through which the highest and happiest results may be obtained. However, as actually practiced, it was not favorable to originality; it rather tended to enforce that amiable mediocrity of opinion and imagination that still prevails. For that reason, a foreigner living in the interior cannot but sometimes long for the sharp, erratic inequities of Western life, with its larger joys and pains, and its more comprehensive sympathies; but only sometimes, for the intellectual loss is really more than compensated for by the social charm, and there can remain no doubt in the mind of one who even partly understands the Japanese, that they are still the best people in the world to live among.

V

As I write these lines, there returns to me the vision of a Kyōto night. While passing through some wonderfully crowded and illuminated street, of which I cannot remember the name, I had turned aside to look at a statue of Jizō, in front of the entrance to a very small temple. The figure was that of a *kozō*, an acolyte, a beautiful boy; and its smile was a bit of divine realism. As I stood gazing, a young lad, perhaps ten years old, ran up beside me, joined his little hands in front of the image, bowed his head, and prayed for a moment in silence. He had only just left some friends, and the joy and glow of play was still on his face. His unconscious smile was so strangely like the smile of the child of stone, that the boy seemed like the twin brother of the god. Then I thought, "The smile of bronze or stone is not only a copy, but that which the Buddhist sculptor symbolizes must be the explanation of the smile of the race."

That was long ago; but the idea, which then suggested itself, still seems true to me. However foreign to Japanese soil the origin of Buddhist art is, the smile of the people signifies the same concept as the smile of the bosatsu: the happiness that is born from self-control and self-suppression. "If a man conquers a thousand times a thousand in battle, and another conquers himself, he who conquers himself is the greatest of conquerors." "Not even a god can change into defeat, the victory of the man who has conquered himself."[i] Such Buddhist texts as these, and there are many, surely express, although they cannot be assumed to have created, those moral tendencies that form the highest charm of the Japanese character. The whole moral idealism of the race seems to me to have been personified in that marvelous Buddha of Kamakura, whose countenance, "calm like a deep, still water,"[ii] expresses, as perhaps no other work of human hands can have expressed, the eternal truth: "There is no higher happiness than rest."[iii] It is toward that infinite calm that the aspirations of the Orient have been turned; and the ideal of the supreme self-conquest it has made its own. Even now, though agitated at its surface by those new influences that must sooner or later move it even to its extreme depths, the Japanese mind

---

[i] Author's Footnote: *Dhammapda*.
[ii] Author's Footnote: *Dammikkasutta*.
[iii] Author's Footnote: *Dhammalpada*.

retains, as compared with the thought of the West, a wonderful placidness. It little dwells, if at all, on those ultimate abstract questions about which we most concern ourselves. Neither does it comprehend our interest in them, as we desire to be comprehended. "That you should not be indifferent to religious speculations," a Japanese scholar once observed to me, "is quite natural; but it is equally natural that we should never trouble ourselves about them. The philosophy of Buddhism has an insightfulness far exceeding that of your Western theology, and we have studied it. We have sounded the depths of speculation only to find that there are depths unfathomable below those depths; we have voyaged to the farthest limit that thought may sail, only to find that the horizon recedes forever. And you, you have remained for many thousands of years like children playing in a stream, but ignorant of the sea. Only now, you have reached its shore by another path than ours, and the vastness is for you a new wonder; and you would sail to Nowhere because you have seen the infinite over the sands of life."

Will Japan be able to assimilate Western civilization, as she did Chinese, more than ten centuries ago, and nevertheless preserve her own peculiar modes of thought and feeling? One striking fact is hopeful: that the Japanese admiration for Western material superiority is by no means extended to Western morals. Asian thinkers do not commit the serious blunder of confusing mechanical with ethical progress; nor have they failed to perceive the moral weaknesses of our boasted civilization. One Japanese writer has expressed his judgment of things Western, after a fashion that deserves to be noticed by a larger circle of readers than that for which it was originally written:

> *Order or disorder in a nation does not depend on something that falls from the sky or rises from the earth. It is determined by the disposition of the people. The pivot on which the public disposition turns towards order or disorder is the point where public and private motives separate. If the people are influenced chiefly by public considerations, order is assured; but if by private, disorder is inevitable. Public considerations are those that prompt the proper observance of duties; their prevalence signifies peace and prosperity in the way similar to families, communities, and nations. Private considerations are those suggested by selfish motives: when they prevail, disturbance and disorder are unavoidable. As members of a family, our duty is to look after the welfare of that family; as members of a nation, our duty is to*

work for the good of the nation. To regard our family affairs with all the interest due to our family, and our national affairs with all the interest due to our nation, that is to fitly discharge our duty, and to be guided by public considerations. On the other hand, to regard the affairs of the nation as if they were our own family affairs, this is to be influenced by private motives and to stray from the path of duty.

Selfishness is born in every man; to indulge it freely is to become a beast; therefore, sages preach the principles of duty and propriety, justice and morality, providing restraints for private aims and encouragements for public spirit. What we know of Western civilization is that it struggled on through long centuries in a confused condition, and finally attained a state of some order, but that even this order, not being based on such principles as those of natural and indisputable distinctions between sovereign and subject, parent and child, with all their corresponding rights and duties, is liable to constant change; according to the growth of human ambitions and human aims. Admirably suited to persons whose actions are controlled by selfish ambition, the adoption of this system in Japan is naturally sought by a certain class of politicians. From a superficial point of view, the Western form of society is very attractive; in as much as, being the outcome of a free development of human desires from ancient times, it represents the very extreme of luxury and extravagance. Briefly speaking, the state of obtaining things in the West is based on the free play of human selfishness, and can only be reached by giving full sway to that quality. In the West, little notice is given to social disturbances; yet they are at once the evidence and the factors of the present evil state of affairs. Do Japanese, enamored with Western ways, propose to have their nation's history written in similar terms? Do they seriously contemplate turning their country into a new field for experiments in Western civilization?

In the Orient, from ancient times, national government has been based on benevolence, and directed to securing the welfare and happiness of the people. No political creed has ever held that intellectual strength should be cultivated for the purpose of exploiting inferiority and ignorance. The inhabitants of this empire live, for the most part, by manual labor. No matter how industrious they are, they hardly earn enough to supply their daily needs. They earn, on the average, about twenty sen daily. For them there is no question of aspiring to wearing fine clothes or to inhabit handsome houses. Neither can they hope to reach positions of fame and honor. What offense have these poor people committed that they also, should not share the benefits of Western civilization? Indeed, by some, their condition is explained on the hypothesis that their desires do not prompt them to better themselves. There is no truth in such a supposition. They have desires, but nature has limited their capacity to satisfy them; their duty as men limits it, and the amount of labor physically possible for a human being limits it. They achieve as much as their opportunities permit. The best and finest products of their labor they reserve for the wealthy; the worst and roughest they keep for their own use. Yet, there is nothing in human society that does not owe its existence to labor. Now, to satisfy the desires of one luxurious man, the work of a thousand is needed. Surely, it is monstrous that those who owe to labor, the pleasures suggested by their civilization, should forget what they owe to the laborer, and treat him as if he were not a fellow being. But civilization, according to the interpretation of the West, serves only to satisfy men of large desires. It is of no benefit to the masses, but is simply a system under which ambitions compete to accomplish their aims. That the Western system is gravely disturbing to the order and peace of a country is seen by men who have eyes, and heard by men who have hears. The future of Japan, under such a system, fills us with anxiety. A system, based on the principle that ethics and religion are made to serve human ambition, naturally agrees with the wishes of selfish individuals; and such theories as those, embodied in the modern formula of liberty and equality, annihilate the established relations of society, and outrange decorum and propriety. Absolute equality and absolute liberty being unattainable, the limits prescribed by right and duty are supposed to be set. But as each person seeks to have as much right and to be burdened with as little duty as possible, the results are endless disputes and legal contentions. The principles of liberty and equality may succeed in changing the organization of nations, in overthrowing the lawful distinctions of social rank, in reducing all men to one nominal level; but they can never accomplish the equal distribution of wealth and property. Consider America...It is plain that if the mutual rights of men and their status are made to depend on degrees of wealth, the majority of the people, being without wealth, must fail to establish their rights; whereas the minority who are wealthy, will assert their rights; and, under society's sanction, will exact oppressive duties from the poor; neglecting the dictates of humanity and benevolence. The adoption of these principles of liberty and equality in Japan would annul the good and peaceful customs of our country, render the general disposition of the people harsh and unfeeling, and finally prove to be a source of calamity to the masses...

Though at first sight, Western civilization presents an attractive appearance, adapted as it is to the gratification of selfish desires; yet, since its basis is the hypothesis that men's wishes constitute natural laws, it must ultimately end in disappointment and demoralization. Western nations have become what they are after passing through conflicts and deviations of the most serious kind; and it is their fate to continue the struggle. Just now, their motive elements are in partial equilibrium, and their social condition is more or less ordered. But if this slight equilibrium happens to be disturbed, they will be thrown once more into confusion, and change; until, after a period of renewed struggle and suffering, temporary stability is once more attained. The poor and powerless of the present may become the wealthy and strong of the future, and vice versa. Perpetual disturbance is their doom. Peaceful equality can never be attained until built up among the ruins of annihilated Western states and the ashes of extinct Western people.[104]

Surely, with perceptions like these, Japan may hope to avert some of the social perils which menace her. Yet, it appears inevitable that her approaching transformation must be coincident with a moral decline. Forced into the vast industrial competition of nations whose civilizations were never based on altruism, she must eventually develop those qualities of which the comparative absence made all the wonderful charm of her life. The national character must continue to harden, as it has begun to harden already. But it should never be forgotten that old Japan was quite as much in advance of the nineteenth century morally, as she was behind it materially. She had made morality instinctive, after having made it rational. She had realized, though within restricted limits, several among those social conditions which our ablest thinkers regard as the happiest and the highest. Throughout all the grades of her complex society, she had cultivated both the comprehension and the practice of public and private duties after a manner for which it were vain to seek any Western parallel. Even her moral weakness was the result of an excess of that which all civilized religions have united in proclaiming virtue: the self-sacrifice of the individual for the sake of family, of the community, and of the nation. It was the weakness indicated by Percival Lowell in his *Soul of the Far East*, a book of which the consummate genius cannot be justly estimated without some personal knowledge of the Far East.[105] The progress made by Japan in social morality, although greater than our own, was chiefly in the direction of mutual dependence. And it will be her coming duty to keep in view the teaching of that mighty thinker whose philosophy she has wisely accepted;[i] the teaching that "the highest individuation must be joined with the greatest mutual dependence," and that, however seemingly paradoxical the statement, "the law of progress is at once toward complete separateness and complete union."

Yet to that past which her younger generation now affect to despise, Japan will certainly on day look back, even as we ourselves look back to the old Greek civilization. She will learn to regret the forgotten capacity for simple pleasures, the lost sense of the pure joy of life, the old loving divine intimacy with nature, the marvelous dead art which reflected it. She will remember how much more luminous and beautiful the world then seemed. She will mourn for many things — the old-fashioned patience and self-sacrifice, the ancient courtesy, the deep human poetry of the ancient faith. She will wonder at many things; but she will regret. Perhaps she will wonder most of all at the faces of the ancient gods, because their smile was once the likeness of her own.

---

[i] Author's Footnote: Herert Spencer.

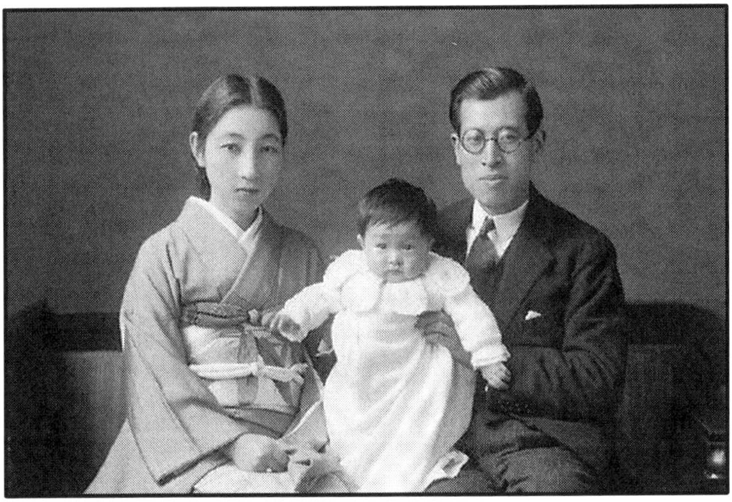

XXVII

Sayōnara!

I

I am going away: very far away. I have already resigned my post as teacher, and am waiting only for my passport.

So many familiar faces have vanished that I now feel less regret at leaving than I would have felt six months ago. Nevertheless, the quaint old city has become so dear to me by habit and association, that the thought of never seeing it again is one I do not venture to dwell on. I have been trying to persuade myself that someday, I may return to this charming old house, in shadowy *Kitaborimachi*, although all the while painfully aware that in past experience, such imaginings invariably preceded perpetual separation.

The facts are that all things are impermanent in the Province of the Gods; that the winters are very severe; and that I have received a call from the great government college in Kyūshū, far south, where snow rarely falls. Also I have been very sick; and the prospect of a milder climate had much influence in shaping my decision.[1]

But these few days of farewells have been full of charming surprises. To have the revelation of gratitude, where you had no right to expect more than plain satisfaction with your performance of duty; to find affection where you supposed only goodwill existed: these are assuredly delicious experiences.

The teachers of both schools have sent me a farewell gift; a superb pair of vases, nearly three feet high, covered with designs representing birds, and flowering trees overhanging a slope of beach, where funny pink crabs are running about; vases made in the old feudal days at Rakusan: rare souvenirs of Izumo. With the wonderful vases came a scroll bearing, in *kanji*, the names of the thirty-two donors; and three of these are names of ladies: the three lady teachers of the Normal School.

The students of the Jinjō-Chūgakkō have also sent me a present; the last contribution of two hundred and fifty-one pupils to my happiest memories of Matsué: a Japanese sword of the time of the *daimyō*. Silver *karashishi* with eyes of gold — in Izumo, the Lions of Shintō — swarm over the crimson lacquer of the sheath, and sprawl around the exquisite hilt. The committee who brought the beautiful thing to my house, requested me to accompany them forthwith to the college assembly room, where the students were all waiting to bid me goodbye, after the old-time custom.

So I went there. And the things which we said to each other are hereafter set down.

II

> DEAR TEACHER: *You have been one of the best and most beloved teachers we ever had. We thank you with all our heart for the knowledge we obtained through your kindest instruction. Every student in our school hoped you would stay with us at least three years. When we learned you had resolved to go to Kyūshū, we all felt our hearts sink with sorrow. We entreated our director to find some way to keep you, but we discovered that could not be*

---

[1] In fact, Mrs. Hearn frequently said that her husband suffered terribly during the bitterly cold winters of Matsué.

done. We have no words to express our feeling at this moment of farewell. We sent you a Japanese sword as a memory of us. It was only a poor, ugly thing; we merely thought you would care for it as a mark of our gratitude. We will never forget your kindest instruction; and we all wish that you may ever be healthy and happy.

MASANOBU ŌTANI,[i]

Representing all the Students of the Middle School of Shimane-ken.

MY DEAR BOYS: I cannot tell you with what feelings I received your present; that beautiful sword with the silver *kara-shishi* romping on its sheath, or crawling through the silken cords of its wonderful hilt. At least I cannot tell you all. But there flashed to me, as I looked at your gift, the remembrance of your ancient proverb: "The Sword is the Soul of the Samurai." And then it seemed to me that in the very choice of that exquisite souvenir you had symbolized something of your own souls. For we English also have some famous sayings and proverbs about swords. Our poets call a good blade "trusty" and "true"; and of our best friend we may say, "He is true as steel," signifying in the ancient sense, the steel of a perfect sword, the steel to whose temper a warrior could trust his honor and his life. And so in your rare gift, which I shall keep and prize while I live, I find an emblem of your true-heartedness and affection. May you always keep fresh within your hearts, those impulses of generosity and kindliness and loyalty, which I have learned to know so well, and of which your gift will ever remain for me, the gracious symbol!

And a symbol not only of your affection and loyalty as students to teachers, but of that other beautiful sense of duty you expressed, when so many of you wrote down for me, as your dearest wish, the desire to die for His Imperial Majesty, your Emperor. That wish is holy: it means perhaps even more than you know, or can know, until you will have become much older and wiser. This is an era of great and rapid change; and it is probable that many of you, as you grow up, will not be able to

---

[i] Masanobu Ōtani, some years later, became Hearn's personal assistant in Tokyō. Later he became a Professor at Shinshu University in Tokyō and wrote of many of his personal memories of Hearn. [See *The Annotated Reminiscences of Lafcadio Hearn*, by Setsuko Koizumi, Edited by Hayato Tokugawa.]

believe everything that your fathers believed before you; though I sincerely trust you will at least continue always to respect the faith, even as you still respect the memory of your ancestors. But however much the life of New Japan may change around you, however much your own thoughts may change with the times, never allow that noble wish you expressed to me to pass away from your souls. Keep it burning there, as clear and pure as the flame of the little lamp that glows in front of your household shrine.

Perhaps some of you may have that wish. Many of you must become soldiers. Some will become officers. Some will enter the Naval Academy to prepare for the grand service of protecting the Empire by sea; and your Emperor and your country may even require your blood. But the greater number among you are destined to other careers, and may have no such chance of bodily self-sacrifice: except perhaps in the hour of some great national danger, which I trust Japan will never know. And there is another desire, not less noble, which may be your compass in civil life: to live for your country though you cannot die for it. Like the kindest and wisest of fathers, your government has provided for you these splendid schools, with all opportunities for the best instruction this scientific century can give, at a far less cost than any other civilized country can offer the same advantages. And all this in order that each of you may help to make your country wiser, richer, and stronger than it has ever been in the past. And whoever does his best, in any calling or profession, to ennoble and develop that calling or profession, gives his life to his Emperor and to his country no less truly than the soldier or the seaman who dies for duty.

I am not less sorry to leave you, I think, than you are to see me go. The more I have learned to know the hearts of Japanese students, the more I have learned to love their country. I think, however, that I shall see many of you again, though I never return to Matsué: some I am almost sure I shall meet elsewhere in future summers; some I may even hope to teach once more, in the government college to which I am going. But whether we meet again or not, be sure that my life has been made happier by knowing you, and that I shall always love you. And, now, with renewed thanks for your beautiful gift, goodbye!

III

The students of the Normal School gave me a farewell banquet in their hall. I had been with them so little during the year, less even than the stipulated six hours a week, that I could not have supposed they would feel much attachment to their foreign teacher. But I have still much to learn about my Japanese students. The banquet was delightful. The captain of each class, in turn, read in English, a brief farewell address which he had prepared; and more than one of those charming compositions, made beautiful with similes and sentiments drawn from the old Chinese and Japanese poets, will always remain in my memory. Then, the students sang their school songs for me and chanted the Japanese version of *Auld Lang Syne* at the close of the banquet. Then all, in military procession, escorted me home and cheered me farewell at my gate, with shouts of "*Manzai!*" "Good-bye!" We will march with you to the steamer when you go."

IV

But I will not have the pleasure of seeing them again. They are all gone far away: some to another world. Yet, it is only four days since I attended that farewell banquet at the Normal

School! A cruel visitation has closed its gates and scattered its students through the province.

Two nights ago, the Asiatic Cholera,[106] supposed to have been brought to Japan by Chinese vessels, broke out in different parts of the city; and among other places, in the Normal School. Several students and teachers died within a short time after having been attacked; others are even now lingering between life and death. The rest marched to the little, healthy village of Tamatsukuri, famed for its hot springs. But there the cholera again broke out, and it was decided to dismiss the survivors at once so they could go to their homes. There was no panic. The military discipline remained unbroken. Students and teachers fell at their posts. The medical authorities took charge of the great college building and the work of disinfection and sanitation is still going on. Only the convalescents and the fearless samurai President, Saitō Kumatarō, remain in it. Like the captain who refuses to leave his sinking ship until all souls are safe, the President stays in the center of danger, nursing the sick boys, overlooking the work of sanitation, transacting all the business usually entrusted to several subordinates, who he promptly sent away in the first hour of peril. He has had the joy of seeing two of his boys saved.

Of another, who was buried last night, I hear this: Only a little while before his death, and in spite of kindliest protest, he found strength, on seeing his President approaching his bedside, to rise on his elbow and give the military salute. And with that brave greeting to a brave man, he passed onto the Great Silence.

V

At last my passport has come. I must go.

The Middle School and the adjacent elementary schools have closed because of the appearance of cholera, and I protested against any gathering of the pupils to bid me good-bye; fearing the risk of exposing them to the chilly morning air by the shore of the infected river. But my protest was received only with a merry laugh. Last night, the Director sent word to all the captains of classes. For which reason, an hour after sunrise, some two hundred students, with their teachers, assemble before my gate to escort me to the wharf, near the long white bridge, where the little steamer is waiting. And we go.

Other students are already assembled at the wharf; and with them wait a multitude of people I know: friends or friendly acquaintances, parents and relatives of students; everyone to whom I can remember having done the slightest favor, and many more from whom I have received favors which I never had a chance to return — persons who worked for me, merchants from whom I purchased little things, a host of kind faces, smiling salutation. The governor sends his secretary with a courteous message; the President of the Normal School hurries down for a moment to shake hands. The Normal students have been sent to their homes, but many of their teachers are present. Most of all I miss my friend Nishida. He has been very sick for two long months, bleeding in the lungs; but his father brings me the gentlest of farewell letters from him, written in bed, and some pretty souvenirs.

Now, as I look at all these pleasant faces around me, I cannot but ask myself the question, "Could I have lived in the exercise of the same profession for the same length of time, in any other country, and have enjoyed a similar, unbroken experience of human goodness?" From each and all of these, I have received only kindness and courtesy. Not one has ever, even by accident, addressed to me a single unkind word. As a teacher of more than five hundred boys and men, I have never even had my patience tried. I wonder if such an experience is possible only in Japan?

The little steamer shrieks for her passengers. I shake many hands; most heartily perhaps that of the brave, kind President of the Normal School, and climb onboard. The Director of the Jinjō Chūgakkō, a few teachers of both schools, and one of my favorite pupils, follow: they are going to accompany me as far as the next port, from where my way will be over the mountains to Hiroshima.

It is a lovely, vapory morning, sharp with the first chill of winter. From the tiny deck, I take my last look at the quaint vista of the Ōhashigawa, with its long white bridge; at the peaked host of strange, dear old houses, crowding close to dip their feet in its glassy water; at the sails of the junks, gold-colored by the early sun; at the beautiful, fantastic shapes of the ancient hills.

Magical indeed is the charm of this land, like that of a land genuinely haunted by gods; so lovely is the spectral delicacy of its colors; so lovely the forms of its hills, blending with the forms of its clouds; so lovely, above all, those long trailings and bendings of mists which make its heights appear to hang in the air. A land where sky and earth intermingle so strangely, that what is reality may not be distinguished from what is illusion: that all seems like a mirage, about to vanish. For me, alas, it is about to vanish forever.

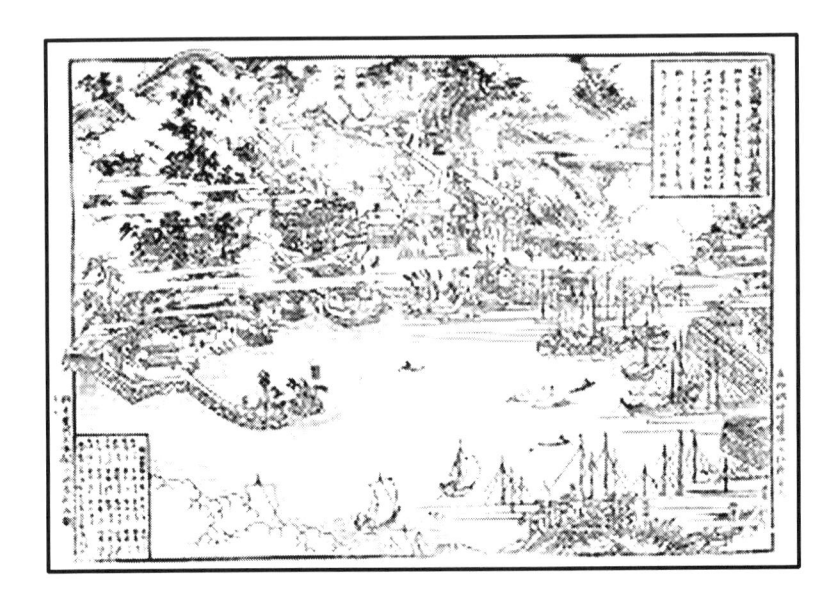

The little steamer shrieks again, puffs, backs into midstream, and turns from the long white bridge. As the gray wharves recede, a long "Aaaaaaaaaa" rises from the uniformed ranks, and all the caps wave, flashing their *kanji* of brass. I scramble up to the roof of the tiny deck cabin, wave my hat, and shout in English, "Good-bye, good-bye!" And there floats back to me the cry, "*Manzai, manzai!*" (Ten thousand years to you! Ten thousand years!) But already, it comes faintly from far away. The small boat glides out of the mouth of the river, shoots into the blue lake, turns a pine-shadowed point; and the faces, the voices, the wharves, and the long white bridge have become memories.

Still, for a little while, looking back as we pass into the silence of the great water, I can see, receding on the left, the crest of the ancient castle, over grand shaggy heights of pine; the place of my home with its delicious garden, and the long blue roofs of the schools. These too swiftly pass out of vision. Then, only faint blue water, faint blue mists, faint blues, greens, and grays of peaks looming through varying distances; and beyond all, towering ghost-white into the east, the glorious specter of Daisen.

My heart sinks for a moment, under the rush of those vivid memories which always crowd on one the instant after parting, — memories of all that make attachment to places and to things. Remembered smiles; the morning gathering at the threshold of the old *yashiki* to wish the departing teacher a happy day; the evening gathering to welcome his return; the dog waiting by the gate at the accustomed hour; the garden with its lotus flowers and its cooing doves; the musical boom of the temple bell from the cedar groves; songs of children at play; afternoon shadows on many-tinted streets; the long lines of lantern fires on festival nights; the dancing of the moon on the lake; the clapping of hands by the river shore in salutation to the Izumo sun; the endless merry pattering of *geta* over the windy bridge. All these and a hundred other, happy memories come back to me, with almost painful vividness, while the far peaks, whose names are holy, slowly turn away their blue shoulders, and the little steamer carries me, more and more swiftly, ever farther and farther from the Province of the Gods.

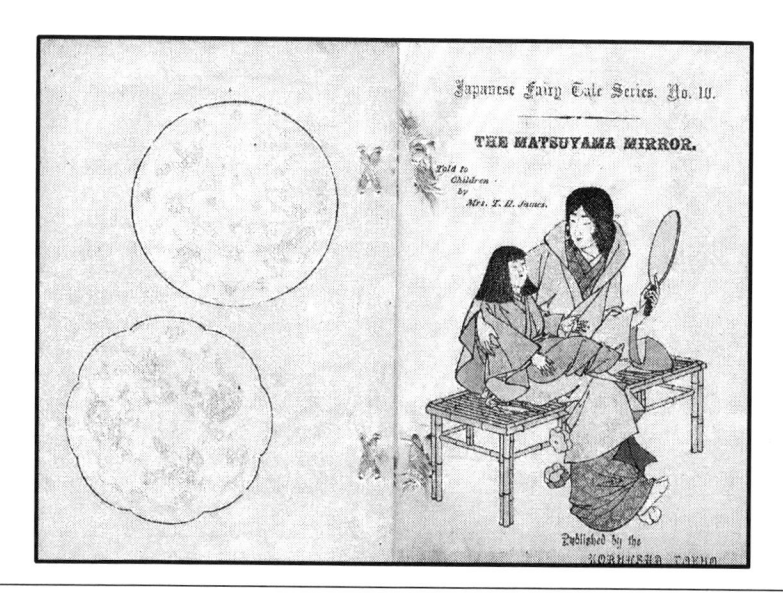

APPENDIX A

The following story, mentioned by the author in Chapter XVIII was originally published as *Japanese Fairy Tale No. 10* in December of 1886 by T. Hasegawa. Mrs. T. H. James was the translator/transliterator, and the illustrations were created by Sensei Eitaku. The same story included here, later appeared in a collection of Japanese "fairy stories" which included tales by Mrs. James, Basil Hall Chamberlain, Lafcadio Hean, and others, published in 1898 (with subsequent reprints).

339

THE MATSUYAMA MIRROR

By

Mrs. T. H. James

A long time ago, there lived in a quiet spot, a young man and his wife. They had one child, a little daughter, whom they both loved with all their hearts. I cannot tell you their names for they have been long since forgotten; but the name of the place where they lived was Matsuyama, in the province of Echigo.

It happened once, while the little girl was still a baby, that the father was obliged to go to the great city, the capital of Japan, upon some business. It was too far for the mother and her little baby to go, so he set out alone, after bidding them good-bye, and promising to bring them home some pretty present.

The mother had never been further from home than the next village, and she could not help being a little frightened at the thought of her husband taking such a long journey; and yet, she was a little proud too, for he was the first man in all that countryside who had been to the big city where the Emperor and his great lords lived, and where there were so many beautiful and curious things to be seen.

At last the time came when she might expect her husband's return, so she dressed the baby in its best clothes, and she herself put on a pretty blue kimono which she knew her husband liked.

You may guess how glad this good wife was to see him come home safe and sound, and how the little girl clapped her hands and laughed with delight when she saw the pretty toys her father had brought for her. H had much to tell of all the wonderful things he had seen upon the journey, and in the town itself.

341

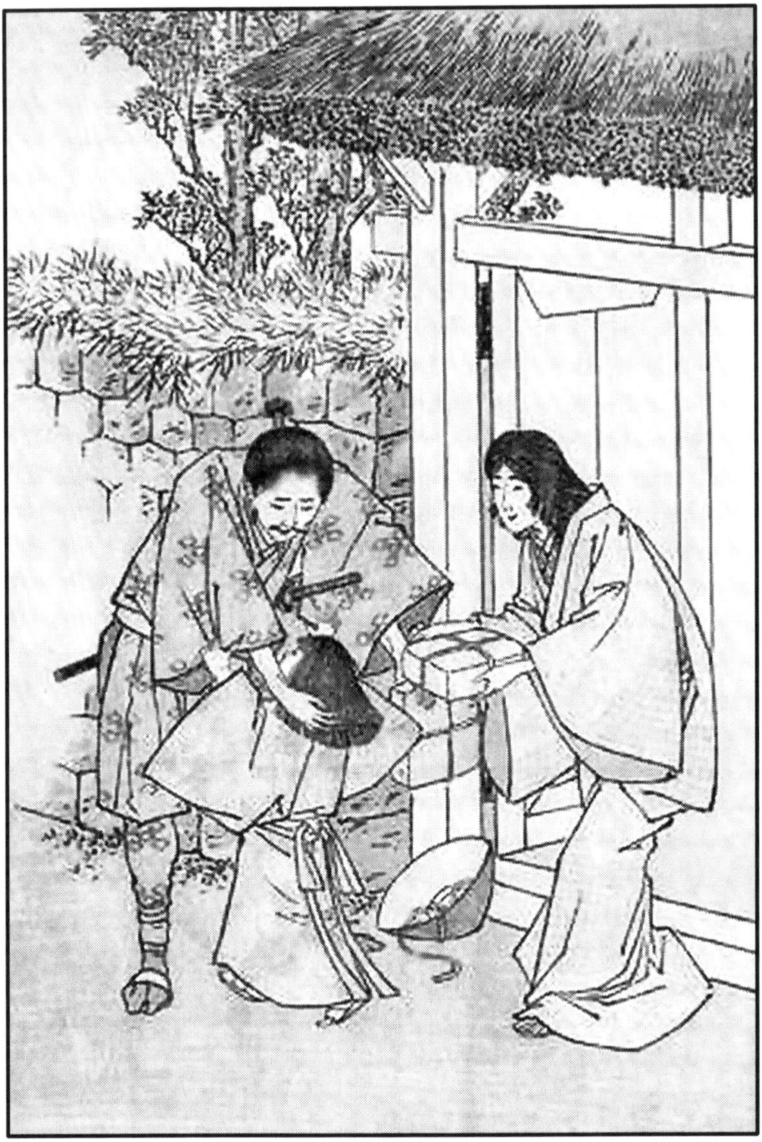

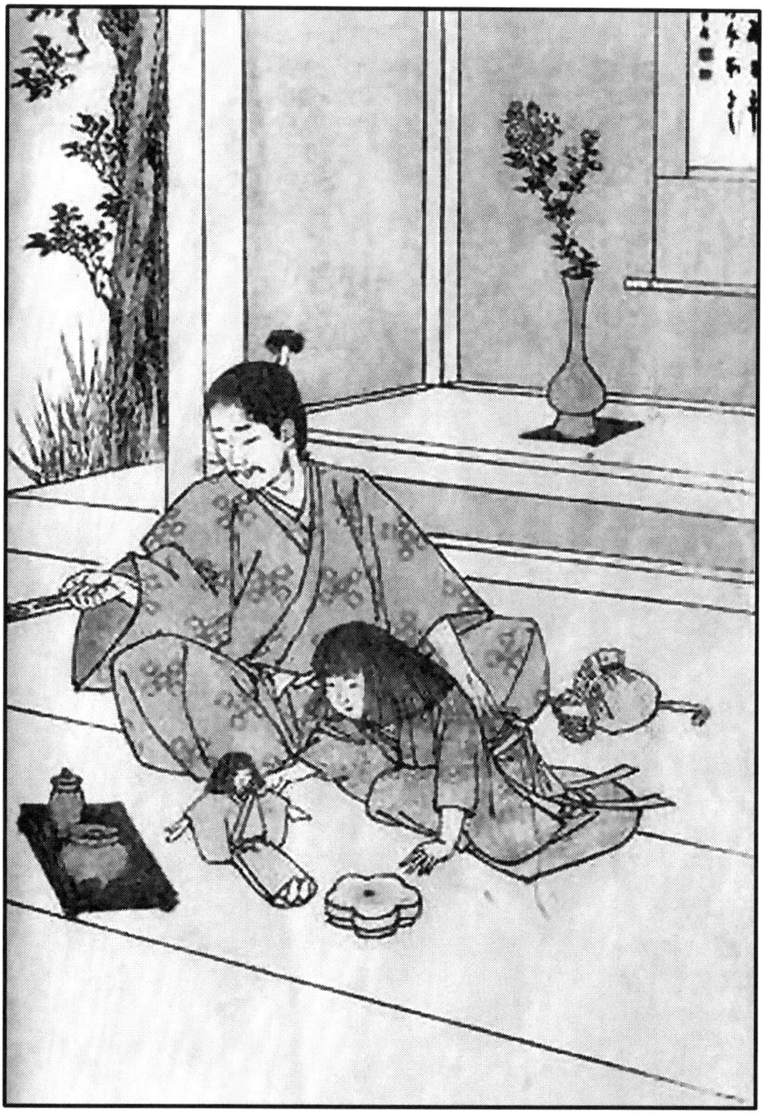

"I have brought you a very pretty thing," he said to his wife. "It is called a mirror. Look and tell me what you see inside." Then he gave her a plain, white wooden box, in which, when she had opened it, she found a round piece of metal. One side was white like frosted silver, and ornamented with raised figures of birds and flowers; the other was as bright as the clearest crystal. The young mother looked into it with delight and astonishment; for, from its depths a smiling, happy face was looking at her with parted lips and bright eyes.

"What do you see?" asked the husband, pleased at her astonishment and glad to show that he had learned something while he had been away.

"I see a pretty woman looking at me, and she moves her lips as if she was speaking; and…dear me…how odd! She has on a blue kimono just like mine!"

"Oh, you silly woman! It is your own face that you see," said the husband, proud of knowing something that his wife didn't know. "That round piece of metal is called a mirror, and in the city, everybody has one, although we have not seen them in this country place before."

The wife was charmed with her present, and for days could not look into the mirror often enough; for you must remember that this was the first time she had ever seen a mirror, so of course it was also the first time she had ever seen the reflection of her own pretty face. But she considered such a wonderful thing far too precious for everyday use, and soon shut it up in its box again, and put it away carefully among her most valued treasures.

Years passed and the husband and wife still lived happily. The joy of their life was their little daughter, who grew up to be the very image of her mother, and who was so dutiful and affectionate that everybody loved her. Mindful of her own little passing vanity on finding herself so lovely, the mother kept the mirror carefully hidden away, fearing that the use of it might breed a spirit of pride in her little girl.

She never spoke of it, and as for the father, he had forgotten all about it. So it happened that the daughter grew up as simple as the mother had been, and knew nothing of her own good looks, or of the mirror which would have reflected them.

But bye and bye, a terrible misfortune came to this happy little family. The good, kind mother fell sick; and, although her daughter waited upon her day and night with loving care, she got worse and worse, until at last there was no hope but that she must die.

When she found that she must soon leave her husband and child, the poor woman felt very sorrowful, grieving for those she was going to leave behind, and most of all for her little daughter. So she called the girl to her and said, "My darling child, you know that I am very sick. Soon I must die and leave your dear father and you alone. When I am gone, promise me that you will look into this mirror every night and every morning; there you will see me, and know that I am still watching over you." With these words, she took the mirror from its hiding place and gave it to her daughter. The child promised, with many tears, and so the mother, seeming now calm and resigned, died a short while later.

Now, this obedient and dutiful daughter never forgot her mother's last request, but each morning and evening took the mirror from its hiding place and looked into it long and earnestly. There she saw the bright and smiling vision of her lost mother. Not pale and sickly as in her last days, but the beautiful

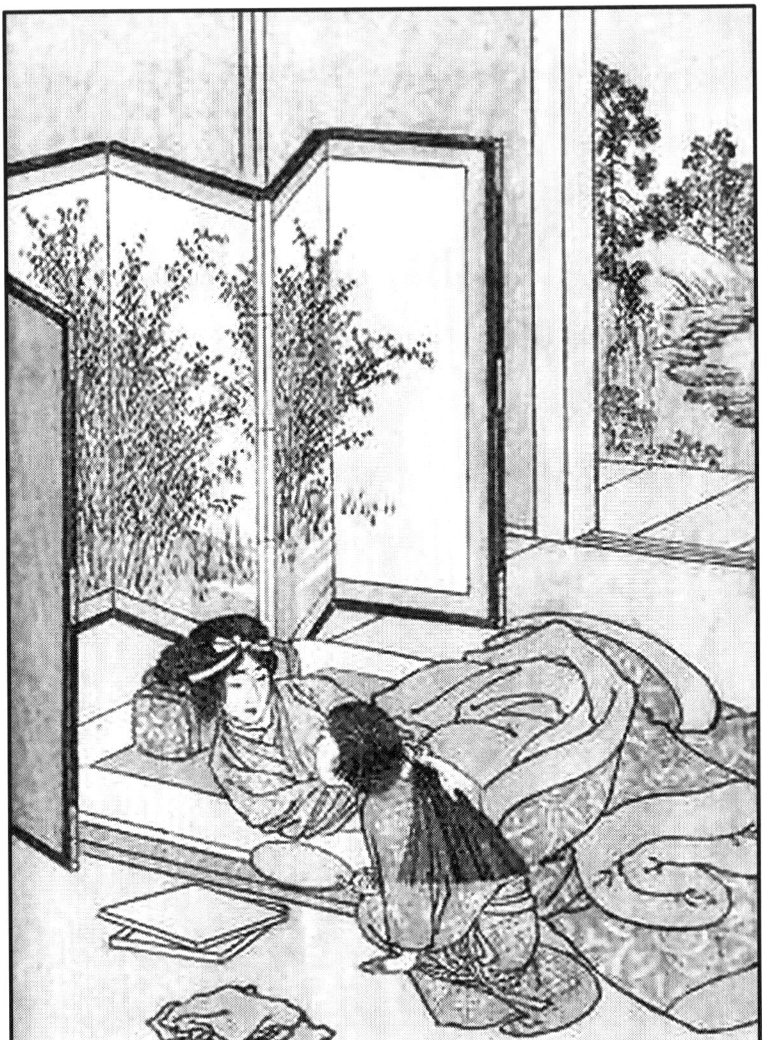

young mother of long ago. To her, at night, she told the story of the trials and difficulties of the day, and in the morning she looked for sympathy and encouragement in whatever might be in store for her. So day by day, she lived as in her mother's sight, striving still to please her as she had done in her lifetime, and always careful to avoid whatever might pain or grieve her. Her greatest joy was to be able to look in the mirror and say, "Mother, I have been today what you would have wanted me to be."

Seeing her every night and morning, without fail, look into the mirror and seem to converse with it, her father at length asked her the reason for her strange behavior. "Father," she said, "I look in the mirror every day to see my dear mother and to talk with her." Then she told him of her mother's dying wish, and how she had never failed to fulfill it.

Touched by so much simplicity and such faithful, loving obedience, the father shed tears of pity and affection. Nor could he find it in his heart to tell the child that the image she saw in the mirror, was but the reflection of her own sweet face; by constant sympathy and association, becoming more and more like her dead mother's day by day.

NOTES

1 Captain Mitchell McDonald, United States Navy, while assigned to duty in Japan, became the principal owner of Yokohama's Grand Hotel, at the time one of the best-known hotels in Japan. He was well known as an unpretentious man, frank, outgoing, warmly affectionate, and for his unrelenting loyalty: qualities that Hearn greatly admired. Despite his shyness, Hearn and McDonald struck up a very strong friendship; in fact, Hearn would frequently travel the twenty miles or so from his home in Tōkyō to Yokohama where he would often entice McDonald away from the hotel on a short excursion to Kamakura for steak, beer, swimming and some relaxed conversation. In time, McDonald assumed the role of Hearn's biggest fan as well as his protector, to such an extent that he assumed the task of looking after Hearn's personal and business affairs, as well as those of his family.

McDonald made frequent trips to the author's home as well, usually on Sundays, where he would spend the day with the family, bringing toys and candy for the children and playing with them for hours at a time. Often, after entertaining the children, if Hearn was working, Setsuko Hearn would guide him to the writer's study where he would sit in a rocking chair, placed there for his exclusive use, and the two men would then spend hours talking, joking, and laughing.

Perhaps out of a foreknowledge of what was to come, Hearn had his will drawn up and named McDonald as executor. Following the writer's death, McDonald maintained a compassionate watch over both the family and Hearn's literary estate, up until the time of his own death in the collapse of his hotel during the Great Kantō Earthquake of September 1, 1923.

2. Basil Hall Chamberlain (October 18, 1850 – February 15, 1935) was a professor at Tōkyō Imperial University and the foremost British Japanologist present in Japan during the late 19th century. He was also, for many years, one of Lafcadio Hearn's closest Western friends and confidants. He wrote some of the first translations of *haiku* into English, as well as the first English translation of the *Kojiki*, the oldest existing chronicle of ancient Japan, dating from the early 8th century.

Chamberlain is best remembered for his popular encyclopedic work *Things Japanese* (1890).

He arrived in Japan on May 29, 1873 and taught at the Imperial Naval School in Tōkyō from 1874 through 1882. His most prestigious position however, was as Professor of Japanese at Tōkyō Imperial University, starting in 1886. There he gained his reputation as a student and scholar of Japanese language and literature as well as an authority on the Ainu and Ryukyuan languages of Hokkaidō and Okinawa respectively. Chamberlain's other works include: *The Classical Poetry of the Japanese* (1880), *A Handbook of Colloquial Japanese* (1888), *A Practical guide to the Study of Japanese Writing* (1905) and (with W. B. Mason) *A Handbook for Travelers in Japan*.

3. Today the best-known Romanization system for Chinese and Japanese is the Wade-Giles system. In 1867, Sir Thomas F. Wade, who was then the Secretary of the British Consulate in Beijing, wrote *A Mandarin Language Reader* using a Roman alphabet of his own construction, which was subsequently modified by Herbert A. Giles (British Consul) for his Chinese-English dictionary published in 1912. The system has since been in use for decades but has been superseded, at least for words in Chinese, by the new Roman alphabet called Pinyin in the People's Republic of China.

4. Algernon Bertram Freeman-Mitford, the First Baron Redesdale (February 24, 1837 – August 17, 1916), was a British diplomat, collector, and writer. He entered the Foreign Office in 1858, and was appointed Third Secretary of the British Embassy in St Petersburg, Russia. Later, after service in the Diplomatic Corps in Peking, he went to Japan as Second Secretary to the British Legation, at the time of the turbulent and violent Meiji Restoration. There he met Ernest Satow and wrote *Tales of Old Japan* (1871), a book which made such classical Japanese tales as the "Forty-seven Rōnin" first known to the Western public. He resigned from the diplomatic service in 1873.

5. William Edward Hartpole Lecky, O.M. (March 26, 1838 - October 22, 1903), was an Irish historian of rationalism and European morals. The passage here is from his 1869 book, *History of European Morals from Augustus to Charlemagne*.

6. Engelbert Kaempfer (September 16, 1651 – November 2, 1716), was a German naturalist and physician most noted for his trips to Russia, Persia, India, Southeast Asia, and Japan, between 1683 and 1693. He wrote three books about his travels; *Amoenitatum Exoticarum*, published in 1712, itself significant for its medical observations; the

first extensive description of Japanese plants, *Flora Japonica*; and *The History of Japan*, published posthumously in 1727, which became the chief source of Western knowledge about the country for the 18th and early 19th centuries.

In May 1690, he set out for Japan as a physician to Vereenigde Oost-Indische Compagnie, or the Dutch East India Company's trading post in Nagasaki, then the only Japanese port open to foreign (Dutch and Chinese) ships, arriving there in September. Kaempfer stayed in Japan for two years, during which time he visited Edo and the Shōgun, Tokugawa Tsunayoshi, twice. In February 1691, he visited Buddhist monks in Nagasaki, becoming the first Western scientist to describe the tree *Ginkgo biloba*. During his stay in in the country, his tact, diplomacy, and medical skill overcame the cultural reserve of the Japanese, and enabled him to gather a sizeable quantity of valuable information. He left Japan in November 1692.

7. When Hearn first arrived in Matsué, he lived at a hotel on Zaimoku-cho (street), at the north end and just to the right of the large, white bridge he described in the first volume of *Glimpses of Unfamiliar Japan*; soon however, in that October, he moved into a small two-story, rented "cottage" on Sueji Honmachi-cho: the house he was later married in. There might have been other reasons, but the main cause of his departure was a little girl who suffered from a disease of the eyes. He often thought of her with sorrow, and begged the little one's relatives to let her go to be treated at the hospital; but the landlord would only answer, "Yes, yes," and postponed doing anything, indefinitely. Hearn became angry, and left the hotel with the words, "Strange and unsympathetic man, who is without a parent's heart!" Then he rented a *hanaré-zakishi* (a detached dwelling in a garden). "However," said Hearn, "the girl is not in the least to blame, only I am sorry for her." So he had a doctor treat her and cure her. In the spring of the following year, he and his wife Setsuko moved again to Kitabori-cho. a few streets northwest of a hill where stood an ancient castle. This is the house with its garden that he describes in this chapter.

8. In classic Japanese architecture, a *shōji* (障子) is a door, window or room divider made of translucent paper (typically washi paper) over a light lattice frame of wood or bamboo. Shōji doors are designed to slide open, and thus conserve space that would be required by a swinging door for example. Formerly the word "*shōji*" could apply to both *fusuma* and *shōji*, although with a formal distinction

of "*karagami shōji*" (唐紙障子、*fusuma*) and "*akari shōji*" (明り障子), the more commonly known variety.

9. As noted above, after his arrival in Matsué, Hearn spent a few days in a small Japanese inn on Zaimoku Street; however, in October, with the help of his dearest friend in life, and colleague, Sentarō Nishida, he was able to rent a two-story house on Sueji Honmachi Street: the house in which he was later to embark upon life as a married man. Apparently his rooms were rather spartan as described by his wife, Setsuko: "I married him a short time after he moved to his new quarters from the hotel...when I went to him, I found only one table and a chair, a few books, one suit of clothes, and one set of Japanese kimono."

It was in the following spring that they moved to the new, larger *yashiki* on Kitabori-cho. As stated by Setsuko: "After we moved to our estate, Kitabori, we missed the view of the lake, but we had left the noise of the city. There was a running stream directly in front of the gate, and on the other bank, we could see the spire of the castle through the woods. This estate was different from others, being a samurai estate. We found it in very good taste, and the reception hall and all the rooms were well arranged. At the back were a hill and the garden, and this garden was a favorite spot where we enjoyed walking about in our *yukata* (light kimono for lounging), wearing garden clogs. The mountain pigeon coos, '*Te-te-pop, ka-ka-po-po!*' When he heard the mountain pigeon coo, Hearn used to call me to come to him. 'Do you hear that? Isn't that delightful?' And he himself would imitate the sound, – '*Te-te-pop, ka-ka-po-po!*' – and ask, 'Did I do it right?'

10. A *tokonoma* (床の間), is an alcove, a place specially designated for the display of revered objects, in a room within a Japanese home, inn, or teahouse (*chashitsu*, 茶室).

11. A *torii* (鳥居, literally, "bird abode") is a traditional Japanese gate most commonly found at the entrance of or within a Shintō shrine, where it symbolically marks the transition from the profane to the sacred. The presence of a *torii* at the entrance is usually the simplest way to identify Shintō shrines, and a small *torii* icon represents them on Japanese road maps. They are however a common sight at Japanese Buddhist temples too, where they stand at the entrance of the temple's own shrine, called *chinjusha* (鎮守), and are usually very small. The first appearance of *torii* in Japan can be reliably placed at least in the mid-Heian period. The oldest existing stone *torii* was built in the 12th century and belongs to a Hachiman shrine in Yamagata Prefecture.

The oldest wooden *torii* is a *ryōbu torii* at Kubō Hachiman Shrine in Yamanashi Prefecture built in 1535. *Torii* were traditionally made from wood or stone, but today they can be also made of reinforced concrete, copper, stainless steel or other materials. They may be found either unpainted or painted vermilion with a black upper lintel. Inari shrines typically have many *torii* because those who have been successful in business in gratitude often donate a *torii* to Inari, *kami* of fertility and industry. Fushimi Inari-taisha in Kyōto has thousands of such *torii*, each bearing the donor's name.

12. Tsurugaoka Hachimangu (鶴岡八幡宮) is Kamakura's most important shrine, founded by Minamoto Yoriyoshi in 1063, and enlarged and moved to its current site in 1180 by Minamoto Yoritomo, the founder and first Shōgun of the Kamakura government. The shrine is dedicated to Hachiman, the patron god of the Minamoto family and of the samurai in general. The deified spirits of the ancient Emperor Ojin, who has been identified with Hachiman, Hime-gami, and Empress Jingu, are enshrined at Tsurugaoka Hachimangu Shrine.

13. The "Death Stone" is certainly one of the most remarkable of Japanese fox legends, illustrating a malignant fox taking the form of a seductive woman in more than one life. She is a creature who comes and goes, with alluring but destructive power — a Japanese version of "Taga Morgana." The legend has also been translated into a noh drama, *Sesshôseki*.

14. The *daimyō* (大名) were the powerful feudal provincial lords in pre-modern Japan who ruled most of the country from their vast, hereditary land holdings. The word is derived from the terms "*dai*" (大), meaning "large," and "*myō*," itself derived from *myōden* (名田), meaning "private land." Subordinate only to the Shōgun, *daimyō* were the most powerful feudal rulers from the 10th century to the middle 19th century in Japan.

15. *Shimenawa* (標縄 注連縄 七五三縄, literally "enclosing rope") are lengths of rice straw rope used for ritual purification in Shintō. They can vary in diameter from a few centimeters to several meters, and are often seen decorated with *shide*. A space bound by *shimenawa* often indicates a sacred or pure space, such as that of a Shintō shrine. *Shimenawa* are believed to act as a ward against evil spirits and are often set up at a groundbreaking ceremony before construction begins on a new building. They are most commonly found at shrines, *torii*, and sacred landmarks. They are also used around *yorishiro* (objects capable

of attracting spirits, hence inhabited by spirits) which include certain trees, in which case the inhabiting spirits are called *kodama*, and cutting down these trees is thought to bring misfortune. In the case of stones or rocks, the stones are known as *iwakura* (磐座、岩座).

16. Motowori was a Buddhist scholar and poet of Japan's classical age.

17. *Jorō* refers in general to mid-level down to lower-level courtesans of the Yoshiwara, Shimibara, or other pleasure quarters of old Japan; however within that general reference, there existed several additional sub-levels of *jurō*.

18. Kōjin, also known as Sambō-Kōjin or Sanbō-Kōjin (三宝荒神), is the Japanese *kami* (god) of fire, the hearth, and the kitchen. He is sometimes called Kamado-gami, literally the god of the stove. He represents violent forces that are turned toward the good of humankind. The name "Sambō-Kōjin" means "Three-way rough deity," and he is considered a deity of uncertain temper. Fire, which he represents, is a destructive force, as shown in the myth of Kagu-tsuchi, the original fire deity, whose birth caused his mother's death. However, Kōjin embodies fire controlled and turned toward a good purpose. He is said to destroy all impurity. He is also responsible for watching over the household and reporting any misdeeds to the *kami* of the village or city. These reports are discussed, and the according rewards or punishments assigned by an assembly of gods in Izumo Province in the tenth month of the traditional lunar calendar. Kōjin is sometimes identified as an incarnation of Fudō Myō-Ō, who is likewise depicted as surrounded by flames and tasked with dealing with misdeeds. As Kamado-gami, he is sometimes depicted as female. Traditionally, a representation of Kōjin is placed near the hearth. This representation might be a simple *fuda* (memorial tablet) in many homes, or it might be as elaborate as a statue, as is common in Buddhist temples. In his statues, Kōjin is depicted with flaming hair, fangs, and a contorted face, and he often wields a bow and arrows. He has two pairs of hands. Some representations of Kōjin present him as possessing three heads. The *Kōjiki* mentions an imperial script detailing instructions for worshipping Kōjin, in the form of Kamado-gami.

19. Himeji (姫路市, Himeji-shi) is a city located in Hyōgo Prefecture in the Kansai region of Japan, and has been the center of Harima Province since the Nara period. Following the Battle of Sekigahara (October 21, 1600), Ikeda Terumasa received a fief at Harima Province

and established the Himeji Domain, expanding the castle and the town.

20. The *koku* (石 or 石高) is a Japanese unit of volume, equal to ten cubic *shaku*. In this definition, 3.5937 *koku* equal one cubic meter, i.e. 1 *koku* is approximately 278.3 liters. The *koku* was originally defined as a quantity of rice, historically defined as enough rice to feed one person for one year (one *masu* is enough rice to feed a person for one day). A *koku* of rice weighs about 150 kilograms (330 pounds). During the Edo period, each *han* (fiefdom) had an assessment of its wealth, and the *koku* was the unit of measurement. The smallest *han* was 10,000 *koku* and Kaga, the largest (other than that of the Shōgun), was called the "million-*koku* domain." (Its holdings totaled around 1,025,000 *koku*.) Many samurai, including *hatamoto*, received stipends in *koku*, while a few received salaries instead. In the Tōhoku and Hokkaidō domains, where rice could not be grown, the economy was still measured in *koku* but was not adjusted from year to year. Thus some *han* had larger economies than their *koku* indicated, which allowed them to fund development projects. In the Meiji period (1868–1912), Japanese units such as the *koku* were abolished and the metric system was installed.

21. According to Setsuko Koizumi: "Early in the summer of the twenty-fourth year of Meiji (1891), we moved over to a samurai estate and kept house. We moved with a maid and a pussycat. One evening in the early spring of that year, while the air was yet chill and penetrating, I was standing on the veranda admiring the sunset on the lake, when I saw, directly below the veranda along the shore, four or five naughty children dunking Pussy up and down in the water, and cruelly teasing her. I begged Pussy of the children, brought her back to the house, and told the story to Hearn. "Oh, poor puss!" he exclaimed. "What cruel children they were!" And he held the shivering Pussy right in his bosom to warm her. That time I felt a great admiration for him." (From *The Annotated Reminiscences of Lafcadio Hearn, By Setsuko Koizumi*, edited by Hayato Tokugawa, Copyright 2013, published by Shisei-Dō Publications).

22. A kite is a type of bird of prey, the most common in Japan being the Black Kite, (*Milvus migrans*), which is a medium-sized member of the family *Accipitridae*, which also includes many other diurnal raptors. It is thought to be the world's most abundant species of *Accipitridae*, although some populations have experienced dramatic declines or fluctuations.

23. The thick, fine, straw mats, fitted on the floor of every Japanese room, are always six feet long by three feet wide. The largest room in the ordinary middle-class house is a room of eight mats. A room of one hundred mats is something worth seeing.

24. In general, *kyō* is a reference to the *Lotus Sutra*. *Nam Myōhō Renge Kyō* (南無妙法蓮華經), also *Namu Myōhō Renge Kyō*, ("Devotion to the Mystic Law of the Lotus Sutra or Glory to the Sutra of the Lotus of the Supreme Law") is a mantra that is chanted as the central practice of all forms of Nichiren Buddhism — *Myōhō Renge Kyō* being the title of the *Lotus Sutra*. The mantra is referred to as *daimoku* (題目) or, in honorific form, *O-daimoku* (お題目) and was first revealed by the Japanese Buddhist teacher Nichiren on the 28th day of the fourth lunar month of 1253 AD at Seichō-ji (also called Kiyosumi-dera) near Kominato in current-day Chiba. The practice of chanting the *daimoku* is called *shōdai* (唱題) and its purpose is to attain perfect and complete awakening.

25. Empress Jingū (神功天皇, Jingū-tennō), who is also known as Empress-consort Jingū (神功皇后, Jingū-kōgō), (c. 169–269 AD) was a legendary Japanese Empress. The Empress-consort to Emperor Chūai, she also served as Regent from the time of her husband's death in 201 until her son, Emperor Ōjin, acceded to the throne in 269. Up until the Meiji period, Empress Jingū was considered to have been the 15th Japanese imperial ruler, according to the traditional order of succession; nonetheless, a re-evaluation of the existing historical records caused her name to be removed from that list, and her son, Emperor Ōjin, is today considered to have been the 15th sovereign. Legend has it that she was anything but a docile woman, and led an army in an invasion of Korea, returning to Japan victorious after three years.

26. A *kannushi* (神主, "god master") also called *shinshoku* (神職), is the person responsible for the maintenance of a Shintō shrine (*jinja*) as well as for leading worship of a given *kami*. The characters for *kannushi* are sometimes also read *jinshu* with the same meaning. Originally, the *kannushi* were intermediaries between *kami* and man; and thus, could transmit their will to common humans. A *kannushi* was also capable of miracles. Later, the term evolved to being synonymous with *shinshoku*; that is, a man who works at a shrine and holds religious ceremonies there.

27. The Meido (冥土) is regarded as the realm of the dead.

28. At the entrance to the underworld is Shide-no-yama, the Mountain of Death. It is a steep cliff veiled in mist that the soul must claw its way up. After entering the gate, the soul then faces the River of the Three Passages. The first is a small stream for those who have committed only minor offenses in life. Over the second river is a bridge of precious metals that the saved pass on their way to paradise. The third is a gulf of monsters and fierce storms that must be forged by the worst sinners.

29. *Maiko* (舞妓) is the term used to refer to an apprentice geisha in western Japan, especially Kyōto. Their jobs consist of performing songs, dances, and playing the *shamisen* (a three-stringed Japanese musical instrument) for guests during parties and feasts. *Maiko* are usually aged 15 to 20 years and become geisha after learning how to dance (traditional Japanese dances), play the *shamisen*, and learning Kyō-kotoba (the dialect of Kyōto), regardless of their origins.

30. In Confucian philosophy, filial piety is a virtue of respect for one's parents and ancestors. In more general terms, filial piety means to be good to one's parents; to take care of one's parents; to engage in good conduct not just toward parents but also outside the home so as to bring a good name to one's parents and ancestors; to perform the duties of one's job well so as to obtain the material means to support one's parents as well as to carry out sacrifices to the ancestors; to not be rebellious; to show love, respect and support; to display courtesy; to ensure male heirs; to uphold fraternity among brothers; to wisely advise one's parents, including dissuading them from moral unrighteousness; to display sorrow for their sickness and death; and to carry out sacrifices after their death.

31. The *uguisu* or Japanese bush warbler (鶯) is a perching bird more often heard than seen, tending to remain deep in the shadow of foliage during the day. Its distinctive breeding call can be heard throughout much of Japan beginning at the start of spring. Some other Japanese names are *haru-dori* ('spring bird"), *haru-tsuge-dori* ("spring-announcing bird") and *hanami-dori* ("hanami bird" or "spring-flower-viewing bird"). The bird is drab, olive-colored and secretive. It is normally only seen in spring before there is foliage in the trees.

32. *Rigor mortis* (Latin: *rigor* "stiffness," *mortis* "of death") is one of the recognizable signs of death, caused by chemical changes in the muscles after death, causing the limbs of the corpse to become stiff and difficult to move or manipulate. In humans, it commences after about three to four hours, reaches maximum stiffness after 12 hours, and

gradually dissipates until absent again, approximately 48 to 60 hours after death.

33. Nichiren (日蓮) (February 16, 1222 – October 13, 1282) was a Buddhist monk who lived during the Kamakura period (1185–1333). Nichiren taught a devotion to the *Lotus Sutra* (entitled *Myōhō-Renge-Kyō*) that contained Gautama Buddha's teachings towards the end of his life, as the exclusive means to attain enlightenment. Nichiren believed that this *sutra* contained the essence of all of Gautama Buddha's teachings relating to the laws of cause and effect and karma. This devotion to the *sutra* entails the chanting of *Nam(u)-Myōhō-Renge-Kyō* (referred to as "*daimoku*") as the essential practice of the teaching.

Nichiren Buddhism includes various schools with their own interpretations of Nichiren's teachings, the most prominent being Nichiren-shu and Soka Gakkai; however, despite the differences between schools, all Nichiren sects share the fundamental practice of chanting the *daimoku*. While virtually all Nichiren Buddhist schools regard him as a reincarnation of the Lotus Sutra's *Bodhisattva* of Superior Practices, Jōgyō Bosatsu (上行菩薩), some schools of Nichiren Buddhism's Nikkō lineages regard him as the actual Buddha of this age, or the "Buddha of the Latter Day of the Law."

34. In the late Edo period, numerous scholars of *kokugaku* (a national "revival," largely comprised of various oligarchs) believed that Shintō could become a unifying agent to center the country around the Emperor while a process of modernization was undertaken. After the Meiji Restoration, the new Imperial Government needed to rapidly modernize the politics and economy of Japan, and the Meiji oligarchy felt that those goals could only be accomplished through a strong sense of national unity and cultural identity. In 1868, the new Meiji government established a government bureau, the Shintō Worship Bureau (神祇事務局, Jingi Jimukyōku) to oversee religious affairs and to administer the government-ordered "separation" of Buddhism from Shintō. In actual fact, beginning in 1871, all Shintō shrines throughout Japan were declared to be the property of the central government. These were assigned an official rank within a hierarchy, and each received a subsidy for their upkeep based on that ranking. The hierarchy of shrines consisted of twelve levels, with Ise Shrine (dedicated to Amaterasu, and thus symbolic of the legitimacy of the Imperial family) at the top. Furthermore, all citizens were required to register as a parishioner of their local shrine, and each parishioner was automatically also a parishioner of the Ise Shrine. This was a major

reversal from the Edo period, in which families were required to register with Buddhist temples rather than Shintō shrines.

In 1872, the Office of Shintō Worship decreed that all Shintō priests were to officially become government employees. Thus, from a legal perspective, State Shintō was not a religion and its values came under the heading of moral instruction rather than religious teaching.

This system concentrated on the more important shrines; folk Shintō practices were mostly left unmolested, and various Shintō fringe movements dating from the Edo period were allowed to continue.

In 1890 the Imperial Rescript on Education was issued, and students were required to ritually recite its oath to "offer yourselves courageously to the State" as well as protect the Imperial Family. The imperial cult was further spread by distribution of imperial portraits for esoteric veneration. All of these practices, used to fortify national solidarity through patriotic observances at shrines, gave pre-World War II Japanese nationalism a tint of mysticism and cultural reserve.

Article 28 of the Constitution of the Empire of Japan reaffirmed the privileged position of Shintō, but also guaranteed freedom of religion "within limits not prejudicial to peace and order, and not antagonistic to their duties as subjects." In practice, this meant that religious groups required government approval, their doctrines and rituals coming under close government scrutiny.

During World War II, the government used State Shintō to encourage patriotism and to support efforts towards militarism. Noted figures in government, including Kuniaki Koiso, Heisuke Yanagawa, Kiichirō Hiranuma and Prince Kan'in Kotohito, participated in public rituals modeled after ancient ceremonies to foster a sense that supporting the war was a sacred duty.

State Shintō officially came to an end after the surrender of Japan.

35. What the author is referring to is commonly referred to as "The Ōtsu Incident" (大津事件, Ōtsu Jiken), a failed assassination attempt on Nicholas Alexandrovich, Tsesarevich of Russia (later to become Emperor Nicholas II of Russia) on May 11, 1891, during his visit to Japan as part of a official visit to the Far East.

Nicholas had gone to Far Eastern Russia for ceremonies in Vladivostok marking the start of construction of the Trans-Siberian Railroad. On his way (by sea) he made an official visit to Japan. The Russian Pacific Fleet with the Tsesarevich first stopped in Kagoshima, then Nagasaki, and then Kobé. From Kobé, Nicholas journeyed overland to Kyōto, where he was met by a delegation headed by Prince Arisugawa Taruhito. This was the first visit by such an important foreign prince to Japan since Prince Heinrich of Prussia in 1880 and two British princes in 1881, and the military influence of the Russian Empire was growing rapidly in the Far East. The Japanese government therefore placed heavy emphasis on using this visit to foster better Russo-Japanese relations. Nicholas showed interest in the Japanese traditional crafts, got a dragon tattoo on his right arm, and bought an ornamental hairpin for a Japanese girl who happened to be near him.

The assassination attempt occurred on May 11, while Nicholas was returning to Kyōto after a day trip to Lake Biwa in Ōtsu, Shiga Prefecture. He was attacked by Tsuda Sanzō (1855–1891), one of his escort policemen, who swung at the Tsesarevich's face with a saber. The quick action of Nicholas's cousin, Prince George of Greece and Denmark, who parried the second blow with his cane, saved the Tsesarevich's life. Tsuda then attempted to flee, but two rickshaw drivers in Nicholas' entourage chased him down and pulled him to the ground. Nicholas was left with a 9 centimeter long scar on the right side of his forehead, but his wound was not life-threatening.

Nicholas was then rushed back to Kyōto, where Prince Kitashirakawa Yoshihisa ordered that he be taken into the Kyōto Imperial Palace to rest, and messages were sent to Tōkyō. Fearful that the incident would be used by Russia as a pretext for war, and knowing that Japan's military was no match for Russia at the time, Prime Minister Matsukata Masayoshi advised Emperor Meiji to go immediately to visit the Tsesarevich. The Emperor boarded a train at Shimbashi Station, and traveled through the night so as to reach Kyōto the following morning.

The following day, when Nicholas expressed a desire to return to his fleet in Kobé, Emperor Meiji ordered Prince Kitashirakawa, Prince Arisugawa Takehito, and Prince Arisugawa Taruhito to accompany him. Later, Emperor Meiji, ignoring protests from some senior statesmen that he might be taken hostage, paid a personal visit to the Tsesarevich, who was recuperating onboard a Russian warship in the harbor.

The Emperor publicly expressed sorrow at Japan's lack of hospitality towards a state guest, which led to an outpouring of public support and messages of condolences for the Tsesarevich. More than 10,000 telegrams were sent wishing the Tsesarevich a speedy recovery. One town in Yamagata Prefecture even legally forbade the use of the family name "Tsuda" and the given name "Sanzō." When Nicholas cut his trip to Japan short in spite of Emperor Meiji's apology, a young seamstress, Yuko Hatakeyama, slit her throat with a razor in front of the Kyōto Prefectural Office as an act of public contrition, and soon died in a hospital. Japanese media at the time labeled her as a *"retsujo"* (literally a "valiant woman") and praised her patriotism.

The government applied pressure to the Court to try Tsuda under Article 116 of the Criminal Code, which demanded the death penalty for acts against the Emperor, Empress or Crown Prince of Japan. However, Chief Justice Kojima Iken ruled that Article 116 did not apply in this case, and sentenced Tsuda to life imprisonment instead. Although controversial at the time, Kojima's decision was later used as an example of the independence of the judiciary in Japan and one of the justifications for the revision of the unequal treaties.

Accepting responsibility for the lapse in security, Home Minister Saigō Tsugumichi and Foreign Minister Aoki Shūzō resigned. The Russian government officially expressed full satisfaction in the outcome of Japan's actions, and indeed formally stated that had Tsuda been sentenced to death, they would have pushed for clemency; however, later historians have often speculated on how the incident (which left the Tsesarevich Nicholas permanently scarred), may have later influenced his opinion of Japan and the Japanese, and how this may have influenced his decisions in the period up to and during the Russo-Japanese War of 1904–1905.

36. Herbert Spencer (April 27, 1820 – December 8, 1903) was an English philosopher, sociologist and liberal political theorist. He developed an all-embracing concept of evolution, theorizing that it was the progressive development of not only biological organisms, but of the physical world, the human mind, and human culture and societies. He is best known as the initiator of the term "survival of the fittest".

37. Hirata Atsutane (平田 篤胤, October 6, 1776 – November 2, 1843) was a Japanese scholar, ranked as one of the four great men of Kokugaku (nativist) studies, and one of the most significant theologians of the Shintō religion. His literary name was Ibukinoya.

38. Motoori Norinaga (本居 宣長, June 21 1730 – November 5, 1801) was a Japanese scholar of Kokugaku (National Revival) active during the Edo period. He is probably the best known and most prominent of all scholars in this tradition.

39. Arthur Schopenhauer (February 22, 1788 – September 21, 1860) is regarded as the quintessential pessimist among Western philosophers. In his work and writings, he attempted to grasp the forces at work in the human psyche and felt that such forces could not be overcome by mere rationalism; thus, they must be met on their own

ground. In terms of ethics, Schopenhauer tended towards determinism. For him, one was free to decide what one wanted, but not fee to will what one wanted. Though one is somehow responsible for his own actions, they are still fully determined by the will under its various forms. Under similar circumstances, he maintained, similar results are inevitable. According to his theory, will inevitably overpowers one's life; hence, the only solution is a denial of the will: to step outside of reality. Simply put, Schopenhauer's sense of ethics can be stated as "it would be better for us not to exist." The removal of oneself from the life of the will must be attained through asceticism or suffering; and can only be achieved gradually through advancing age. He strongly disapproved of suicide, referring to it as an illusion; suicide being a powerful attempt to escape the will, but nonetheless, actually an affirmation of one's desire: such an act could never snuff out the will.

40. Numa Denis Fustel de Coulanges, (March 18, 1830 - Sept. 12, 1889) was a French historian, and is regarded as the originator of the scientific approach to the study of history in France.

After studying at the École Normale Supérieure, he was sent to the French school at Athens in 1853 and directed some excavations at Chios. From 1860 to 1870 he was professor of history at the Faculty of Letters at the University of Strasbourg, where he had a brilliant career as a teacher. His subsequent appointments included a lectureship at the École Normale Supérieure in February 1870, a professorship at the University of Paris Faculty of Letters in 1875, the Chair of Medieval History at the Sorbonne in 1878, and the directorship of the École Normale in 1880.

Fustel's historical thought had two main tenets: the importance of complete objectivity and the unreliability of secondary sources. By his teaching and example, he consequently established the modern idea of historical impartiality at a time when few people had any qualms about combining the careers of historian and politician. His insistence on the use of contemporary documents led to the full use of the French National Archives in the 19th century. Fustel, however, was no paleographer, and his fondness for manuscript sources was occasionally responsible for major errors of judgment.

Apart from *La Cité Antique* (The Ancient City, 1864,), a study of the part played by religion in the political and social evolution of Greece and Rome, most of Fustel's work was related to the study of the political institutions of Roman Gaul and the Germanic invasions of the Roman Empire.

41. Ryōbu Shintō (Duel-aspect Shintō) is also referred to as Shingon Shintō, a constructed sect that combines traditional Shintō with the teachings of the Shingon sect of Buddhism, formed during the late Heian and Kamakura periods (794 A.D. – 1333 A.D.), and has as its foundation the concept that *kami* are simply manifestations of Buddhist deities. Prime among these was the equation of the sun goddess Amaterasu with the Buddha referred to as Mahāvairocana or Dai-nichi Nora, the Great Sun Buddha; that the two realms of *dai-nichi* conform to the *kami* honored at the Ise Grand Shrine, Amaterasu-ō-mikami and Toyouke-no-ō-mikami, the deity of agriculture and industry. Amaterasu was compared to the Taizo-kai or "Womb World" and Toyouke-no-ō-mikami to the two mandalas used in the representation of the dual nature of Dai-nichi.

42. A *kakemono* (掛物, sometimes referred to as a *kakejiku* (掛軸, hung or hanging scroll) is a Japanese scrolled painting or work of Shodō (calligraphy) which has been mounted, usually on a flexible backing with silk fabric edges , so that it can be rolled for storage. As opposed to *makimono*, which are meant to be unrolled laterally and placed on a flat surface, a *kakemono* is intended to be hung against a wall as part of the interior decoration of a room. It is traditionally displayed in the *tokonoma*, or alcove, of a room. When displayed in a *chashitsu*, or teahouse for the traditional tea ceremony, the choice of the *kakemono* and its complementary flower arrangement (*ikebana*, 生け花) help set the spiritual mood of the ceremony. Often the *kakemono* used for this will bear calligraphy of a Zen phrase done in the hand of a distinguished Zen master. Because of their relatively small size, when compared for example to a *byōbu* (folding screen) or to a *shohekiga* (a wall painting), a *kakemono* can quickly be changed with ease to match a season or particular occasion. The *kakemono* was first introduced during the Heian period (794 - 1185) as a means of displaying venerable Buddhist images, works of Shodō, or particularly poetic works. From the Muromachi period (1337 – 1583) on, landscapes, flowers, paintings of birds, and portraiture also became favored subjects.

43. *Gohei* (御幣), *onbé* (御幣) or *heisoku* (幣束) are ostensibly wooden wands, decorated with two *shide* used in Shintō rituals. A *shide* (紙垂, 四手) is a zigzag-shaped paper streamer, often seen attached to *shimenawa* used to mark sacred precincts. The streamers are usually white, although they can also be gold, silver, or a mixture of several colors. *Gohei* are used to bless or sanctify in various Shintō rituals but their usual purpose is to cleanse the sacred places in temples and to purify, bless, or exorcise any object that is thought to have negative energy.

44. Simply put, *Ō-mamori* are amulets or charms. The practice of obtaining amulets from shrines and Buddhist temples is almost universal in Japan. *Ō-mamori* are traditionally small brightly colored brocade bags with drawstrings, usually with an inscription giving the name of the shrine and perhaps the benefit (*remake*) for which the amulet has been obtained. *Ō-mamori* are acquired by children, by people who are sick, at the New Year, for passing an examination, for traffic safety, and at the time of a pilgrimage or occasional shrine visit. *Mamori* means "protection" so strictly speaking the function of an amulet is to protect against bad influences, disaster etc.; while a talisman (*Ō-fuda*) is supposed to attract or channel good fortune; but good fortune is the absence of bad so there is considerable overlap in the function of *Ō-mamori* and *Ō-fuda*.

45. Emperor Jimmu (神武天皇, Jimmu-tennō) was the first Emperor of Japan according to the traditional order of succession. He is also known as Kamuyamato Iwarehiko no mikoto (神日本磐余彦尊) and personally as Wakamikenu no mikoto (若御毛沼命) or Sano no mikoto (狹野尊). The Imperial House of Japan has traditionally based its claim to the throne on its descent from Jimmu. While his accession is traditionally dated to 660 BC, no historically firm dates can be assigned to this early Emperor's life or reign, nor to the reigns of his early successors.

46. A prominent feature of Japanese architecture, particularly in the Edo period and the Early to mid-Meiji period, is the *fusuma* (襖): vertical rectangular panels that can slide sideways to redefine the spaces within a room or house, or to act as doors. Typically, they measure about 90 cm. wide by 180 cm. in height; coincidentally, the same dimensions as a *tatami mat*, and normally are 2-3 cm. thick. They consist of a latticework wooden substructure that is covered in cardboard and a layer of paper or cloth on both sides, and typically have a black lacquer border and a circular "finger catch" rather than a handle or doorknob. Historically, *fusuma* were painted, often with such scenes from nature as forests, plants, trees, animals, birds, or sea life. The *fusuma*, as well as *shōji* (translucent paper room dividers) run on wooden rails located both above and below, which were typically waxed but now utilize a vinyl lubricating strip instead.

47. The *Book of Deuteronomy* is the fifth book of the Hebrew *Bible*, and of the Jewish *Torah/Pentateuch*. The book consists of three sermons or speeches delivered to the Israelites by Moses on the plains of Moab, shortly before they entered the Promised Land. The first sermon reviews the forty years of wilderness wanderings which have led to

that moment, and ends with an exhortation to observe the laws (or teachings); the second reminds the Israelites of the need for exclusive allegiance to one God and observance of the laws he has given them, on which their possession of the land depends; and the third offers the comfort that even should Israel prove unfaithful and so lose the land, with repentance all can be restored.

48. The *sakaki* (*Cleyera japonica*) is a flowering evergreen tree native to warm areas of Japan, Korea and mainland China. *Sakaki* is considered a sacred tree in Shintō, along with other evergreens such as *hinoki* (檜) or "Japanese cypress," and *kansugi* (神杉, "sacred *cryptomeria*"). In Shintō ritual offerings to the *kami*, branches of *sakaki* are decorated with paper streamers (*shide*) to make *tamagushi* (玉串, literally, "jewel skewer"). At Japanese weddings, funerals, *miyamairi* and other ceremonies at Shintō shrines, *tamagushi* are ritually presented to the parishioners by *kannushi* (priests).

49. A *butsudan* (佛壇 or 仏壇, literally "Buddha altar") or *butsuma* is a shrine commonly found in temples and homes. A *butsudan* is a wooden cabinet with doors that enclose and protect a *gohonzon* or religious icon, typically a statue or painting of a Buddha or *bodhisattva*, or a mandala scroll. The doors are opened to display the icon during religious observances, and closed before sunset. A *butsudan* also usually contains an array of subsidiary religious items, called *butsugu*, such as candlesticks, incense burners, bells, and platforms for placing offerings such as fruit, tea or rice. Some Buddhist sects place *ihai*, memorial tablets for deceased relatives, within or near the *butsudan*.

50. Jōdo Shinshū (浄土真宗, "True Pure Land School"), also known as Shin Buddhism, is a school of Pure Land Buddhism, founded by the former Tendai Japanese monk Shinran. Shinshu Buddhism is considered the most widely practiced branch of Buddhism in Japan, with 20% of the population of Japan identifying membership with the sect.

Nichiren (日蓮) (February 16, 1222 – October 13, 1282) was a Buddhist monk of the *Kamakura* Period (1185 – 1333) who taught that devotion to the *Lotus Sutra*, *Namu-Myōhō-Renge-Kyō*, was the sole means by which to attain enlightenment: the chanting of "*Nam Myō hō Renge Kyō*" being a key means of worship. Nichiren is recognized as the founder of Nichiren Buddhism, which has had great influence on certain parts of Japanese society during various eras, such as the merchant class of the *Edo* Period and the ultra-nationalists of the pre-World War II, or early *Shōwa* era. According to the doctrines of Nichiren Buddhism, all people have an innate Buddha nature and are therefore, essentially capable of attaining enlightenment in their present lifetime.

51. San-indō (山陰道, literally, "northern mountain circuit" or the "northern mountain region") is a Japanese geographical term. It refers to both an ancient division of the country and also the main road running through it. *San-in* translates to "the shaded side of a mountain," while *dō*, depending on the context, can mean either a road, or a circuit, in the sense of delineating a region. This name derives from the idea that the northern side of the central mountain chain running through Honshū was the "shaded" side, while the southern side was the "sunny" (山陽, *san-yō*) side. The pre-modern region corresponds for the most part with the modern concept of the San-in region.

The region was established as one of the Gokishichidō (Five provinces and seven roads) during the Asuka period (538-710), and consisted of the following eight ancient provinces: Tamba, Tango, Tajima, Inaba, Hōki, Izumo, Iwami and Oki. This system however gradually disappeared in the centuries leading up to the Muromachi period (1333-1467).

The San-indō, however, continued to be important, and highly travelled throughout the Edo period (1603-1867). Running mostly east-west, its eastern end, along with those of most of the medieval highways (街道, *kaidō*), was at Kyōto. From there it followed the coast of the Sea of Japan to Hagi, near Shimonoseki, the western end of both the San-yōdō and the San-indō, very near the westernmost end of the island of Honshū. Though the road originally terminated in the west at Hagi, the lords of Chōshū Domain at some point during the Edo period changed it to end at Yamaguchi.

As might be expected, the road served an important strategic and logistical role in a number of military situations over the course of the years. Ashikaga Takauji in the 14th century, Akechi Mitsuhide in the 16th century, and many others used it to flee from conflict, to return to the core of the country (*kinai*), or to move troops. Many *daimyō* also used this road as part of their mandatory journeys (*sankin kotai*) to Edo under the Tokugawa Shōgunate. Of course, the road also served the more everyday purpose of providing a means of transportation for merchants, traveling entertainers, pilgrims, and the average people as well.

52. *Kaimyō* ((戒名), literally "precept name," also referred to as a "Dharma name") is a new name acquired during a Buddhist initiation ritual in Mahayana Buddhism and monk ordination in Theravada

Buddhism. The name is traditionally given to a Buddhist monastic, but is also given to newly ordained monks, nuns and laity. In Japan, other than the standard usage of Dharma names for monastics and laity, it is also tradition for the deceased to receive a Dharma name written in *kanji* by a priest. This name supposedly prevents the return of the deceased if his name is called from the living. The length of the name depends also on either the virtue of the person's lifespan, or more commonly, the size of the donation of the relatives to the temple, which may range from a generally common name to the most elaborate names for 1 million *yen* or more. The high prices charged by the temples are a controversial issue in Japan, especially since some temples put pressure on families to buy a more expensive name. The *kanji* for these *kaimyō* are usually very old and rarely used ones, and few people nowadays (with the exception of Chinese scholars) can read them.

53. Obon (お盆) or just Bon (盆) is a Japanese Buddhist custom to honor the spirits of one's ancestors. This Buddhist-Confucian custom has evolved into a family reunion holiday during which people return to ancestral family places and visit and clean their ancestors' graves, and when the spirits of ancestors are supposed to revisit the household altars. It has been celebrated in Japan for more than 500 years and traditionally includes a dance, known as Bon-odori.

The festival of Obon lasts for three days; however, its starting date varies within different regions of Japan. When the lunar calendar was changed to the Gregorian calendar at the beginning of the Meiji era, the localities in Japan reacted differently and this resulted in three different times of Obon. "Shichigatsu Bon" (Bon in July) is based on the solar calendar and is celebrated around July 15th in eastern Japan (the Kantō region such as Tokyō and Yokohama. and the Tohoku region), coinciding with Chūgen, the mid-year gift giving time. "Hachigatsu Bon" (Bon in August), based on the lunar calendar, is celebrated around the 15th of August and is the most commonly celebrated time. "Kyū Bon" (Old Bon) is celebrated on the 15th day of the seventh month of the lunar calendar, and so differs each year. "Kyū Bon" is celebrated in areas like the northern part of the Kantō region, Chūgoku region, Shikoku, and Okinawa Prefecture. These three days are not listed as public holidays but it is customary that people are given leave. Also refer to *The Annotated Glimpses of Unfamiliar Japan*, Vol. I, Chapter VI.

54. *Nukekubi* (抜首), meaning "detachable neck." are monsters of Japanese folklore. By day, *nukekubi* appear to be normal human beings;

by night however, their heads detach from their bodies at the neck and travel about independently in search of human prey. These heads attack by screaming (to increase their victims' fright), then closing in and biting. While the head is detached, the body of a *nukekubi* becomes inanimate. In some legends, this serves as one of the creature's few weaknesses; if a *nukekubi's* head cannot locate and reattach to its body by sunrise, the creature dies. Legends often tell of would-be victims foiling the creatures by destroying or hiding their bodies while the heads are elsewhere. By day, *nukekubi* often try to blend into regular human society. They sometimes live in groups, impersonating normal human families. The only way to tell a *nukekubi* from a normal human being is a line of red symbols around the base of the neck where the head detaches. Even this small detail is easily concealed beneath clothing or jewelry.

55. Maruyama Ōkyo (円山 応挙, June 12, 1733 – August 31, 1795), was a Japanese artist active in the late 18th century. As a young man, he moved to Kyōto, where he studied artworks from Chinese, Japanese and Western sources. A personal style of Western naturalism mixed with Eastern decorative design emerged, and Ōkyo founded the Maruyama School of painting. Although many of his fellow artists criticized his work as too slavishly devoted to natural representation, it proved a success with laymen. He is perhaps best known today for his numerous illustrations of Japanese ghosts.

56. Nishida Sentarō was without doubt Hearn's dearest friend in life: certainly in Japan. He depended greatly on Mr. Nishida, who constantly worked to smooth Hearn's way in literally every facet of life in Matsué, and even after Hearn's departure from that city, in linguistic, scholastic, and domestic matters. It wasn't long after Hearn's departure for Kumamoto, Kyūshū, that he would begin to deeply miss Nishida.

57. *Hakama* (袴) are a type of traditional Japanese clothing, simply put, pleated, skirt-like trousers, typically worn in formal Japanese ceremonies and in martial arts over a kimono, which were originally worn only by men, but today they are worn by both sexes. Hakama are tied at the waist and fall approximately to the ankles.

There are actually two types of *hakama*, divided *umanori* (馬乗り, literally "horse-riding hakama") and undivided *andon hakama* (行灯袴, literally "lantern hakama"). The *umanori* type have divided legs, similar to trousers. Both these types appear similar. *Hakama* are secured by four straps (*himo*); two longer *himo* attached on either side of the front of the garment, and two shorter himo attached on either side of the

368

rear. The rear of the garment has a rigid board-like section, called a *koshi-ita* (腰板), and below that is a *hakama-dome* (袴止め), a spoon shaped component sometimes referred to as a *hera*, which is tucked into the *obi* or *himo* at the rear, and helps to keep the hakama in place.

Hakama have seven deep pleats, two on the back and five on the front. The pleats are said to represent the seven virtues of *bushidō*, considered essential to the samurai way. Although they appear balanced, the arrangement of the front pleats, (three to the right, two to the left) is asymmetrical, and as such is an example of asymmetry in Japanese aesthetics.

58. The *haori* (羽織) is a hip- or thigh-length *kimono* jacket that is commonly worn by men over their kimono on formal and semi-formal occasions. With a change in fashions at the end of the *Meiji* period, both men and women now wear the *haori*, though women's jackets tend to be longer.

59. A *hibachi* (火鉢) or "fire bowl," is a traditional Japanese heating device. It consists of a round cylindrical or a box-shaped, open-topped container, made from or lined with a heat-proof material and designed to hold burning charcoal.

60. *Hanetsuki* is a traditional Japanese game, played with a wooden paddle called a *hagoita* and a shuttlecock called a *hane*. The game is quite similar to the Western game of badminton, but is played without a net. The game can be played in two ways; one in which one person attempts to keep the shuttlecock in the air as long as possible; the other is played by two people who bat the *hane* back and forth. There exists an old tradition that the longer the *hane* remains in the air, the greater protection from mosquitoes the player will receive in the coming year.

61. Thomas Henry Huxley (May 4, 1825 – June 29, 1895) was an English biologist known as "Darwin's Bulldog" for his advocacy of Charles Darwin's theory of evolution. Huxley's famous 1860 debate with Samuel Wilberforce was a key moment in the wider acceptance of evolution, and in his own career. Huxley had been planning to leave Oxford on the previous day, but, after an encounter with Robert Chambers, the author of *Vestiges*, he changed his mind and decided to join the debate. Huxley was slow to accept some of Darwin's ideas, such as gradualism, and was undecided about natural selection, but despite this he was wholehearted in his public support of Darwin. He was instrumental in developing scientific education in Britain, and

fought against the more extreme versions of religious tradition. In 1869, Huxley coined the term "agnostic" to describe his own views on theology, a term whose use has continued to the present day.

62. *The Imperial Rescript on Education* (教育ニ関スル勅語, *Kyōiku ni Kansuru Chokugo*) was signed by Emperor Meiji of Japan on October 30, 1890 to articulate government policy on the guiding principles of education in the Empire of Japan. The 315 character document was read aloud at all important school events, and students were required to study and memorize the text.

63. Kusunoki Masashige (楠木 正成, 1294 – July 4, 1336) was a 14th century samurai who fought for Emperor Go-Daigo in his attempt to take control of Japan away from the Kamakura Shōgunate and is remembered as the ideal of samurai loyalty.

64. *Tom Brown's School Days* (1857) is a British novel by Thomas Hughes. The story is set at Rugby School, a public school for boys, in the 1830s (Hughes himself attended Rugby School from 1834 to 1842). The novel was originally published as being *By an Old Boy of Rugby*, and much of it is based on the author's experiences. Tom Brown is largely based on the author's brother, George Hughes, and George Arthur, another of the book's main characters, is generally believed to be based on Arthur Penrhyn Stanley. The fictional Tom's life also resembles the author's in that the culminating event of his school career was a cricket match. The book overall is a drama about life at Rugby School in Victorian England where the headmaster is fair but not effective and life is brutal for the young boys because of bullying and its consequences.

65. *Cuore* (Heart) is a children's novel by the Italian novelist, journalist, poet, and short story writer Edmondo De Amicis (October 12, 1846 - March 11, 1908) The novel is regarded as his best-known work, and was inspired by his own children, Furio and Ugo, who had been schoolboys at the time of its writing. It is set during the Italian Unification, the political and social movement that combined different states of the Italian peninsula into the single state of Italy in the 19th century, and includes several patriotic themes.

66. Ono no Michikaze or Ono no Tōfū (小野 道風, 894 – February 9, 966) was a prominent *shodōka* or Japanese calligrapher, who lived in the Heian period (794–1185). One of the so-called Sanseki (三跡, "Three Brush Traces"), along with Fujiwara no Sukemasa and

Fujiwara no Yukinari. Tōfū is considered the founder of Japanese style calligraphy or *wayōshodō* (和様書道). In the story of Ono no Tofu, he was feeling despondent about failing to be promoted in the Imperial Court. As he sat, feeling badly, he watched a frog repeatedly trying, but failing, to leap up a willow branch. Finally the frog succeeded and Ono no Tofu was encouraged to persist

67. *Kana* are syllabic Japanese scripts, a part of the Japanese writing system contrasted with the logographic Chinese characters known in Japan as kanji (漢字). *Hiragana* (平仮名, ひらがな or ヒラガナ) is a Japanese syllabary, just one basic component of many, along with *katakana*, *kanji*, and *rōmaji* (the Latin alphabet). *Hiragana* and *katakana* are both *kana* systems, in which each character represents one *mora* (most simply put a sound-syllable). Each *kana* is either a vowel such as "*a*" (あ); a consonant followed by a vowel such as "*ka*" (か); or "*n*" (ん), a nasal sonorant which, depending on the context, sounds either like English m, n, or ng ([ŋ]), or like the nasal vowels of French.

Hiragana is used to write native words for which there are no *kanji*, including particles such as から (*kara*, "from"), and suffixes such as さん ~*san* (Mr., Mrs., Miss, Ms.). Likewise, *hiragana* is used in words for which the *kanji* form is obscure, not known to the writer or readers, or too formal for the writing purpose. Verb and adjective inflections, such as, for example, *be-ma-shi-ta* (べました) in *tabemashita* (食べました, "ate"), are written in *hiragana*, often following a verb or adjective root (here, "食") that is written in *kanji*. *Hiragana* is also used to give the pronunciation of *kanji* in a reading aid called *furigana*.

There are two main systems of ordering *hiragana*, the old-fashioned *iroha* ordering, and the more prevalent *gojūon* ordering.

68. Amida Nyorai, Amida, or Amida Butsu is the central figure of Amida Buddhism or Pure Land Buddhism (浄土教, *Jōdokyō*), referred to as *Amitābha* in Sanskrit, the Buddha of Everlasting Light, a previous incarnation of Siddhartha Gautama, the Buddha. Tradition holds that in this previous incarnation as a *bodhisattva*, he refused to accept Buddhahood unless he was able to grant eternal happiness in the Pure Land to whoever called upon him: a promise that became known as the Original Vow. Anyone who calls his name, *Namu Amida Butsu* with sincere devotion, faith, and trust, will be granted enlightenment, eternal life and happiness in the Pure Land, which had been established explicitly for those who call on him.

Pure Land was not an invention of Japanese Buddhism, but rather came from Mahayana Buddhism in India and then spread through China. The advance of Pure Land Buddhism in Japan reflected a significant change in Japanese thought, from a religion which stressed individual endeavor directed toward achieving enlightenment to a singular reliance for salvation by Amida Butsu; thus opening Buddhism to all social classes in Japan, including those on the periphery of society, such as prostitutes, who had been denied salvation through previous mainstream traditions.

69. Hidari Jingorō (左 甚五郎) was a possibly fictitious Japanese artist, sculptor, and carpenter. Although various studies suggest he was active in the early Edo period (around 1596-1644), there are controversies about the historical existence of the person. Jingorō is believed to have created many famous deity sculptures located throughout Japan, and many legends have been told about him. His famous "Nemuri-neko" (Sleeping Cat) carving is located above the Kuguri-mon Gate amidst the sacred mountain shrines and temples of Nikkō.

It is told that after someone cut off his right hand, he learned to work with his left hand and became Hidari Jingorou (*hidari* (左) means "left") Stories about Jingorō are spread in wide regions in Japan. According to one, he once saw a woman of such exceptional beauty that he made a sculpture of her. Jingorō began to drink in the company of the sculpture, and it eventually began to move, following Jingorō's lead. At first it had no emotion and could only imitate Jingorō's movements; however, when he placed a mirror in front of the sculpture, the woman's spirit entered and it came to life.

70. Ōtani Masunobu was a former pupil of Hearn's at Matsué and later became his literary assistant when he lived in Tokyō. Subsequently, Ōtani became a renowned writer in his own right.

71. The *shō* (笙) is a Japanese reed musical instrument that was introduced from China during the Nara period (710 to 794). It is modeled on the Chinese *sheng*, although the *shō* tends to be smaller in size. It consists of 17 slender bamboo pipes, each of which is fitted in its base with a metal reed. Two of the pipes are silent, although research suggests that they were used in some music during the Heian period. The instrument's sound is said to imitate the call of a phoenix, and it is for this reason that the two silent pipes of the shō are kept — as an aesthetic element, making two symmetrical "wings." Like the Chinese *sheng*, the pipes are tuned carefully with a drop of wax. Because moisture collected in the *shō's* pipes prevents it from sounding, performers can be seen warming the instrument over a small charcoal brazier when they are not playing. The instrument produces

sound when the player's breath is inhaled or exhaled, allowing long periods of uninterrupted play.

The *shō* is one of the three primary woodwind instruments used in *gagaku*, Japan's Imperial Court music. Its traditional playing technique in *gagaku* involves the use of tone clusters called *aitake* (合竹), which move gradually from one to the other, providing accompaniment to the melody. A larger size of *shō*, called *u* (derived from the Chinese *yu*), is little used although some performers, such as Hiromi Yoshida, began to revive it in the late 20th century.

72. The term *taiko* (太鼓) means "drum" in Japanese — more accurately, "great" or "wide" drum. Outside Japan, the word is often used to refer to any of the various Japanese drums, (和太鼓, *wa-daiko*), and to the relatively recent art-form of ensemble *taiko* drumming (sometimes called more specifically, "*kumi-daiko*" (組太鼓)).

73. The *shōko* (鉦鼓) is actually a small bronze gong, struck with two horn beaters, used in Japanese *gagaku*. It is suspended in a vertical frame and comes in three sizes.

74. The *hichiriki* (篳篥) is a double reed Japanese flute used as one of two main melodic instruments in several forms of Japanese music. The *hichiriki* is difficult to play, due in part to its double reed configuration. Although a double reed instrument like the oboe, the *hichiriki* has a cylindrical bore and thus its sound is similar to that of a clarinet.

75. Spencer's *First Principles*, published in 1867, was an attempt by Herbert Spencer to synthesize his thoughts on the first systematic theory of evolution.

76. George Henry Lewes (April 18, 1817 – November 30, 1878) was an English philosopher and critic of literature and theater. He became part of the mid-Victorian uproar of ideas which encouraged discussion of Darwinism, positivism, and religious skepticism; however, he is perhaps best known today for having openly lived with George Eliot, a soul-mate whose life and writings were enriched by their friendship, although they were never married.

77. John Fiske (March 30, 1842 – July 4, 1901) was an American philosopher and historian.

78. François Marie Charles Fourier (April 7, 1772 - October 10, 1837) was a noted French philosopher. An influential thinker, some of Fourier's social and moral views, held to be radical in his lifetime, have

become mainstream thinking in modern society. Fourier is, for instance, credited with having originated the word "feminism" in 1837. Fourier's views inspired the founding of the community of Utopia, Ohio.

79. Tokoji Temple (東光寺) was founded in 1691 and belongs to the Obaku School of Japanese Zen Buddhism. Its beautiful wooden temple buildings stand within the tranquil woods east of downtown Hagi, offering visitors a moment of serenity. Like most temples of the Obaku sect, Tokoji comes with an architectural style that displays more Chinese influence than that of the average Japanese temple. This is quite obvious when entering the temple through its Chinese style, red entrance gate. The approach to the main hall then leads under an even larger wooden gate, the Sanmon Gate, and passes an old bell tower built in 1694. Tokoji's main hall is also built in Chinese Zen architecture style and houses a statue of the historic Buddha (Shaka Nyorai). Behind the temple buildings lies the graveyard of half of the Mori *daimyō*, who governed from Hagi during the Edo period. The odd numbered *daimyō* in the succession of Mori lords were buried here, while the first and the even numbered lords were buried at Daishoin Temple. The burial site makes for quite an impressive sight, and its location within the woods lends it a peaceful and spiritual atmosphere.

80. Ōei (応永) was a Japanese era after Meitoku and before Shōchō. This period spanned the years from July 1394 through April 1428. Reigning emperors were Go-Komatsu-tennō (後小松天皇) and Shōkō-tennō (称光天皇).

81. A *magé* (髷) is the historical Japanese hair style often seen worn by samurai; now commonly seen as the hairstyle of sumo wrestlers.

82. *Ohaguro* (お歯黒) was a custom of dyeing a married woman's teeth black. It was most popular in Japan until the Meiji era, as well as in the southeastern parts of China and Southeast Asia. The practice was considered beneficial in addition to being cosmetic, said to prevent tooth decay, in a similar fashion to modern dental sealants.

83. Tottori-shi (Tottori City) is the capital of Tottori-ken or Tottori Prefecture, located in the southwest, coastal Chūgoku area of Honshū, east of Shimane Prefecture, and the nation's least populated prefecture.

84. The *takamakura* and *makura* are Japanese pillows which support the neck but allow one's hair to in effect hang freely; that is, so it doesn't

touch anything and thus retains its style in pristine condition. These types of pillows were generally used by women.

85. Gionzan An'yō-in Chōraku-ji (祇園山安養院長楽寺) is a Jōdo-shū Buddhist temple in Kamakura, Kanagawa Prefecture. The temple itself has a complex history and is the result of the fusion of three separate temples called Chōraku-ji, Zendō-ji, and Tashiro-ji. It was first opened in 1225 as Chōraku-ji in Hase Sasamegayatsu by Hōjō Masako for her dead husband, Minamoto no Yoritomo, founder of the Kamakura Shōgunate. At the time it was a Ritsu sect temple. After being burned to the ground by Nitta Yoshisada's troops in 1333 at the fall of the Kamakura Shōgunate, it was fused with Zendō-ji, moved to this spot and renamed, but it burned again in 1680. It was then once more rebuilt and a Senju Kannon (Thousand-armed Goddess of Mercy) was transferred to it from Tashiro-ji in Hikigayatsu.

86. This is fundamentally untrue, as geisha do not routinely engage in sex with their customers but are regarded more directly as entertainers and companions; furthermore, they are discouraged from having or "entertaining" male friends on their own while they are under contract. The author here has somewhat confused geisha and oiran (花魁), who were courtesans in Japan, a type of *yūjo* (遊女) or *jōro*; that is to say, a "woman of pleasure" or prostitute.

87. *Shirabyōshi* (白拍子) were female dancers, prominent in the Japanese Imperial Court, who performed traditional Japanese dances dressed as men. Interestingly, the dances were themselves also called *shirabyōshi*. The profession of *shirabyōshi* developed in the 12th century. Typically, they would perform for nobles and high-ranking samurai, and at celebrations. They are sometimes referred to as courtesans in the English language, but that term refers to a high-class prostitute, so this is rather incorrect because, by their very nature, they were performers; although some *shirabyōshi* would give birth to nobles' children. Still, this was not their purpose.

88. The *eta* were a caste group whose employment in jobs considered unclean set them apart in the feudal economy of Japan. Their major line of work was with leather; however they performed other services such as executioners, butchers, handlers of the dead, disposers of offal, and other jobs avoided by people in general as being unclean. Because of their association with occupations considered to be degrading, they were even refused work as domestics, and thus, evolved into the bottommost social class. *Eta*, as a social class, still exists in modern

Japan and the people assigned to that class are very frequently discriminated against.

89. The Oki Islands (隠岐諸島, Oki-shotō) are a group of volcanic islands in the southwestern part of the Sea of Japan, situated between 40 to 80 km. north of the coast of Honshū, with a population of approximately 24,500 people. It is uncertain as to when the islands were discovered; however, they are mentioned in the *Kojiki* and *Nihon Shoki*. Even during the Nara period, the islands were used as a place of exile for persons from the mainland. From the Kamakura period on, the islands were administered as Oki no kuni (Oki Province) and were governed by the governor of Izumo Province.

In 1198 Emperor Go-Toba was sent to exile to Dōgo, the largest island, where he stayed until his death in 1239. Between 1331 and 1333 Tennō (Emperor) Go-Daigo was exiled to Nishinoshima.

From the Muromachi period the islands were ruled successively by the Sasaki clan, the Yamana clan, and the Kyogoku clan, concluding with the Amago clan in the Sengoku period. During the Edo period, the Tokugawa family took control over the islands and placed them directly under the control of the Shōgun through a governor. Later, they became part of the Matsué Domain. During that time the islands were a stopover point for trading boats travelling to and from Asia. After the Meiji Restoration, which introduced a succession of reforms to restructure the Japanese state, the islands first became part of Tottori Prefecture in 1871, and then was transferred to the Shimane Prefecture in 1888. On October 1, 2004, the town of Saigō and the villages of Fuse, Goka and Tsuma were administratively merged into the town of Okinoshima, even though the townships still exist as separate towns.

90. The Ryukyu Islands (琉球諸島, Ryūkyū-shotō) are a chain of islands in the western Pacific at the eastern edge of the East China Sea and southwest of Kyūshū, comprising the southernmost island group of Japan, including Okinawa, Miyako, and Ishigaki. From 1829 until the middle of the 20th century, they were also known as the Luchu or Loo Choo Islands. There are a total of 73 islands, some uninhabited. The inhabited islands are populated by people with the same features as the Japanese, and while Ryukyu dialects are related to Japanese, they are generally unintelligible to speakers of Standard Japanese.

91. *Terra incognita* or terra *ignota* (Latin for "unknown land") is a term that was used in cartography for regions that had not been mapped or documented, first being used in the sixteenth century. An urban legend

claims that cartographers labeled such regions with "Here be dragons," believing that the fantastic creatures existed in remote corners of the world and depicting such areas as decorations on their maps. The phrase is now used as a metaphor by researchers to describe any unexplored subject or field or research.

92. Hoki (伯耆国; Hōki-no-kuni) was an old Japanese province in what is today the western part of Tottori Prefecture. Hōki bordered on Inaba, Mimasaka, Bitchū, Bingo, and Izumo Provinces. The ancient capital was in the area that is now Kurayoshi, and a major castle town was at Yonago.

93. Hearn was at this time, just beginning to learn Japanese and has rendered the short conversation between the sailors and the *mochiya* translated almost word for word, in the order spoken. In Japanese, the verb almost always comes at the end of the sentence. The reader may arrange their own translation from Hearn's words.

94. The author is no doubt having a bit of fun and at the same time being sardonic with this biblical reference:

> *"They that go down to the sea in ships, that do business in great waters; these see the works of the Lord, and his wonders in the deep. For he commandeth, and raiseth the stormy wind, which lifteth up the waves thereof. They mount up to the Heaven, they go down again to the depths: their soul is melted because of trouble. They reel to and fro, and stagger like a drunken man, and are at their wits' end. Then they cry unto the Lord in their trouble, and he bringeth them out of their distresses. He maketh the storm a calm, so that the waves thereof are still. Then are they glad because they be quiet; so he bringeth them unto their desired haven. (Psalms, 107:23-30, KJV)*

95. Daisen (大山) is a volcanic mountain located in Tottori Prefecture, the highest mountain in the Chūgoku region, and the most important volcano on the Daisen volcanic belt.

96. According to legend, Mongaku Shōnin had been in love with a married woman, whom he pursued and whose husband he demanded that she kill. Rather than betray her marriage and her honor, the woman tricked her husband into leaving on a trip. She then told Mongaku Shonin the husband was at home on that night and to come kill him. She dressed as a man and pretended to be asleep. Thinking it was the husband, Mongaku Shōnin beheaded her. Finding he had

really killed his beloved, Mongaku, in horror, ran away and became a wandering monk.

97. Sasaki Takatsuna (佐々木 高綱, 1160 – December 8, 1214) was a Japanese samurai commander in the Genpei War, the great conflict between the Minamoto and Taira clans. An infant at the time of the Heiji Rebellion (1159–1160), Takatsuna grew up with an aunt in Kyōto, and joined the forces of Minamoto no Yoritomo in 1180, when Yoritomo called for aid against the Taira. Takatsuna saved Yoritomo's life at the battle of Ishibashiyama, and aided in the destruction of the Taira following the end of the war. As a result, he was rewarded with the position of *shugo* or governor of Nagato Province. In 1195, Takatsuna retired to Mount Koya to become a Shingon priest. He left his son with his title, land, and all his material possessions. He is said to have died in 1214 in Matsumoto, Nagano (then Shinano Province). Nogi Maresuke was one of his descendants.

98. Legend has it that Gaken Chōja was the vassal of the Indian King Jihi Daiken Ō, who accompanied the king to Japan in order to save the Japanese people. Immediately after the king and Gaken Chōja arrived in Japan, Chōja visited Ise to inform Amaterasu that he was the messenger of both Kumano and Zaō Gongen. He requested Amaterasu's permission to allow him and his king to stay in Japan. Amaterasu responded that only the (mythical) Emperor Jimmu could grant his request, so Gaken went to ask the Emperor's permission, which was granted, and Gaken Chōju began his training at Mount Omine. In his seventh manifestation, Gaken became En no Gyōja, thus creating the lineage that positioned En no Gyōja within a direct line originally founded in Indian sources.

99. According to Basil Hall Chamberlain in his *Things Japanese* (page 267):

> *The generic meaning of kago is "basket"; but the word is applied specifically to one particular kind made of split bamboo, having a light lid atop and sometimes a strip of cotton stuffed on one side to ward off the sun's rays and swung on a pole which two men — one in front and one behind — bear on their shoulders. This is the country kago, but still the general means of conveyance in mountainous districts, where jinrikishas are not practicable, — sometimes even where they are. The person carried squats much in the same way as the Japanese are accustomed to sit, except that the posture is more semi-recumbent. He does not experience any difficulty in (so to say) abolishing his legs. The*

kago has been variously modified as to details at different times and places. The old norimono of the towns, so often mentioned by travelers of an early date in their descriptions of daimyo's processions, was but a glorified kago. Being larger and more stately, it might perhaps be termed a palanquin. The specimens preserved (for instance at the Ueno Museum in Tokyō) show the extent of which luxury was carried in this conveyance, for the costly lacquer, where carefully fitted slides having jalousies bound with silk kept out the profane gaze of passers-by, and finely wrought metal fastenings at every available point proclaimed in heraldic language the occupants aristocratic birth.

100. In Buddhism, *bosatsus* or b*odhisattvas* are enlightened beings who have put off entering paradise in order to help others attain enlightenment. There are many different *bodhisattvas*, but the most famous in Asia is Avalokitesvara, known in Chinese as Guanyin (Kwannon in Japan). *Bosatsus* are usually depicted as less austere or inward than the Buddha.

101. Zenkō-ji (善光寺) is a Buddhist temple located in Nagano. The temple was built in the 7th century. Nagano City, established in 1897, was originally a town built around the temple. Historically, Zenkō-ji is perhaps most famous for its involvement in the battles between Uesugi Kenshin and Takeda Shingen in the 16th century, when it served as one of Kenshin's bases of operation. Currently, Zenkō-ji is one of the last few remaining pilgrimage sites in Japan. Zenkō-ji was founded before Buddhism in Japan was split into several different sects, so it currently belongs to both the Tendai and Jōdo-shū schools of Buddhism, and is co-managed by twenty-five priests from the former school, and fourteen from the latter. The temple enshrines the image of the Amida Buddha. According to legend, the image, having caused dispute between two clans, was dumped into a canal. It was later rescued by Yoshimitsu Honda; and the temple was thus named "Zenkō," according to the Chinese transliteration of Yoshimitsu's name.

102. The Boshin War (戊辰戦争, Boshin Sensō, "War of the Year of the Yang Earth Dragon") was a civil war in Japan, fought from 1868 to 1869 between forces of the ruling Tokugawa Shōgunate and those seeking the return political power of the Imperial Court. The war found its origins in dissatisfaction among many nobles and young samurai with the Shōgunate's handling of foreigners following the opening of Japan during the prior decade. An alliance of western samurai (particularly the domains of Chōshū, Satsuma and Tosa) and

court officials secured control of the Imperial Court and influenced the young Emperor Meiji. Tokugawa Yoshinobu, the sitting Shōgun, realizing the futility of his situation, abdicated political power to the Emperor. Yoshinobu had hoped that by doing this, the Tokugawa house could be preserved and participate in the future government.

However, military movements by imperial forces, partisan violence in Edo, and an imperial decree promoted by Satsuma and Choshu abolishing the house of Tokugawa, led Yoshinobu to launch a military campaign to seize the Emperor's court at Kyōto. The military tide rapidly turned in favor of the smaller but relatively modernized imperial faction, and after a series of battles culminating in the surrender of Edo, Yoshinobu personally surrendered. Those loyal to the Tokugawa retreated to northern Honshū and later to Hokkaidō, where they founded the Ezo Republic. Defeat at the Battle of Hakodaté broke this last holdout and left the imperial rule supreme throughout the whole of Japan, completing the military phase of the Meiji Restoration.

Around 120,000 men were mobilized during the conflict, and of these about 3,500 were killed. In the end, the victorious imperial faction abandoned its objective to expel foreigners from Japan and instead adopted a policy of continued modernization with an eye toward eventual renegotiation of a series of unequal treaties with the Western powers. Due to the persistence of Saigō Takamori, a prominent leader of the imperial faction, the Tokugawa loyalists were shown clemency, and many former Shōgunate leaders were later given positions of responsibility under the new government.

The Boshin War testifies to the advanced state of modernization already achieved by Japan barely fourteen years after its opening to the West, the already high involvement of Western nations (especially Britain and France) in the country's politics, and the rather turbulent installation of imperial power. Over time, the war has been romanticized by Japanese and others who view the Meiji Restoration as a "bloodless revolution," despite the number of casualties.

103. The *Book of Rites* (*Li Ki*) is a compilation of ancient Chinese religious ceremonies and rituals practiced during the eighth to the fifth century BC. Propriety (*Li*) is one of the cardinal virtues to be cultivated by a practicing Confucian or Daoist.

104. Author's Footnote: These extracts from a translation of the *Japan Daily Mail*, November 19, 20, 1890, of Viscount Tōrio's famous conservative essay do not give a fair idea of the force and logic of the whole. The essay is too long to quote entirely; and any extracts from

the *Mail's* admirable translation suffer by their isolation from the singular claims of ethical, religious, and philosophical reasoning, which bind the various parts of the composition together. The essay was furthermore remarkable as the production of a native scholar, totally uninfluenced by Western thought. He correctly predicted those social and political disturbances which have occurred in Japan since the opening of the new parliament. Viscount Tōrio is also well known as a master of Buddhist philosophy. He holds a high rank in the Japanese army.

105. Author's Footnote: In expressing my earnest admiration of this wonderful book, I must, however, declare that several of its conclusions, and especially the final ones, represent the extreme reverse of my own beliefs on the subject. I do not think of the Japanese as lacking individuality; but their individuality is less superficially apparent, and reveals itself much less quickly, than that of Western people. I am convinced that much of what we call personality and force of character in the West represents only the survival and recognition of primitive aggressive tendencies, more or less disguised by culture. What Mr. Spencer calls the highest individuation surely does not include extraordinary development of powers adapted to merely aggressive ends; and yet, it is rather through these, than through any others, that Western individuality most commonly and readily manifests itself.

Now there is, as yet, a remarkable scarcity in Japan, of domineering, brutal, aggressive, or morbid individuality. What does impress one as an apparent weakness in Japanese intellectual circles is the comparative absence of spontaneity, creative thought, original perceptivity of the highest order. Perhaps this seeming deficiency is racial: the people of the Far East seem to have been, throughout their history, receptive rather than creative. In any event, I cannot believe Buddhism, originally the faith of an Aryan race, can be proven responsible. The total exclusion of Buddhist influence from public education would not seem to have been stimulating; for the masters of the old Buddhist philosophy still show a far higher capacity for thinking in relations than that of the average graduate of the Imperial University. Indeed, I am inclined to believe that an intellectual revival of Buddhism, a harmonizing of its loftier truths with the best and broadest teachings of modern science, would have the most important results for Japan. A native scholar, Mr. Inoue Enryō, has actually founded, in Tōkyō, with this noble object in view, a college of philosophy which seems likely, at the present writing, to become an influential institution.

106. Cholera is an infection in the small intestine caused by the bacterium *Vibrio cholerae*. The main symptoms are watery diarrhea and vomiting. Transmission occurs primarily by drinking water or eating food that has been contaminated by the feces (waste product) of an infected person, including one with no apparent symptoms. The severity of the diarrhea and vomiting can lead to rapid dehydration and electrolyte imbalance, and death in some cases. The primary treatment is oral rehydration therapy, typically with oral rehydration solution, to replace water and electrolytes. If this is not tolerated or does not provide improvement fast enough, intravenous fluids can also be used. Antibacterial drugs are beneficial in those with severe disease to shorten its duration and severity. A pandemic of Asiatic cholera was rampant in Central and Eastern Asia form 1881 - 1896.

Made in the USA
Coppell, TX
25 April 2020